D1508847

ALL
ABOUT
MEAT

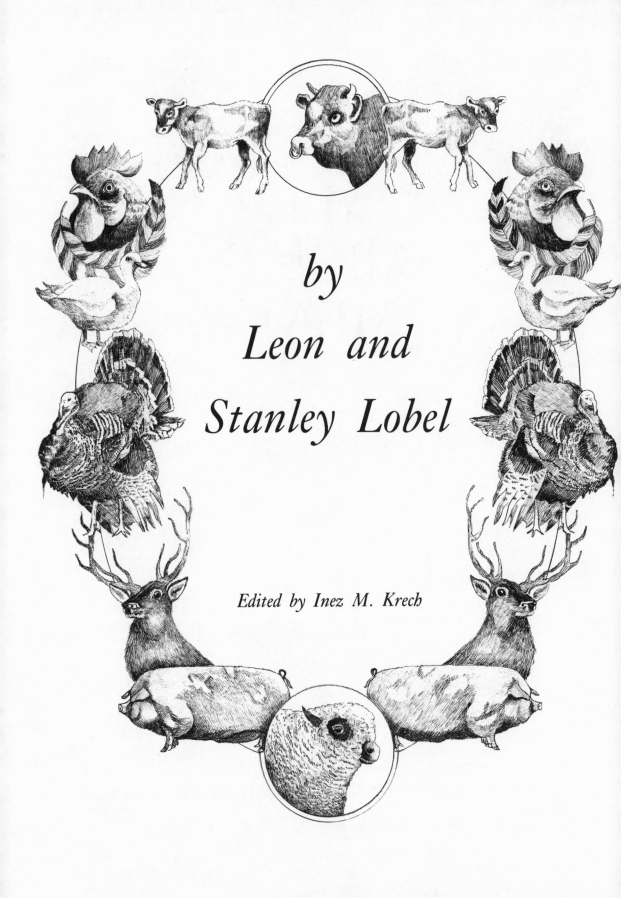

by

Leon and

Stanley Lobel

Edited by Inez M. Krech

ALL
ABOUT
MEAT

HARCOURT BRACE JOVANOVICH

New York and London

Printed in the United States of America

Text illustrations by Birney Lettick

Chapter opening illustration by Loretta Trezzo

Library of Congress Cataloging in Publication Data

Lobel, Leon.
All about meat.

Includes index.
1. Meat.   2. Cookery (Meat)   I. Lobel, Stanley,
joint author.   II. Title.
TX373.L6   641.6'6   75-5928
ISBN 0-15-104390-6

First edition

B C D E

To my four dearest loves: my wife and friend, Anita, and my three precious children, Linda, Ava, and Wendy. For all the world to see, one four three.

—LEON LOBEL

Lovingly dedicated to three very special people, my darling wife, Evelyn, and my two dear children, David and Mark, who with myself make a foursome united by love and understanding.

—STANLEY LOBEL

CONTENTS

CONTENTS

ALL
ABOUT
MEAT

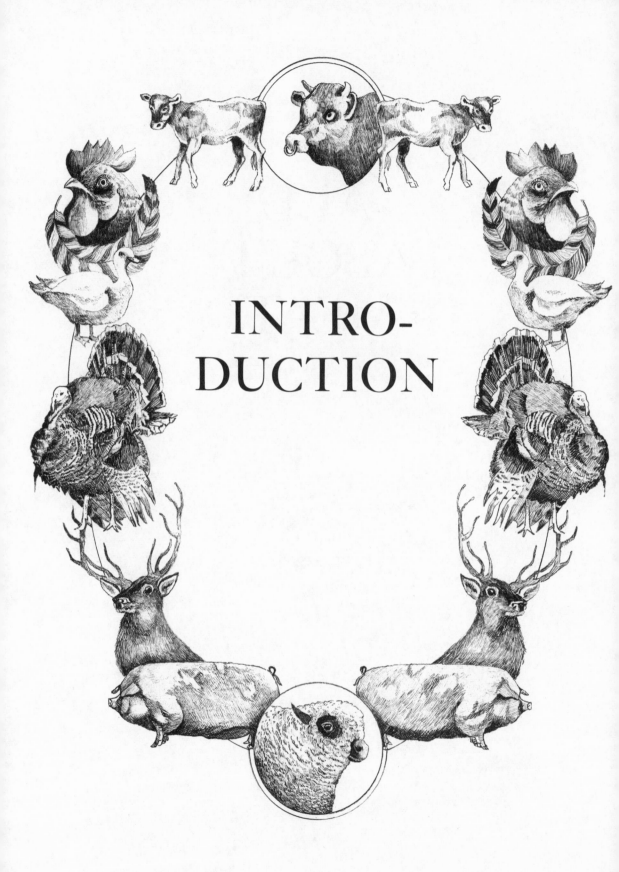

INTRO-
DUCTION

IN 1865, GREAT-GRANDFATHER LOBEL AND HIS son were running a beef cattle farm near Czernowitz, now Chernovtsy, in Bukovina, a part of the Austrian Empire from 1775 to 1918. The city, on the slopes of the Carpathians, became the capital of Bukovina and eventually an important commercial center. As Czernowitz grew, so did the cattle business.

When Grandfather Lobel took over, he added a slaughterhouse and began selling meat wholesale, directly from the farm. He also found time to serve as mayor of Czernowitz for many years.

When Morris Lobel, our father, was only eight years old, his father began teaching him all about the family business—how to care for cattle and what to look for in a good meat animal—conformation, health, and so on. Young Morris learned to recognize the beasts that had been fed on higher ground, on alpine meadows rich with grass; these better-fed animals were stronger and healthier. By the time Morris was fourteen he was buying and selling cattle on his own.

Grandfather Lobel's fair price for live cattle was 14¢ a pound. Son Morris sold some for 14½¢ to a buyer who had previously paid 14¾¢ elsewhere; he thought he was giving the buyer a bargain while making more money for the family. Grandfather slapped him for overcharging the customer. He had a reputation to uphold, a reputation for honesty, for fair value for money, for quality cattle. When he had cattle of poorer quality to sell, he sold them for less.

At the age of seventeen, Morris Lobel, like so many men of his generation, left Europe to avoid compulsory conscription and to find a new life in America. He settled in Boston with one of his sisters. Although he already knew everything there was to know about meat, from live animals to retail cuts, he went to work at a wholesale meat house until he could earn enough money to buy a horse-drawn delivery van. Then he purchased whole steers and delivered the meat to retail markets in his truck. With the training he had received from his father, he was able to select and sell quality meat. Two years later, he had two delivery vans. He worked his route for two and a half more years. When he was about twenty, he opened his own shop, retaining the vans and still delivering to other retailers. He trained a group of men to run the shop his way, and it was an immediate success. Eventually he was supervising six men in the shop and three men in the wholesale end of the business.

Then, in the early twenties, Boston was hard hit by an epidemic of influenza.

Morris and all his help were sick for many weeks. He had to give up the shop and the delivery vans, and most of his savings went for the care of his employees.

With two dear friends, Morris decided to make a fresh start in New York City. He opened a shop in the Bronx with the last of his funds. As soon as he could, he added the wholesale facet to the business and, with an automobile as his delivery van, began selling quality meat to other retailers. Even during the Depression the business prospered, and later Morris opened a shop on the West Side of Manhattan.

During his first years in New York, Morris met Etta, the girl who was to become his wife. Morris and Etta used to walk together along Fifth Avenue, but one day they walked up Madison and passed an old apartment house where workmen were just starting to break down the ground-floor walls to make room for shops. Etta said, "Morris, this is the store you should have." In the years following her death, when many of his customers moved across town, Morris set up his shop at that address. Even after a leg amputation, he continued to work.

Morris Lobel set a standard that we, his sons, have tried to follow. He was always pleasant, never brusque; he believed in warm personal relationships with his customers. He sold the same kind of meat to all—quality meat that was consistently excellent. He did not insist that any of us go into the meat business, but he taught us nevertheless. Actually, our late brother Nathan had planned to be an electrical engineer, and Leon wanted to work in dentistry. On weekends all of us helped in the shop, and little by little we became more interested in meat than in anything else. Stanley had always wanted to follow in our father's footsteps. It was a harmonious family then, as it is now.

We learned about meat in a completely pragmatic way. Morris was a patient teacher, firm but never cross; he never belittled us for our mistakes. Every morning he went to the wholesale market to buy meat; when we began to work in the shop, we went too, all of us together. For two years we watched as he made his selections and taught us to recognize quality when we saw it. After those years of training, he would stay in the car and send us inside to choose; he would examine our selections and make us take them back if they were wrong. Eventually he felt confident of our ability to buy according to his standards, and he could stay home during those early-morning hours.

Buying and preparing meat twenty years ago was much more difficult than it is now. The hours were longer, the work more arduous—even the concept of the business was different. Yet it was immensely more difficult in the twenty years before that. Today, many preparatory steps are done by packer or specialist, and we have machines to help us in a variety of ways. Unfortunately, the more machines and specialists there are, the further the individual consumer is removed from a basic knowledge of meat. With the help of our father and our brother Nathan, we have tried to educate the buyer. We have supplied material for articles on meat published in major magazines and in the newspapers of New York City; we have been consulted and interviewed on radio and TV; we have lectured on TV and in schools. During the meat crisis of 1973–74, we were consulted often, and we were proud to be consulted.

Our first book, *Meat*, was published in 1971. All three of us worked on it, and although Nathan did not live to see it in finished form, he was involved in the preparation of the manuscript from the beginning. Nathan had remarkably skillful hands. He was instrumental in developing the boneless capon, which became one of our specialties, and he was equally deft at boning other birds, small and large. He also had a great talent for cooking, and shared both these gifts with us and with our customers. We valued his participation in our harmonious family group and in all our projects to educate people about meat.

From our shop, we have sold meat to some of the wealthiest and most important people in the United States and the world. We have supplied recipes to cooks and chefs preparing dinners for heads of state and small households alike. Great restaurants have sought our advice on buying meat, preparing it, cooking it, serving it. The chapters that follow are based not only on our experience, but on the combined experience of four generations of a family working in the meat business. We like to think we have had a hand in raising public opinion of the retail meat business and of the word "butcher." We have tried to encourage the buyer to read labels and learn how to choose quality even in packaged meats. We have urged the discontinuation of the use of additives to meat, because of their harmful effects. We have tried to stop the selling of poorly grazed animals as good quality. Through our articles we have tried to teach the consumer to recognize meats of higher quality that are often for sale at approximately the same prices as poorer grades; a little more money can frequently buy much better quality. We have worked to educate the buyer in the storing and freezing of meat, both small portions and wholesale quantities.

In one very tangible way, we hope to enable retail and wholesale buyers to provide good aged meat: we have developed a process for aging that should revolutionize the meat industry. We already have two patents on our process.

There is no doubt that the services of the United States Department of Agriculture (USDA) have greatly improved the quality of meat reaching the retail customer. We also owe greater cleanliness, better preparation of the carcass and improved merchandising to government inspection, grading and regulation. These changes have led inevitably to the mass marketing in today's huge supermarkets. It is the pace of American life that has produced the demand for fast food resulting in a loss of personal customer relations and a failure of communication between producer and individual buyer. Though the housewife of a century ago could influence her butcher directly, could insist that his meat be clean or that he prepare the cuts in a certain way, today the customer is remote from the source and generally uninformed about how to choose meat and prepare it. To us, this lack of general knowledge seems a dangerous trend. Before all the information becomes the sole property of technicians and the only meat for sale is precut and prepackaged, we want to teach the home shopper what makes a good bird or a good piece of meat, how to choose it for specific purposes, how to prepare it and how to serve it.

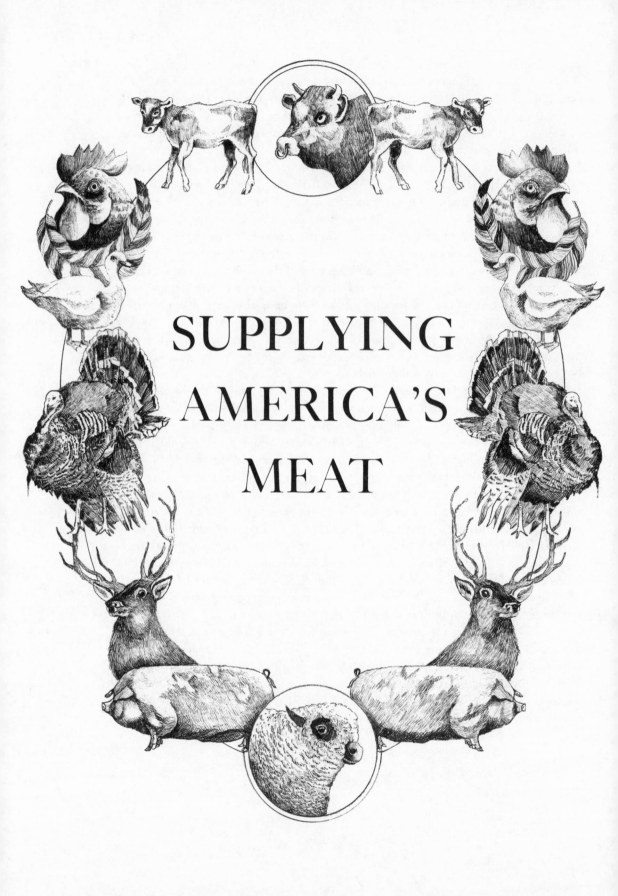

SUPPLYING AMERICA'S MEAT

Chapter 1

As THE CIVIL WAR DREW TO A CLOSE, Chicago was busy building the Union Stockyards. They were completed on Christmas Day, 1865, and sixty years later they embraced an area of 475 acres. For many years it seemed that all the country's meat was destined to come from Chicago. As railroads spread over the expanding United States, Chicago mushroomed from a village of twelve families in 1830, encompassing less than one-half mile, to become the greatest railroad center in the country. It was the growth of the railroads that originally made Chicago the nation's meat-packing center. Those massive cattle drives that have become familiar to Americans from countless Westerns are not so far back in the past. Only a hundred years ago, herds moved along the cattle trails that led ultimately to the railhead. But as the railroads proliferated, the drives disappeared.

Shipping cattle live requires a lot of space, and beasts do not like long trips any more than humans do; there are even some cattle illnesses related to travel. In 1869, an inventive fellow named George H. Hammond decided to ship meat—precut quarters of beef and pork—in a refrigerated car. Chicago was cool to this idea, so Hammond set up his business in Indiana—hence, the great city of Hammond. With the spread of the rails and the development of refrigeration, meat packing moved closer to the producers.

Today, most meat-packing is done much farther west than Chicago. Many producers like to control all aspects of production: raising, fattening, slaughtering, cutting, packing in plastic, shipping to wholesalers all over the country. The largest companies have regional depots, and some have subsidiaries specializing in a single aspect of the business.

These huge corporations want to be dependent on nobody. In this they are like the early-American farmer, who performed all the steps necessary to provide food for his family. But the United States was a wilderness then, and a large part of its meat supply was wild game, which was shot as needed. Early settlers imported livestock, but they used it chiefly for breeding.

Going back thousands of years meat production was a matter for society's concern. The written laws concerning Kosher meat—meat that is ritually clean—represent centuries of customs kept alive by oral tradition. Kosher laws are still in effect today for Orthodox and many other Jews, and some other religions require meat to be prepared according to similar regulations. Kosher markets, even those in the poorer sections of large cities, are known to offer high-quality meat.

In the Middle Ages, butchers, like many other skilled workers, banded together in guilds. These organizations had to submit to the rules of their city-states or kingdoms regarding cleanliness and avoidance of fraud.

As the thin line of settlements on the eastern seaboard of what was to become the United States grew, regulations ensuring a wholesome meat supply were worked out between butcher and buyer. This personal relationship with the butcher, who bought live animals, slaughtered them and marketed them, continued until recent times. But community action to control slaughtering and care of meat was found only here and there.

In 1706, the first meat-inspection law in North America was passed, in New France, today's Quebec Province. The connection between veterinary medicine and meat production became official: the animals brought to the slaughterhouse had to be certified as healthy before they could be slaughtered. The priest (*curé*) was one of those empowered to certify, a role not so different from that of the rabbi who examines animals for ritual slaughter.

NATIONAL INSPECTION

In 1889, the first federal law in the United States requiring inspection of cattle at the time of slaughtering was passed, not for protection of American citizens, but for protection of overseas trade. European buyers had complained that certain animal diseases made American meat products unfit to eat. This early law eventually led to the Federal Meat Inspection Act of 1906 and to subsequent acts.

Today, federal inspection is required for all meat-packing plants that sell their

Kosher tag indicating that meat is ritually clean

USDA stamp indicating that meat has passed federal inspection

products over state lines or to any foreign country. By 1972, about 91% of the meat sold commercially in this country was slaughtered under federal inspection. For the remaining 9%, some packers requested federal inspection, others were content with state or city inspection. According to the Federal Wholesome Meat Act of 1967, each state was obliged, by 1970 at the latest, to provide inspection conforming to federal standards. Some small amounts of meat are still slaughtered on farms, as was done centuries ago, but these are, of course, for home consumption only.

Inspection is a complicated process. Animals are inspected before slaughter, and any that are unfit, for whatever reason, are marked Condemned. Doubtful cases are marked Suspect and set aside for extensive post-mortem examination. Post-mortem examination of all carcasses is extremely thorough, and includes head, glands, viscera, pelvic cavity, and bones. Condemned animals are destroyed or treated so that they cannot be used for food.

The plants in which inspection takes place are also subject to stringent rules. A great deal of water is used in preparing a carcass, and for most purposes it has to be water good enough to drink. The plants themselves have been designed for cleanliness; stainless steel or other impervious surfaces are used, and everything is made as automatic as possible.

TRICHINOSIS

Those animal diseases that European buyers complained of before 1889 were significant because humans too can contract them. Animals can contract many diseases usually thought of as strictly human—pneumonia and arthritis, for example. The most notable is trichinosis, found, not only in swine, but also in all species of American wildlife, from mouse to polar bear. Trichinosis is a serious and painful disease for humans and has not yet been eradicated. Unfortunately, it is impossible to detect in living animals, and when man eats either raw or inadequately cooked pork he becomes a host to the parasite, a roundworm only a few millimeters long. Even careful microscopic examination may fail to detect the parasite, and such tests have not been carried out in the United States since 1906, although they are still done in Europe. If these tests were made, inevitably without complete success, the consumer would logically assume the meat to be safe—an unfounded assumption in many cases. Instead, the law requires all pork that is to be eaten without being cooked further to be processed in some way that will kill the parasite, such as heating the meat to 137° F. or holding it at −20° F. for 6 days or at −10° F. for 10 days, under specified conditions.

Since 1906, a tremendous effort has been made to educate producers in better ways of raising swine, particularly in regard to their feed, and this has reduced the incidence of trichinosis. In the years 1944 through 1953, nearly 400 cases of trichinosis in humans were reported annually. By 1960, the number was 160, and by 1971, only 103. But the progress has been uneven; for example, there were 222 cases in 1969. More recent figures can be found in *Statistical Abstracts of the United States*. Trichinosis is a disease that the law requires be reported, and national records are kept at the U.S. National Center for Health Statistics in Atlanta, Georgia.

Despite the decline in the incidence of trichinosis, it is still necessary for unprocessed fresh pork to be cooked by the consumer—not until it is dried out and tasteless, but to an internal temperature of 170° F. Americans have never had a taste for uncured raw pork, although many Europeans like it. (Cured and smoked pork are special cases; see Chapter 3.)

Poultry was not covered by the inspection laws passed in 1889 and 1906. Until fifty years ago it was usually bought live or freshly killed, and the housewife did everything else. Federal inspection of domestic birds was finally made mandatory on January 1, 1959. Since then, poultry-packing plants have been subject to inspection just like those handling meats. Both ante- and post-mortem inspections are carried out. A newer law, the Wholesome Poultry Products Act of 1968, requires inspection of all poultry, whether it moves in interstate commerce or not.

GRADING

Inspection does not reveal much about the quality of meat or poultry other than that it is clean and free from disease. Quality is monitored by another service of the USDA—grading. The first step in the development of a grading system was to identify beef by the region in which it was raised, but with general improvements in livestock feeding, this soon became a meaningless distinction. Various producers used terms of their own, and the consumer was confused. In 1924, after some limited experiments, the first federal grade standards were published, and grading and stamping of beef were officially adopted in 1927. This service is voluntary and is paid for by the meat packers themselves, but reliable producers know that it is to their advantage to use it. Consumers should never buy ungraded meat of any kind.

The symbol indicating approval by the inspection service and the symbol de-

USDA stamp indicating grade

USDA tag for poultry, the shield indicating the grade, the stamp indicating that the bird has passed federal inspection

noting the grade are both stamped on the meat in a vegetable dye (harmless if eaten) so extensively that you should find them on the retail cut you purchase before it is specially trimmed for you. The following are the government meat grades, based on conformation of the animal, quality (tenderness, juiciness, flavor) and cutability (the amount of usable meat on the carcass):

Beef	Veal	Lamb	Pork
Prime	Prime	Prime	U.S. No. 1
Choice	Choice	Choice	U.S. No. 2
Good	Good	Good	U.S. No. 3
Standard	Standard	Utility	U.S. No. 4
Commercial	Utility	Cull	Utility

Beef also has Utility, Cutter and Canner grades, and veal has Cull, but these will never appear in retail markets. In fact, retailers seldom sell anything below Good. In addition, beef has cutability grades of 1 to 5.

Poultry is graded too. Birds are identified as to species (chicken, turkey, duck, etc.) and as to class of bird according to age and sex. The grade mark A, B or C is usually found with the inspection stamp. Some packers care enough about their birds to have even the parts tagged with this information.

DEVELOPING TENDER MEAT

In comparing recipes from other countries with their American counterparts, you will notice that many of the former specify much longer cooking times. If you were to follow some of these recipes exactly, you would have meat so overcooked and dried out as to be totally unappetizing. The reason for this is that American meats are of better quality, from better-fed animals that are far tenderer. The development of domestic meat animals is the product of generations of work in animal husbandry. First the distinction was made between cattle breeds that were good milk producers and those that were good meat producers. Then the meat producers were carefully bred to produce animals with a characteristically blocky shape—wide, deep chest, short legs and neck, well-developed hindquarters. These cattle have a good proportion of meat to bone, and they are well developed in those body areas that provide the most popular cuts. Feeding experiments have indicated that while animals fed with corn develop more fat, their meat is 30% tenderer. Concentrated feeds produce even tenderer meat.

Other experiments in breeding were conducted to develop early-maturing cattle. For more than twenty years, DES (diethylstilbestrol), a synthetic hormone, was implanted in livestock to promote growth, which it did; it also decreased food costs by 11%. Fortunately, research continued. It was discovered that the hormone remained in the meat after slaughtering, and that in humans and animals treated with it the hormone could be linked to the development of cancer. On April 27, 1973, the FDA banned the use of this hormone; the expectation was that, without

DES, increased feed costs would raise the price of beef. But so many other factors helped to do this that it is hard to be sure just what part the banning of DES played.

Another development designed to produce very tender meats was the use of enzymes. Today, various packers inject live beef cattle with papain or other enzymes just before slaughtering. Some producers inject the enzyme solution into the less-tender primal cuts, rather than the whole carcass, after slaughtering. The FDA has cleared all these enzymes as safe within specified limits; and, of course, the meats containing them must be so labeled. However, most of the testing of these tenderizers was done by their manufacturers. We are very much opposed to this use of enzymes, and we have tried—so far, in vain—to persuade the FDA and the USDA to ban their use.

A further experiment involved the sale of enzyme-coated paper to butchers; of course, we are not in favor of this either, but the practice is disappearing, we are glad to report.

Breeding experiments similar to those conducted on cattle have been conducted on sheep. The distinction between meat producers and wool producers was made, and it was discovered that crossbred lambs provided better meat than their purebred ancestors. Feeding experiments have shown that sheep can synthesize B vitamins from feed composed of pasturage and harvested forage, and that the only mineral supplement they need is salt, though ewes do need extra feed during gestation. Like cattle raising, lamb production has been greatly improved by increased control of diseases and parasites. Since lambs are marketed at such a young age, it has not been necessary to breed them for early maturing.

In addition to the developments in hog feeding that have so markedly reduced the incidence of trichinosis, there has been a tremendous change in the hogs themselves. The roly-poly pig, with a thick layer of fat between flesh and hide, was desirable when lard was the chief fat used in cooking and pastry making. Today, leaner hogs grow heavier on less feed. With these animals also, crossbreeding has resulted in increased growth rates and healthier animals that are more efficient in turning feed into meat. When hogs come to market, they average slightly under 250 pounds and are 6 months old or less. Half a century ago, hogs were marketed at at least 9 months and were almost 100 pounds heavier (most of this excess weight was fat).

IDENTITY LABELING

The most recent aid for the meat consumer, worked out by the Industrywide Cooperative Meat Identification Committee, is the Meat Identity Labeling Program. A new code has been established that reduces the more than 1,000 names currently used by retailers to about 300. This program is voluntary, but if it is widely adopted you will be able to buy the same cut by the same name all over the country, which has certainly not been the case up to now. Meat labels will list the weight of the piece, the price per pound and the total price. They will also list the meat name, the primal (wholesale) cut of the animal and the standard name of the retail cut. This will not only simplify selection, but also make it easier to match the cut with the best cooking method. On certain items, such as ground beef, there will be a listing of the percentage of fat. The new meat charts of the National Live Stock and Meat Board recommend cooking methods for each retail cut as well.

Another recent development is that some producers are slaughtering beef at an earlier age. It's too soon to estimate how far-reaching this will be or how well accepted by the consumer. It is hoped that this step will conserve corn and other grains used for animal feeds and will help to slow the upward spiral in the price of these commodities. The animals are slaughtered 2 or 3 months earlier than usual, which still allows for beef with good flavor and reasonable tenderness, but does eliminate some of the quality of older beef. This younger meat will need slightly less cooking time. There may be some changes in grading to adjust to this.

The changes in chicken have been even more striking than those in other meats, because the bird has been subject to national attention for so few decades. Chickens are now bred for better appearance and for more meat per bird. The development of the fast-growing broiler has been another significant change. These smaller chickens, broiler-fryers, are produced in Del-Mar-Va Peninsula and in the Southeast. The older birds, stewing chickens or fowls, also used as egg layers, are grown wherever eggs are produced. DES has also been used in poultry to produce fatter birds, but, as with meat, the practice has been discontinued.

The biggest change in American birds was the breeding of the Beltsville white turkey, developed by the USDA at its research center in Maryland. This bird—smaller, meatier and rounder than its predecessors—has made turkey a popular year-round commodity. Today, a large percentage of the turkeys eaten in this country are Beltsville whites, although they are actually grown mostly in the Midwest and California.

Because of the quality of American meat, the generally good distribution of food and the high standard of living, Americans eat more meat per capita than people in most other nations. Even in a year of problems like 1973, the United States produced nearly 40 billion pounds of meat, and the average American ate about 190 pounds. Of this amount, 61% was beef, 36% pork; the tiny percentage remaining was divided between veal and lamb. Even though veal is very popular in Italy and Austria and lamb the favorite meat all around the Mediterranean, neither is a big item here. One reason for the popularity of beef in the United States and Argentina is the abundance of space for grazing and acreage for the grain that builds a calf to a steer of 1,000 pounds. It takes thousands of pounds of grain to make those 1,000 pounds of steer, plus protein supplements, hay and pasture. By the time such an animal has been reduced to a carcass, more than a third of the weight has been trimmed away; still more is lost in trimming into retail cuts.

Supply and demand affect the price of meat, but it takes time for a change in demand to be reflected in supply. When the supply is finally altered, the demand may be quite different. It takes longer to change the supply of beef than it does that of other meat products, because cattle are large and take a relatively long time to reach maturity. In the last twenty years beef production has nearly doubled, pork production has remained almost steady, and lamb production has decreased. Over the same period the price has increased for all, the most for calves. In 1972, 135.4 million animals were slaughtered in the United States, and the country imported an additional 2,653 million pounds of meat. Poultry moved in the opposite direction; both chicken and turkey prices were greatly reduced during those twenty years, and, surprisingly, Americans began eating more turkey and less chicken. A further striking change was the drastically increased use of frozen poultry—from 411 million pounds in 1950 to 2,236 million pounds in 1972.

Now that you are up to date on the history of meat production in the United States, you are ready for a lesson in how to buy fresh meat and poultry—how your retailer buys it, and how you should buy it from him.

FRESH MEATS
AND
POULTRY

Chapter 2

BEFORE FRESH MEAT PRODUCTS ARRIVE at your grocery store or butcher shop, they have already undergone a number of processes, including inspection and grading. Each wholesale cut of meat has been numbered, beginning with the carcass. Each carcass has been inspected and graded, the quality ranging from upper to lower within each grade. The carcasses of beef have been shipped from packing plants to local wholesalers. From this point, meat reaches retailers in several ways.

Large retail chains purchase whole steers and ship them to distribution centers, where they are cut into wholesale portions. These basic wholesale cuts are called "primal cuts," not to be confused with the term "Prime," used for grading. Chains may send the primal cuts to stores, or they may cut them into retail portions at the distribution center. The same chain might ship slightly different selections to their various stores, according to the known preference of customers in particular sections of the country or in neighborhoods of large population centers.

At present, many large supermarkets have butchers in the store, even though you may need to push a buzzer or knock on a window to find them. In these markets the wholesale cuts may be butchered to suit the customer, and some special preparation, like boning, may be available. But the trend is toward elimination of individual butchers in chains; eventually, standard prepackaged cuts may be all they will offer.

Fresh wholesale cuts often reach chain supermarkets in heavy plastic packaging. The best-known and most-used brand is Cryovac. To eliminate air and moisture, the plastic is shrunk to the meat with dry ice or hot water. Such packaging prolongs freshness for up to 2 months. Meat in these packages gets older, but it does not "age" in the ordinary sense. Although this wrapping is used for both fresh and cured wholesale meats, it is not used for fresh retail cuts.

The retail shopper can buy all kinds of meat in his shop or supermarket, but the wholesale buyer has to work harder. Since meat wholesalers specialize in one kind of meat, the independent butcher has a lot of shopping to do.

A butcher whose shop is not part of a chain may buy entirely by telephone, ordering so many forequarters or hindquarters of beef and whole carcasses of other animals, specifying the grade of each. Another may go to the wholesaler and look at the meat, buying what looks good to him. We follow the second procedure. At 4:30

A.M., when most of the world is still asleep, we are examining those wholesale meats, to handpick the best for our customers.

A good wholesale shopper looks for animals with good conformation, those with all portions well shaped. The shopper also checks for indications of broken, damaged or abnormally thick bones, which might signify a healed break or injury; for instance, there should be equal spacing between rib bones.

The age of the animal is important, and the smart buyer will pass up animals with dark-colored bones. These animals are older and less desirable than those with brighter-colored bones.

Any evidence that an animal has been mistreated would immediately disqualify it for us. The meat should not be bloodshot. Tiny particles of blood looking like little clots, bubbles or splotches spread throughout a wide area of the meat can be seen easily if present and indicate that the animal has been in an accident or has been damaged.

MARBLING AND GRAINING

The fat content of beef is important; the amount of exterior fat should be reasonable, not excessive, and its color should be creamy white, not yellow. The interior fat, or marbling, is also significant. While the best steak will have marbling that looks like dotted pencil marks, good meats for pot roasts or stews will have marbling that is more like pencil strokes. Extremely heavy marbling resembling crayon marks will be found in the meat of an animal that is too old to be purchased for any purpose. An overfed animal can reach its peak and pass it; the quality goes backward, as it were. In such animals, the graining will be substantial and white in color; but the meat will feel quite hard and the external fat will be yellow—both signs of old age. This meat will be fatty and tough. Double-thick crayonlike marks with little meat between the fat strokes may indicate an injury that was callused but never healed. Meat showing such marks will be like that of extremely young animals with inadequate graining—it will lack tenderness. If a buyer finds evidence of any injury in a quarter, he should return it.

To judge the quality of the beef itself, wholesale buyers look for good color: It should be pink rather than deep fiery red; the latter would suggest poor quality, as would a dark red or bluish color.

The wholesale buyer should beware of any excess on the carcass—too much fat or rind, or a heavy flank. These are simply waste products, and it is senseless to pay for them.

When the halves have been chosen, a forequarter and a hindquarter from the same side of the same animal, they are weighed, priced and tagged for the wholesale buyer. The meat is shipped to his shop later.

AGING

At this point both wholesale and retail cuts of meat can be aged, the length of time depending on the desired taste and tenderness. The maximum time for beef is 6 weeks. Meat to be aged is hung in a chamber refrigerated to 34 to 40° F. During this time any blood not removed at slaughtering is drained, and moisture is extracted by evaporation. Enzymes in the meat cause autolysis, a process of digestion that breaks down tendons and fibers, making the meat tenderer and more flavorful. At the same time, the meat itself becomes firmer because of the loss of liquids. The exterior surfaces become very hard, and must be cut off and discarded before the meat is sold. The total loss from eliminating hard surfaces and from evaporation is about 2% by weight of a large retail piece. While this does not sound like much, if you multiply it by the total number of cuts and the huge volume of wholesale meat, you will see that the loss to a wholesaler or supermarket chain is substantial. As a result, meat shipped to most chains and supermarkets is not aged. If you are willing to pay a little more for better-tasting, tenderer meat, buy at a shop that takes the trouble of aging.

Aged meat will look moldy if there was too much moisture in the aging chamber. But if the humidity is maintained at 70% and the temperature is also kept constant, there will be a minimum of discoloration and little action by microorganisms. Speeding the process by increasing the humidity and the temperature for part of the time is, in our opinion, undesirable.

The meats in the heavy plastic packages become more tender because of enzyme action, but there is no evaporation because the meat is resting in all its extracted liquids. Most of these packages are not dated, so they could be held too long. If so, an unpleasant smell will be present when the plastic is opened; such meat would be returned to the wholesaler. In our opinion, this too is an unsatisfactory kind of aging.

Veal requires no aging, since it already has tenderness and good consistency. Lamb can be aged for 1 week, pork for 10 days. While these three meats are naturally tender because the animals are young, lamb and pork have more fatty covering than veal and can thus be aged for better consistency.

Kosher meat is not aged, for Kosher laws require meat to be eaten within 72 hours of slaughtering.

BEEF

In the paragraphs that follow we will explain how we cut beef quarters to get the most out of every portion. The forequarter includes five primal cuts: rib, brisket, plate, foreshank and chuck.

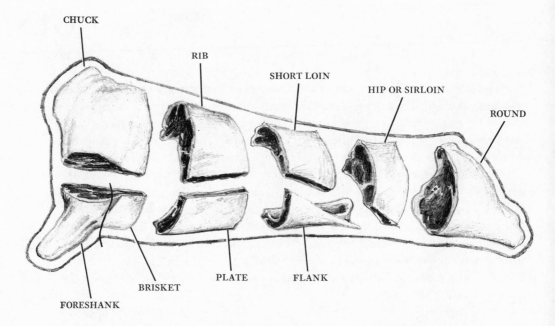

CHUCK

RIB

SHORT LOIN

HIP OR SIRLOIN

ROUND

PLATE

FLANK

BRISKET

FORESHANK

Beef carcass, divided into wholesale (primal) cuts

Rib

Remove the layer over the top of the ribs to be used for a pot roast. Cut off the section including the 3 bones nearest the chuck for boiling beef. Since the rib portion is the most desirable and expensive, it calls for greater attention in cutting. The remaining 7 rib bones can be used for a single large rib roast or can be butchered into a 3-bone and a 4-bone roast, or divided in various other ways. For instance, rib steaks, called *entrecôtes* in French terminology, can be cut.

The eye of the rib in the portion closer to the hind is a solid round of meat known as the "first cut." To remove the short ribs, measure 2 inches from the edge of the eye toward the ends of the rib bones; measure at both ends so the cut will be straight across; at this line cut off the whole bones. Trim the fat, and use the ribs for beef spareribs.

For boneless rib roasts, cut around the bones, following each indentation, and remove the bones in one piece. Replace the bones in the indentations and tie them on; they will serve as a rack for roasting and add flavor.

Brisket

Trim out the whole brisket to make one huge pot roast to feed 10 to 12 people; or cut it into halves or thirds for small pot roasts. The first cut, nearer the hind, is heavier. As you go toward the shoulder there is more fat and fibrous graining.

Therefore the second cut is better for boiled beef and corned beef. Ask your butcher for the cut you prefer; if you use the wrong cooking method the dish will be much less successful.

Plate

The plate includes the ends of the rib bones described in the rib section. Plate short ribs, or plate flanken, are near the brisket and closest to the rib portion. They must be trimmed well; they can be braised, potted or boiled. Also in this section is the skirt steak; part of the skirt is a loose piece, about 15 inches long, 4 inches wide and ½ inch thick; the top portion is attached to the plate and is less tender. Both parts are boneless but require good trimming. If your beef is of high quality, the loose piece will have good flavor and can be broiled; the other piece makes good cubed steaks. If the beef is of lower grade, grind the skirt steak; ask your butcher's advice about the quality.

The lower part of the plate, toward the head, is often used for pastrami. The remaining portion, toward the flank, can be cut into long-bone flanken. The meat from this portion is chewier and not as flavorful as the plate short ribs. But long-bone flanken can be used to contribute to the nutrition of dishes that need long, slow cooking; or they can be boned completely and the meat ground. This section is not the best choice for boiled beef because it has too much bone in proportion to meat.

In the foreshank, separate the shin meat from the bone and grind it, or use the shin with its bones for soup or stock, or for long, slow pot-roasting, or for beef *osso buco*.

Chuck

To divide the chuck in the most economical way, remove the top portion, the blade, of the entire chuck first. Halve it diagonally as close to the blade bone as possible, because there is meat hidden near this bone. Remove the blade bone, leaving one oval-shaped piece of meat and another flattened oval; the flattened oval can be cut into slices to make "chicken steaks," individual minute steaks or top blade steaks. Use the other oval-shaped piece for a pot roast or as soup meat. Use all trimmings for grinding.

There remain 4 ribs on the bottom of the chuck and the balance of the neck bones toward the end of the chuck. Use the first 2 ribs, closer to the hind, for a rib roast (blade roast); it will not be as good as prime ribs, but it will be fine for a dinner at home. Ask your butcher to remove the remaining 2 ribs and the neck bones in the chuck, and keep them for soup.

The 6-inch piece of meat next to the blade roast can be pot-roasted or cut for stew. The 4-inch piece closer to the head, the neck, can be used for pot-roasting or soup meat. The closer to the neck end you go, the tougher the meat. Keep all the scraps for hamburger.

In the lower portion of the chuck, also called the "shoulder" or "arm," the section closest to the rib is called a cross-rib roast. If the beef is of high quality (high Choice or Prime), you can oven-roast this piece; with beef of lower grade it is best to braise it. The front part of the shoulder can be cut into two 3-inch pieces or three 2-inch pieces; in good-quality beef these can be cooked like London broil. Braise or pot-roast if the beef is of lower grade. Any remaining portions in the chuck can be used for pot-roasting, but eliminate the bones and remove the heavy tendons.

There are other ways to butcher the chuck; some variations you may find in your retail market are chuck short ribs, blade steak and arm pot roast or steak. The flat, thick "California roast" is an underblade pot roast. Unless the beef is of good quality, this roast will be more successful if cooked with moist heat.

Only the forequarter is used for Kosher beef, because the hindquarter cannot be drained of blood. This is true of beef, veal and lamb; pork is not eaten.

The hindquarter includes four primal cuts: short loin, hip or sirloin, round and flank.

Short Loin

The short loin lies next to the ribs. From this portion we get shell steaks and *filets mignons*, or Delmonico, T-bone and porterhouse steaks, these last three including a part of the tail.

The first cut, nearer the head, provides the Delmonico or club steak. The second cut, 3 inches in, has a larger filet and a different bone conformation; this cut is butchered into T-bone steaks. Porterhouse steaks come from the third cut, the next 3 to 4 inches, which has an even larger filet.

If the filet portion running through all these steaks is removed, the remaining section makes shell steaks, also called strip steaks, New York strips or Kansas City strips. In French terminology this is the *contrefilet*, or *faux filet*. The shell portion can be cut into roasts, into double-thick steaks, or into 13 to 15 individual steaks about 1 inch thick. We'll get back to the filet itself later.

In good markets, you will have noticed little grooves cut into the fat edges of these and other steaks. They may look decorative, but that's not why they are there. In allowing the meat to expand during cooking, these incisions prevent curling due to shrinkage of the membrane between meat and fat.

Hip, or Sirloin

This portion contains the sirloin steaks. The most economical way to butcher it is to cut 6 to 8 sirloins 1 inch thick, each large enough to serve 3 or 4 people, or to cut thicker steaks, up to 2 inches, for barbecue. There are also other ways to divide it. Through this section runs the butt portion of the tenderloin, the continuation of the tender filet in the short loin.

Round

The round includes the top, or tip, sirloin, rump, top round, eye round, bottom round and shin.

From the top sirloin, cut 1 or 2 steaks, each 1 inch thick. Use the balance for roast beef.

The rump, or the top of the rump, is called in French the *aiguillette*. This can be roasted if the meat is of good quality.

From the top round, cut 2 pieces 2 inches thick for London broil. Then remove the entire top section of the part remaining for hamburger. Slice the balance into ¼-inch-thick slices, no thicker, for Stroganoff; or use as a roast, cut for a lean beef stew, or grind this portion too, if you prefer.

The eye of the round should be trimmed of all cartilage and membrane; it can be used for an elegant pot roast or, with care in preparation, for a good oven roast. This is called the silverside, or silvertip, in British terminology.

The bottom round, a piece about 10 pounds in weight, can be cut into pieces of various sizes for pot roast. The shin, like the shin of the forequarter, can be used for soup meat, for grinding, for pot-roasting or for beef *osso buco*.

Flank

This portion contains the tails of the steaks. They can be left on the steaks, ground for hamburger, or cut for beef stew. The boneless flank steak can be used for London broil. The wholesale flank cut includes, in addition, large chunks of fat. Ask the butcher to slice these into strips, or have it cut by machine into slices. The slices can be used to wrap any roasts that require moisture in cooking, the eye round, for instance. (Beef fat can be used for veal roasts, too.) The fat strips can be used to wrap around *filets mignons*, veal *noisettes* or similar pieces of meat lacking a fatty covering.

Filet, or Tenderloin

The tender, boneless filet, or tenderloin, is a cut that runs through the short loin and sirloin. It tapers to a smaller circumference at each end; the end toward the head is quite small, about 1½ inches across, the end nearer the hind about 5 inches across. The entire filet can be roasted for a special occasion; it will serve 10 to 12 people. The filet can also be divided into two portions, one from the short loin and one from the sirloin. The wider piece, from the sirloin, can make a roast for 6 to 8 people, or it can be cut into 1-inch small sirloin steaks, each large enough for 2 or 3 servings.

From the center of the filet, the porterhouse section, comes the Chateaubriand, a double-thick steak that is adequate for 2 servings. Two of these can be cut from the filet. Moving toward the head end, slices 1 to 1½ inches thick are cut to make the *filets mignons* ("little threads"). Usually these have the outside cartilage still

23

HEAD OF FILET
(THE SIRLOIN END)

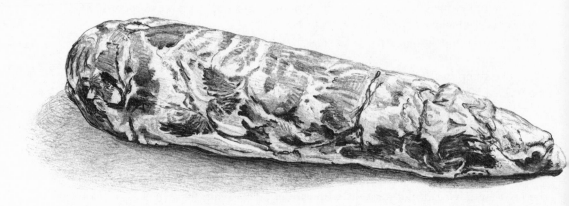

Beef filet or tenderloin, whole

TAIL OF FILET
(THE SHORT LOIN END)

around them, although we prefer to remove it entirely. The little pieces can be sautéed or quickly broiled close to the heat source without wrapping, but usually they are wrapped with bacon, pork fat or, our preference, beef fat.

The *tournedos* is cut thinner than the *filet mignon*, never more than 1¼ inches. To prepare it, a small extra layer of meat is removed, as well as all cartilage and membrane. Usually a *tournedos* weighs 3½ to 4 ounces. It is also called a *médaillon*, but that name applies better to the little rounds specified by Escoffier. According to him, *tournedos* are cut from a single slice to make round nuggets of meat like the *noisette* of a rib lamb chop; if they are cut in this fashion, each person needs 2 or 3 *tournedos* for an adequate serving. However the *tournedos* are prepared, they serve as a foil for garnishes or sauces; Escoffier lists more than 60 ways to serve these little nuggets. Going on toward the narrow end, you may cut slices smaller than our *tournedos*, called *petits filets;* either of the little ends can also be cut into cubes for kebabs—to be sure very superior kebabs—prepared for a small London broil, or sliced for beef Stroganoff.

You may find differences in various references, but the drawings on page 25 show one way to divide the filet.

If it is important to you to have perfectly round slices cut from the filet, then your butcher should tie them, because the meat is naturally shaped like a flattened oval. Since the tenderloin is usually found as part of a steak in this country, it seems a true luxury cut by itself. You might be surprised to learn that in the past it was a far more common cut than steak in Europe, especially in Italy and Hungary, and routinely served to people who had trouble chewing.

All the bones that remain from cutting the quarters can be used for soups and stocks; the long bones can be used for marrow.

The only remaining piece is the beef kidney, which can be braised, stewed or

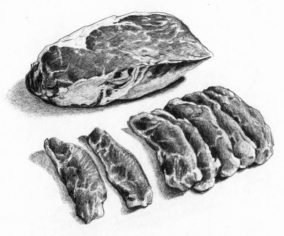

Filet mignon (little thread), a slice cut from the head end of the filet, and slices for Stroganoff cut from the same portion

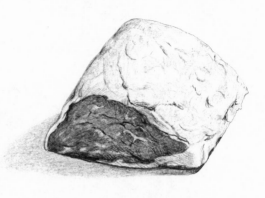

Chateaubriand, a double-thick steak cut from the center of the filet, the porterhouse section

A small London broil, made from the tail end of the filet

used in beef pie. If your animal was young and of good quality, beef kidney can be sautéed (see p. 296).

The head, tongue, tail, liver and heart are removed from the animal when it is butchered into the wholesale quarters. A retail butcher who wants any of these has to order them specially. The tail is sold as "oxtail." Tongue is sometimes sold fresh, but many are cured and smoked. For more on variety meats, see Chapter 11.

VEAL

Young animals can be slaughtered at various ages, the youngest being baby calves of 8 to 12 weeks, fed only on milk and consequently called "milk-fed veal." Even younger animals are imported from New Zealand for use as canned veal. These animals are so immature that the real character of the meat is missing.

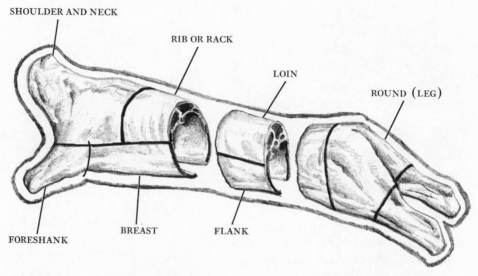

SHOULDER AND NECK

RIB OR RACK

LOIN

ROUND (LEG)

FORESHANK

BREAST

FLANK

Veal carcass, divided into wholesale (primal) cuts

Vealers are older, larger, and have been fed on grain and grass. They are usually slaughtered at about 12 weeks and weigh 150 to 200 pounds. These animals are just beginning to display the true color of veal and the quality that is expected of this meat. The vealer is usually more tender and whiter in color than the calf. Calves are older and weigh 250 to 300 pounds at slaughtering. The calf that is allowed to grow past 6 months becomes a young steer, and after 11 months the steer becomes a young bull.

In the market you will have difficulty detecting any difference between veal and calf. When we look at the animals in the wholesale market, conformation is the first consideration. The meat should be as white as possible; the fat should be even whiter than the color of the flesh. Dark fat indicates that the animal is older than it should be, and tough. The bones of young animals are red; if they are brown, the animal is old and we won't buy it. Any skin should be white. These same factors, except conformation, can guide you when shopping retail. In addition, look at the cartilage around the spinal cord, evident in chops; that cartilage should be white, never dark.

In the wholesale market, veal is delivered as the whole carcass. It can be divided into a hindsaddle, consisting of 2 hindquarters, and a foresaddle, consisting of 2 forequarters, or it can be divided into sides of 1 hindquarter and 1 forequarter. In the forequarter there are the rack, breast, shoulder and neck, and foreshank. (In the foresaddle the double rack and double breast are called the "bracelet," and the double shoulder and neck are called the double chuck.)

Forequarter

The breast of veal can be cut into halves, a pocket can be made in the half nearer the loin, and this piece can be stuffed if desired. Or the breast can be cut into strips and trimmed to use as veal spareribs. Another alternative is to cut the whole veal breast, bones included, to use for a messy veal stew.

The rack—the first 8 ribs—can be cut into chops or left in one piece for a rib roast of veal, to be cooked like a beef roast. The chops can be single, double for broiling, or double with pockets for stuffing and baking. The balance can be boned, rolled and roasted. Or, leaving the bones in the meat, crack them and use the piece for pot-roasting. Yet another way of using this portion is to remove the bones and cut the meat for *blanquette;* don't be afraid that this section is too fancy for a stew—a *blanquette* requires tender boneless meat with a minimum of sinews. You can even grind this meat for an extremely healthy vealburger.

In the chuck portion, remove the shank with its bone; use that for *osso buco* or veal stew, or bone and grind the meat for burgers. Bone the shoulder, remove all cartilages, sinews and membranes, and roast. This will be a good alternative to roast leg of veal. You may find arm or blade roasts with bones, but they are difficult to carve.

Hindquarter

Remove the flank; use this for grinding only.

The loin portion can be cut into regular loin chops, or the kidney can be cut with the chops to make "kidney chops." Of course, this portion can be made into a roast, or it can be boned and rolled with the kidneys inside.

The rump makes a good roast, either with or without bones. If you bone and roll it, be prepared to have it fall apart when carved.

The round (the leg) can be properly prepared in only one way: Separate it into its various sections and remove veins, cartilage and membranes. Once this is done, cut into thin slices and flatten for *scaloppini,* or use the round as a roast for a buffet or other special occasion. Or cut into slightly thicker cutlets, ¼ to ½ inch thick. The old-fashioned cutlet, a slice across the leg, is still sold, but not often. In a thin slice, the membranes make the sections separate and curl in cooking, but a thicker slice can be cooked like a steak. All cuts from the leg need careful preparation.

For the Kosher trade, *scaloppini* are cut from the leg of the forequarter. Little slices cut from any part other than the leg are not truly *scaloppini.*

In addition to the skeletal cuts, veal has brains, tongue, head, kidneys, heart, liver and sweetbreads. As with beef, only the kidneys remain with the carcass. All other portions are removed in butchering the meat.

LAMB

Like calves or vealers, lambs arrive at the market as whole carcasses. Mutton, which comes from older animals, is seldom found in our markets, but when it is, it is cut in the same way as lamb.

Spring lambs are born in February or March, and they appear in markets from the first of April to the beginning of October of the same year. These animals are able to graze, and the quality of the meat reflects their better feed. Winter lamb is older and drier, and has a more pronounced lamb taste; the winter feed does not produce as good a quality of meat. Spring lamb has no odor, while the older animals do. Spring lamb has pink bones, winter lamb red. The leg of spring lamb weighs a maximum of 7 pounds, but the legs of winter lambs will weigh up to 8 or 9 pounds. The spinal cord of the winter animal is yellower than that of the younger animals, and a small amount of grain will show in the eye of the chop in older animals. Obviously, winter lamb is less tender and needs longer cooking at lower heat.

The whole carcass contains 2 legs, 2 loins, 2 racks, 2 breasts and the entire chuck. It can be split into quarters or into a foresaddle and hindsaddle.

The most familiar portion is the leg. Here are five ways your butcher can prepare it:

1) Crack the chops (for ease in carving later), but leave them attached to the roast. Roast plain.
2) Bone the leg and butterfly it. This is fine for barbecue. With spring lamb that is young and tender, it can be broiled indoors; of course, it can be roasted also.
3) Cut the leg into halves; roast half, and cut the rest into chops for broiling.
4) Bone the leg and roll it for a rolled roast.
5) Cut the leg into chunks for shish kebab.

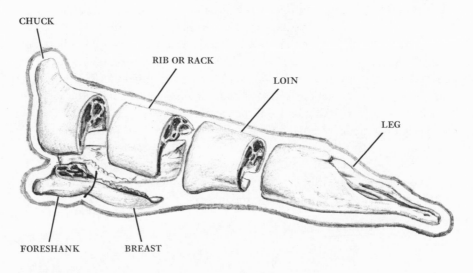

Lamb carcass, divided into wholesale (primal) cuts

The double loin is called the saddle. The whole saddle or a single loin can be roasted. The loin can also be cut into single or double chops.

The section next to the loin is the rack. The whole round section of the animal is the bracelet, including the double rack and the attached flank, or breast. The rack without the flank portion can be roasted as a double, or as two singles, or it can be cut into single or double rib chops. The two racks can also be cooked together as a crown roast.

The flank beneath the rack, the remaining breast portion and the foreshank are sometimes cut off in one piece. This is most often divided into chunks for stew, and the flank is usually ground. The breast can be cut into lamb spareribs or riblets. You may see large pieces of the breast in some markets, and these can be braised—they are messy to eat but have good flavor. The breast can be stuffed like a veal breast, but it is not as meaty as veal, since the animal is smaller.

Another way to butcher the lamb is to cut the foresaddle into the bracelet and the double chuck. The double chuck includes the neck, shoulder, shoulder lamb chops and shanks. Shanks can be braised or stewed, and the neck is usually used for stew only. The shoulder can be made into an elegant stew or good shish kebab.

Lamb also has brains, heart, kidneys, liver, sweetbreads and tongue. Kidneys are generally available, but you'll have to ask for and perhaps order in advance the other variety meats. As with beef and veal, only the kidneys remain with the carcass.

There are two other well-known kinds of lamb. Hothouse, or milk-fed, lamb is a tiny animal, fed only on its mother's milk. In France, this lamb is called *agneau de lait* or *agneau de Pauillac;* Pauillac is a small town near Bordeaux where some of the finest red wines of the world are produced; they go well with lamb, of course. There is American hothouse lamb too, and it must be specially ordered. The meat from these animals should be cooked gently, for a short period of time and with little seasoning. *Agneau de pré-salé* is salt-marsh lamb, slightly older than hothouse lamb but still young. Fed on the salt marshes near the coast in northern France, these lambs have a distinct flavor all their own.

French recipes for lamb generally result in juicy pink meat; for some American tastes this is quite a shock. Is there a difference in the lamb? Yes, French lamb is generally smaller, and there is no American lamb fed like the salt-marsh lamb. But the difference is chiefly a question of taste. Lamb is so young and tender that it does not need to be cooked forever. Consult Chapter 6 for how long to cook pinker lamb if you would like to try it; you might like it!

The United States also imports lamb from New Zealand and Australia, and this is clearly identified as such. We do not think it is as good as domestic lamb.

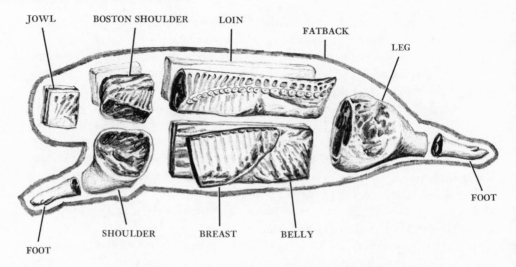

Pork carcass, divided into wholesale (primal) cuts

PORK

Pork is treated differently from other meats in several respects. As you have already noticed, the grading system is different. In addition, much pork is cured or processed in various ways, and different packers have their own ways of preparing it.

Like lamb and veal, pork is young meat, so it is naturally tender. Look for the same specifications as for veal: light pink to white meat, white fat, deep pink to red bones. However, the meat itself should look grainy, like beefsteak. Because the graining in pork is not fatty tissue but muscle, moisture is needed in cooking it.

The primal cuts of pork are leg, loin, belly, breast, shoulder, jowl and foot.

The leg can be used for a huge roast, it can be cut into a butt half or shank half, or steaks can be cut from the center, although this procedure is more common with cured ham.

The loin can be divided into sirloin, center loin and blade loin roasts; and these sections can in turn be cut into chops, single or double. The whole loin or any of its separate sections can be boned, and the bones can be tied to the roast to serve as a rack and add flavor. Also in this section is the pork tenderloin, which weighs ¾ to 1 pound, is tender and delicious, and can be roasted plain, stuffed and roasted, or braised. The loin can also be made into a crown, using 16 chops.

The belly is used for salt pork (called side meat in the Southern and Midwestern parts of the United States) and for bacon; as a result, this part seldom arrives at retail stores fresh, but goes to the packers who salt or cure it. Streak lean from the belly is sold fresh, but it must be ordered in advance.

The breast is the source of spareribs; they can be purchased in "sheets," or your butcher can crack the bones or cut them into sections. A large portion of the weight is bones.

The shoulder can be cut into a picnic ham, smaller than the leg ham but not quite as tender, an arm roast or arm steaks, a Boston butt or blade steaks. The hocks are cut from the shank end of the picnic ham; and fresh hocks are usually used for stew or soup.

Only in markets serving customers of particular cultures will you be apt to find jowl, ears and tail. Bacon is made from the jowl, and feet are smoked and pickled as well as being sold fresh; there is more about these parts in Chapter 11.

Country-style spareribs, cut from the shoulder end of the loin, are not true spareribs but are actually meatier and not too fatty. They are good braised.

Although pork neck bones have almost no meat on them, they can be used to make broth or give inexpensive protein to soup or stew.

Fatback and lard come from the layer of fat over the back of the hog and the layer covering the butt. Fatback can be found fresh or salted.

As you can see, there are parts of the pig that are never purchased by the retailer. Most retailers buy according to the demands of customers, and for pork the demands are frequently for only the leg, loin and spareribs of fresh pork, and ham, bacon and other cured cuts.

VENISON

Venison is sometimes sold in retail markets. Because deer are not raised as domestic animals, all venison is hunted. To be sold, it needs the game warden's seal. The meat is cut similarly to veal, into breasts, chops, steaks, roasts, filet, and chunks for stew. Less tender portions are ground, and they make good venison-burgers.

Bones and fat left over after cutting meat carcasses for wholesale and retail are used for soap and soap powder, detergent and fertilizer. Of course, some bones that remain after retail cutting can be purchased for stock making and for marrow, and some fat can be used for cooking (see p. 23). Suet, the fat around the kidneys of beef, is used for pastry making and cooking souffléed potatoes. Lard and fatback from pork are regularly sold, and leaf lard, from the ribs of the pig, also used for pastry, can be purchased from some shops if it is ordered.

POULTRY

Chicken

Would you believe that in 1901 chicken was priced at 20¢ per pound and cost a lot more than roast beef? Yes, it's all different now!

Among protein foods, chicken is one of the best buys. Besides its nutritional values, it is reasonable in cost, easy to prepare, and quickly cooked. It can be ready for the table in simple fashion for any informal occasion or an emergency, and serves equally well for festive meals if you make just a little extra effort.

Butchers generally buy their poultry from some one supplier who specializes in the kind and class of birds they need. A careful buyer, wholesale or retail, looks for birds with perfect conformation, more breast than leg, no bruises or blood marks, and a healthy yellow color. A good butcher will not sell a bird that he would not eat himself.

Chickens can have many labels: young chicken, broiler, fryer, broiler-fryer, roaster, stewing chicken, fowl, hen, mature chicken.

Weighing from 1 to 2½ pounds, broilers, or young chickens, are 6 to 8 weeks old and have very little fat. Fryers weigh between 2½ and 3½ pounds, and the broiler-fryer ranges from 2 to 3½ pounds. Your market will use one term or the other for these little birds; you can fry broilers and broil fryers or roast either if you do it right. The roaster, or pullet, ranges from 14 weeks to 8 months of age and is more fleshy and rounded than the younger birds. Its usual weight is from 3½ to 6½ pounds. The older birds, hen or fowl, can weigh up to 8 pounds, and they are about a year old. Today these large birds are not as common in markets as they once were because they take much longer to cook than the younger birds. But for certain purposes they are without parallel—especially for stock making and as cold chicken for salad.

When buying broiler-fryers, look for a coating of yellow fat, which indicates that the bird has been fed on corn. A bird with a plump breast is of prime quality; but a pointed breast and thin white skin are signs of poor quality. It is futile to poke the breastbone—the true tests are those we have mentioned.

The pullet is naturally good for roasting or baking, but it is the most tender bird for fricassee and can be used for quick cooking indoors and for barbecuing on the outdoor spit. These chickens have been bred for tenderness. Look for plump-breasted birds with short rather than long bodies and yellow skin. Pullets of 4 pounds are just the right size for making *suprêmes*, cutlets or *scaloppine*, and for chicken Kiev—all made from the breast. We will get back to these later. Larger pullets, of 6 to 6½ pounds, can be roasted, but they can also be diced for chicken kebabs—1½-inch squares of the whole bird, light and dark meat. You can also bone and skin the bird, and grind the meat for chickenburgers.

Older birds are usually recognizable by their weight, so much greater than that of the common broiler-fryer. They also have much more fat. Remember that older

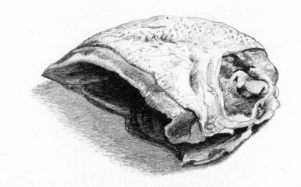

Chicken breast, whole

Chicken breast, split

Chicken breast, split and boned, with skin removed

birds require longer and moister cooking, but they are certainly more flavorful than small broilers.

In addition to whole birds, many markets sell chicken parts—breasts, whole legs, drumsticks, thighs, wings, gizzards, livers, hearts—separately and in various combinations. It is possible to find split birds and quartered birds as well. Sometimes each part is sold for a different price per pound, and sometimes they are sold for the same price as whole birds. Good chicken producers will take the same care of the parts as of the whole birds. Recently, boneless and skinless chicken breasts have been available; these cost more, and they are easy to prepare yourself. You do not know how long these little pieces have been drying in the market; they will be juicier and more flavorful if you skin and bone them just before you need them.

There are many terms for the chicken breast. The whole breast is made of 2 half-breasts. Each half-breast has 2 fillets, a larger and smaller, joined at the shoulder. The boneless half-breast includes both these fillets. We have used the term *scaloppine* for the fillets because they can be treated like veal scallops; this is not customary usage, but we think it makes sense. Some culinary writers call one of these boneless half-breasts a cutlet, others use that term (French *côtelette*) for the half-breast with the upper joint of the wing attached. Some famous chefs, including Escoffier, say that the *suprême* is the same as the fillet; Escoffier adds that the *suprême* may include the large and small fillets or only the larger one. Other great chefs use the term *suprême* to mean one side of the breast, including both fillets, with a small piece of the wing bone, not the whole joint, still attached and the blade bone, the main bone running down each side of the breast, still in place; the small rib bones are removed from the *suprême*, as well as all skin and tendons. The meat is removed from the attached piece of wing bone; the bone then sticks out as a sort of handle and is trimmed and often covered with a frill. When prepared with these few bones, the breast has less tendency to dry out, and the retained bones help the meat keep its shape.

In our shop we prepare the half-breasts still another way: We remove all the bones except the upper joint of the wing bone, which is shaped to hold a frill. We think removing the bones makes the piece much easier to serve, but we leave the skin on to keep the meat from drying out. The *suprême* can be cooked with or without the skin.

You can have your butcher prepare your chicken breasts in any way that suits you, or you can do it yourself. Even if you buy whole chickens to make *suprêmes*, it will not be a wild extravagance because you can use the rest of the birds for so many other things. Although boneless chicken breasts can be found prepared in many markets, a *suprême*, whichever version you like, has to be prepared for you.

When you examine a boned half-breast or *suprême*, you will see that there is a natural pocket in the larger fillet, perfect for stuffings of many kinds.

Some other chicken parts we should mention are the feet and cockscombs. It has been discovered that the spongy texture of these parts can serve as a repository for disease-producing cells. Since January 1, 1973, chicken feet can be legally processed for human food only when handled in an approved manner in specific cases. What this boils down to is that feet cannot be sold over state lines for ordinary use, and you will not find either feet or combs for sale in general markets. Even though classic texts say to use feet for their gelatin and cockscombs as garnishes, you do not need either. A veal knuckle will provide good gelatin for aspic, or you can use commercial packaged gelatin. Many prettier garnishes can supplant the cockscombs. Now most poultry feet are used for fertilizer.

Capon

A capon is a castrated male bird under 7 months old. Because of the removal of the reproductive organs, these birds are lazier and they become larger and fatter. In most markets capons must be specially ordered. They are excellent for a large beautiful roast, stuffed inside and between skin and flesh. They are also the ideal poultry for a *galantine* (p. 224) if you should be that ambitious.

Rock Cornish game hens can be had fresh only by special order, but they are available everywhere frozen, so you can read about them in Chapter 4.

Squab

Squabs are young pigeons, weighing about 1 pound each. They are for sale fresh all year long, but usually they must be ordered in advance. Since they are sold with viscera still inside, your butcher will eviscerate them when you buy them. All squabs are raised domestically; a Northern squab is like a round apple, firm in texture; Southern squabs, a different species, are larger, have somewhat dry flesh, and are pointy breasted.

Turkey

Turkeys are no longer a one-season bird; you can find them all year long. Young turkeys of 4 to 6 pounds, available only in the spring, can be quartered to broil or barbecue. Holiday birds are bigger and are almost always roasted whole. The broad-breasted female, or hen, turkeys are sweeter than males, more succulent, juicier, and fattier for their weight. These birds seldom exceed 19 pounds. Because the male, or tom, turkeys are drier, they require longer cooking over lower heat for best results. Usually the male can be identified by his pointed breast. If you buy a jumbo-sized bird during the holidays, when birds of 16 to 40 pounds are sold, you can be sure it's a male. Fresh birds are more delicious and juicy than frozen, so it's worth while ordering them in advance.

Duck

Though most ducks and geese come to market frozen (see Chapter 4), fresh birds are marketed seasonally. Sold in the spring, little ducks of 2½ to 3 pounds are good for broiling and barbecuing. Later in the season, 4-pound birds, good for potting and deep-frying, can be purchased. The fall birds of 4½ to 5 pounds are usually roasted but can be potted.

If you read some French and Chinese recipes for duck, you may find them puzzling because the birds referred to are either smaller or larger than those usually available in the United States. For instance, a *nantais* duck of 3 pounds can be divided into 2 good servings, whereas one of our more usual 5-pound birds is too much for 2 servings and adequate, maybe, but not generous, for 4 servings.

Goose

Few fresh geese are readily available; you must order one in advance. Although most frozen geese weigh about 8 pounds, larger birds of up to 18 pounds can also be found in some markets. The heavier the bird, the fattier and older it will be. Smaller, younger birds will be tenderer.

Game Birds

Guinea fowl and pheasants are wild birds, but both have been also raised commercially for many decades. Their taste is similar to that of other domestic birds, but they do have the rather dry flesh common to game birds. Guineas are quite expensive, and not many are raised commercially.

Female pheasants are recommended over males because they have a little more fat, making the meat smoother, less dry, and tenderer. An eviscerated female weighs 2½ to 3 pounds, which is more than a male. Females also require less roasting time than males. These elegant birds are good flambéed or served under glass. A male weighs 1¾ to 2½ pounds, has somewhat dry and stringy flesh, and retains more of the gamey flavor of wild birds than does the female. Males are best cooked with slow, moist heat to retain whatever juices there are. Flambé one of these birds with brandy when serving it at table.

Mallards, served frequently on Edwardian tables, are very scarce today. Other wild birds—partridges, grouse, quail, and the waterfowl—are in hunters' catches. Unless you are an experienced hunter, you may have trouble determining whether or not your bird is young and tender. If in doubt, use moist heat for cooking, and compensate for the lack of fat by outer-larding.

Poultry organ meats sold with the birds include heart, gizzard and liver. These, along with the neck, are usually packed in paper and inserted in the cavity of the whole bird. Be sure to remove the package before starting to cook. These are good for stock or to add to your gravy.

CURED AND
PRESERVED
MEATS AND
POULTRY

Chapter 3

PRESERVING MEAT FOR LATER USE began very long ago. We know the Chinese had sausages long before the Christian era. As for the Romans, Petronius, once a crony of Nero's, wrote so much about food in *Satyricon* that we would expect him to mention sausages if he knew about them, and, to be sure, he does: "There were sausages too, smoking hot on a silver grill, and underneath (to imitate coals) Syrian plums and pomegranate seeds." A pretty conceit! In another place he describes the presentation of a cooked hog stuffed with sausages and black pudding. Since Petronius turned up his toes in 66 A.D., we can be sure sausages have been around for at least 2,000 years. And since they are among the most sophisticated of our cured meats, we can be just as sure that the whole idea is extremely ancient.

Traditionally in the United States, hog slaughtering in the fall was an important occasion at every farm; lots of the meat was put down in salt to tide the family over the winter. Even farms concentrating on something else—wheat, dairy products, chicken—raised a pig or two, fattened on table scraps and garden excess for home consumption. This old tradition may have been the reason why pork is butchered and marketed differently from other meats in this country. As was noted in the last chapter, some parts of the pig never reach the retailer fresh, but go straight to a packing house that will process them in some fashion.

Salt Pork

One process is dry-salt curing, which produces salt pork. Salt alone is rubbed on pieces cut from various fatty sections of the pig, especially the belly. Cured fatback is similarly prepared from pieces along the back and butt. This process is also the first step in many more complex curing recipes.

Salt pork is available to retailers in large pieces, 8 to 20 pounds, and fatback in pieces of 6 to 12 pounds. An individual shopper can buy a small chunk of ¼ pound. It will keep for at least a month, but if stored for much longer, it begins to turn rancid. These fats have varying degrees of saltiness too, which can't be determined by their appearance.

From the part of the pig near the bacon section, streak lean, containing a tiny line of meat in the fat, is often cured in brine but is also available fresh (see p. 30).

Years ago, "pickled pork"—pork in brine with additional preservatives—was packed in barrels and carried on shipboard to feed American seamen and those of other countries on long voyages. This barrel pork is no longer available, and the sailors of today eat fresh meat. However, some meats are still prepared this way, notably corned beef, which, by the way, has nothing to do with the vegetable corn. This usage of "corn" is derived from the Norse word *Korn*, meaning grain, used to refer to a grain of salt. The salt used in corning is coarse, more like kernels of grain than refined table salt. (Table salt is also different in that it contains additional ingredients, which are listed on the box.)

Corned Beef

The brisket and bottom round are the usual cuts used for corned beef. Because the meat of the brisket is sweeter, however, it is preferred. Tongues of beef, veal and lamb are also corned. Actually, any type of red meat that can be used for pot-roasting or poaching can also be corned or pickled. Corning mixtures include salt, sugar and spices in a brine; the recipe of each packer is secret, and the type of spicing depends on the meat being used and the flavor that is wanted. More cloves, less salt, the length of time the meat is allowed to remain in the brine—these factors will affect the final taste. Whole corned briskets can weigh 12 to 16 pounds; these are shipped to butchers in kegs or individually packed in heavy plastic. Portions of the whole brisket can be purchased retail, and in some markets small plastic-wrapped pieces are available.

If a butcher buys less than a keg, the pieces will be shipped to him in plastic bags, and he may transfer them to his own pickling solution once they reach his shop. Many butchers also do their own corning according to their own secret recipes.

Cooking corned beef or any corned meat is simple. Remove the plastic wrapping if there is one, and place the meat in a large kettle, making sure to shake all the spices in the wrapping into the cooking pot too. Cover with room-temperature water, bring to a boil, and simmer for about 3 hours, according to taste. After it is cooked, let the meat cool in the water. If you want extra flavor, an onion, a carrot, some additional spices and a bay leaf can be added to the cooking water. Corned meats that have had a long stay in brine may need a preliminary soaking; consult your butcher if the packer's style is unknown to you.

Well, that's the bare bones of boneless corned meat; you can go on from here to make very handsome dishes for buffets, parties, picnics, and so on. After the poaching step just described, glaze the meat and bake it in the oven to give it a beautiful finish. Any glaze recipe for ham can be used. Madeira has a good flavor for these meats, and fruits make excellent accompaniments or garnishes. An aspic glaze on a chilled cooked corned meat is another possibility. The classic New England boiled dinner is made with corned beef, whole potatoes, whole carrots, whole onions and wedges of fresh cabbage, all cooked together. The vegetables are added when the meat is almost done, allowing just enough time for them to cook. This plain hearty food makes a perfect winter dinner.

SWEET AND SOUR TONGUE AND CORNED BEEF   6 servings

1 pound tongue	1 tablespoon sugar
1 pound corned beef	3 plums, washed but not peeled
1 lemon	3 tablespoons pineapple juice
2 oranges	3 pineapple rings
1 tablespoon honey	2 tablespoons Southern Comfort
3 tablespoons raisins	

Cut the tongue and corned beef into slices ⅛ inch thick. Peel completely three quarters of the lemon and both oranges. Cut off the unpeeled quarter of the lemon and both ends of the oranges; cut the peeled fruits into wafer-thin slices, leaving the unpeeled quarter of lemon whole for later. Use a sturdy medium-sized pot with a cover. In a single layer arrange most of the lemon slices in a circle on the bottom of the pot, completely covering it. Set remaining lemon slices aside for later. On top of the lemon slices, place about one quarter of the tongue and corned-beef slices. Next, add a layer of orange slices and the rest of the lemon slices, then another quarter of the meat. Arrange the remaining orange slices to cover the entire meat layer, then add another quarter of the meats. Spoon the honey around the top of this meat layer, sprinkle on the raisins and sugar, and squeeze the juice of the reserved lemon quarter over everything. Add a few more slices of meat; slice the plums and place them over the meat. Arrange the rest of the meat in a circular pattern over the plums, and spoon the pineapple juice over all. Cover the pot, and let it cook over low heat on top of the stove for 1½ hours.

With a sturdy spatula or pancake turner, try to reach to the bottom of the pot, and, with one or two strokes, turn over the entire contents in one piece; do not mix more than that. Place the pineapple rings on top. Heat the Southern Comfort in a large ladle, ignite it, and pour flaming over the meats and fruits. Cover the pot and let everything simmer over *very low* heat for 1 hour longer.

Lift out the pineapple rings and transfer the meat to a platter. Spoon out the other fruits and arrange on top of and around the meats. Replace the pineapple rings on top of the entire dish. The sauce remaining in the pot can be served separately, to be spooned over rice or noodles.

Pig's feet, hocks and spareribs are also pickled. To prepare the pickled spareribs, poach them first, as you would corned beef, but for a shorter length of time. Then drain, cover with a mixture of brown sugar and honey, and sprinkle with caraway seeds. Bake until glazed, and you will have a good informal dish.

The cured meats most familiar to us are bacon and ham. Although the variety in the preparation of these meats is enormous, the basic steps are salt-curing for preservation and smoking for flavor. This type of curing can be done with many other cuts and kinds of meat.

Salt-cured and smoked meats are subject to all sorts of government inspections. They must be good fresh meats that have never been frozen; the salt must be evenly distributed, with no large deposits in any one place; there must be no bruises or other damage, no areas imperfectly cured, and no discoloration from the smokehouse—every piece must show an even healthy color appropriate for the nature of the meat used and the style of curing; the meat must smell good. In addition, such meats are tested for fat and salt content. Wrappings are likewise examined carefully; if plastic is used, it must be of regulation thickness; if paraffin- or plastic-coated paper is used, this too must comply with standards. The casing or wrapping may not be split or torn, and there must be no air pockets. Containers are inspected as well as the plants where the meats are processed. Cartons must be labeled, and samples from the cartons inspected.

Bacon

Bacon has a moderately high ratio of fat to lean, but within specified limitations there is a lot of variety. If you have a preference in this respect, note the particular packer who has just what you want. The flavor will vary too, depending on the smoking process used. We have more to say about bacon in Chapter 7.

Canadian bacon is made from boneless pork loins from which all bones, cartilages and blade meat have been removed. The meat is smooth and round, with few sinews. The layer of fat surrounding the meat is very thin, no thicker than ¼ inch. From end to end the entire piece must be meat that can be cut into even slices. Ideally the meat is stored under refrigeration after curing and smoking, but some is frozen. Before slicing, pieces of Canadian bacon weigh from 3 to 9 pounds; sliced for wholesale they are packed in 5- to 10-pound containers. Small packages of slices wrapped in greaseproof packing and vacuum-sealed are sold retail.

Do not limit your consumption of this delicious meat to the occasional breakfast slice. Canadian bacon is good roasted whole and cooked on the barbecue. Treat it like ham, with glazes if you like.

Some bacon is cured but not smoked. The fat of this bacon is very white, and the meat is paler than that of smoked bacon. Use it as you would salt pork, or to line baking dishes, or for outer-larding if the salt is agreeable to your recipe. Blanch it first if you want to reduce the salt content.

Because bacon is perishable, it will develop molds if you keep it in your refrigerator too long. If you have purchased a large amount, it can be frozen, but not for long periods. Vacuum-packed packages sealed in heavy plastic will not lose flavor or aroma, but those that have been opened or wrapped differently may lose some flavor in the freezer. Be sure to defrost before cooking.

Ham

Escoffier considered fresh pork unworthy of first-class cookery, but he did think well of ham. All the hams he wrote about, including the Virginia and Kentucky varieties, were different from those usually found for sale today. We will discuss so-called country hams, or hard-cured or dry-cured hams, later. Aside from these, all smoked hams sold today are fully cooked and ready to eat; the labels will tell you how to heat and serve. The term "ham," correctly referring only to the leg of the pig, is also used for other parts of the animal prepared in the same fashion. With the new meat terminology devised by the Industrywide Cooperative Meat Identification Board in use, you should be able to tell from the label which cut was used for the piece you buy.

Leg ham can be bought with the skin or skinned, partially boned or completely boned, or boned, rolled and tied. Shoulder ham is available either regular or skinned. Picnic shoulder ham comes regular or boneless, skinless, rolled and tied. There is also boneless shoulder butt. In addition, pork loins, both regular and bladeless, spareribs, jowl squares and shoulder hocks are cured and smoked as ham is. Some of these are ready to eat, others require cooking, and still others, because they are fatty, need only enough cooking to be well heated. Be sure to read the labels or ask your butcher how you should prepare the ham you buy.

The jowl squares, or jowl bacon, are not usually used as bacon but as flavoring meats. Hocks add good flavor to soups and stews, but they can be prepared in other ways if you like; the problem with hocks is that they contain much cartilage and bone and not much meat.

Almost all of these cured and smoked pork products are also available cured and *not* smoked. If you find these in your markets, remember that they will need cooking.

Old-fashioned curing and smoking methods resulted in a dry, rather hard product. Today, water is added to ham to make it juicier. If a product contains water, it must be so labeled, but the water may never exceed 10% of the weight of the fresh meat. At the curing stage, brine is pumped into the meat, curing and adding water at the same time. In addition to accelerating the curing process, this distributes the dissolved salt more evenly throughout the meat. The amount of water used will make a difference in the texture of the finished product.

How does a piece of fresh pork become a smoked ham? First, the meat is cured with dry salt or brine. If dry salt is used, it is rubbed over the outside of the hams, and they are stacked in a cool place until the salt has been absorbed by the liquids in the meat; at the same time, the salt extracts some of the liquids, drying the meat in the process. If enough salt were used, the meat could be completely preserved, but even a low salt content has a strong preservative effect and destroys organisms that could cause the meat to spoil. According to each packer's recipe, a mixture of salt, sugar and spices is used for conventional hams.

The sugar is added for flavor and to counteract the hardening effect of the salt as it dries the meat. The rosy color of most cured meats is actually a denatured protein, resulting from the action of nitrite on the muscle tissue. After this step any excess salt is brushed off.

If brine is used for the curing step, the meat is completely immersed in it. With brine too, spices and herbs can be used. After brining the meat is rinsed in fresh water and dried, allowing a glossy coating composed of proteins from the meat to form. Hams with brine pumped into them are soaked in brine as well. For some special meats seasoning is spread over the entire surface before smoking.

It may be that smoking originated with the smudge fires that were used to keep insects, birds and animals away from salted meat while it dried. Smoking is not needed for preservation because there are so many other possibilities, but it is done today for the delicious flavor it gives the meat. However, by drying the meat smoking does have a preservative effect. If meat is completely cooked and dried, like the jerk meat, or jerky, of the Western game hunters and cowboys, it can be kept for years without refrigeration. This odd name comes from *charqui,* which in turn is derived from an Indian word; drying meat for traveling and for winter is a truly American tradition. Most smoked meats of today are only dried a little, so they still need refrigeration.

A whole smoked ham can weigh from 8 to 20 pounds, while boneless and skinless hams weigh up to 14 pounds. The little smoked butt usually weighs 1½ to 3 pounds. Made of the Boston butt, and quite fatty, the butt is boned and rolled; it may be cured as ham is, but it does not really taste the same. These cuts are also called "cottage butts" or "cottage rolls." Chunks of rolled, boneless ham in airtight wrapping are available in various sizes. Pork tenderloins are also cured and smoked.

For the picnic shoulder, weighing from 4 to 12 pounds, the blade and shoulder are trimmed in the shape of a true ham; the shank is cut exactly at the knee joint. Hams made from the shoulder are not as lean as those from the leg, and, because they are bony, they do not have such a large even layer of pink meat. Due to its boniness, its abundance of cartilage and its pore structure, which is different from that of the true ham, this cut is always pickled-cured instead of dry-cured. To dry-cure shoulder hams would take so long that they would become much too salty. Pickling and smoking picnics also take longer than it would for a regular ham. Even in this there are regional differences; some picnics are cut slightly differently for various sections of the country. The picnic is easiest to prepare and serve when boned and rolled.

In shopping for a domestic ham, choose one weighing no more than 16 pounds. Heavier hams may be from older animals and therefore less tender, or the extra weight may indicate that excess water has been pumped into the meat. The skin should be removed, or most of it at least, as should the long shank; if these are sold with the ham, they simply add to the weight and, as a result, to the price.

Let us return for a moment to those hams Escoffier considered superior. It is natural enough for a Frenchman to like ham, since the Gauls probably invented the process; they salted pork, smoked it for 2 days, then rubbed it with oil and vinegar and hung it up to dry. In the Middle Ages each region of what is now France developed its own style of curing. Until the nineteenth century, a ham fair was held in the square in front of Nôtre Dame de Paris for three days before Good Friday; even then ham was an Easter specialty. Bayonne and Toulouse hams are sliced very thin and eaten raw, usually as appetizers; such hams are never boiled, but they can be sautéed or mixed with other dishes and cooked. *Jambon de Paris* is lightly smoked or not smoked at all and requires cooking; it tastes more like the conventional hams of the United States than do the other French hams.

Prague ham is salted, cured in brine for several months, and then smoked over burning beechwood; this also needs cooking. Said to be smoked over burning juniper bushes, Westphalian ham, like Bayonne, is eaten raw. Danish ham is cured the same way as bacon and only lightly smoked.

The most famous of the dry-cured raw hams is Parma ham, usually called *prosciutto.* This is cured and dried but not smoked. The meat has an almost translucent look, and it is delicate and delicious. One secret in making *prosciutto* is the curing ingredients; the other is the way it is dried—in air-swept caves. *Prosciutto* is imported, but there is an American version, available in large chunks in heavy plastic packages and in smaller packages of slices. *Prosciutto* is eaten raw but can add flavor and color to countless preparations. Spain makes *jamon serrano* in Huelva, not unlike *prosciutto*, rosy and delicate; the story goes that this is aged in snow. A similar ham, *presunto*, is made in northern Portugal.

The best-known English ham is York ham, tender, pink and very good; there are also excellent hams from Wiltshire and Suffolk. Irish hams are dry-salt cured, boned, and smoked over peat.

Some of the European hams can be found at specialty shops in the United States, especially Parma and Westphalian hams. American-made Parma-style ham is boneless and a lot easier to carve than the Italian original.

Country-Style Hams

No European hard-cured ham is any better than the well-known American hams—from Virginia, Kentucky, Tennessee, and even Pennsylvania and New York State. The first commercial pork curing in the thirteen colonies may have been done in Massachusetts in 1636, but the place best known for ham is Smithfield, Virginia. For these hams, razorback pigs are raised on acorns, beechnuts and hickory nuts for 9 months, then on peanuts and corn. The leg is prepared in a "long cut"—butchered at the joint where the pelvic bone meets the backbone and at the fetlock joint, which makes them look different from the more familiar chunky short-cut ham. The hams are dry-salted until cured, then covered with black pepper and smoked over hickory fire—low heat and lots of smoke—for weeks. They are aged for a year or longer. Other Virginia hams come from pigs fed on peanuts or peaches, and they may be cured more quickly or smoked over other woods.

Kentucky hams are from Hampshire pigs fed on acorns and clover and then on grain. They are dry-salted for a month, then smoked over hickory bark and sassafras wood, or apple wood or corncobs for an additional month. These hams are aged for up to 2 years.

You can buy these "country hams" by mail from the packer or in specialty shops. They differ from most other American hams in that they do require cooking. When you open the package, you may be horrified to see the ham covered with mold and salt, appearing inedible. Scrub it in hot water with a nylon scrubber or a stiff-bristled brush; then soak all night covered in water. The next day, submerge the ham in fresh room-temperature water and bring to a boil slowly, letting the water barely simmer until the bone at the shank end sticks out of the meat about 1½ inches. Let the meat cool in the liquid. It is ready to eat at this point, but usually the cooled meat is skinned, glazed and baked. You can vary these steps by simmering less and baking longer, and the glazes you may use are many.

With such a range of hams on the market—those that require cooking, those that do not; those that must be soaked, and those that have already been soaked—you can pick the kind that suits your taste, but be sure to read package labels to make sure your next preparatory step will be the right one for that particular ham.

Two other cured and smoked pork products are *Lachsschinken* and *capocollo* (also spelled *capicola* and *capacola*). *Lachsschinken*, or "salmon ham," is cured boneless pork loin stuffed into a casing made of the large intestine and smoked by hot or cool smoke. This salmon-colored meat is usually found in specialty shops. *Capocollo* is cured pork butt rubbed with paprika and hot peppers and stuffed into a beef bung; it is then smoked and air-dried. This is often found with other delicatessen meats, and it makes a delicious sandwich meat.

Looking at the labels of the many kinds of cured and smoked meats, from large hams to various sausages, you may be astonished to read the same ingredients on all of them—water, salt, sugar, spices, sodium nitrite—and occasionally something special. The differences will be in the proportions of each ingredient and in the choice of spices. Current knowledge of the chemical action of each ingredient enables packers to produce any special flavor or to make all cured meats taste alike, if that's what consumers wanted.

Pastrami

Other meats besides pork are smoked. Lamb, mutton and beef are delicious that way, but they are usually prepared only in small smokehouses from which a shopper must buy directly.

The exception is pastrami, which is made by large packers and is a great favorite in New York. Pastrami is beef from the boneless plate or the boneless flank lying next to the brisket. It is probably a descendent of the Balkan smoked meats, especially Romanian *pastramă*; in fact some packers specify that their pastrami is Romanian in style. The meat is coated with pepper and smoked long enough for the cartilage to break down. Pastrami is available in large pieces or in small amounts of slices packed in plastic. It can be eaten as it is, baked until heated well, or served in gravy. If the pastrami is very peppery, a good trick is to cook it in water. Bring 1½ quarts water to a boil, then drop in the piece of pastrami. Continue to boil for 20 to 25 minutes, then drain briefly and serve hot.

Smoked Turkey

Smoked birds are now quite familiar, and turkeys are one of the specialties of New York State. It is important to have good-quality birds for smoking. Unless turkeys of at least 15 pounds are used, the finished product will be stringy and dry. Salt and seasoning are spread on the birds and allowed to work for a brief curing time. Then they are cooked and smoked simultaneously. The process is more delicate than that used for meats; and since birds are not dried and hard like a country ham, they are still perishable. If they are not to be sold within a week they are frozen, which is usually the case for shipment across state lines. Smoked turkeys must be thoroughly wrapped because they are already somewhat dehydrated and freezing can dehydrate them even more. After thawing they can be eaten without further cooking, or they can be heated with a little water—1 tablespoon to 1 pound of poultry—in a covered container over low heat or in a low oven. If you have someone to carve for you, one of these makes an excellent choice for a buffet or party.

Other birds are sometimes smoked, at specialty smokehouses. Capons and chickens, ducks and geese, even the little Rock Cornish game hens are sometimes found prepared this way. The fattier birds are very successful, but even pheasant and quail can be smoked. Like turkeys, these birds are not cured or pickled in the conventional way, but are rubbed with seasoning before smoking.

Sausages

Now let's get back to those sausages we mentioned at the beginning of this chapter. Under this heading we will consider briefly—the subject is worth an encyclopedia all by itself—all the products made of ground meat stuffed into casings.

Everyone agrees that sausage making began as an effort to utilize all the bits and pieces left over after animals had been butchered for food; and the intestines of the animal served as the casings, as they do today in some instances. Home farms and then regions developed their own recipes; gradually the products of some areas became so famous that the name of a place became permanently attached to the specialty made there. For example, in Braunschweig (Brunswick in English) they made liver sausage; it was called "Braunschweiger Wurst," "Brunswick sausage"; we've dropped the word for sausage and call that type by the adjective for the city. The same thing happened with "frankfurter," "wiener" and many others. "Baloney," as we pronounce it, is the sausage from Bologna, Italy.

While it is possible in the home kitchen to grind meat, season it, and stuff it into a casing to make an acceptable sausage, commercial sausage making can include a huge number of ingredients, each for a specific purpose. Among them are antioxidants, binders and extenders, chilling media (chiefly salt, acting just as it does in the old-fashioned ice-cream freezer), both natural and synthetic coloring, curing agents (some to preserve color, some to fix color), emulsifying agents, flavoring agents (including sugars and that mysterious thing called "hydrolyzed plant protein"), gases (CO_2 and N), sodium bicarbonate to neutralize excess acidity, calcium propionate to retard molds, phosphates, and synergists (various acids to increase the effectiveness of antioxidants). Additives may be used only if approved, if they are not injurious to health, and if their use is not intended to deceive the consumer. Sometimes today when one reads the label on a package of knackwurst, for instance, it is hard to find "meat " among all the other ingredients. No one sausage would have all the ingredients mentioned, and they must be listed on the label. The vague term "spices" is generally used to conceal the packer's secret recipe for the particular taste of his product. Usually it includes both herbs and spices.

Casings are made from the small and large intestines of pig, lamb and beef. These are prepared with great care—the larger ones are actually turned inside out for thorough cleansing—and then they are salted and chilled. Besides the intestines, some of the other inner membranes of the animals have special uses. There are also synthetic casings, at least two types made of plastic and one of hydrocellulose.

Animal casings are edible, and at least one of the nonanimal casings is too, but all of them can be peeled off if you prefer, after cooking for cooked sausages. In addition some sausages, the fatter ones, are packed in cloth bags, which are sewn closed.

Fresh sausages are made of uncured, uncooked meat, and they are not smoked. The salt or seasoning used in the recipes is not enough for curing. You must treat these as you would any other fresh meat: Refrigerate and plan to cook them within a week. You can freeze them if they are well wrapped, but the maximum freezer storage time is 6 months. You can find fresh sausages made of all pork, all beef, or meats mixed with various extenders or binders. You can also buy fresh sausage without casings (sausage meat) or in a single large casing.

Fresh smoked sausages are also uncooked, but they have been smoked over hardwoods, as ham or bacon are, to develop a particular flavor. The smoking is not enough to cook them, so these also must be treated like fresh meat and used within a week.

Cooked sausages are usually made of uncured meats, although some cured meats are also cooked. These have been completely precooked and can be served without further preparation. However, like all cooked fresh meat, they must be refrigerated and used within 2 weeks.

Cooked smoked sausages are ready to eat as purchased, but most of them taste better hot. These include the most familiar types—frankfurters, wieners, knackwurst, bologna—which are similar in texture and taste. As they are made in the United States, mortadella, kielbasy and berliner sausages are also in this category. Although these are made with fresh meats, a kind of curing, emulsion curing, takes place within the casing, the action of the salt and seasonings mixed with the ground or chopped meat before it is packed. Afterward it is smoked; with mortadella and kielbasy the cooking and smoking are completed together. The others are cooked in water after smoking. These meats should be refrigerated also, and for best flavor they should be used within 2 weeks.

Semidry or summer sausages were so named because they would keep in the summer, which was an important consideration before the development of refrigeration. These have been smoked long enough to dry and are usually left to dry further. The meats used are usually mixed with curing ingredients and allowed to cure for 1 or 2 days before being stuffed into casings, but the exact procedure varies with the specific kind of sausage. These will keep longer than most sausages and will not spoil if left unrefrigerated for a day or two—on a camping trip, for instance—but to keep them in top condition refrigerate them; plan to use them within 3 weeks. Cervelat is an example.

Dry sausages are drier and firmer than semidry because more moisture has been extracted from them. The drying can last from 1 to 6 months and has to be done with great care, very slowly and evenly. Some of these are cured before being packed in casings, some are smoked before they are dried, some are never smoked, and some are cured in the casing. Chorizos, frizzes or frizzie, salami and pepperoni are all dry sausages. Even if you have seen charming pictures of these hanging on strings in European kitchens, it is better to refrigerate and use them within 3 weeks.

As you already know from Chapter 1, the chief concern with any meat product including pork is the destruction of all live trichinae. For the product to be safe without further cooking, the internal temperature must reach 137° F. Freezing pork at −20° F. for 6 days or at −10° F. for 10 days will also kill the organisms. The freezing step is used only for "certified pork" used in sausages that are lightly cured and lightly smoked, because otherwise it would not be safe to eat them; mettwurst, or schmierwurst, is the chief example of this type. Other sausages must reach 137° F. by smoking or various cooking methods. If they have not been adequately smoked or cooked, the consumer will have to cook them before serving. Therefore it is important when you buy any product of this kind to read labels carefully. If in doubt, consult your butcher.

Although frozen certified pork is used for mettwurst, most other sausages *must* be made of fresh meats that have never been frozen. *Frankfurters* are made of fresh boneless skeletal meat from beef, veal, calf or pork, and the meat must be made into frankfurters within 7 days of slaughtering. Liquid smoke is permissible as a flavoring agent for frankfurters but not as a substitute for actual smoking over hardwood. The usual meat mixture is half beef and half pork, but there are also all-beef frankfurters as well as other mixtures. Kosher franks are all beef, packed in sheep casings. The seasoning in frankfurters includes salt, sugar, black pepper, red pepper, nutmeg and coriander. Dry skim milk or soy protein may be used. Ice or water may be added to help in mixing, and links may be naturally or artificially colored. The number of links per pound must be specified, and the casings are tested for surface resistance.

Liverwurst is made from pork livers with gall bladders removed and pork meat trimmings from skeletal cuts, none of which has been frozen. Salt, sugar, spices, onion powder, nitrate, nitrite and additives are mixed with the ground meats, but no extenders are allowed. The mixture is stuffed into casings, cooked to 160° F., and cooled. The fat content may not exceed 30%.

Breakfast pork sausages are made of fresh pork that has not been frozen or cured. Salt, sugar, sage and perhaps other spices as well as antioxidants are mixed with the ground meat. Dry ice is used in the process of stuffing, and at no time is the meat allowed to be hotter than 50° F. The finished sausages are chilled to 40° F. or cooler before packing. If the sausages are frozen, they must be kept at exactly 0° F. As with franks, the number of links per pound must be specified, and the fat and moisture content is tested. Some multisyllable preservatives may be used, but they may not represent more than .3 gram per 1,000 grams of the sausage.

Since frankfurters, liverwurst and fresh pork sausages are only the most familiar and simple fresh meat sausages, you can imagine what a huge book this would be if we went on to describe the many kinds.

There are countless sausages and other ground meats made in France—*saucisses, saucissons, boudins blancs* and *noirs, crépinettes, gayettes, rillettes*—and in Italy—different varieties of *salami, mortadella, pepperoni, bologna*—and in Germany and Spain and Poland—everywhere the pig is eaten. If you see one of these names in your market though, it is not a French or Italian or Spanish or German sausage you're looking at, but an American-made meat product. All the sausages sold in the United States are made in the United States. If you arrived at the port of New York with a sausage you picked up abroad, that would be as far as you would get. By such careful control, the incidence of food-related illnesses has been sharply reduced.

Trichinosis is not the only problem to be confronted in smoked and cured meats. Bacteria and molds are potential dangers, and careful curing, smoking or cooking is designed to destroy most of them while at the same time contributing to the characteristic taste of each product. "Hot smoke" reaches a far higher temperature than "cool smoke," and the use of one or the other and the length of smoking time make a considerable difference in the texture and taste of such meat.

Many sausages, as well as meat loaves, are available in small portions in vacuum-sealed packages or freshly sliced from delicatessens.

Dried Meats

Yet another kind of curing is done by drying. We mentioned jerky earlier, a perfect example. Probably chipped beef is the best known but two other famous dried meats are biltong, an African jerky made of beef, venison or ostrich (!), and *Bündnerfleisch*, beef air-dried in the Swiss Alps, in Grisons, the largest of the Swiss cantons. Imported *Bündnerfleisch* can sometimes be found in specialty shops. Salt is used in preparing domestic dried beef, and it is indeed salty. It can be found vacuum-packed in jars or plastic packages, and it is a great meat for emergencies. There are also smoked sliced beef, different from chipped, and freeze-dehydrated meat, which can have a moisture content as low as 2%; this can be rehydrated successfully.

Canned Meats

Meat canning is a complicated industry. The manufacture of cans could fill a chapter, and the methods of filling, sealing and heat processing could fill another. Heat processing must destroy enzymes, molds, yeasts and bacteria, especially anaerobic bacteria, which can survive without oxygen. Most canned hams are still perishable and require refrigeration, so treat them like fresh meat. If in doubt, be sure to read the labels. The United States imports some canned hams, chiefly from Poland and Denmark. Some people think these are superior to American hams, but we do not.

There are many other canned meat products. The famous or infamous "luncheon meat"; corned beef and corned-beef hash; frankfurters and wieners; bacon; and countless preparations made with meat and other ingredients—stews, meat spreads, chili and so on. Many of these products are good for the emergency shelf.

Also canned are various poultry products, boned chicken and various poultry spreads. One of the most successful of all the canned meats is tongue, whole or sliced, which is packed in tins and jars.

Besides all these products, from salt pork to canned tongue, there are so many others that it would take a lifetime to sample them all.

Here is a simple recipe made with knackwurst; you can adapt the recipe to other sausages and vary the filling. It makes a good lunch or supper dish, especially for children.

KNACKWURST CANOES

Rinse off the knackwurst and drop into boiling water for 5 minutes. Split them down the middle, but not all the way through, making a canoe shape. Have hot mashed potatoes ready, and sprinkle some cornmeal into them. Stuff the canoes with the potatoes until they cover most of the top of the wurst. Sprinkle with chopped chives and ground peppercorns, and bake in the oven until the top is crusty and golden brown. A hungry person can eat two of them.

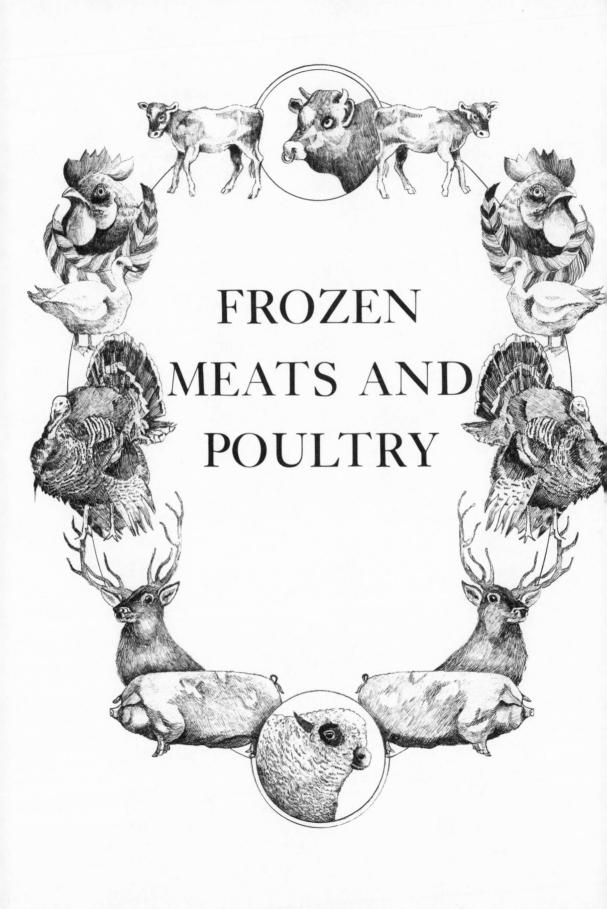

FROZEN
MEATS AND
POULTRY

Chapter 4

Aʟʟ ᴋɪɴᴅꜱ ᴏꜰ ᴍᴇᴀᴛ ᴀɴᴅ ᴘᴏᴜʟᴛʀʏ can be found frozen in the retail markets of the United States. Some housewives in this country buy these exclusively and never know how fresh meat tastes. There is no doubt that the successful freezing of these foods has simplified food shopping for those who are far from good markets or who have limited time.

If you regularly buy frozen meats from your retail shop or supermarket, you already know some of the disadvantages. First, the frozen portions may be too large or too small for your family. Perhaps you can use the excess in some leftover preparations; if it cannot be used, the purchase is not really economic. Second, you cannot really tell much about the quality of frozen meat in the retail market; it is usually completely covered with wrapping, but the freezing process alters the appearance anyway, making it impossible to determine the consistency.

If you buy many frozen meats, you should find a market you can absolutely trust. You should be confident that the packages have not been defrosted and refrozen, that they were well wrapped to prevent freezer burn, and, most important, that the meat was of good quality to begin with. In the retail market, you may find meats that have come from the big packing houses; these have usually been packaged in conveyor systems and have never been touched by human hands. In larger markets, you may find meats and poultry that have been packed and frozen by the store itself. These can be fine if your store is dependable. No matter how good the meat was originally, it can lose quality through poor handling before it gets to you. Do not buy a package containing a layer of frozen liquid, for you can be sure that the package has been defrosted at least once. If you cannot see into the package, be sure you cannot hear any liquid sloshing around when you shake it.

Obviously, we think buying frozen meats is a second choice. It is far better to see your meat before freezing it and to have it cut into the portions you want. You can be certain then that it has never been defrosted and refrozen.

Buying meat wholesale to freeze is not the ideal solution for every family. The family must be large enough to use all the meat before its optimum storage time has elapsed, and proper storage must be available.

If you have adequate freezer space, it is practical and economical to buy meat wholesale and have it cut into portions to suit your own family size and your own habits. You will also be sure of the quality of meat you are buying. None of the frozen meat will be wasted if you decide exactly how to use each portion when you buy it.

In 1974, the average retail price of a Prime half-steer was $450. By the time the half-steer has been divided into packages ready for the freezer, 30% of the weight—fat, excess bone and trimmings in bulk—will have been discarded. This loss, however, is balanced by a 30% savings on the cost of buying all the cuts separately in a retail market. But because the lump sum necessary to buy in bulk is large, it is important to have adequate freezer storage space and to be sure everything is in good working order.

FREEZERS

Freezers come in various sizes, 12, 15 and 21 cubic-foot capacities being among the most common. They also come in a variety of styles: upright, like conventional refrigerators, or chest types. In addition, freezers can be frost free or require manual defrosting. To determine the size you need, consider how much space you have to put a freezer in your home and the number of people in your family. A freezer of 15 cubic feet will hold about 500 pounds of food. Your available space may determine the style you choose, but we recommend the upright because it is easy to lose things in a deep chest, and you will have to move many packages to get to those on the bottom. We also recommend that you get the frost-free type, because to defrost manually you must disconnect the power, remove all the packages, and scrape down the box. Not only is this a lot of work, but also, more important, due to the temperature change, your frozen foods will suffer deterioration while all this is going on.

It is true that the frost-free box is more costly, but you pay that sum only once, and it will result in a better storage arrangement since the meat will remain at the correct temperature until you are ready to cook it.

Be sure your freezer has a thermostat, and make it a habit to check the temperature every time you take something out. If the temperature alters significantly, do not wait to check the mechanism. By the time the temperature has risen above 0° F. you are in danger of losing all your meat before repairs can be made.

When you buy your freezer, buy at least enough insurance to protect yourself against the loss of your meat because of power failure or equipment malfunction.

BEEF

If you have a 500-pound capacity freezer and if your family enjoys eating beef, you can seriously consider purchasing half a steer. This will be 300 to 400 pounds gross primal weight. In grades other than Prime, the animals may be smaller.

Looking at the side of beef hanging in the market, you cannot see the face of the various cuts, so you will not be able to judge the quality by the usual indications. To be sure you are buying good beef, accept only government-inspected meat, and only Prime or Choice grade. Look for good conformation; the leg portion should be rounded, curving down almost like a question mark. The fat should be creamy white. There should not be too much exterior fat surrounding the eye of the meat, and the steak portions should exhibit marbling like fine pencil dashes (see p. 18).

Let us assume that you have a family of 4 and that you give a dinner party for 8 to 10 people once a month, with leftovers after the party. The half-steer will be butchered first into wholesale cuts and then into retail cuts. Here are our suggestions for dividing these.

Loin

8 porterhouse steaks, 1 to 1¼ inches thick, each for 2 servings
3 T-bone steaks, each for an individual serving
6 sirloin steaks, 1 inch thick, each for 3 to 4 servings

Note that the porterhouse may be cut into thicker steaks than the sirloin. This is because the face of the porterhouse is smaller, and at the T-bone end the steak would be too small for 2 servings if cut too thin.

Here is another way to cut this section:

15 or 16 shell or strip steaks, 1 inch thick, or double, or triple steaks
1 whole tenderloin (filet) roast, 6 servings

Or try this instead:

Cut half into pieces for fondue—cubes of ¾ to 1 inch
Cut half into pieces for Stroganoff—round or square slices ¼ to ½ inch thick

Round

top round, first 6 inches, 2 London broils, each for 6 servings

This will be a delicious London broil. The balance of the top round will make a good roast beef, like that from a delicatessen, served in thin slices.

1 eye of the round roast, about 5 pounds, 8 servings

If your beef is Prime, this will make a fine oven roast. If the beef is Choice, it is better to pot-roast the eye of round.

3 bottom round roasts, each about 3½ pounds, for 6 servings

All cuts from the round are economical; there is scarcely any waste because there is little fat and very few bones.

2 top sirloin roasts, each about 4½ pounds, for 6 to 8 servings

Be sure your butcher removes all veins, an important factor in preparation.

Flank Steak

This is used for London broil. You can have one large piece or smaller pieces of 1 or 2 pounds. To avoid losing juices, do not have it scored before freezing.

The tail of the porterhouse, which is in the flank section, is often ground, and we prefer that, but it can also be cut into chunks for beef stew or made into cube steaks.

Hindshank

Cut into 2-inch-thick chunks; they will be about 3 inches in diameter, each with a round slice of marrow-filled bone in the middle. Or cut the hindshank into 3 pieces to make *osso buco* of beef.

Rib

The entire section has 7 rib bones. This can be cut into 2 rib roasts, each with 2 bones, each to serve 4 or 5 persons; and a single 3-bone roast to serve 6 or 7 persons.

There is a layer of meat above the eye of the rib section that can be used for pot roast; cut it into 2 sections of 2½ to 3 pounds each, to serve 5 people. Part can also be cut into thin strips for pepper steak.

Remove the end section of rib bones (back ribs) from the beef roasts. Prepare and cook these beef spareribs as you would pork spareribs.

Chuck

The chuck includes the shoulder, or blade, the arm chuck, the entire neck of beef and the foreshank. Cut the foreshank into *osso buco*, as you would the hindshank, or into slices for stew, or grind it for hamburger.

With a shoulder, or blade, of Prime beef, cut a single 3-inch-thick London broil, to serve 6 persons. Tie the balance for pot roast. You can either tie some bones with the pot roast to add flavor or save all the bones for stock making.

With Choice beef, roll the entire piece for a large pot roast that will serve 14 persons.

Remove the entire top portion of the arm chuck. Use the piece, including the first 2 bones of the neck portion, as roast beef, bones still in, to serve 6 people; it will be very tender.

Remove all remaining bones in the neck portion; keep the bones for stock and cut 3 pot roasts from the boneless portion, each to serve 6 persons.

Retain all scraps for grinding.

Plate and Brisket

The whole brisket will have a net weight of 8 to 9 pounds. Cut it into halves, each portion to serve 6 persons. Pot-roast fresh brisket. (See Chapter 3 for corned brisket.)

The butcher's, or hanging, tenderloin is attached next to the kidney and hangs down loosely below it. It makes a good London broil.

Lying under the brisket is the breastbone. Do not remove all the meat from it, but trim it well and use the piece to make boiled beef or a very rick stock, or add it to vegetables or split-pea soup. These bones are rich with gelatin and other good nutrients, which are easily released in cooking (see p. 159).

The plate, lying inside the rib section, includes the plate flanken, or short ribs, which are square in shape and have small bones. Plate flanken are superior to long-bone flanken, near the flank portion, because the latter are stringier and fattier. To prepare the long-bone flanken, crack the bones in 2 or 3 places before freezing. Save to add to slow-cooking dishes rather than serving this separately.

The boneless skirt steak makes superb hamburger. Whether you plan to broil it as steak or grind it, remove the membrane and cut it into 2 pieces to freeze.

In addition to these cuts of substantial size with a large proportion of meat, there will be pieces of meat with many bones. Cut some of these into smaller chunks to make beef stew. As for the rest, bone it, grind it and store it in packages of 1 or 2 pounds; 2 pounds is the maximum because it takes too long to defrost anything larger, and it would be too much for this imaginary family of 4 anyway. You can also make patties of the ground meat before freezing it, separating them with a sheet of freezer paper; this makes defrosting much easier, and you can separate from the package only as many patties as you need.

Cut out all the remaining bones, including neck bones, and divide them into mounds weighing 2 to 3 pounds. For the best flavor, mix bones from different parts of the carcass in each mound, including, for instance, bones from the shoulder with those from the leg. Wrap them in secure packages and label them "bones." These will make excellent stocks and soups.

CALF AND VEAL

As you know, calf and veal are young cattle slaughtered at different ages, but as far as freezing is concerned, the same rules apply to both.

This meat is tender, perishable and fine; it has little fat, and it is not firm. Because freezing causes changes in the consistency, flavor and texture of these meats, do not buy half a calf or veal. If you want to keep some frozen veal on hand, buy retail cuts for specific uses. For instance, purchase a large piece of the leg to be cut into *scaloppini*; do not cut into scallops before freezing, because these slices are quite thin and especially subject to freezer burn. Veal steaks at least ¾ inch thick can be frozen, as can vealburgers—either ground veal shaped into patties or un-ground veal to be used alone or mixed with other meats for burgers or meat loaf (see Chapter 12). Chunks for stew cut from breast, neck or shank of veal can be pack-aged and frozen also. Large pieces and the stew packages can be kept for 3 months, but ground veal and veal for *scaloppini* should be frozen for short periods only: 2 or 3 weeks is safe, with a maximum of 1 month.

LAMB

A lamb is so much smaller than a steer that you can buy a whole carcass, weighing from 35 to 40 pounds, for freezing. Loss due to trimming is 20 to 25% with lamb, and there is an equivalent percentage of savings over buying the same cuts retail. Divide it for freezing as follows:

Leg

2 roasts, with bones or boned and rolled
or bone and flatten one to butterfly for the barbecue
or cut one into cubes, 1½ to 2 inches in size, for shish kebab

Loin

16 single loin lamp chops
or 8 double loin lamb chops
or 1 French saddle of lamb

The saddle is a good cut if you know how to carve it (see p. 328), but it does take considerable space in your freezer.

Bracelet

By removing the breast, you will have a rack. For the moment set the breasts aside, and divide the rack like this:

2 single racks of lamb, each with 8 chops
or 16 single rib lamb chops
or 8 double rib lamb chops
or 1 crown of lamb, made by fastening both racks together (see p. 221)

Neck, or Chuck

Cut 12 shoulder lamb chops, ¾ inch thick. Remaining will be 2 ends of neck, 2 shanks and 2 breasts. Trim all these well and cut them into pieces for lamb stew. After trimming, weigh the pieces, divide them into 3- to 4-pound portions, wrap and label. You may prefer to leave the shanks whole for braising or keep a shoulder in one piece for roasting. Cut to suit your own plans.

In a lamb butchered for freezing, nothing is left over—no bones or bits for grinding—because the bones are still in the cuts.

In addition to these portions, you will have 2 lamb kidneys. These can also be frozen, but you may prefer to take them home and cook them for lunch.

PORK

It is possible to freeze pork, but we do not recommend it. Like veal, good pork is tender, and freezing tends to harden the meat because most of the moisture in pork is in the fat. Because of the youth of the animals, freezer burn occurs more quickly in pork and veal than in beef, even when correctly wrapped.

SMOKED AND CURED MEATS

Smoked and cured meats present special problems for freezing. The salt used in curing slows the freezing process, causing the fat in the meats to suffer changes in taste that can be most unpleasant, especially if you store the meat for longer than a few weeks. Also, in meats such as ham the salt has a tendency to come to the surface. When such a ham is roasted, the outer cuts will taste very salty and the center pieces extremely mild.

Smoked tongue and brisket corned beef can be frozen more successfully because these are usually cooked in water, which equalizes the salt content.

GAME

If someone in your family enjoys hunting, you should know something about freezing the catch. It is possible, but you must face the same problems as you do in cooking game. It is always lean, making it perishable in freezing, as veal is; you have no idea how the animal was fed, so you cannot know the quality of the meat; unless you are an experienced hunter alert to the specific signs of age, you probably will not know how old your animal is. In general, treat game like veal for freezing: Freeze only larger sections and be sure to wrap with great care.

Rabbits are raised commercially in the United States, especially in Arkansas, and some are imported from Australia. They appear in markets already frozen. If you have small game like this in your catch, prepare it for freezing as you would a chicken (see p. 65).

WRAPPING, LABELING, DATING

Before freezing, each cut should be weighed and then double-wrapped with high-grade freezer paper and sealed. Label each package at once with the name of the cut, the weight and the date. Do not delude yourself that you will be able to recognize a particular piece later by its shape or size; after a while everything in the freezer looks exactly alike. There are special tapes for freezer labeling; they are sticky on one side and you can write on the other. Be sure to use this special tape because ordinary sticky tapes come off at such low temperatures. There are also special pens for freezer labels, but indelible felt pens work fine and are sold in many places.

The best wrapping is flexible paper with a polyethylene coat; there are also transparent bags of polyethylene that can be sealed with twisters. Aluminum foil tends to become brittle when frozen, and it may crack, or you may poke a hole in it while wrapping a cut with an awkward shape or a projecting bone. The important thing is that the package be completely airtight; if it is not, the meat can develop freezer burn.

FREEZER BURN

Freezer burn results when the moisture has been forced out of frozen meats and poultry by low temperature, a process like dehydration. The meat so affected is not spoiled in the sense of "contaminated," but it has lost juices and, as a result, some of its nutritive value. And the taste will be spoiled—the meat will take on some of the odors of the storage box through the exposed portions. Because the exposed tissues have lost moisture, the texture will be brittle; the surface will appear dry, brownish and spotted. Since you will have to cut off this exterior portion, it is wasteful to let any of your frozen food be damaged in this way.

To make sure your packages are as airtight as possible, press the wrap closely around the meat. Even better, create a vacuum by sucking the air out with a straw. As with ground beef patties, if you want to freeze individual chops or steaks together, be sure to separate them by sheets of wax paper or freezer paper.

If the meat is oddly shaped, you may have better luck with heavy plastic or transparent plastic wrap. First put a crumpled piece of wrap over any projecting corners or bones, then wrap with a single layer of the flexible wrap, and then overwrap with a second layer, seal, and label.

STORAGE

Recording the name of the meat cut and its weight is obviously useful, but do not forget the date as well. The length of time you can store frozen meat is relatively short; for optimum flavor and nutrition, the meat must be used within a specific period. Frozen meats should be rotated in the freezer so that the packages on the bottom will not get lost. What you froze first should be used first. Also, do not over-stock; if you have more frozen meat than your family can use, the inevitable result will be the storage of part of it for many more weeks or months than is safe for best use.

Although meat stored for too long might not spoil and could well be edible, it will have lost flavor, juiciness and nutritional value. Even when perfectly wrapped, meats will undergo some dehydration during prolonged freezer storage. Long storage at temperatures higher than 0° F. presents still other problems: At 0° F. or below, there will be no enzyme or bacterial action, but if the temperature rises, dormant enzymes could cause detectable changes in taste. This might sound puzzling if you recall the wooly mammoths found frozen in the Arctic, which were edible after incredible eons. The reason for this seeming contradiction is that the mammoths were frozen at temperatures far below 0° F., and for all those ages they were stored without appreciable temperature fluctuations or any exposure to air. But just the opening and closing of home freezers causes such changes to occur.

If you have room in your freezer for the packages you have made—approximately 400 pounds if you purchased a half-steer—put them all in the freezer, at −10° F., and close it. *Do not open it* until 48 hours have elapsed; this will allow the meat to freeze solidly.

If there is not enough room in your freezer for all the meat, you may be able to arrange with your butcher to store part of it until you do have space. Your butcher may even be willing to store it all; consider this option if you have no room for a freezer of your own, or explore possible arrangements with frozen-food lockers, to be found in most large population centers.

Another word of caution: We have been talking about a proper freezer that can be kept at a steady −10° F. Do not even consider freezing such a mass of food in the little freezer compartment of a conventional refrigerator. With these, stick to the rule of storing no more than 3 pounds of unfrozen food for each cubic foot of space in the box. If you add more than this, you will raise the overall temperature in the refrigerator, endangering the other foods stored.

How long can frozen meat be stored? The Department of Agriculture suggests these maximum storage times:

beef	12 months
lamb	12 months
fresh pork	8 months
ground beef and lamb	4 months
pork sausage	3 months

We would like to make a further distinction in storage times, based on the kind of equipment you have:

refrigerator with freezer compartment
    with a separate door   3 months
side-by-side refrigerator-freezer,
    freezer with separate door and thermostat   6 months
self-contained freezer   12 to 16 months

The 16-month time for the self-contained freezer applies to larger pieces of meat and to beef, not to ground, cured or excessively fatty meats. If you follow these guidelines, your meat will not change noticeably in either appearance or flavor.

One last word about planning: Do not buy a specific piece of meat expecting to use it for a specific recipe some time in the future. One piece can so easily be lost among the dozens of packages in your freezer. Rather, purchase that cut fresh. Buy a half-steer or a whole lamb with general purposes in mind, and have it cut into basic pieces that you know you can use.

COOKING FROZEN MEATS

We recommend that all frozen meat be defrosted before cooking. When cooking meat from the frozen state, it is impossible to see how it is progressing in the oven or pot. Inevitably the outer portions will be overcooked or worse before the interior is done. In addition, you cannot season frozen meat properly because all seasoning will stay on the outside and slide off into the bottom of your cooking vessel. Unless the meat is something you froze yourself, you may not even be sure of the best cooking method to use.

To defrost meats, remove them from freezer to refrigerator and let them stay there, on a tray or dish with edges, to catch juices, for 24 to 72 hours, depending on the size of the piece. Of course, the larger the piece, the longer it will require to be fully defrosted.

After defrosting, cook the meat as soon as possible. It has undergone some changes as a result of the freezing process—particularly loss of moisture—and you cannot keep it uncooked in the refrigerator for as long as you would a similar piece of fresh meat; 2 days is the limit.

Cook defrosted meat just as you would fresh meat; see Chapter 6 for all the general procedures, and Chapter 16 for barbecue and spit-roasting. Here is an example, using frozen rabbit:

RABBIT WITH MUSTARD-CREAM SAUCE   6 to 8 servings

½ frozen rabbit, about 2¼ pounds
2 tablespoons olive oil
1 tablespoon butter
1 teaspoon salt
½ teaspoon ground white pepper
1 teaspoon drained capers

½ teaspoon dry mustard
¼ cup chicken stock
3 tablespoons prepared Dijon mustard
1¼ to 1½ cups frozen whole tiny white
    onions
½ cup heavy cream

Defrost the frozen rabbit in the refrigerator for 36 to 40 hours or at room temperature for 5 to 6 hours. Most frozen rabbit is sold precut; you may want to cut the pieces into smaller sections.

Preheat oven to 350° F. Heat oil and butter in a heavy skillet and brown the rabbit pieces on all sides. Brown only a few pieces at a time, and as they are browned transfer them to a sturdy casserole, 1½- to 2-quart size. Sprinkle each layer of pieces with some salt, white pepper, capers and dry mustard. When the rabbit is all browned, the casserole should be full. Pour the chicken stock into the skillet and bring to a boil while stirring with a wooden spatula to incorporate all the meat juices in the pan. When the stock boils, reduce the heat and stir in the prepared mustard. (Do not use less mustard than specified; it will not be overpowering, but very delicate in taste.) When the mustard and stock are well blended, pour the mixture over the rabbit. Cover the casserole and bake in the oven for 1½ hours. Check the casserole after ½ hour; if the stock has cooked away, add another ¼ cup; this will not be necessary if the rabbit just fits the casserole and if the cover is tight.

After 1½ hours, add the onions. When the liquid is at a simmer again, add the cream, cover, and let the dish bake for another 30 to 45 minutes. The longer it cooks, the thicker the sauce will be, but the rabbit will be very tender after 30 minutes.

Note: You can use only oil for sautéing if you prefer. You can eliminate the cream and instead add ½ cup additional stock at the outset; the dish will taste different, but it will be less caloric. If you have a whole rabbit, double the other ingredients and use a 3½-quart casserole.

If you plan to marinate a piece of frozen meat, you can unwrap it, put it directly into the marinade, and let it defrost there. But if it is a large piece that requires several days to defrost, the marinade will probably overpower the taste of the meat. For a more delicate flavor, let the meat defrost, still wrapped, for 24 hours, then unwrap it and put it in the marinade. Any juices that are extracted during defrosting will be collected in the marinade, so it can be used to good advantage in cooking or in making a sauce or gravy to be served with the meat.

Defrosting can be done at room temperature too, and you can cut the refrigerator time to one third or one quarter, but slower defrosting at a cooler temperature helps retain more of the juices in the meat.

As a last resort you can defrost in the broiler, placing the meat as far as possible from the source of heat. If your broiler heat is adjustable, set it at "moderate." Let the meat rest in the broiler for 3 to 5 minutes on each side, according to its thickness. Of course, this will work only for meat cuts of even thickness—steaks, chops, flat slices; do not try it with a roast. Do not try it for any cut that is less than 1½ inches thick either; they will defrost reasonably quickly in other ways, and the broiler method will dry them out.

If you are forced to cook your meat from the frozen state, here are some suggestions. First, be prepared for the cooking to take longer; a roast normally requiring 2 hours to be done will need 3 when frozen. Start the roast in a very hot preheated oven (450° F.), and let the meat cook for 20 to 30 minutes; this will prevent some of the steaming effect that would result from starting at a lower temperature. Then reduce heat to slightly lower than the standard temperature for your particular cut, and roast until done. As soon as the meat is cooked enough to allow it, insert the meat thermometer; try to have the point centered. If your finished roast isn't browned to your taste, you can raise the temperature at the end to brown it.

In cooking frozen meats with moist heat, simply allow a longer time for braising, poaching or stewing than you would for unfrozen meats.

To broil frozen meats, preheat the broiler, oil the grill, set the heat as high as possible, and place the frozen steak or chop almost twice as far from the heat source as you would thawed or fresh meat. Cook for 2 to 3 minutes longer on each side than for thawed meat, or until done to your taste. Test by cutting a small slice near the center. Do not attempt to broil pieces 1½ inches thick or thicker while still frozen; this method is possible only for pieces thinner than 1½ inches.

If your frozen pieces are less than ¾ inch thick, it will be better to panfry them. Frozen hamburgers and other ground meats are better panfried, but we do not recommend ever cooking these ground meats while still frozen. Nor do we recommend it for very thin cuts like cube steaks or sandwich steaks; these defrost quickly enough because they are so thin.

We do not suggest deep-frying frozen meats. The temperature of the oil is critical for good deep-frying, and dropping still-frozen meats into the oil will reduce it too much. In addition, the moisture in the frozen meat will cause splashing.

Frozen bones for stock can of course be put directly into water, since the long slow cooking will be more than enough to defrost them.

Microwave cooking, still somewhat experimental, may offer the solution for cooking solidly frozen meats, since the foods in such appliances cook from the inside out, whereas conventional methods cook from the outside in. Until this device has been perfected, however, it is best to defrost and cook using conventional methods.

CHICKEN

Buy fresh chickens when they are plentiful and least expensive, and freeze your own. Commercially frozen chickens that are not sold immediately are stored and sold past the time when they taste their best. In some markets frozen chickens are thawed for sale, and any not sold are refrozen; these birds will have lost juiciness and flavor. For the same reasons, you yourself should never refreeze poultry that has been frozen and thawed.

If you are buying frozen chickens and find that there is a lot of frozen liquid in the package, you can be sure that the chicken in that package has been defrosted and refrozen. While the chicken may not be spoiled, it will not taste the way a good bird should; that frozen liquid contains the juices that would have made your chicken flavorful.

Unless you are buying from a farmer, all the chickens in markets today will be eviscerated. If your chickens are not so prepared, this must be done before freezing. All the birds we have been talking about should be completely drawn and dressed.

Broilers

Broilers can be frozen whole, but you must have adequate space for them. They can also be split or quartered. Prepare them for cooking before you freeze them: Wash them in water, pat dry and season. Pack in flexible freezer wrapping and suck out the air with a straw.

Fryers

Follow the same procedure for fryers as for broilers, but cut the birds into smaller pieces.

If you plan to fry the pieces with breading, do not bread them before freezing; the coating has a tendency to crack and dry, and the meat underneath will dry also. In cooking, the frozen coating will not become crisp. For these reasons, it is better to bread the pieces *after* defrosting.

Defrost the frozen pieces of broilers or fryers, still in their wrappings, in the refrigerator overnight. Then bring them out to your countertop and allow them to reach room temperature, which will take about 4 hours.

Roasters

Roasters are pullets of 3½ to 6½ pounds. They can be frozen whole, but remember, you need adequate space.

If you are buying a bird to freeze for later roasting, look for one with a coating of fat that will act as a lubricant during roasting; this reduces the need for basting. The fat under the skin should be clean milky-white; if it is blue-white, indicating a very thin fatty layer, do not pick the bird. Season your roaster, inside and out, but do not stuff it. The seasoning will sink into the bird and will not be lost in the liquids during defrosting.

To defrost frozen whole chickens—broilers or roasters—put them, still wrapped, in a bowl or clean sink and *cover* with cool water. If the breast sticks up too high, cover it with a wet towel. This assures that the moisture of the bird is not lost as it defrosts.

If you get ambitious and bone your poultry to make a roll or a *galantine*, you can freeze these too. However, do not soak boneless rolls or *galantines* in water to

Chicken disjointed (cut up) for freezing. The same procedure is used to prepare chicken for fricassee or for other stews, or for frying, or for the broiler or barbecue.

defrost them. Instead, leave them in the refrigerator for 2 days, then let them rest on the countertop for 4 hours before roasting or poaching.

Frozen chicken parts—legs, wings, breasts, etc.—can be good buys when they are cheaper than whole chickens. Use legs and wings for stew, for stock and for potting. Frozen breasts can be used in any way that fresh breasts can.

Chickens can be boned and cut into cubes for chickenburgers or kebabs. Place the cubes in 1-pound packages, wrap, seal and label. The bones left after cutting chickens for burgers or kebabs can be stored for future use in stock in the same way as bones of beef. Wrap them in 2- to 4-pound packages.

Giblets can also be frozen for stocks. However, chicken livers should be used fresh, and in any case they would make a cloudy stock.

CAPON AND TURKEY

You could buy capons and turkeys to freeze whole, but it is not practical. To begin with, turkeys are plentiful all year round nowadays, and capons can be ordered in advance from your butcher. Unlike chicken, neither of these birds makes the sort of dish you think of cooking in an emergency; they are usually party fare or for special occasions, and they require a long time for defrosting and cooking. And they will occupy far too much space in your freezer. However, if you should want to freeze a turkey or capon, follow the general rules for choosing a good bird and proceed as you would with a roasting chicken.

As for choosing an already frozen bird from the market, you just have to proceed by trial and error. When you find a packer whose birds seem just right to you, make a note of the name and buy that kind the next time.

When fresh turkey is available at low cost, you can buy it and freeze parts. These will not take up so much space in your freezer, and they will defrost more rapidly. Another good trick is to cut turkey *scaloppine*—thick breast slices—from fresh birds, which will be ideal for parties at a later date. Wrap carefully, with a slice of freezer paper between each 2 pieces. When you are ready to use them, defrost in the refrigerator overnight—still wrapped, of course.

ROCK CORNISH GAME HEN AND SQUAB

Rock Cornish game hens are always sold frozen in a vacuum pack, because if they were not, they would dry out within a day. These hens weigh 1 to 1¼ pounds. The Rock Cornish roasters of 2 to 3 pounds are also found frozen.

In large population centers, frozen squabs are available in markets. If you raise your own and intend to freeze them, dress them in the usual way, eviscerate, and season before freezing.

To defrost these little birds, let them rest, still wrapped, in the refrigerator for at least 24 hours. The cooking time for squabs is so short that unless they are fully defrosted before cooking, the interior may be still raw when you serve them. If you are working with commercially frozen birds, do not forget to remove the little package of giblets before cooking. You can speed the defrosting process if you pull the package out as soon as the bird is defrosted enough to permit it.

DUCK AND GOOSE

Almost 75% of the ducks on the market in the United States are sold frozen. Long Island ducks are still plentiful, although some ducks are raised in other states. Almost 95% of all geese will be frozen when you buy them. Many of these come from Maine and some from European sources.

Because it is difficult to determine the quality of a frozen bird, it is important to know where the bird was raised and who the packer was.

Ducks are sold already eviscerated, and their average weight is about 5 pounds. However, there are smaller birds, and it is better to choose a duck of 4 to 4½ pounds because the larger ones are too fatty.

Geese can range in weight from 8 to 18 pounds. The heavier the bird, the fattier it will be and the more care you must take in preparation.

To defrost a duck or goose, put the wrapped bird in the refrigerator, allowing 2 days for a duck and 3 for a goose. When the specified time is up, remove the bird from the refrigerator and let it come to room temperature before proceeding. If you are planning to poach either type of bird, you can reduce the defrosting time somewhat, but be sure the bird has defrosted sufficiently to remove the bag of giblets before you begin poaching.

Even with frozen birds, it is possible after defrosting to loosen the skin from the body and insert a layer of flavorful, but not fatty, stuffing between skin and flesh. Before roasting, prick the skin to release excess fat, or dump the defrosted bird in *boiling* water and *boil* for 30 minutes to release fat; then pat dry and roast as usual.

Occasionally frozen game birds are sold in markets, even something so exotic as woodcock or grouse. Defrost these as you would a domestic bird of the same size. The major difference between domestic and game birds is that game is lean, with little fat, and it will need the same care after defrosting as fresh game. Be sure the game is eviscerated before you cook it.

If you catch your own birds—such as pheasant, partridge, mallard or grouse—dress and clean them carefully, chill, and then wrap and freeze as you would a domestic bird. Small birds can be frozen whole, but you may prefer to split or quarter larger birds.

PREPARING
MEATS AND
POULTRY
FOR
COOKING

Chapter 5

I<small>N CHAPTER 1 YOU READ</small> about federal efforts to ensure a safe meat supply. Your butcher shop and supermarket can defeat these efforts if they fail to take precautions for food sanitation. Most cities have health inspectors who examine all shops that sell food, and they withhold the right to sell from any establishment that fails to comply with standards. So the meat you buy has been approved by federal inspectors and sold in a shop approved by local authorities. Now *you* can defeat all these efforts unless you too follow good practices.

First, try to get the meat or poultry home and into your refrigerator as soon as possible; do not leave it in the car trunk for hours. If your butcher says you can put your purchases in the refrigerator just as he handed them to you, do that. But in most cases the meat should be unwrapped enough to allow air to circulate freely, enabling the meat to breathe. Tight wrappings suffocate uncooked meat; an unpleasant smell and a smeary texture, caused by anaerobic organisms, can result. Since moisture also speeds the growth of microorganisms, do not wash or rinse meat until you are ready to cook or process it in some way. For best results, refrigerate large pieces of meat for 3 days, smaller pieces for 2 days, ground meat and variety meats for 1 day. If you keep them longer, there will be subtle changes in flavor and eventually obvious signs of spoilage. (Cooked meat presents different problems; see Chapter 19.)

Be sure all your working surfaces in your kitchen are clean, as well as all your utensils and tools, especially equipment for grinding, chopping, mixing and blending. Your refrigerator should be clean, and you should keep the door open only as long as is absolutely necessary. Do not overload your refrigerator; there should be enough room for air to circulate around the food you have stored. When you are ready to work, make sure your hands are really clean. Be sure to clean the blade of your can opener after every use, and to wipe the tops of your cans before you open them.

You can prepare superb meals with very few utensils, but it does help to have good tools. One good professional knife, which should be sharpened professionally, for slicing, carving and cutting chickens, is the basic essential. A French chef's knife is best for chopping; we do not recommend cleavers for the home. A mallet will be useful if you plan to flatten your own scallops. Your chopping block should be a good 3-inch-thick block; you can cut on thinner cutting boards, but a sturdy nonskid block is safer. Plastic cutting boards can slip and skid; wood is definitely superior. You will also need a grater, a sifter, and a good food grinder with blades of several sizes. A food mill can be used for some recipes, but we strongly recommend a good all-purpose blender that dices, chops, purées, etc. Every year brings some new utensil that can work wonders. If it will solve your kitchen problems, fine; but first make sure the tools you already have will not work just as well.

Now let's consider some preparations that precede the actual cooking: marinating, larding, seasoning, tenderizing and trussing.

MARINATING

The word "marinate" comes from the Latin word *marinus*, an adjective meaning "of the sea." Salt was probably the first preservative, and salt water, or brine, was used even before Roman times to preserve fish. The action of the brine altered the taste of the fish, and eventually this slightly "pickled" flavor became popular. A favorite Roman sauce called *garum* was made from the brine used to pickle various saltwater fish; after the pickled fish were pressed to extract liquid, the mixture of brine and fish juices was flavored to taste with vinegar, pepper or other seasonings. The kind of fish used made a difference in the taste of the *garum*. In Japan small plums pickled in very salty brine, *umeboshi*, are shredded and simmered in water; the juice thus obtained is used as a flavoring agent. All these somewhat salty liquids serve the same purposes as marinades: to tenderize and flavor the foods soaked in them.

A marinade is a mixture of liquids and seasonings, but it is never as salty as the liquids from which it evolved because preservation is no longer its primary purpose. There is always an acid ingredient, which can be wine, vinegar, lemon juice or another acid. The acid has a softening effect on meat fibers. There is usually oil in a marinade, which carries the flavors of the seasonings into the meat once the acid has softened it. This softening, or tenderizing, is an important preparatory step if you are dealing with less-tender cuts. The action of the acid is almost like precooking. The fish preparation called *seviche*, made in Peru and Ecuador, is "cooked" only by acid action. Originally the acid used in *seviche* was orange juice, which is only weakly acid compared to wine or vinegar. However, the flesh of fish is more tender than meat, and for *seviche* it was usually cut into small pieces. Marinating a large piece of meat will not have such a thorough effect; only the outer portions will be appreciably tenderized. While it is unlikely that anyone uses a marinade for its original purpose—to keep meat from spoiling—it is true that a marinade, because of the acid and salt in it, can retard bacterial growth and depress enzyme action. In emergencies this knowledge might be helpful to a cook. Certainly marinated meat can be stored for longer under home conditions than meat not so treated.

You may find directions for a so-called "dry marinade" in some cookbooks. We consider this a misnomer. Since it is almost impossible to spread the dry mixture evenly onto the meat, the concentration will be too heavy in one spot and too light in another.

When is marinating indicated? When the meat you are using is less tender or less flavorful than you would like. Round steak, flank steak and London broil are examples of such meats. However, if you are braising these less-tender cuts, do not marinate them first. In the braising process there is an exchange of flavors between the meat and the ingredients used in braising. The meat fibers are softened by the moist slow heat, enabling the meat to absorb other flavors and juices. Marinating would be a duplication.

Usually only large pieces of meat are marinated. If you are preparing small pieces by a dry-cooking method, it is better to baste them during cooking. Marinating small chunks is not advised because the multiple surfaces allow too much meat juice to be extracted, actually toughening the meat instead of tenderizing it. Because the many surfaces absorb so much flavor from the marinade, the natural meat flavor is disguised.

Marinating cannot develop quality that is not there, but it can enhance what is. However, the longer you marinate, the more the meat will taste of the marinade and the less it will retain of its own natural flavor. If simple flavoring is your purpose, marinate for 1 to 2 hours. If tenderizing is your goal, marinate for longer—up to 2 days.

Liquid ingredients for marinades are usually in the proportion of one-fourth acid to three-fourths oil. Olive oil is what we recommend; it is nutritious (vitamins A, E, F) as well as digestible. (But see p. 357 if you have a dietary problem.) The acid can be red or white wine; vinegar, plain or flavored; lemon or orange juice, cider. Sherry, vermouth and beer are also possibilities. In addition to their primary roles in marinating, both oil and acid contribute flavor.

The choice of seasonings for marinades is wide. Add salt and pepper, but go easy on both, unless you definitely want a peppery taste. If the marinade is to be cooked before use, it is preferable to season it with fresh herbs. Dried herbs have an already concentrated flavor, and in cooking they could become overpowering. Even in uncooked marinades fresh herbs are preferred. However, spices (peppercorns, cloves, juniper berries) usually do their work best in a cooked marinade because they release their flavors better in hot liquid. Spices do not dissolve, but remain as tiny bits suspended in the solution. Cooking a marinade produces a stronger-flavored, better-blended mixture. It is possible to achieve almost the same result with an uncooked marinade by mixing all the ingredients and letting them stand, covered, at room temperature for 24 hours. Most marinades include flavoring vegetables—onion, carrot, celery and garlic. The first three can be cut into small pieces, and garlic can be minced, mashed or put through a garlic press. Walnuts, an excellent flavoring ingredient, can be pressed or wrapped in a cloth and pounded to bits. Pulverized cooked bacon is another zesty flavoring for marinades.

The many recipes for marinades are usually designed for a particular meat or poultry, but the same marinade can actually be used for anything. Make your own adjustments; for instance, red wine or dark vinegar will discolor white meats, so for these use white wine or white-wine vinegar. For beef use only red wine. Either cooked or uncooked marinades will do, but, because of its more intense flavor, a cooked marinade will have a stronger effect on the taste of the finished dish. There will be no difference in tenderizing effects between the two, since the degree of tenderizing depends only on the length of time the meat soaks. Use a marinade of low acidity for a meat with delicate texture or flavor.

Another kind of marinade that we use is a moist paste made of crushed garlic with its own juice, minced onion and oil.

NATURAL MARINADE

2 heads of garlic
1 medium-sized onion
2 cups olive oil

Separate the garlic into its cloves, peel the cloves, and crush them in a mortar or bowl until they are reduced to small bits. Mince the onion to bits about $1/16$ inch square. Stir both, with all the juices, into the oil and mix well.

To use, pat the mixture all over the outside of the meat, wrap the meat in foil, and refrigerate it overnight. Do not be afraid that the garlic will be overpowering; as it cooks with the meat, both its smell and taste will diminish. Any little bits that remain in the pan drippings or cooking liquid can be removed by straining.

The next recipe, for a cooked marinade, is somewhat unusual.

ROSE-PETAL MARINADE (for rack or leg of lamb)   about ½ cup

6 fresh red roses
½ cup fresh orange juice
2 tablespoons sugar

2 sprigs of fresh mint, or 2 tablespoons
mint jelly
2 tablespoons Cognac

Separate the rose petals, cut the white edges off the ends near the stems, wash the petals and dry them. Put petals in a small saucepan with orange juice, sugar and mint sprigs or jelly. Simmer over the lowest possible heat, stirring every few minutes, for 1 hour. Add Cognac and continue to stir for a few more minutes. Remove from heat and let cool. Strain before using.

Brush or spread over lamb before roasting. You can roast it at once, or you can let the lamb wait for 1 hour or overnight.

After lamb is cooked, use drippings in the roasting pan for gravy. If it is necessary to thicken the gravy, use cornstarch (see p. 315).

An uncooked marinade can be utilized as part of the cooking liquid in several processes: strained or as is, as part of the liquid for braising or pot-roasting; as a basting sauce for broiling or barbecuing; and in the preparation of a sauce. Store uncooked marinade under refrigeration for only about 1 week. Before storing, bring it to a boil over moderate heat, let it cool, then strain into glass or plastic containers with lids. Press hard on the lid to create a vacuum, and be sure to label the container as to the kind of meat used. Use leftover marinade a second time only with the same kind of meat that was soaked in it, because the meat, while absorbing some flavors from the marinade, will release some of its own juices. (Too much meat juice can be lost this way if the marinade is highly salted.)

A cooked marinade can be used as part of a sauce if you have planned for it; an example is the classic poivrade sauce for venison, made with the cooked marinade used to tenderize the meat. Aside from such a planned use, it's better not to use a cooked marinade a second time. The flavor is too strong and there will be a large amount of meat juice in the marinade, which may cause it to turn rancid. Plan to use it promptly, or discard it.

Here are two recipes using marinades, the first uncooked, the second cooked.

CHICKEN WITH ORANGE-SOY MARINADE
(for broiling or barbecuing)   4 servings

2 broiler chickens (2 pounds each),
   quartered, with wings cut off
¾ cup orange juice
½ cup soy sauce
2 tablespoons honey
1½ tablespoons minced onion

1 tablespoon grated orange rind
1 teaspoon dry mustard
1 teaspoon curry powder
½ teaspoon dried parsley flakes
½ teaspoon cayenne pepper

Wash chicken pieces and pat dry. Mix all the marinade ingredients. Arrange chicken pieces in a single layer on a large flat pan and brush the pieces on all sides with marinade. Refrigerate the chicken and any remaining marinade separately.

Bring chicken to room temperature before cooking. Broil or barbecue the chicken, turning the pieces carefully so as not to burn them (see p. 267). If you are doing this on the barbecue, be sure the wood or charcoal is well reduced to coals before you start. Chickens of this weight are very young and tender and need to be treated delicately. Use remaining marinade to baste the chickens as you turn them.

OVERNIGHT STEAK   4 servings

4 tablespoons beef marrow (see p. 170)
4 tablespoons butter
2 slices of bacon, cooked and pulverized
1 large onion, minced
3 garlic cloves, minced

pinch of dried or fresh thyme
¼ teaspoon salt
¼ teaspoon freshly ground pepper
steak for 4 servings (T-bone, shell or strip,
   sirloin, porterhouse, rib or chuck)

The day before serving slowly melt the marrow in a medium-sized skillet over low heat; mash it as it melts. Add the butter and blend well. Add bacon, onion, garlic and thyme; mix well. Cover the skillet, and cook over very low heat for 20 minutes. Add salt and pepper and continue cooking, uncovered, for 15 minutes longer, stirring often.

Brush the steak all over with the warm marinade. Wrap steak well in wax paper or foil and place the package on a platter or baking sheet to catch any juices that may leak. Refrigerate overnight. Store remaining marinade in the refrigerator.

The day you serve, remove steak from refrigerator 2 hours before broiling, and let it reach room temperature, still wrapped. Shortly before starting to cook, reheat the remaining marinade. Broil the steak on one side, turn over, and spread marinade evenly over the steak. Broil on the second side until done.

LARDING

Fats and oils used in the preparation of meats and poultry are relatively few. As with marinating, we prefer olive oil here. Meats and poultry can be rubbed or brushed with oil before cooking, especially when they are to be broiled or barbecued. (More about barbecuing in Chapter 16.) The purpose of oiling is twofold: to add flavor and to prevent excessive drying of the outside surfaces during cooking.

Do not make the mistake of thinking that every piece of meat must be treated with oil or fat before cooking. On the contrary, if the kind of meat and the particular cut you are using has sufficient exterior fat, do not use any; adding grease to grease serves no purpose.

Adding fat to meat before cooking is called "larding." The word "larding" comes from the Latin word *lardum*, which means cured swine's flesh, or bacon, and the French noun *lard*, meaning fat, especially of the hog, and bacon. However, when we refer to pork fat for use in larding, we mean, not bacon or cured or salted fat, but fresh pork fat (fatback) that has not been frozen.

As you can guess from the terminology that has developed over the centuries, pork fat is the kind of larding most often used. While the home cook may use the term "larding" to apply to any use of extra fat, it has a more specific meaning for the professional chef, especially one trained in the techniques of French cooking. To such cooks, larding means inserting narrow strips of fat into the flesh. This is done to add richness of flavor and additional moisture, especially with lean or less-tender meats that require long cooking; the little strips of fat, "lardoons," slowly melt as cooking proceeds and lubricate the meat. The lardoons are forced into the meat with a needle of special design, with a hollow to hold the fat; these come in several sizes. Place the fat strip in the hollow, and insert the needle into the meat. Hold the end of the strip with one hand while you slowly withdraw the needle, leaving the fat in position. Sometimes lardoons are soaked in brandy or rolled in herbs or a mixture called *gremolata* (garlic cloves, grated lemon rind and parsley, all chopped together to fine bits), used by Italian cooks.

Short strips of fat are sometimes inserted only an inch into the meat, and a row of little tufts is allowed to protrude from the surface; this method also has a professional name, *piquer* in French.

We have described these processes so you know what they are, but we do not follow them ourselves and do not recommend that you do. The reason is simple: Making holes in the meat allows much juice to escape, appreciably depleting flavor and juiciness, which the addition of the fat cannot replace. If your meat is very lean and lacks tenderness, choose instead a cooking method that will counteract these characteristics. Try moist heat and long, slow cooking for such cuts.

Outer-larding

There is one kind of larding we do use, the kind the professional chef calls "barding," but which we shall refer to as "outer-larding." In this process a piece of meat is wrapped on the outside with sheets of fat. You might be amused to know that the origin of the term "barding" is a French word, *barde*, that in the Middle Ages meant iron armor for a horse. Fat for outer-larding is cut into thin slices, and it can be flattened slightly between two sheets of paper. It is arranged around the meat and tied in place at regular intervals with lengths of butchers' string.

As with other types of larding, most people use pork fat for outer-larding, but we do not. Pork fat can become rancid, and it has a distinctive taste and odor of its own that are released during cooking. If you do not want a pork flavor, do not use fatback for outer-larding; if you want it, however, by all means use it.

We have sometimes been asked to freeze slices of pork fat for future larding, but we will not do it because the fat absorbs moisture during freezing, which changes its flavor markedly. It is not possible to freeze a chunk of fatback for later slicing either, because the fat becomes crumbly, making it difficult to slice. Only fresh pork fat is desirable for larding.

Since we do not recommend pork for larding, there must be something else. Yes, beef, veal and poultry fats can be used, and each kind of meat requires its own special larding and preparation.

For beef, use only beef fat from near the flank for outer-larding. It should be cut on a slant into slices ¼ inch thick. This fat is solid and workable, while suet, the hard fat surrounding the kidney and loins, is crumbly.

You can also save fat from trimming steaks and freeze it for future use. It will not crumble, and it is smooth and pliable. Before freezing, put the trimmings between two sheets of paper and flatten them with a mallet to produce the wider pieces needed for outer-larding.

If you are working with veal, use beef or veal fat. Because it has no taste, veal fat is also an excellent choice for larding poultry. But even better than outer-larding for both veal and poultry is rubbing the meat with oil. If you do use veal fat, have it cut from the flank, as you would beef fat.

Outer-larding can be used with less-expensive cuts of meat to add juiciness; it does not tenderize—only internal fats do that. The filet of beef, which has no fat of its own, is often outer-larded. Do not outer-lard really good roast beef, especially if you want the outside of your roast to be crisp and browned. Consider what the final appearance of your meat will be. It is not desirable to lard lamb, and we definitely advise against larding meat to be pot-roasted; in pot-roasting, the extra fat would make the whole dish too fatty.

If you have meat with a lot of external fat, you would do well to trim away some of it. A steak that is cooked relatively quickly should have only a thin layer of fat, ¼ inch thick or less, to be cooked and served with the meat. To make the fat more digestible, score it at ¼-inch intervals so it will become crisp.

The fat on large roasts can also be trimmed and scored; this is often done with baked ham, and the scoring is decorative as well as functional.

Most meal planners today are interested in limiting the calorie and cholesterol contents of foods. If these are your goals, it is probably better to skip the addition of extra animal fats if you can prepare moist and tender meats in other ways. There are two exceptions we will mention here: If game and game birds for spit-roasting are not well outer-larded, they will dry out before they are done, because they have so little fat (for more about this, see Chapter 16); sheets of fat are also necessary in the preparation of pâtés and terrines (see Chapter 9).

Here is an idea for "larding" without fat. If you are cooking a roast or pot roast that needs additional moisture, use leaves of lettuce or red or white cabbage instead of fat—white only for pork and veal. After seasoning the roast, wrap the leaves around it, and tie them in place. The leaves will supply additional liquid and keep the outer surfaces of the roast from drying, without imparting a cabbagy taste to the meat. Discard the leaves when the meat is done.

Poultry Fat

Poultry fat cannot be prepared as other fats are, because it is soft and can never be used in sheets. There are two ways to use it for larding. The little lumps of fat inside the cavity near the tail can be pulled out and skewered on top of the bird with poultry pins.

You may also render poultry fat, with onions if you like, and use it for basting during cooking. If you render ahead of time or have some rendered fat left over, be sure to store it in the refrigerator.

SEASONING

Perfectly cooked prime meats may be so delicious that you could eat them without embellishment, but most Americans have become so accustomed to well-seasoned food that eating unseasoned meat is almost unthinkable. We think all meats taste better when seasoned *before* cooking.

One simple trick, used in Indian cookery, is to rub the outside fat of meat with a fresh lemon 2 hours before broiling.

Here is a delicious seasoning for steaks and chops: Mix walnut extract (walnuts puréed through a garlic press), freshly crushed peppercorns and olive oil. If you like the flavor, add a little Drambuie. Mix together well. Brush the mixture on steaks or chops 1 hour before you plan to cook them, and leave them at room temperature. If you do this many hours ahead of time, refrigerate the meat. The meat will absorb the flavors, and the mixture will prevent the escape of meat juices as the meat comes to room temperature and as it cooks.

People who like garlic insert little slivers of it into meats. Do not do this unless you enjoy the flavor.

Poultry can be most successfully seasoned between skin and flesh. This is not

Stuffing a bird between skin and flesh

as difficult as it sounds. Gently insert your thumbs beneath the skin at the neck end, while holding the wings down with your index fingers. Starting with the skin over the breast, which is loose, work your thumbs in a heart-shaped pattern toward the tail. Do this gently, being careful not to tear the skin. Mix seasoning with butter or a chilled oil. As the oil cools, it thickens and becomes easier to handle. Pat the seasoned butter or oil on the flesh of the bird, under the skin. As the bird reaches room temperature before cooking, the flavors are absorbed by the meat.

Classic French cookery includes a dish called "chicken in half-mourning," in which truffles are inserted between the flesh and skin of a chicken, usually in a carefully arranged pattern. The chicken is also stuffed; then it is poached and beautifully sauced. When fresh truffles are used, the meat becomes well perfumed with the truffle flavor. Truffles are found only in southern France and northern Italy. Canned truffles can be purchased in the United States, and a few stores sell fresh truffles flown in from Europe. The canned fungus is much less delicious than the fresh, and the imported fresh truffle is costly, so we will not recommend it. Even without truffles, you can make a bird look beautiful and taste delicious by using the method we have described, and the possible flavorings are many. The same procedure can be used with other birds—capons, ducks, etc. The recipe that follows is an example; the cornmeal stuffing helps absorb some of the duck fat while adding flavor.

DUCK WITH PEACHES   3 or 4 servings

5-pound duck

cornmeal stuffing for duck (recipe follows)

24 seedless green grapes

8 peach halves, fresh or canned

grated rind of 1 orange

8 chestnuts, cooked, peeled and pulverized

3 tablespoons Grand Marnier

½ teaspoon dried thyme

Have butcher loosen the skin of the duck so that it is separated from the flesh but both skin and body are still in place. Make the stuffing. Squeeze the juice from the grapes in a press, or whirl them in an electric blender to extract the juice, or mash with a potato masher.

Preheat oven to 350° F. Sew the neck opening of the duck closed. Insert the cornmeal stuffing between skin and body, making the layer as even as possible. Place the peach halves in the body cavity and sew the vent closed. Mix together orange rind, chestnuts, grape juice, Grand Marnier and thyme, and rub the mixture over the skin of the duck on all sides; save remaining mixture for basting. Place the duck, breast down, on a rack and roast for 1 hour. Turn duck breast up and return to the oven for 20 minutes. Reduce heat to 300° F., and continue to roast the bird for 1 hour and 15 minutes longer, basting every so often with remaining grape-juice mixture or with the drippings in the pan. If your duck weighs less than 5 pounds, reduce the cooking time by 20 to 25 minutes.

If you like, you can make gravy with the pan drippings (see p. 314).

CORNMEAL STUFFING FOR DUCK

¼ pound butter

1 tablespoon light raisins

¾ teaspoon curry powder

3 garlic cloves, crushed

¼ teaspoon ground sage

1 teaspoon minced fresh chives

⅛ teaspoon salt

6 peppercorns, cracked

1 cup light cream or half-and-half

½ cup yellow cornmeal

2 cups dry bread crumbs

Melt butter in large skillet, and add next seven ingredients. Cook slowly for 30 minutes. Stir occasionally to mix and prevent sticking. Cool slightly. Add cream, and mix well; add cornmeal, and mix well; add bread crumbs and mix. Use to stuff under the skin of the duck.

Boned Meats

Boned meats can be seasoned before they are reshaped or tied. Parsley or other green herbs can be used for color contrast, as can mixtures of herbs with minced garlic or onion. Fruits too can be used for flavoring in these preparations. A mixture of fresh herbs and sliced onions is perfect for a leg of pork that has had all pelvic, hip, leg and shank bones removed. Mix with whatever other seasoning you like. Another good way to prepare leg of pork is to butterfly it, lubricate well with butter or oil, add a stuffing, and roll. Still another: Bone the leg, and then marinate it in lots of white wine and herbs for 2 days; use no onions in this. Roll the meat with seasoning and fresh herbs inside and roast, in the oven or over a spit, with low heat, using the remainder of the marinade for basting.

A boned center shoulder of veal is enhanced by being stuffed with marrow, scraped out cold and well seasoned with salt and pepper. Roll and tie for roasting. Another tasty idea is to stuff celery stalks with seasoning, even with cheese, and place these in a boned meat to add flavor.

If you season meats and poultry as soon as you take them from the refrigerator, they will absorb the flavor as they reach room temperature. But do not do this with those meats that should be kept refrigerated to prevent spoilage until you are ready to cook them: pork, variety meats and ground meats. Another reason for seasoning ground meats only when they are ready to be cooked is that the many surfaces allow too much loss of moisture from the hygroscopic action of the salt in the seasoning mixture.

Bacon, sautéed and then ground, can be rubbed over a shell roast or a filet to add salt and flavor. Or mix the ground bacon with barbecue sauce to be spread on spareribs for barbecue or pork loin for spit-roasting. For chickens, mix 1 tablespoon ground cloves, 1 tablespoon powdered onion or onion juice, and 1 tablespoon brown gravy mix into ½ cup honey; add orange juice if you like. Rub the mixture over the chickens to be roasted or spit-roasted at least an hour before you cook them. Adjust the amount of spices and honey to taste.

TENDERIZING

If you have a fine cut of Prime meat, you will probably not have to do anything to make it juicy and tender, but meat of other grades or cuts from less-tender parts of the animal may be far from that ideal state. You may be tempted to use some sort of meat tenderizer to help things along. We recommend that you resist the temptation. The active ingredients in meat tenderizers, as in some soaps that have been the subject of controversy, are enzymes produced by plants. The enzyme most often used is papain, which is obtained from green (unripe) papayas. Papain breaks proteins down into their components, such as proteose and peptin. Although this might seem like a good thing, in our opinion it is not. The problem is that the tenderizing action is effective only on the outer portion of the meat, while the inside remains as it was. In cooking meats treated with these products, by the time the interior is finally tender, the outside will be dried to tasteless shreds.

Some cooks maintain that they have solved this problem by piercing the meat with a skewer or steel fork, allowing the tenderizer to get to the center. While this lets the tenderizer in, it also lets meat juices out; you will end up with reasonably tender meat from which most of the juiciness and flavor is gone.

All research on enzymes has been done in the last fifty years, and only a few have been isolated. It is known that cold inactivates them, so they probably have no effect on refrigerated meat. They are reactivated when warmed, but they become inactive once again before the temperature reaches 100° C. (212° F.). They are destroyed in water considerably below the boiling point. Their effectiveness is limited to the short time meat is at room temperature and during the early stages of cooking, excluding moist-heat methods.

Actually, tenderizing can be achieved by combining most fruits with meats, since enzymes are present in all fruits. Pineapple contains bromelin, crab apples contain pectinase, and enzymes have been found in bananas and figs. All these fruits have been used with meats or poultry. Inhabitants of the Tropics used to tenderize meat by wrapping it in papaya leaves. The little kiwi (Chinese gooseberry), from Australia, has a distinctly tenderizing effect when added to less-tender beef in the braising pot. Fruits and fruit leaves are more delicate in effect and flavoring than commercial tenderizers. You will notice several dishes including fruits with meat or poultry in this book.

We think tenderizers alter the taste of meat significantly. The best way to tenderize your meat is to cook it properly, by a method suited to the cut and grade.

TYING AND TRUSSING

Meats that are not firm or that are in more than one piece are generally tied for cooking. For tying, use white butchers' string, which is not stretchy or bristly and will not bruise or tear the meat.

Some examples of tied meats are boned loin of veal, either plain or rolled around the veal kidney; boned and stuffed shoulder of any meat; boned leg of lamb; beef pot roast, with or without bones. Any boned meat should be tied so that it will keep its shape during cooking. By hand, shape the meat to the desired form: its original shape before boning, a roll or a cushion; then tie at regular intervals. Do not tie your meat too tightly or juices and flavor will escape, and there will be string scars when the meat is cooked. The general shape can also be spoiled by tying too tightly. Any kind of knot will do, as long as it does not come untied.

Another type of meat frequently tied is an already boneless cut, such as a whole filet of beef. This is sometimes tied at even intervals so that the *filets mignons* cut from it will be perfect rounds when served; without tying, the natural shape of the cut would yield slightly elongated slices rather than round ones.

Of course, meats that are outer-larded, wrapped in sheets of fat or in cabbage leaves, will need to be tied to keep the wrapping in place.

In some cases the strings are cut before the cooked meat is served; this is the proper procedure with meats tied only to keep outer-larding in place. With boned meats, it is better to remove the strings as you come to them in carving, so the meat does not fall apart.

Completely boned meat to which the bones are returned for roasting is also tied. See Chapter 20 for examples. Because the meat will pick up and retain flavor from the bones, this is done only when the bones are not overaged. The rack of bones is untied and removed before serving.

Chicken trussed with a single string, following the Lobel method

Trussing Poultry

Poultry that is tied for cooking is said to be "trussed." There are many ways to do this. You can loop a long piece of string around legs and wings in a crisscross pattern, ending up with a knot at the back of the bird. Using either a one-thread or a two-thread technique, you can sew the bird through the shoulders and thighs with a trussing needle, like a giant sewing needle. All French cookbooks direct you to use the needle; these instructions might make more sense when we remind you that most French chickens come to market looking different from American birds: with the wings cut off and the entire leg down to the middle toe of the foot still attached. The chickens sold in the United States are more compact, with shorter and fatter legs. We do not recommend either of these trussing methods, because they make the bird look like a package ready to be mailed. We think they are much too complicated and not really necessary. We also disapprove of piercing the flesh with the trussing needle, because this causes loss of juices.

Poultry is trussed for cooking processes in which the bird is cooked whole: roasting, spit-roasting, braising, poaching. If your bird is stuffed, you may want to sew the skin that closes the vent over the stuffing. The neck end can also be sewn, however, you can close both openings with small skewers or poultry pins (see p. 223 for more on preparing stuffed poultry). If you have a good bird that has been properly eviscerated, you will have ample skin to close over the stuffing, and if you follow either of the methods we are about to suggest with such a bird you will not need to sew the vent at all.

First, fold the neck skin over the back, then flip the wing tips over the shoulders, where they will hold the neck skin in place. If your bird has insufficient neck skin for this, sew the neck opening. Now position the bird with the tail toward you; hold the legs, one in each hand, and firmly push them back toward the chest and close to the body, making the bird more compact. With a single string, tie the ends of the drumsticks and the end of the body together. At serving time there is only one string to cut, and there will be no scars on the perfect golden-brown surface of your bird.

If you have a larger bird—capon or turkey—here is another method that does require either a trussing needle or a roast-beef tier. Arrange the neck skin and wings as just described, and push the legs toward the body. Guide the needle through the knee joint at the end of the drumstick, then through the flap of skin covering the vent, through the tail, through the opposite side of the flap of skin, and through the opposite knee joint. Tie the two ends of the string together, and that's all. This method holds the legs together in such a way that the vent is closed, and you will not need to sew it or pin it in any other way. As with our other technique, at serving time there is still only one string to cut.

Tie all whole birds whether they are stuffed or not, because they will keep their shape for better appearance when served.

A Note About Recipes and Menus

The recipes in this book are intended as illustrations of the procedures we describe. You can follow them exactly if you like, but it is better to adjust the amounts of seasoning, herbs and spices to suit your own taste. If you do not like wine, substitute another liquid. If you like your meat or poultry cooked more or less than we specify, do so. We hope the recipes will serve as examples or suggestions, starting points from which you can improvise.

The menus are intended as illustrations of ways to use and combine various meats and poultry. If you do not care for the vegetable or starch we suggest, substitute another choice.

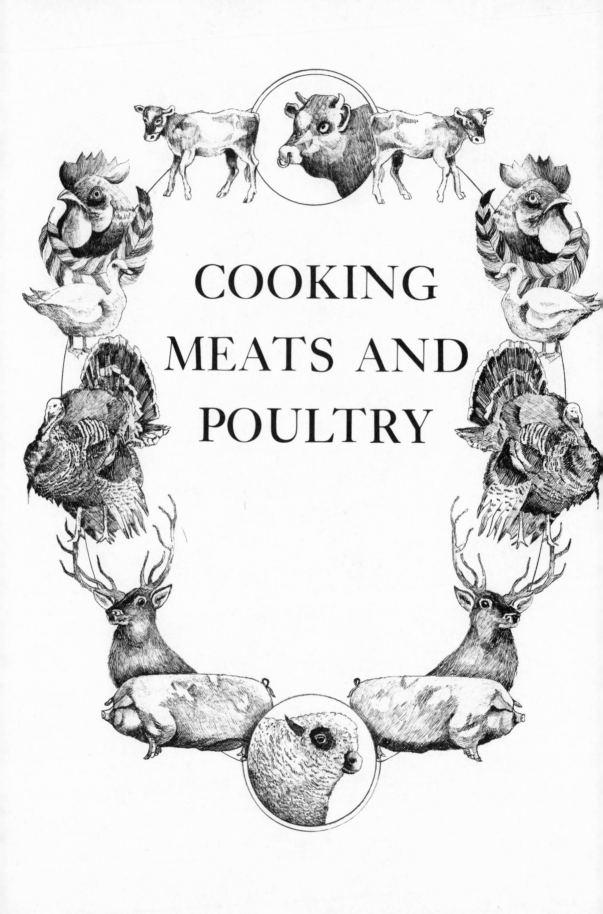

COOKING

MEATS AND

POULTRY

Chapter 6

W HEN MEAT IS COOKED, the heat breaks down muscles and tough fibers, causing the meat to become tender. There are three kinds of liquid in meat: body moisture, blood and fat. In cooking, the fine grains of fat are melted and the other liquids are extracted; the mixture of fat and juices is spread through the meat, making it tender.

In cooking processes like roasting, the outside layer of meat becomes coagulated, sealing in most of the juices. However, body moisture does escape through the pores and evaporates. If the moisture did not evaporate, the meat would be more steamed than roasted. To prevent "steaming," it is best to place meat on a rack for roasting.

For outdoor cooking, such as barbecuing and spit-roasting, the moisture evaporates more readily. During broiling also, moisture evaporates, and extracted fats fall into the pan under the broiling rack.

The delicious smell of meat cooking is caused by the melting of the mixture of fat and blood. Each type of meat and poultry has its own distinctive aroma.

In raw and rare meats, enzymes are alive. Enzymes and bacteria are destroyed by intense heat, but so are vitamins. This means that well-done meat is less nutritious than meat cooked for a shorter period of time, but because of the destruction of enzymes and bacteria it is easier to chew and digest. By "well done" we do not mean cooked to a tough leathery state; meat done to this point would be hard to chew and digest. Because rare meat takes longer to digest, you will not feel hungry nearly as soon as after eating a meal of well-done meat.

ROASTING

Roasting is a cooking method that uses dry heat. In oven roasting, the heat source is arranged so that the entire enclosed space is heated, and hot air on all sides of the meat does the cooking. Because lean cuts lack internal fats, which tenderize meat as they melt during cooking, they require special care if they are to be roasted. Young tender meats such as young poultry and veal have very little natural fat, so you must compensate for this by rubbing the outside with oil and by cooking at a low temperature. Roasting is the wrong choice for tough or sinewy meats, since moist heat is needed to make these tender.

On the whole, we advise against marinating meats to be roasted, but of course you may do it if you wish.

Spit-roasting is a process in which the meat is constantly turned, thus exposing all sides evenly to the heat source. Although we usually think of this as taking place outdoors, there are indoor ovens equipped with spits, both permanent installations and portable equipment. All general information about roasting applies to spit-roasting as well; for the specifics see Chapter 16.

Unless a specific recipe gives contrary directions, always *preheat* your oven to high heat to sear the meat. If you were to start roasting in a cold oven, the length of time needed for the heat to reach the center of the meat would result in a steaming effect. After 5 to 10 minutes reduce to 350° F. or whatever temperature your particular meat requires.

Except for pork and variety meats, allow meat to reach room temperature before starting to roast it. Season meat as soon as you take it out of the refrigerator, to give the meat time to absorb the seasoning; if you season just before putting the meat in the oven, the seasoning tends to run off with the melting fat.

An important factor in roasting is the true temperature of your oven. Even the best equipment can vary with time and use. If your oven needs adjustment, the cooking charts on the following pages will be only approximate. If in doubt, purchase a separate oven thermometer—they are quite inexpensive—and check to see if the true temperature agrees with the setting. If not, ask someone from your utility company to adjust the oven for you.

Also, we have based our suggested roasting temperatures on the assumption that the meat to be cooked is fresh and at room temperature (for frozen meats see Chapter 4). If your meat is colder than this, the timing will be different.

Meat Thermometer

The meat thermometer is an excellent device that will be especially helpful if your oven is not adjusted exactly, because the internal temperature of meat is the crucial test of doneness. If you are an experienced cook, you can probably tell by the appearance of a roast when it is done to your taste. If you are not sure how the roast should look, use a thermometer. Do not feel that this will mark you as a novice; many good cooks would not think of roasting without a meat thermometer. This device has a stainless-steel or aluminum spike, pointed at one end and fitted into a gauge at the other; it is washable and watertight. Insert the spike into the thickest portion of the roast so that the tip is in the center of the meat. Do not let the thermometer touch any bones in the roast, and avoid the fat; the true reading must come from the center of the meat itself. If you have a flattish piece or one of awkward shape, insert the thermometer horizontally or at an angle, but try to place it so that the dial can be seen easily, either through your oven window or when you open the door to check. Some books suggest making a hole in the meat with a larding needle before inserting the thermometer, but we advise against it; the fewer holes you make, the less juice you will lose. Most meat thermometers have a movable red arrow that you can set for the temperature you want. If you let a roast cook until the temperature indicator reaches the red arrow, you will discover that even after you turn off the oven the temperature keeps rising, past the ideal point you had decided on. Even though the oven is turned off and the temperature in it is slowly decreasing, the meat continues to cook because it has retained all the heat it absorbed. If you want your meat rare, turn the oven off before the indicator reaches the red arrow; the temperature of the meat will rise to that point while "resting" in the turned-off oven.

Another factor that will affect the temperature in roasting is opening the oven door. Do not do this any more than necessary because each time you open the door the temperature in the oven itself changes slightly, giving the meat a mild shock.

Other factors can affect the roasting process: the shape of the piece of meat, its fat content, the presence of bones. Even if you roast it properly, your meat will not be tender and delicious unless it was a good piece to begin with.

Still another variable in roasting could be an unexpected change in your dinner schedule. You may be planning to eat at 6:30, and your family misses the train home; or your guests are delayed. In such cases, take the roast out of the oven as soon as you hear of the delay, and let it rest at room temperature. You can place a sheet of foil loosely over it, but do not cover it tightly or wrap it because then it will steam. Calculate backward from the new time at which you plan to serve, and determine when the roast needs to be replaced in the oven to complete the roasting. When the time comes, return the meat to the oven at a *slightly higher temperature* and finish roasting. Do not use a lower temperature than specified, or you will ruin the roast. If the reverse happens, and everyone comes early, serve them an appetizer and conversation. It is not possible to rush the roasting process without reducing the quality of the finished dish.

Beef

Beef cuts good for roasting are top sirloin, top round, prime ribs and the first cut only of the shoulder (blade roast) and chuck (cross-rib roast). Start these at 500° F. for 10 minutes; then reduce the heat to 350° F. and cook as long as the recipe indicates, or until done to taste. With larger pieces of meat that require longer cooking, use a lower temperature, 325° F., so that the meat does not dry out excessively as it cooks.

A beautiful-looking roast is the eye of the round, or silverside, outer-larded for extra moisture; but only a Prime eye should be cooked in this way. Another good cut is the shell roast, with or without its bones. And the filet, or tenderloin, is especially tender. If you are preparing either shell roast or filet, roast until done at 500° F. The eye of the round may look like the tenderloin, but it needs much longer cooking at a lower temperature; the eye of lower grades is better pot-roasted.

Obviously, a roast will weigh more with its bones than without. The heavier roast needs to cook longer at a slightly lower temperature. If you have difficulty determining cooking time, a meat thermometer will be a great help (see p. 88).

When the roast is done to your taste, let it rest in the turned-off oven for 15 minutes; this will give the meat juices a chance to be redistributed. If you transfer the meat directly from hot oven to room temperature, the "shock" of the temperature change will draw out much of the juice. If you start carving before this resting period, you will see the juices run out. The rest will make the meat easier to carve, and it will still be hot.

ROASTING BEEF

Cut	Weight (pounds)	Oven Temperature	Cooking Time (minutes per pound)	Interior Temperature (roasting thermometer)
Standing rib	6 to 8	350° F.	18	140° F. (rare)
			22	160° F. (medium)
			25	170° F. (well done)
Half standing rib	5 to 7	350° F.	18	140° F. (rare)
			22	160° F. (medium)
			25	170° F. (well done)
Rolled rib	4 to 6	325° F.	15	140° F. (rare)
			20	160° F. (medium)
			22	170° F. (well done)
Shell roast	6	350° F.	15	140° F. (rare)
			18	160° F. (medium)
			20	170° F. (well done)
Top sirloin	4	325° F.	20	140° F. (rare)
			25	160° F. (medium)
			30	170° F. (well done)
Tenderloin	4 to 6	450° F.	30 (total)	140° F.
Eye of round	5	375° F.	1 hour (total)	160° F. (rare)
		350° F.	20 to 25	170° F. (well done)

Since this is the first cooking chart in the book, this is a good place to explain that the charts are meant to be guides only. If you like your meat cooked less or more than indicated, adjust accordingly.

Beef can also be roasted in salt. We do not recommend this as a practical alternative, but it is an interesting method. This is how to do it. First preheat the oven to 500° F. Moisten the beef with water, then rub it all over with coarse salt (edible rock salt). Measure a large sheet of heavy-duty foil about three times the size of the meat, and center it in a shallow pan approximately the same size as the roast. Spread salt on the foil, and place the meat on top. Fold the foil and salt around the meat, covering it completely. A 2-inch-thick roast should be roasted for 35 to 40 minutes; for larger roasts, up to 6 inches thick, add 15 more minutes for each additional inch. Halfway through the roasting, after about 20 minutes for the 2-inch roast, pull off the foil, leaving the meat encased in salt. When the roasting time is up, turn off the heat and leave the beef in the oven for 2 hours. Then scrape off the remaining salt, and serve. The beef will be rare.

Veal

Veal cuts for roasting are the rump, shoulder, rib or rack, leg and loin. Veal must be treated gently; do not use intense heat. Rub the veal with olive oil before cooking, and use no other fat with the seasoning. Roast at 325° F. for the necessary time, and at the end of the cooking brown the roast at higher heat for a few minutes if you like.

ROASTING VEAL

Cut	Weight (pounds)	Oven Temperature	Cooking Time (minutes per pound)	Interior Temperature (roasting thermometer)
Leg	5 to 8	300° F.	20 to 25	170° F.
Loin	4 to 6	325° F.	25 to 30	170° F.
Rib, or rack	3 to 5	325° F.	35 to 40	170° F.
Shoulder (rolled or stuffed)	4 to 6	300° F.	25 to 30	170° F.
Rump	4 to 6	325° F.	25 to 30	170° F.

Pork

Pork cuts for roasting are loin, leg, shoulder, rump and spareribs. To be properly done, pork requires longer cooking at a lower temperature than beef. Extra fat is not usually necessary when cooking pork, but pork does need to be seasoned well. For many years it was thought necessary to eat only well-done pork because of the danger of trichinosis. This has resulted, over the past 100 years or so, in countless servings of dry, tasteless pork. It is now known that the parasite is killed at a temperature of 137° F. Juicy and flavorful pork can be eaten without concern; the internal temperature should be 170° F.

Roast pork at 325 to 350° F. Because of its close grainy texture, pork can dry out during cooking. This is why many recipes call for basting pork as it roasts; basting adds flavor as well as moisture, and helps crisp the external fat. Fruits are particularly complementary to pork, and fruit juices alone or mixed with other ingredients can make good basting sauces for it. Sweet and Pungent Sauce (p. 266) is also good for basting. So is olive oil. Another way to add moisture is to cover the meat for the first quarter of the roasting time, and then remove the cover and let the meat brown. You can also combine a moist-heat method with a dry-cooking method by steaming or parboiling the meat for part of the cooking time. Keep this in mind when cooking fresh pork by any method; the added moisture will give you much more delicious meat.

ROASTING PORK

Cut	Weight (pounds)	Oven Temperature	Cooking Time (minutes per pound)	Interior Temperature (roasting thermometer)
Loin				
center	3 to 5	325° F.	30 to 35	170° F.
blade or				
sirloin	3 to 4	325° F.	35 to 40	170° F.
rolled	3 to 5	325° F.	35 to 40	170° F.
Leg				
whole	12 to 16	325° F.	20 to 25	170° F.
half	5 to 8	325° F.	30 to 35	170° F.
Shoulder				
picnic	5 to 8	325° F.	25 to 30	170° F.
butt	4 to 6	325° F.	35 to 40	170° F.
Rump	6 to 10	325° F.	25 to 30	170° F.
Spareribs	2½ to 4	325° F.	25 to 30	170° F.

Ham

The reason we did not mention roasting smoked ham in the discussion of fresh pork is that the old-fashioned smoked hams that required lengthy boiling or roasting are no longer sold, with the exception of the cured hams, or "country hams," of the Southern states. They call for special handling. (See Chapter 3.) The cured hams generally available in retail markets are precooked. It is hard to give general rules for roasting ham because each packer has his own way of preparing it. Consult your butcher when you buy, and read the labels on the wrapping carefully.

In general, a precooked ham should be baked at 350° F. for 1½ hours, just long enough to be thoroughly heated and glazed to taste. Roasting half a ham will require more than half of this time: Allow at least 1 hour.

Lamb

Lamb cuts for roasting are leg, loin and saddle, rack and crown, and shoulder.

The leg of spring lamb in season is quite tender and will cook quickly. Marinate it lightly, for 1 to 2 hours, if you like. Then roast the leg for 1½ hours for a perfect dish.

The saddle, consisting of both loins in one piece, is a good cut for special occasions. With bones, roast either the loin or the saddle as you would a leg. The double loin can be boned to make a rolled roast; for a festive touch, buy extra kidneys and have them rolled inside, or add chopped kidneys to a stuffing of other ingredients.

The rack is both sections of rib chops. When split, each half makes a rib roast like a miniature beef rib roast. Roast either single or double rib sections as you would the leg. The sections can be attached to form a crown; for more about that, see page 221.

Because the shoulder has so many bones, it makes a good roast only when boned. After boning, it can be cooked as a flat roast, called a "cushion shoulder," or it can be rolled.

Winter lamb must be cooked with more precision than spring lamb. It requires more time and moisture for tenderizing. To provide this moisture, cover the roast when you put it in the oven, and leave the cover in place for a quarter of the cooking time, adding an extra 10 to 15 minutes to the total specified time.

Mutton, as we have already noted, is not an American favorite and as a result is scarcely to be found. If you do find some, remember that the meat is fattier, redder and more strongly flavored than spring lamb. Roast it as you would winter lamb.

ROASTING LAMB

Cut	Weight (pounds)	Oven Temperature	Cooking Time (minutes per pound)	Interior Temperature (roasting thermometer)
Leg	5 to 8	350° F.	15	145° F.
Loin	3 to 4	350° F.	40 to 45 total	145° F.
Saddle	6 to 8	325° F.	15 to 18	145° F.
Rack (rib)	3 (before trimming)	350° F.	40 to 45 total	145° F.
Crown (unstuffed)	4 to 5	350° F.	40 to 60 total	145° F.
Shoulder	4 to 6 (before boning)	325° F.	20 to 25	145° F.

All the cooking times listed in the chart are for medium-rare lamb, which will be juicy, tender and still somewhat pink inside. If you prefer your lamb well done, double the cooking times, set the meat thermometer for 160 to 170° F., and reduce the oven temperature to 325° F. for all cuts. Remember, however, that the loin and rack are tender and have a relatively thin layer of meat; these cuts can easily over-cook and become dry if you try to roast them until well done.

For an unusual way to roast a leg of lamb, try the following recipe.

CURRIED LEG OF LAMB OVERNIGHT   6 or 7 servings

6-pound leg of lamb
1 tablespoon curry powder
1 teaspoon salt
1 teaspoon ground cinnamon
½ teaspoon cracked peppercorns
¼ teaspoon ground ginger
¼ teaspoon ground cardamom
¼ cup orange-flavored yogurt
2 tablespoons orange juice
½ teaspoon crumbled cooked bacon
2 tablespoons minced onion
3 garlic cloves, crushed

Have your butcher trim the lamb and crack the first two chops about 1½ inches apart, to make it easier to carve later. Stir curry powder, salt and spices into yogurt and orange juice and mix very well. Add bacon, onion and garlic, and mix. Place the leg of lamb on a large sheet of heavy-duty foil. Rub all the yogurt and spice mixture over the lamb. Wrap the foil around the meat to make sure that no juices will escape from the package, and store in the refrigerator overnight.

The next day, about 4 hours before serving, take the package from the refrigerator. Leaving it wrapped, allow it to come to room temperature. Preheat oven to 400° F. Unwrap the lamb, and place it on a rack, fat side up, in a baking pan. Roast at 400° F. for 5 minutes, then reduce heat to 325° F., and roast for 1½ hours. Turn off heat, but leave the meat in the oven for 10 minutes longer. Then serve.

Large Poultry

Roasted poultry for Sunday dinner and roast turkey for Thanksgiving and sometimes Christmas are American traditions. Today turkey is available all year long, and you do not need to wait until Sunday to roast chicken.

Turkey must be kept moist during roasting. It can be outer-larded or basted. (For more on holiday birds, see Chapter 23.) Use an oven preheated to 275 to 375° F., and maintain the same temperature throughout cooking. For large birds, which need to roast longer, set the oven at the lower temperature, and cook the bird breast down for three quarters of the cooking time. Fresh turkeys are definitely superior to frozen in flavor and juiciness. Even if you live in a frozen-poultry area, it is worth while to order a fresh bird in advance.

Chickens of 3½ to 4½ pounds are usually roasted, but you can roast smaller birds too. Roast a large chicken at 325° F. for 1¼ to 1½ hours. Then turn off the oven, leaving the bird there for ½ hour before carving and serving it.

Capons of 6 to 7 pounds make good roasts, and one such bird can provide 10 servings. Treat capon like chicken: Roast in a 325° F. oven for 1¾ hours, then increase the heat to 375° F., and roast for 15 minutes longer, for added browning. As with chicken, let the bird rest in a turned-off oven for ½ hour before carving.

If your poultry is stuffed, cook it for 20 to 30 minutes longer than you would if it was not, so that the stuffing is completely done.

Poultry does not have to be at room temperature before roasting because it is cooked relatively slowly and has no meat in the middle that must be reached by the heat. Nevertheless, it will slow the process a little if the bird goes directly from refrigerator to oven.

If you want to, you can make any bird self-basting by inserting slivers of butter between skin and flesh. You can also protect the drier breast meat by roasting the bird breast down for three quarters of the cooking time. Other good tricks are brushing the bird with a sauce or marinade containing butter or oil, or spooning pan drippings over it from time to time, but do not open the oven door more than necessary.

Ducks and geese are fatty birds, but if you are careful with them they will be digestible. One way to eliminate some of the fat is to prick the skin of the bird and put it in boiling water for about 30 minutes. Then drain, pat dry and roast. If you skip the boiling step, at least prick the sides of the bird to release fat. During cooking, baste the bird to develop color and crisp the skin. Roast ducks and geese at 350 to 400° F. A 5-pound duck will need 2 hours at the lower temperature, a 12-pound goose about 4 hours. Be sure to remove excess fat from the roasting pan periodically during cooking because it tends to burn, and burning fat can spoil the flavor of the birds.

Small Poultry

Small birds like squabs and Rock Cornish game hens require care in cooking. Outer-lard the squabs with fresh beef fat and cook at 300° F. for 1 hour. Outer-lard the Rock Cornish game hens with beef fat also, or baste them as they roast to keep them moist. Put little birds in a preheated 400° F. oven; after 10 minutes reduce heat to 350° F., and roast for 50 to 65 minutes longer, according to the weight of the bird. Almost all small birds will be done in 1 to 1¼ hours. They can be basted with herb butter or with a mixture of butter and jelly or marmalade, to glaze them. After the squabs or Cornish hens are done, turn off the oven and let them rest in the oven for 15 minutes before serving.

Pheasants and guinea hens, originally wild birds, are now raised commercially. Like game birds, they are somewhat dry, with little fat, and therefore need some extra care. Outer-lard them, and cook them covered for about half the roasting time. After they are uncovered, baste them frequently.

If you are using frozen poultry, be sure it is fully defrosted before roasting. This is especially necessary with the small birds, which need only a brief cooking time.

Use a meat thermometer with the larger birds, but you will not find it as easy as with meats. Insert about three quarters of the length of the spike diagonally into the breast. The internal temperature should be 185° F. when done. Since pheasants and guinea hens have flat breasts, insert the meat thermometer between leg and thigh instead.

ROASTING POULTRY

Bird	Weight (pounds)	Oven Temperature	Cooking Time (minutes per pound)
Chicken	3½ to 5	350° F.	18 to 25
Turkey	6 to 12	350° F.	18 to 25
	13 to 24	325° F.	15
Capon	6 to 7	325° F.	20 to 25
Duck	5	350° F.	25 to 30
		400° F.	18 to 25
Goose	12	350° F.	20
Squab	1	300° F.	60 (total)
Rock Cornish game hen	1 to 1¼	350° F.	60 to 75 (total)
Guinea hen	2 to 4	350° F.	60 to 75 (total)
Pheasant	2¼ to 3	350° F.	25 to 30

Like the charts for meat, the chart for poultry is a guide, not a rule. If you start your bird at a higher temperature, you can reduce the roasting time slightly. You may want to increase the temperature at the end for browning; in this case too the overall cooking time should be slightly reduced. Whether your bird is stuffed or unstuffed will also make a difference in cooking time (see p. 94).

All-Day Roasting

Here's another idea for roasting large pieces of meat, which may seem very radical even though people have been talking about it for over a decade; it is sometimes called the "all-day" method. Set your oven at the internal temperature you want the cooked meat to reach, for instance, 170° F. for well-done beef. Preheat the oven, and insert the meat thermometer in a large beef roast—18 to 23 pounds, either boneless or with bones. Put the meat in the oven uncovered, and cook overnight or all day. The meat will never exceed the temperature you want; when the internal temperature reaches 170° F., your meat is ready to serve. This can be done with lamb too, but not with pork or veal.

The same method can be used with a large turkey of 30 to 35 pounds. Make sure the turkey has been out of the refrigerator for a few hours before you start. Then set the oven at 185° F., and preheat it. Insert the thermometer into the thickest part of the thigh muscle. The turkey can either be outer-larded or roasted in a covered pan. Cook the bird all day or overnight.

Obviously, this method cannot be used for small pieces of meat or small birds. If the desired temperature is reached and your large roast remains in the oven after that point, even it will dry out, so plan to serve it when it is beautifully juicy and tender.

BROILING

Because broiling, like roasting, is a dry-cooking method, some of the same considerations apply. For instance, meats with insufficient natural fats are better cooked by other methods, like panbroiling; very thin pieces of meat will dry out in the intense heat; delicate meats are not usually enhanced by broiling; less-tender meats need more moisture than this method provides.

In broiling, meats are exposed to a direct heat source, which may be gas, electric, wood or charcoal. Usually the meat or poultry is turned so that both sides can become browned. The type of fuel makes a difference. Gas broilers provide an extremely hot heat, and foods broiled in them burn more readily than those broiled with other fuels. To prevent burning and overcooking, the meat must be at least 5 inches from the heat source. The same is true of wood and charcoal fires, which give heat of the same intensity as gas broilers. Electric broilers, on the other hand, give much less heat, and foods can be placed as close as 3 inches to the electric heat source. Moisture can accumulate in the less-intense heat of the electric broiler, so to prevent a steaming effect, keep the door open as you broil.

In gas and electric broilers the heating unit is usually above the meat; obviously, in charcoal fires the heat is below the meat. When the heat is above the meat, you must place it on a rack or other device so that the fats and juices extracted can be drained off as they accumulate and discarded as waste. In charcoal broiling the fat and juices fall into the fire and are consumed. (For charcoal cookery, which we usually call barbecuing, see Chapter 16.)

Meats cooked close to the heat source for a short time will be seared on the outside and quite juicy in the middle. When broiled farther from the heat for a longer time, meats cook more evenly, and the external surfaces will be less crisp and well done. These are the two extremes in broiling, and you will adjust your cooking to achieve the balance that suits you best. The first alternative will not work well for thick cuts of meat because, after such a short cooking time, these pieces will emerge, not with a juicy interior, but a raw one. The second method is out for thinner pieces because they will be too dried out. In general, thicker pieces need longer cooking at lower heat (farther from the heat source) to be cooked through, and thinner pieces need faster cooking in order to remain juicy and flavorful.

These are the differences between broiling and barbecuing: The heat of the barbecue fire is more intense, and as a result the meat or poultry is usually cooked farther from the fire; to prevent drying and to add flavor, the food is often basted as it cooks; the coals themselves flavor the food, which neither gas nor electric heat sources can do.

As with roasting, allow the meat, unless it is pork, to come to room temperature before cooking. Season the meat when you take it out of the refrigerator, but do not salt it until you are ready to broil, because salt tends to extract juices; in broiling, which by its very nature has a drying effect, early salting could ruin your meat. Pepper can develop a bitter taste during broiling, so use it for a coating—it will flavor the meat—but brush off the bits of spice after cooking.

Lemon brushed on the fat of meats will keep it from flaring up in the broiler, and you will not detect the taste.

If you are broiling good-quality Prime beef, lamb or pork, you need not add fat or oil. Veal has some of the drawbacks for broiling that we have mentioned: It has little fat, and it is delicate. Nevertheless, veal of good quality that is thick enough can be broiled. Of course, veal should be rubbed with oil before broiling.

Preheat the broiler. You do not need to grease the grill, but you can rub it with lemon to prevent flaring.

Is there a difference between "grilling" and "broiling"? No. The word "broil" evolved from Latin words meaning to burn or singe over embers. "Grill" was derived from the name of the utensil on which the food was placed. Although most indoor broilers no longer look like gridirons or grills, the device for outdoor barbecuing does. The grill influenced European taste for the appearance of broiled dishes. Europeans like broiled meats to be marked with a checkerboard pattern seared into the surface by the hot grill; the meat is moved at right angles to achieve the crisscross pattern. If you want to, you can accomplish this easily enough by

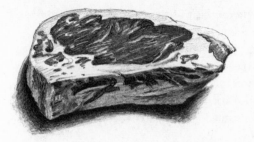

Delmonico or club steak, from
the short loin, the portion nearest
to the head

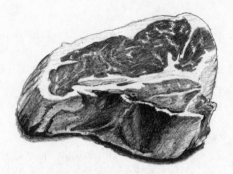

T-bone steak, also from the short
loin; this is larger than a club steak.

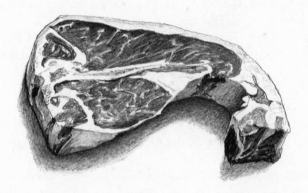

Porterhouse steak, the third cut from the short loin

Shell or strip steak from the short loin, with the filet portion removed

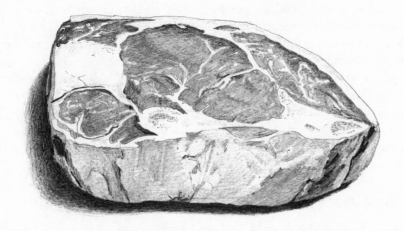

Sirloin steak from the hip or sirloin portion

Round steak cut from the top sirloin portion of the wholesale round

using a small grill; heat it to red hot, then place it on top of the meat for about 2 minutes, first with the bars one way, then the other. But it will not make the steak taste any better.

Meats

Good meats for broiling are steaks of all kinds; chops of all kinds; veal birds and cutlets; leg of lamb that has been boned and butterflied; rack, saddle and loin of lamb that have been prepared for broiling; hamburger and other chopped meats; regular bacon and Canadian bacon; ham steaks; frankfurters and salami; liver, both calf and chicken; sweetbreads, brains and kidneys; poultry, split or in pieces; young tender game.

It is not necessary to baste everything you broil, but it is a good idea with thinner pieces and drier meats, especially pork.

When is broiled meat done? Broiled cuts are usually thinner than roasts, and for this reason alone it is easier to tell by their appearance when they are done. Another way to tell is by touch: If the meat feels spongy, it is not done; if it feels hard, it is overdone; medium-rare meat with a juicy interior feels almost firm but gives a little under gentle finger pressure. Restaurant chefs test broiled meat by touch only. If you try this a few times it will not seem difficult. Just remember this basic rule: The more flexible the meat, the rarer it is.

If you cannot trust your judgment on this, make a tiny incision in the middle of the meat, lift out a very small slice and see how that looks. Do not cut the slice from the edges, because they will be done in any case, and be sure to make your incision as small as possible to avoid losing juices.

BROILED HAMBURGERS

Buy 1 pound of your favorite beef cut for hamburger, and shape the meat into 3 patties, each 1 inch thick. Make a hole in each pattie and insert 2 flat thin slices of dill pickle. Wrap a slice of uncooked bacon around each pattie, not around the edges, but over the middle. Fasten the bacon with a wooden food pick; do not allow more than ¼ inch of the pick to stick out at the edges; you do not want the wooden ends to burn. Grind peppercorns over the bacon wrapping and onto the meat. Place the broiling pan 3 or 4 inches from the heat source. Broil the hamburgers for 6 minutes on each side, until well browned and done to your taste. Turn only once during broiling. If you make burgers smaller than 6 ounces each, adjust the time and distance from the heat source accordingly.

Poultry

Poultry is excellent broiled. Chickens, usually broiler-fryers, are cut into halves or quarters. Open the wing joint so that it will lie flat, and sever the joint between leg and thigh so the leg will not curl up. *Do not* remove the skin. Season the pieces on both sides. If you marinate chicken in advance, you will not need to baste it. However, you can brush pieces of unmarinated chicken with oil as you turn them. Turn the pieces 2 or 3 times, broiling longer on the bone side to cook the interior.

If you are cooking chicken halves, you may discover that when the white meat, which is drier and more delicate, is done, the dark meat is still too rare. An easy solution—and one you can apply to broiling anything with parts that cook unevenly—is to cover the fast-cooking portion with foil. Remove the foil at the last moment to be sure the entire piece is hot and browned.

Pieces of turkey, duck and goose, and split small birds like squabs can be broiled too, but the fatty duck and goose may cause flaring in the broiler. You can avoid this by precooking them just as you would for roasting (see p. 94).

Opening wing and thigh joints on a chicken half so that it will lie flat for broiling. The same procedure is used in preparing chicken halves for the barbecue.

PANBROILING

This alternative to regular broiling for thin or lean pieces of meat is a top-of-the-stove method. The meat is cooked in a preheated skillet or frying pan, but not in fat. The pan must be heavy—an iron skillet is ideal—with an even, flat bottom, which will expose all surfaces of the meat to the same degree of heat. You can use pans lined with a nonstick coating like Teflon.

This method is best for pieces of meat 1 inch thick or less; do not panbroil any cut thicker than 1½ inches. Thicker pieces will be seared on the outside before the interior is done. It is usually not necessary to grease the pan, but if you have pieces 1½ inches thick it is better to do so.

A variation of panbroiling is salt broiling. When you have heated the heavy skillet, fill it with a *thick layer* of edible coarse salt, and let it get very hot. Place a thin piece of meat on the salt, and let it cook over moderate heat for about 5 minutes on each side for medium rare. The meat will not be extremely salty, but people on salt-free diets should certainly avoid this method. We do not recommend salt broiling because it does not offer any advantages over plain panbroiling and it is not economical because the salt is all discarded after each use.

COOKING WITH FATS

There are three methods called frying: sautéing, panfrying and deep-frying. When a French chef says "frying," he means only what Americans refer to as "deep-frying"; he does not count sautéing as frying at all. Panfrying is such a common technique in the United States that it seems to be an American invention.

Sautéing

In sautéing, the amount of fat used is very small—just enough to form a thin layer between pan and food so that food will not stick. Meats and poultry to be sautéed should be quite tender and rather thin, because sautéing is a fast process. The French verb *sauter* means "to leap" or "to jump"; in sautéing, food should practically jump in and out of the pan.

Because the cooking time is so short, oil, butter or margarine can be used for sautéing, but both butter and margarine present problems. Margarine, especially the soft or whipped kinds, burns more quickly than butter, and the flavor of margarine changes subtly during cooking, even when it has not been burned. With whole butter, little particles of milky residue form as the butter melts, and these can burn in a hot pan. If you use salted butter, the salt is separated as the butter melts, and it browns rapidly, becoming slightly bitter in taste. To prevent bitterness, use unsalted butter. To eliminate the milky particles, clarify the butter. Another solution to these problems is to mix the butter with oil, which keeps the butter from burning.

Olive oil is fine for sautéing, but it does impart a flavor of its own. If you do not like the flavor, use a bland oil like corn or peanut oil.

If you want to regulate the cholesterol content of your diet, use a margarine made of approved ingredients or a polyunsaturated oil, like corn oil.

Good foods for sautéing are boneless chicken breasts, plain or flattened; *scaloppine* of veal, pork, lamb or beef; livers of chicken, calf and young beef; small kidneys, split; *tournedos* and *filets mignons*.

The meat should be dry; if not, pat it with absorbent paper towels. Your pan should be large enough so that the pieces are not crowded; if you have more meat than fits in one pan, use more pans, or sauté the pieces in several batches. The meats should be at room temperature before sautéing, because if they are put directly from the refrigerator into the pan there will be splashing due to the moisture in the meat. If you want to, you can coat the meat with seasoned crumbs or a thin layer of flour.

Heat the pan, and let the small amount of oil or butter come to a simmer. If you have trouble gauging this point, fling a drop of water into the pan; it should dance across the surface and evaporate in about 1 second.

Put the dry unseasoned meat in the pan; brown on one side for 2 to 4 minutes according to the thickness of the piece; turn over, and season the cooked side; cook the second side, season it, and serve. If you allow sautéed meats to sit before serving, they will lose their crispness.

After sautéing, delicately flavored chicken and veal can be sauced and garnished in countless ways. For a quick pan sauce, transfer the cooked meat to a platter, and keep it hot. Then add a small amount of hot liquid to the sauté pan—wine, stock, fruit juice, whatever suits your recipe; use 1½ to 3 tablespoons per serving. Bring the liquid to a boil while carefully mixing into it all the browned meat juices from the pan. Let the mixture boil for a few minutes, until somewhat reduced, strain it if you want to, then spoon a little over each serving. The garnish—mushrooms, onion rings, green-pepper slivers, etc.—can be sautéed in the same pan, to be mixed with the pan sauce. The sauce can be seasoned, and butter or marrow can be added to make it glossy.

There is a cooking method that starts with sautéing and ends with simmering in a small amount of liquid; this process has no special name in the United States, although French cooks refer to it as "sautéing." This method is useful for pieces of meat and poultry that are slightly thicker than those you would normally sauté. Still using a small amount of oil or butter, sauté the meat until it is delicately browned. Then, without transferring the meat to another container, add to the pan whatever liquid suits your recipe, about ¼ cup per serving. Bring the liquid to a boil, then lower the heat to a simmer, and cook until the meat is done. The liquid will be reduced in cooking and can usually be served as a sauce just as it is, but it can be further elaborated if you like. This is a good method for cooking cut-up chickens.

Panfrying

Panfrying requires more fat than sautéing does, and it takes more time. This method is ideal for meats that need a longer cooking time than sautéing would provide—thick pieces and those with an egg-and-crumb or a batter coating. Some examples are chops, thick pieces of liver, chicken pieces with bones, small steaks, steak strips, stuffed *scaloppine*, hamburgers, lambburgers and croquettes made of raw meat.

Preheat the pan as you would for sautéing, but use a little more fat. If your meat or poultry is coated, season the coating; otherwise season as for sautéing. Do not cover the pan. After both sides are browned, reduce the heat, and cook a little longer, until the meat is done to your taste.

HOW TO COOK A CHEESEBURGER

Use a Teflon-coated pan. Let it get quite hot, then sprinkle seasoning *on the pan*. Add hamburger patties 1½ inches thick. Cook for 4 minutes, turn, cook for 2 more minutes; then cover each hamburger with a slice of cheese. Cover each pattie with a metal cap; the 4-inch cover of a coffeepot is ideal. Cook for 2 minutes longer; then transfer the cheeseburger to a toasted bun. Total cooking time is 8 minutes.

We have been discussing frying in a *sauteuse*, skillet or frying pan on top of a conventional gas or electric stove, but we should mention the electric skillet, which can be used anywhere, even at the table. For more ideas about using this device, see Chapter 17.

Another receptacle for frying is the wok, a round iron pot used in Chinese cooking. The sides of the wok are not perpendicular to its bottom, but curve gradually into it, forming a small circular base that was originally designed to be set into a round opening in a charcoal-burning brick stove. Because of its parabolic shape, the wok requires an extremely small amount of oil for frying. Stir-frying, the type of Chinese cooking most familiar to Americans, is easy in a wok; for stir-fried dishes, all pieces of meat or poultry and any vegetables used are cut into thin strips or cubes of the same size. Those ingredients that need the longest cooking are fried first; then the others are added. When the pieces cooked first are browned, they are pushed up the sides of the wok, and the oil on them drains to the bottom, where the pot is the hottest. Beef round steak and squares of duck or chicken are perfect for stir-frying. Add squares of red or green peppers, mushrooms, snow peas, Chinese cabbage, water chestnuts, almonds—whatever you like—to make a dish that is like a quick stew, with everything still crisp and retaining its color.

Browning, which is the first step in many recipes, is like panfrying except that the food is not completely cooked in the frying pan; it is usually transferred to a baking dish or casserole for the remainder of the cooking time. Other ingredients or liquids may be added to the casserole, but the fat left over after browning is discarded. The recipe that follows will illustrate this process.

BUTTERFLY PORK CHOPS
WITH TOMATO-MUSHROOM SAUCE   4 servings

4 pork chops, each 2 inches thick	1½ pounds potatoes, peeled
6 tablespoons oil	1 teaspoon salt
2 tablespoons chopped fresh chives	3 tablespoons butter
1 cup fresh tomato sauce, or 1 can (8 ounces)	6 tablespoons dry bread crumbs, seasoned or unseasoned (optional)
8 fresh mushrooms, peeled and chopped	2 slices of Swiss cheese, cut into small pieces
¼ teaspoon sesame seeds	

Have pork chops split to look like butterflies with open wings. Preheat oven to 350° F. Pour the oil into a large skillet, and add the chives. Heat oil with chives; then add the chops and brown them on both sides. Brown only 2 chops at a time, making them lie as flat as possible in the pan (one side will not be perfectly flat because of the butterflying). As chops are browned, transfer them to a large shallow baking pan (a lasagna pan is the right size). When all the browned chops have been placed in the baking pan, add tomato sauce, mushrooms and sesame seeds to the oil remaining in the skillet. Mix well, and heat for 10 minutes. Pour over the pork chops, and bake them for 25 minutes. While the chops bake, boil potatoes with salt until *very* tender, then drain and mash. Stir in the butter and beat the potatoes until smooth. Divide into 4 large balls, and roll each ball in bread crumbs (use more than specified if needed) until coated on all sides.

Remove baking pan from oven, and turn chops over. Put 1 potato ball in each corner of the pan, and sprinkle the cheese over the chops. Return the pan to the oven, and bake for 20 minutes longer. Put under a preheated broiler for 5 minutes to brown the top of the entire dish.

Deep-Frying

Of all the frying methods, deep-frying presents the most problems. A deep kettle or a thermostatically controlled electric fryer and a frying basket to fit are essential. If you have only the kettle, you should acquire a frying thermometer. The famous bread-cube temperature test may work well as you start to fry, but the temperature of the fat is lowered each time another piece of food is added, and you cannot conveniently repeat the bread-cube test at a later stage in frying. Also, the longer the kettle stays over the heat source, the hotter the fat. If you have a lot of food to fry, the last batch may be overbrowned or even overcooked. With the thermometer as a guide, you can adjust the heat when necessary, or, if you are using an electric stove, you can move the kettle to another burner, keeping it at a steady temperature from start to finish.

Lard is the fat most often used for deep-frying, and purified lard is the least expensive of the fats you can use; however, it is not a practical choice for home cooking because its odor is strong. The fat around beef kidneys is often recommended for such dishes as souffléed potatoes, but it is not readily available to everyone. Hydrogenated vegetable shortenings are probably better for general use; they do not absorb odors from the foods cooked in them, and they can be purified for later use by cooking a heel of bread in them for 5 minutes. Discard the bread and strain the fat. Use this trick for other fats and oils too.

Vegetable oils are good for deep-frying too, especially peanut oil. Do not use butter, margarine or chicken or bacon fat, because they will burn at the temperature required for deep-frying. We do not recommend olive oil for deep-frying either, because its odor becomes extremely pungent at high temperatures.

Fried chicken is an all-American favorite. Other meats suitable for deep-frying are 1-inch-thick chunks of tender beef from the shell, filet or sirloin; the eye of the lamb chop; croquettes and fritters. *Tempura* is a delicious Japanese dish of fried batter-coated foods; the batter is a simple mixture of egg, water and flour. Usually *tempura* consists of shrimps, other seafood, and vegetables fried and served together, but pieces of poultry are sometimes used. The Italian favorite *fritto misto* also includes an assortment of vegetables with pieces of chicken, sweetbreads and so on, which are usually just floured before frying. Using either of these ideas, you can prepare a delicious "mixed fry." The secret is to have all the ingredients in pieces of similar size and ready to cook so that some of each kind can be served together. Cauliflowerets, whole mushrooms, pepper squares and small beef chunks, for example, are delicious together.

Prepare all the ingredients; then heat a kettle or electric fryer half full of oil or shortening to the correct temperature. Your recipe will probably tell you what the temperature should be; if not, the owner's manual for your electric fryer may provide the proper information. As a general rule, the oil or shortening for uncooked meats should be heated to 360° F. Cooked meats, for example chopped or ground meats used in meatballs or croquettes, need hotter oil, 375° F., because they will be in the oil only long enough to become browned and puffed up. Dip your frying basket into the oil, then lift it out and place a few pieces of meat or poultry in it. To avoid cooling the oil to a point below that necessary to seal the exterior of the food, do not overload the basket. When the pieces are golden, lift the basket, let it drain briefly, then transfer the food to absorbent kitchen paper. If you are cooking a large amount, keep the portion cooked first in a warming oven or a low oven—200 to 225° F.—until all the pieces are cooked. If you are not sure that the food is done, cut open a piece from the first batch you cook and check it. If it is overdone, reduce the heat of the oil by 5° F. and try again. If it is underdone, cook the next batch a little longer.

It is possible to deep-fry meats and poultry without a coating, as French fried potatoes are cooked, but meats and poultry are usually better with a coating. Coatings add a delicious crispiness to fried foods, but, more important, they seal in the flavor and juices of the meat. Coatings can be made of flour alone, beaten egg and flour, beaten egg and crumbs, or batters like those used for *tempura* and fried chicken. Many cookbooks advise chilling the coated food to set the coating. However we do not recommend this, because the cold food lowers the temperature of the oil far too much, thus preventing the sealing of the exterior. In addition, adding cold foods to hot fat can cause splashing. It is better to have the foods at room temperature when you begin deep-frying.

White meat from chicken and very tender meat like veal present special problems in frying: They tend to dry and overcook. One solution is soaking such meats in milk overnight to give them added moisture. But the best way to avoid drying out and overcooking is to deep-fry dry or tender meats for a shorter time at lower heat. When deep-frying chicken or veal, be sure to test a piece from the first batch for doneness.

Read the directions that come with your electric fryer carefully. If you are deep-frying in an ordinary kettle, remember this basic rule: The hotter the heat, the faster the food cooks. The fat should be heated to 425 or 450° F. for meat that needs only 1 or 2 minutes of frying. Thick pieces, which must be fried longer, require lower temperatures to cook the interior properly.

The recipe that follows uses a large frying pan and less oil than the conventional deep-fryer, but it illustrates how to deep-fry with simple equipment.

SOUTHERN FRIED CHICKEN AND VEAL KEBABS   6 servings

3 whole chicken breasts, each split, skinned and boned

1 pound veal (1 slice), cut from the round, ½ inch thick

18 unpeeled small white onions (silverskins)

18 medium-sized whole fresh mushrooms

4 eggs

½ cup cider

2 cups dry bread crumbs

½ cup all-purpose flour

½ teaspoon salt

2 pinches of ground pepper

½ teaspoon paprika

¼ teaspoon dried orégano

shaker of all-purpose flour

18 one-inch squares of green pepper

2 cups oil or hydrogenated shortening

Separate chicken breasts, and cut each of the 6 halves into 3 pieces. Cut the veal into 1-inch squares. Boil the onions for 10 minutes, then peel them. Clean the mushrooms, and cut the stems off even with the caps.

Beat the eggs well, then mix in the cider. Pour the mixture into a large oval dish like a soup plate or deep platter. Mix bread crumbs, ½ cup flour, salt, pepper, paprika and orégano, and pile this mixture on another plate or a large sheet of wax paper. Have another large sheet of wax paper and the shaker of flour ready.

Place chicken and veal pieces, mushrooms, parboiled onions and green-pepper squares evenly on small metal skewers. Use any system or color scheme you like, but the arrangement on each skewer should be no longer than 5 inches.

Pour some of the oil into a large frying pan and heat it. As it heats, sprinkle flour from the shaker over the skewers on all sides; shake off excess. Dip the skewers into the egg and cider mixture, then into the bread-crumb mixture. Place the coated skewers on the sheet of wax paper and let them rest for 5 minutes.

When the oil is very hot, put as many skewers into the pan as you can. When the breading is golden brown, after 5 to 8 minutes, use tongs to turn the kebabs over, and cook them on the other side for the same length of time. When golden brown on both sides, place the kebabs on absorbent kitchen paper to drain. Then transfer them to a baking sheet, and keep warm in an oven preheated to 250° F. until all the kebabs are cooked and ready to serve. Add more oil to pan as needed.

Idea: If you have a lot of egg and crumbs left over, mix the egg and cider mixture with the crumb mixture to make a batter, and add some cut-up or chopped cooked carrots for color. If the mixture is too soft, use more bread crumbs. Drop spoonfuls of the mixture, like small pancakes, into hot oil, and cook for 5 or 6 minutes on each side, until done to taste.

Another recipe, which we call "Lobels' Northern Fried Duck," does call for a deep-fryer because of the size of the pieces of duck. Cut a 4½-pound duck into 8 pieces, drop them into boiling water, and boil for 45 minutes. Drain, cool, and pat dry. Dip the pieces into egg and crumbs or batter, and deep-fry until crisp. You can use this idea for other fatty meats and birds.

COOKING WITH MOIST HEAT

Moist heat can be used to cook any kind of meat, but it is especially suitable for less-tender meat and meat with little internal fat. Moist heat is necessary for extracting gelatin from joints and, of course, for stock making.

Braising

Braising is the moist cooking method that uses the least amount of liquid. Flavoring vegetables and the meat itself provide all the necessary moisture, and since the food is cooked in a covered pot, the moisture is retained. For the most successful braising, use a pot that is just the right size for the ingredients. If your pot is considerably larger than the meat, leaving a lot of air space around it, the liquid in the ingredients has a chance to become steam, and the result is a dish that is more steamed than braised. In true braising, there is an exchange of liquids and flavors between meat and vegetables. If you do not have a pot small enough for the meat, you can compensate by arranging a sheet of foil over the meat to catch the moisture that condenses on the inside of the cover; make a tiny hole in the foil so that steam forming under it can escape. The type of pot used is just as important as the size; it should be heavy, with a tight-fitting cover.

Good vegetables for braising are celery, leeks, onions, carrots, green pepper, cabbage—almost anything. Cut them into pieces or shred them; they do not have to be of any particular size, or even of the same size, but they will be easier to handle during cooking if diced evenly. Classic French cookery specifies a size—¼-inch cubes—and a mixture of pieces of this size is called a *mirepoix*, which is usually sautéed in butter. Pork rind is sometimes added for the gelatin it contributes, but whether you do this is a matter of taste—the taste of pork. If you decide to use rind, blanch it first. If you like, you can use the cooked rind as cracklings, to provide a garnish for the completed dish. A calf's foot or knuckle is sometimes added for gelatin, but do this only if the piece of meat you are braising is large enough to require quite a long cooking time, because it takes a long time to extract gelatin from the joints.

Before braising, meats are sometimes browned on all sides; this is optional. Browning does enhance flavor as the external meat juices become coagulated, and it is usually a good procedure with red meats, because it helps start the process of flavor exchange. Season both meat and vegetables completely, then roll the meat in flour before placing it on the bed of vegetables.

Many cooks suggest larding meats to be braised; we do not, as was stated in the preceding chapter (p. 76). If your meat is very lean, you may outer-lard it, but remember, the fat will all be retained in the braising pot. Marinating is often suggested for meats to be braised, but we advise against this also (see p. 73).

White meats require more delicate handling than red meats in braising, as in all cooking methods. Gentle heat is especially important for these meats. When braising white meats, be sure to dice the vegetables, because white meats are cooked for a short time and you must do everything possible to hasten the exchange of flavors.

Some meats suitable for braising are beef brisket, chuck, bottom and top round, cross-rib, boiling beef or flanken, eye of round; leg of lamb, boned lamb shoulder, lamb riblets; neck of veal with or without bones, veal shoulder, rump, shanks with bones; center loin of pork with bones—this is costly, but it has few sinews and fat; fresh tongue of all kinds; oxtails.

Poultry suitable for braising includes large chickens, fowls, sections of turkey or duck, and larger game birds.

Whether you put your braising pot on top of the stove or in the oven, the process is the same. When the meat has been braised for about 45 minutes, upset the contents of the pot, and stir the vegetable bed. Return to the heat and finish braising. To make a smooth, thick gravy or sauce, purée the meat juices and vegetables from the pot. Of course, you can simply spoon some of the juices and vegetable pieces over each serving.

Pot-Roasting

Pot-roasting is similar to braising, but more vegetables and liquid are added. To evaporate about 20% of the moisture and reduce the liquid to make more flavorful gravy, the cover is removed for about half the cooking time.

We could suggest approximate times for braising and pot-roasting, but the best way to be sure your meat is done is to test it with a fork. Since these dishes can be kept hot or reheated, it is not critical to have them ready at a particular minute. If the meat does not seem tender enough, simply cook it a little longer.

Both braised and pot-roasted meats can be cooked a day in advance of serving and refrigerated. The period of refrigeration provides more opportunity for flavor exchange, and during this time fat released from the meat will rise to the top of the liquid and harden there, and it can be lifted off and discarded before you reheat the dish for serving. Braised and pot-roasted meats can be served cold, and they make useful leftovers (see Chapter 19).

A new kitchen "appliance" useful for oven braising is the plastic oven bag. For safety, be sure your oven is correctly regulated, and do not use just any plastic bag—*only* those developed for oven use. They can withstand temperatures up to 400° F., and they are simple to use: Put your meat or poultry in the bag, and add the seasoning, flavoring or liquid of your choice. Tie the bag closed, and place it in a shallow oven dish or on a baking pan. With a skewer or long fork, make some holes in the top so steam can escape; look into the oven during cooking, and poke another hole in the bag if it seems to be puffing up. You can braise large or small pieces this way, and when the cooking is finished, the bag is discarded, and you have a minimum of cleaning up. Oven bags are also handy for precooking meats for barbecue.

Clay Bakers

Another sort of braising, done in unglazed earthenware pots, is an old method used by the ancient Romans and the American Indians. Food cooked in earthenware pots tastes delicious, but there is one disadvantage: It is hard to wash the pots afterward. No soap can be used on them, because it would be absorbed by the clay, and some meat juices remain in the clay even if you wrap the meat in parchment cooking paper. Braising in clay bakers differs from ordinary braising in that it must begin in a cold oven. Be sure to follow the directions that come with your baker for care before and after cooking. When using a clay baker, follow any braising recipe, but add about 20 minutes to the cooking time to compensate for starting in a cold oven. Trim external fats from the meat, and place it on a vegetable bed, as in conventional braising, or cook it without vegetables. During braising, steam escapes through the porous clay, and the finished dish will be much less "wet" than if braised in the conventional manner. Juices and vegetables will be extremely flavorful, but green vegetables will lose their bright color. Meats cooked in clay bakers can be kept under refrigeration for at least a day longer than ordinary braised meats because the meat never becomes overly moist. A delicious clay-baked dish can be prepared by adding a little dry vermouth to a roasting chicken stuffed with dill and onions and resting on a bed of carrots and mushrooms. Here is another recipe for clay baking:

CLAY-BAKED VEAL WITH SPINACH AND ORANGE   8 to 10 servings

2 pounds fresh spinach	2 teaspoons salt
5 pounds boneless shoulder of veal	1 teaspoon grated lemon rind
1 tablespoon minced fresh onion	grated rind of 1 orange
¼ teaspoon dried basil	½ cup fresh orange juice
¼ teaspoon dried orégano	2 garlic cloves, peeled
pinch of dried summer savory	

Do *not* preheat the oven. Use a medium-sized clay baker, which holds 3½ to 4 quarts in the bottom section. Put it in a large dishpan or clean sink, cover with cold water, and soak for 10 minutes or longer. Wash and trim the spinach (use only fresh spinach for this recipe); then shake as much water out of it as possible. Drain the baker, place the spinach in the bottom, and put the veal on top. Mix onion, herbs, salt and lemon and orange rinds, and sprinkle them over the veal and spinach; add the orange juice. Put each garlic clove on a wooden food pick, and drop it in. Cover the baker, and put it in the cold oven. Turn the control to 400° F., and bake for about 2 hours. Discard the garlic. Slice the veal and serve with some of the spinach and pan juices. The spinach will have lost its bright color, but it will taste delicious, and the veal will be exceptionally good.

To wash the clay baker, soak it in hot water and scrub with a stiff brush or nylon sponge. Be sure it is completely dry before you put it away.

Steaming

We have suggested a trick to keep braising meat from steaming, but we should mention steaming as another moist cooking method. You can steam in a proper pasta or clam steamer, a pot with holes in it that is suspended inside a larger vessel containing liquid; or in a small basket steamer that fits into a conventional saucepan; or in a pressure cooker. Steaming is used chiefly for extracting juices from meats, as in making beef tea. Because steaming virtually dissolves the soft portions of a cut, meat cooked by this method will be tender but somewhat stringy. Steam meat only for special needs.

Other moist cooking methods—boiling, poaching, stewing—use considerably more liquid than braising, pot-roasting or steaming. Boiling is not a recommended method for cooking meat. At first, the boiling process softens meat, but as it proceeds it toughens and shrinks the fibers, allowing all meat juices—body moisture, blood, fat—to escape into the liquid. Even in stock making, in which the liquid that results is more important than the meat cooked in it, boiling is not the best method to use; too much flavor and too many nutrients escape in the steam produced by boiling. However, boiling is useful for certain preparatory steps, for instance, the extraction of excess fat from such birds as ducks or geese.

Poaching

"Poaching" or "simmering"—both terms indicate the same process—is cooking in liquid at about 200° F.; the liquid should be moving gently in the pot but not breaking into bubbles or releasing volumes of steam. Such gentle heat is fine for tender cuts of meat and for young birds, but poaching tough meats or old birds for a relatively long time can also result in a good dish. This longer poaching is the method used to obtain stocks and soups; see Chapter 10 for more about that.

Do not brown meat or poultry before poaching, but you may roll the pieces in flour. Start poaching in *warm*—not hot or cold—water or stock (preferably your own homemade stock). Season the liquid mildly, and add vegetables if you want to. To extract the most flavor from your vegetables, grate them or cut them into small pieces. When the meat or poultry is almost done, remove the pot from the heat, and let the food finish cooking in the hot liquid. As with braised meats, test for doneness with a fork.

Good meats for poaching include "boiled beef," which is really poached, not boiled, veal shank and beef shank. Country hams are also poached before they are baked.

Poultry is often poached, especially chicken to be served cold. However, other birds—duck, goose, turkey, Rock Cornish game birds—can also be prepared in this way. If you have never poached a duck or goose, you may be surprised at the juicy and tender meat that results; in addition, the fat is released in the poaching liquid, and you will not have to prick the skin or do any preliminary work to eliminate fat, as you would in roasting such birds. You can save the poaching liquid for cooking rice, noodles or vegetables.

Truss whole birds, stuffed or unstuffed, for poaching so they will keep their shape. Young tender chickens will be done in 45 minutes, but older birds, stewing chickens or fowls, will take much longer to become tender. For ways to use fowl, see Chapters 8 and 10. Poultry cut into pieces can be poached too; the cooking time will be the same as for whole birds and will, of course, vary according to the age of the bird.

Boiled Beef

Excellent for boiled beef are short ribs, or flanken, which are sweet but rich (fatty); after boiling them, let them cool in the liquid, lift off the fat, and reheat to serve. Bottom round, or rump, various cuts from the shoulder, the layer on top of the rib, and the brisket are also good boiled. Do not buy long-bone flanken for boiling; this cut has a stringy texture and a large amount of gristle and veins. You can distinguish between the short ribs and the long-bone flanken if you are careful when shopping; the obvious fatty content and large amount of bone will indicate which cut to avoid. Boiled beef is delicious with horseradish sauce.

Stewing

Stews are made by various moist-heat methods. Meat for stewing is cut into pieces, and poultry is cut into sections or individual servings instead of being cooked whole. Other ingredients are almost always stewed with the meat, to be served with it as part of the dish. In this, stewing differs from braising, in which vegetables are used mainly for flavoring; for braising, vegetables are cut into small bits, and by the time the meat is fully cooked they are soft enough to be puréed into sauce, a use that is incidental to their function of flavoring. Flavoring vegetables may be added to stews, but those that are to be served with the meat should be left whole or cut into large pieces. If the liquid used is not allowed to boil, the vegetables will remain whole no matter how long the stew cooks.

Here are a few general rules for stewing, but remember that you can do whatever you like. If you are cooking beef, brown the pieces first, but do not brown veal. Put an inch or less of *hot* stock or whatever liquid you choose in the bottom of a sturdy pot—not enough to submerge the meat. Add meat, vegetables and the seasoning of your choice, but season gently—you can always adjust later. If you have delicate vegetables like little white onions, mushrooms or small tender peas, add them at the end of stewing, allowing just enough time for them to cook. Delicious additions to stews are very tiny white onions, smaller than silverskins, which come frozen in large bags.

Daube

Some stews are cooked like braises; a good example is a *daube*, a French stew cooked in a heavy pot, its cover sealed tightly with dough, allowing no steam to escape. A *daube* can be cooked in the oven or over very low heat on top of the stove. With conventional stews cooked on the stove top in the manner of poaching, it is possible to add ingredients as the cooking progresses. With a *daube*, all ingredients must be added at the outset because the pot may not be opened until everything is done. Beef is the meat most often used in a *daube*. Some cooks suggest that the meat be browned first; others say it should never be browned! Escoffier directs the cook to brown beef, but not mutton. Do as you like about this. Sprinkle a little flour on the meat, and pour in enough stock or wine or a mixture of both almost to cover the meat. You can cook this dish by the all-day method described on page 96. To cook a *daube* in this way, seal the pot, set the oven at 200° F., and let the stew cook all day or night.

Stews require slow cooking over gentle heat; if for some reason you choose to stew a tender meat, the stewing time will be short, but the cooking must be especially gentle.

Blanquette

"White" stews—fricassees or *blanquettes*—are made of light-colored meats, usually veal or chicken, but turkey and duck can be used too. The sauce is always made with some of the stock used in the stewing; it is thickened to a velvety smooth mixture, a *velouté*. Meat for a fricassee is usually browned in butter before poaching, but meat for a *blanquette* should be as nearly white as possible, so it is started in cold liquid and never browned. While a fricassee might contain carrot disks or tiny artichokes or fresh parsley, only white vegetables are used in a *blanquette:* small white onions and mushrooms. Obviously, meat or poultry for a *blanquette* must be tender and free of membranes and tendons. A *blanquette* needs careful handling to be just right, and it is excellent for special occasions. Milk or cream is usually added to the velouté sauce, and it is commonly thickened with egg yolks. You can eliminate the egg yolks if you want to, but the sauce must be very smooth and thick.

Before we close this chapter on cooking, we should mention the microwave oven. Even though several kinds of microwave oven are being manufactured, the device is still, in some ways, in the experimental stage. Since we have not used it, we can only give general information about how it works. Microwaves cause food molecules to move, thus producing heat and cooking the food. Although this appliance is called an "oven," its effect is more like steaming than roasting, and foods cooked in most of the microwave ovens on the market today do not brown as they do in conventional cooking. Microwave cooking has one tremendous advantage: It is extremely rapid, and meats can be put directly into the oven from the refrigerator. It may be the "microwave of the future," but we think the other methods we have described will give you great results.

BREAKFAST

Chapter 7

Despite the emphasis on cereal grains and fruit juices for the first meal of the day, protein-rich meats and poultry are appropriate for breakfast. Taste and tradition limit our choices for this meal more than for any other, though almost any kind of meat would serve. A few exceptions are fresh pork, which is generally too rich for the first meal of the day, and veal, which requires preparations too elaborate for quick service. As good energy producers, nothing can surpass small portions of red meat, which are quick to prepare.

The housewife of today, with little or no staff, must consider primarily short-order meats for breakfast. It was a tradition to cook oatmeal and baked beans overnight in deep-well cookers or in old coal stoves and serve them for breakfast, but this method does not serve well for meats. Precooked meats or poultry that have been stored under refrigeration might do, but the best breakfast dishes are freshly cooked and quickly cooked.

Bacon

Bacon is the most popular breakfast meat in the United States; ham probably rates second. Two obvious reasons for the popularity of bacon are the speed and ease of preparing it and the delicious aroma it releases as it cooks. Today's consumer prefers lean bacon, and not only are hog producers breeding leaner animals than in the past, but also packers are trimming bacon more extensively to make it leaner.

Good packaged bacon is generally available in slices of varying thicknesses, and by trial and error you can find a brand that will suit you. Nevertheless, for the thickest, most delicious bacon, take the trouble to hunt for unsliced slab bacon, and have your butcher slice it to your specifications, or slice it yourself. Although some packaged sliced bacon may have a pronounced smoky taste because it has been cured with heavy smoke, slab bacon retains more of the smoked flavor simply because it has not been sliced in advance.

Most people panfry bacon. If panfrying is your choice, let the bacon reach room temperature before cooking, so that the strips, or rashers, as the British call them, can be separated easily. Place them in a single layer in a cold pan, and cook over low to moderate heat, turning at least once—more often, if you like—to crisp both sides. When the strips are done, lift them out of the pan and place them briefly on a layer of absorbent kitchen paper before serving. Frying over high heat tends to curl the bacon, cooking it unevenly, perhaps burning it in some places while barely heating it in others.

Bacon can also be broiled, of course, and if your broiler allows the released fat to run off, the rashers can be served immediately, without draining. Under the broiler, packaged bacon will be done in 4 to 5 minutes.

Here is Leon Lobel's method for preparing breakfast bacon: From slab bacon, cut slices ¼ to ⅜ inch thick. Place the slices on a rack, and bake them in a preheated 350° F. oven until almost done. Then put them under the broiler to crisp. When cooking slices this thick, score the tops to prevent curling and release excess fat.

Stanley Lobel suggests cooking breakfast bacon like this: Cut slices from a slab, making them about ¼ inch thick. Drop them into boiling water, and boil them for 3 or 4 minutes. Then remove slices from water, pat thoroughly dry with absorbent kitchen paper, and sauté, holding the slices down with a spatula to ensure that they cook evenly. Slices of this thickness will be sautéed in about 3 minutes.

Bacon is an excellent accompaniment to other breakfast foods—eggs in all their preparations, pancakes and waffles, French toast, cornmeal mush. Also, cooked and crumbled bacon can be added directly to other mixtures such as scrambled eggs, waffle batter and pancake batter. A bacon sandwich can be dipped into a French toast mixture to make delicious thick toast. The relatively small amount of animal protein in these bacon preparations combines with the protein content of the other foods to make breakfast far more nutritious.

Canadian Bacon

Canadian bacon, from the eye of the pork loin, is best cooked with moisture. If you are panfrying it, add a little oil to the pan. The meat is done when delicately browned on the edges; do not cook it for too long a time or it will become dry and hard to chew. Or have the Canadian bacon cut into slices about ⅜ inch thick and bake them in a preheated moderate oven (350° F.) for about 20 minutes. This will result in juicier meat. Canadian bacon can also be broiled. Place it on a rack, and broil at moderate temperature about 3 inches from the heat source; if you place it farther from the heat, it will become quite dry before the edges are browned. Slices of ¼ to ⅜ inch thick will be done in about 6 minutes; broil for 4 minutes on one side, then turn and broil for 2 minutes longer. Thicker slices, which take longer to broil, can be placed farther from the heat source because they will not dry out as rapidly as the thinner slices.

Sausages

Sausages are another favorite breakfast meat. Fresh uncured sausage links can be panfried, broiled or simmered. Sausage patties can be panfried, broiled or steamed; they can be simmered too, but they tend to crumble in water. To panfry links, start with a cold pan, as for bacon, but add about 2 tablespoons water for 8

LAMB CHOPS

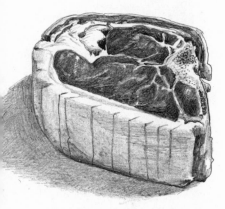

Loin chop, cut from the loin portion

Loin chop containing a slice of the kidney, called a "kidney chop"

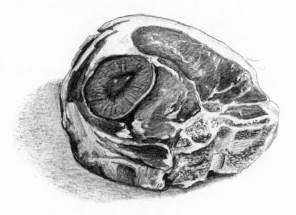

Sirloin chop, cut from the leg, the portion closest to the loin

Arm chop, cut from the arm portion, near the foreshank, of the chuck

Blade chop, cut from the blade portion, near the neck, of the chuck

Rib chop, cut from the rib or rack portion

117

small links. Cover the pan, and cook over low heat for 5 or 6 minutes; by this time the water will have turned to steam, and the sausages will be thoroughly heated and partially cooked. Remove the cover, and brown the links on all sides, completing the cooking. The steaming step helps keep the meat juicy.

Sausage links are sometimes parboiled to release excess fat. However, if you have small, high-quality sausages and enough time, simply move them back and forth in the frying pan until they are cooked and browned on all sides.

Do not prick pork sausage links; this releases too much juice and fat, and with the fat goes part of the flavor. On the other hand, it is useful to prick beef sausages before cooking, because they are packed in heavier casings than pork sausages are. Another trick with beef sausages is to press them down as they cook, to bring more of the surface in contact with the hot pan; their thicker casings make them a little slower to cook.

To simmer, drop sausage links into boiling water; as soon as the water comes to the boil again, reduce the heat, and keep it at a steady simmer. Thin links will be done in 5 or 6 minutes, thicker links in about 10 minutes. Of course, this method will not brown the sausage.

To panfry patties, follow the same process as for links, or substitute about 1½ tablespoons of oil for the water, and cook uncovered; this method is similar to panbroiling. Be sure to turn the patties so that each side is well browned, using a spatula or pancake turner to keep the patties from breaking.

Sausage meat pressed into rolls or blocks can be sliced and treated like patties, and they are not as likely to fall apart in pan cooking.

Brown-and-serve sausages are, of course, much quicker than regular sausages to prepare, and they are good in emergencies.

Other good breakfast meats are chipped beef; sliced ham, cold or sautéed; veal or lamb kidneys, broiled or sautéed; and chicken livers prepared in a variety of ways.

Chipped Beef

Chipped beef needs only to be heated before serving. It is usually heated in white or à la king sauce. The first preparation is called "creamed chipped beef," and it makes an excellent quick dish served on toast or English muffins—perfect for a brunch or luncheon, as well as for breakfast. The fact that chipped beef is salty must be taken into account when preparing it and planning the balance of the menu. Chipped beef can also be shredded into small pieces and used as crumbled bacon is in omelets and pancakes.

Ham

Slices of cold boiled or baked ham are good alone or with egg dishes or pancakes. For company occasions, thin ham slices can be rolled into cornucopias and filled with scrambled eggs or cheese mixtures. This idea can be varied by adding different herbs or vegetable bits to the eggs, or by garnishing the serving in interesting ways.

Kidneys

Because of the short time needed for cooking small kidneys—lamb and veal—they make excellent breakfast fare. Trim lamb kidneys (see p. 179), and place them in a shallow pan, cut sides down. Broil under moderate heat for 3 minutes, then brush lightly with seasoned olive oil or another basting mixture of your choice. Cook for 3 minutes longer, then brush again with oil, and turn them over. Broil on the second side for 2 minutes, brush that side with oil, broil for 2 more minutes, and they should be done. The cut edges will curl, and the cut side will become slightly cup-shaped during cooking; juices and a few drops of the seasoned oil will remain in the little hollow. If you have basted with a light hand, the pan juices may be poured over the kidneys. Preparing lamb kidneys in this way takes only a few minutes longer than broiling bacon. Serve on toast, garnished with parsley sprigs or diced pimientos.

Because veal kidneys are larger than lamb kidneys, they should be sliced and either broiled or sautéed. Broil the slices for about 5 minutes on each side, brushing them all over with oil. Slices of veal kidney sautéed plain, over brisk heat, will be done in 3 or 4 minutes. You can vary this method by dipping the slices into egg and crumbs before sautéing. It is important not to overcook kidneys of any kind, because they become tough and lose flavor.

Because stewing takes considerably longer than broiling or sautéing, stewed kidneys are less practical for breakfast. Kidneys of any kind should be freshly cooked, since they become quite hard and lose flavor when refrigerated after cooking.

Chicken Livers

Chicken livers are delicious for breakfast. Sauté them in oil or butter or a mixture of both; use about 2 tablespoons of either for 1 pound of chicken livers. The livers can be cooked whole or sliced, or each liver can be cut into 2 or 3 pieces. If served alone, 1 pound yields 4 to 6 servings but if the livers are mixed with other ingredients, the same amount will go further. Here is an excellent chicken-liver dish for breakfast:

CHICKEN-LIVER AND MUSHROOM OMELET   1 serving

2 to 3 ounces chicken livers	2 eggs
1 tablespoon bone marrow, softened (see p. 170)	2 tablespoons heavy cream
	salt and pepper
2 to 3 ounces fresh mushrooms	1 tablespoon unsalted butter

Trim chicken livers and cut each lobe into halves. Mix livers with softened marrow, and cook over low heat for 20 minutes. If mushrooms are very fresh and clean, do not peel, but wipe with a damp cloth; cut a slice from the stem end and discard it. Dice raw mushrooms, and cook with liver and marrow mixture for 5 minutes.

Meanwhile make the omelet. Break eggs into a small bowl, add heavy cream, and mix well with a fork. Season lightly with salt and pepper if you wish. Put butter in a small omelet pan (7 inches), and heat it over moderate temperature. When butter is sizzling, pour in egg mixture and reduce heat to low. Do not stir egg mixture; this is a "pancake omelet." When omelet is three-quarters done, in 3 or 4 minutes, sprinkle filling over half of it. Wait for 2 minutes, then flip the other half of the omelet over the filling. Cook for 2 more minutes, and then serve at once. It is always better to make individual omelets rather than larger ones, because the smaller ones cook more quickly and are easier to serve.

Chicken

Although chicken served as a breakfast dish in past decades, it is less common on breakfast tables now because of today's fast-paced life styles. Fried chicken was a Sunday or holiday breakfast in some sections of the United States, but we do not recommend it because it is too heavy a dish. However, small portions of chicken or other poultry simply broiled or sautéed can make good breakfast dishes. Chicken will cook in a matter of minutes if slices of it are prepared like *scaloppini* and slightly flattened. Creamed chicken and waffles make an elaborate breakfast, one for a company occasion perhaps, and if the chicken is prepared from a cold poached bird that has not been overcooked to begin with, it need not take long to prepare such a dish. Prepoached chicken is also good diced and mixed with scrambled eggs.

While small whole birds like squabs and Rock Cornish game hens are sometimes suggested for breakfast on elaborate menus, they are really too much work for a breakfast dish and are better suited for brunch or luncheon.

Regional and local traditions have produced some unusual breakfast menus. Everyone knows about baked beans and salt pork for Sunday breakfast in old New England. Originally the dish was cooked all day Saturday in a bean hole outdoors or in a large iron pot in the home hearth so that it was ready to eat on the Sabbath, when everyone went to church services that lasted for hours. By an odd quirk, the recipe crossed the ocean to become popular in England as a breakfast dish, served on toast, and as a teatime snack. Maine farmers enjoyed salt pork baked in apple pie for breakfast. These salt-pork dishes are nutritious and warming on a cold morning but hardly seem appropriate for a family living in a well-heated home. Another traditional New England breakfast dish is steak, also common in the western United States. Plain broiled steak will certainly send one off to work full of energy. Here is a variation:

STEAK AND EGGS   1 serving

1 small minute steak (3 to 4 ounces trimmed meat)
1 tablespoon unsalted butter
2 large eggs

Broil the steak until done to taste, but do not overcook it. Fry eggs in butter, sunny side up, until partially done. Cut the steak into sections, and arrange them on top of the whites of the eggs. Cover the pan, and finish cooking the eggs. Serve at once; the diner breaks the yolks, which run over steak and whites, making a delicious flavor combination.

The eye of the lamb chop can be prepared in the same way.

Another tasty meat-and-egg favorite is corned-beef hash topped with poached egg. Of course, the corned beef would be previously cooked, but the hash itself could be entirely prepared and ready for sautéing at the breakfast hour.

Scrapple

A Pennsylvania specialty for the start of the day is scrapple or *paanhaas*, made of cooked pork and cornmeal. Like cornmeal mush, scrapple can be made the day before and chilled. At breakfast time simply unmold, slice, and sauté the slices until they are browned to your liking. It is possible to purchase scrapple, although it is less generally available today than it was a generation ago. It is more commonly made at home, and for those who like it the family recipe may be a treasured possession.

Another nutritious breakfast meat is liver, either plain or with a garnish of bacon. Calf's liver and steer liver, both tender and quick to cook, can be sautéed in minutes.

Meal Patterns

If you are accustomed to a small meal at the start of your day, some of these suggestions may seem as hearty as luncheon dishes, and this leads us to a question: Can anything good for lunch serve equally well for breakfast? Probably so, yet your appetite after a morning of activity is likely to be greater than at the start of the day, when the body's metabolism is slower; therefore you may expect most people to eat less food than some of these recipes call for or to avoid those preparations that are overly rich. But the customs of a culture rule people more than we might believe. Histories and diaries indicate that in European countries from the sixteenth to eighteenth centuries breakfast was the same sort of meal as any other. Roasts, whole-grain breads and beer or ale were common breakfast fare for those who could afford them. Even during the twentieth century, a countryman's breakfast in France might consist of pâté sandwiches and white wine, quite different from the *café au lait* and croissants one thinks of as a typical French *petit déjeuner*. It is important to remember that people who lived before the age of mechanization were obliged to perform far more physical labor than most contemporary workers are, that they lived in unheated houses, and that their whole life's rhythm was intrinsically related to the cycle of weather and seasons.

What should be the pattern of daily meals for contemporary Americans? Certainly a coffee and pastry breakfast is insufficiently nutritious. People's daily eating patterns should coincide with their work styles. People doing heavy labor should eat a substantial breakfast, a substantial lunch, and a light dinner if they go to bed early. The size of the dinner should be related to the hour of bedtime; if bedtime comes 5 hours or more after dinner, then the dinner should be a large meal. A person working at a desk job or doing light physical labor should eat a light breakfast, but one including some protein, a substantial lunch and a light dinner. Again, the size of dinner depends on the person's schedule. In general the trend today is toward eating less at most meals. However, breakfast is extremely important for all people, no matter what their daily rhythm; beginning the workday with a good meal will give them the energy they need to perform their jobs efficiently.

Here are a few breakfast menus. Brew a fresh pot of delicious coffee or tea to accompany any of them.

Tomato juice and beef broth
Whole-grain cereal
Scrambled eggs
Bacon muffins

Half cantaloupe
Chicken-Liver and Mushroom Omelet (p. 119)
Croissants with lime marmalade

Orange and grapefruit juice
Corn oysters with bacon crumbles in the batter
Broiled tomato halves

Broiled half grapefruit with honey
French toast bacon sandwiches

Stewed prunes and apricots
Oatmeal
Sausage patties with sautéed apple rings

Applesauce with cream
Corned-beef hash patties with poached eggs
English muffins with apricot preserves

★

BRUNCH

Brunch is sometimes thought of as a kind of elaborate breakfast, but it is actually a buffet luncheon that includes some breakfast dishes. For brunch, breakfast dishes are somewhat embellished and often include more seasoning than would be desirable at the start of the day. Hardly anyone comes to a brunch, usually served around noon, without having had a first meal. At such a meal you can serve meat or poultry dishes that would be too time-consuming to prepare for everyday family breakfasts. Simple brunch dishes are sliced cold ham, tongue, chicken or turkey. Corned-beef hash with poached eggs is as good for brunch as it is for breakfast. For an important occasion roasted small birds can make an impressive show. Here are two special brunch menus.

Bullshot cocktails (beef broth with vodka)
Coffee
Scrambled eggs with chicken and pimientos
Corn sticks
Sliced baked ham
Green spinach pie (baked in filo pastry)
Sticky buns
Fresh fruit bowl

Keep the scrambled eggs at serving temperature over hot (not boiling) water in a chafing dish or double boiler. Keep the spinach pie hot on an electric hot tray.

★

Sherry
Coffee
Veal-kidney stew with mushrooms
Hominy grits
Sliced cold tongue and chicken
Preserved kumquats
English muffins
Cantaloupe and honeydew melon with lime wedges

Keep the stew and hominy warm over hot water in chafing dishes.

LUNCHEON

Chapter 8

LUNCHEON MUST BE THE MOST FLEXIBLE MEAL because of the variety of daily schedules. It is a typical leftover meal, a meal of sandwiches, or a meal of such short-order foods as steak, lamb chops or veal scallops. For many people, the time allotted for lunch is so brief that there is no time for cooking at all, while others eat their main meal at midday. If your family eats a large meal at noon, these luncheon ideas may be used for your evening meal, whether you call it supper, high tea or simply a light dinner.

In the preceding chapter you read that anything good for lunch could serve for breakfast as well. Conversely, any meat or poultry dish suitable for breakfast would be fine for luncheon, but you would probably want a larger portion, more pronounced seasoning and some appropriate accompaniments. For some, lunch may be more of a rush than breakfast, so the quickly prepared bacon with eggs might be the perfect choice if it does not duplicate the breakfast menu. All the breakfast suggestions can be adapted: Simply add a vegetable, salad or both, and finish the meal with a piece of fruit.

Sandwiches

Sandwiches made with meat are American favorites, and they can be a compact nutritional package too, if the bread is made of whole-grain or enriched flour and a vegetable garnish is added. The plain sandwich of 2 slices of bread can be made with any cold cooked meat: oven-roasted or pot-roasted beef, veal, lamb or pork, sliced and trimmed of bones and bits of gristle. These taste good spread with prepared mustard or horseradish, or with slices of pickles or fresh cucumbers added, or with leaves of lettuce and mayonnaise. If you like butter with your meat sandwiches, a good spread can be made with a mixture of softened butter and mustard, in proportions to suit your taste. Cold sliced tongue and ham also make delicious sandwiches; the so-called combination sandwich of ham and Swiss cheese is one of the most popular. Cold sliced chicken or turkey is excellent for sandwiches too; these sandwiches are commonly spread with mayonnaise rather than butter, and garnished with lettuce and tomato.

The sandwich made with only one slice of bread—open-faced—probably had a

Danish origin. The Danes are famous for their *smørrebrød*, which means "butter" (*smørre*) and "bread" (*brød*). Open-faced sandwiches, served for luncheon everywhere in Denmark, and for snacks and late-night suppers as well, have become popular throughout the world. While the original models would never do for a dieter, it is possible to use the open-faced idea to make a low-calorie sandwich. Anything good for a standard sandwich can be used for the open-faced version, but a little more care is usually taken to decorate them: The ingredients may be arranged in a pattern; bouquets of parsley, watercress, mustard cress or dill are often added, and they are sometimes sprinkled with bits of scallion, red onion, pickle, olive or pimiento.

There are also larger sandwiches—double- or triple-deckers. The most famous is the club sandwich, traditionally made of sliced chicken in one layer and bacon in the other, with lettuce, tomato and mayonnaise. Turkey can be used, of course, and you can adapt the idea to any other cold meat: bacon with veal, chicken or turkey with ham, or any cold meat in one layer and a vegetable or salad mixture in the other.

Sandwiches in buns have resulted in the most popular lunch and snack in the world—the hamburger. While a standard hamburger from one of the large chains may pall if you have to eat it daily, a hamburger made at home can be absolutely delicious because you can have high-quality meat, juicy and flavorful, ground especially for your purposes (see Chapter 12). And you can do all sorts of tricks with a homemade hamburger: bury a chunk of cheese in the middle, season it, garnish it, sauce it, spread the buns with flavored butter or mayonnaise—the possibilities are endless. A cheeseburger, also very popular, is simply a hamburger with a slice of American cheese melted on top during the last few minutes of cooking (see p. 103); these are most often served with the top half of the bun on the side, so you can see the cheese.

Another sandwich in a bun is the "hero," variously referred to as a "grinder," a "submarine," a "poor boy" or a "hoagie." "Hero" is the name most often heard around New York, "grinder" is common in New England and "poor boy" in the South. This idea originated with the luncheon of French and Italian workmen—a loaf of crusty bread split lengthwise and filled with whatever there was at home, sometimes only cucumbers and no meat at all. The bread was wrapped in a bandana and carried to work. In the United States a hero always has meat in it, usually several types of dry sausage, plus roasted red peppers or tomatoes, cheese, anchovies and oil-cured olives. A hero can actually be made of any cold meat, and it makes a delicious lunch for a really hungry person.

In France when you order a sandwich (pronounced "sahndweech"), you get half a loaf of French bread, the size called *ficelle* (meaning "thread"), about 1 inch wide and about 20 inches long, filled with *jambon* (ham), *fromage* (cheese) or pâté. You can use this idea for a quick lunch instead of using standard bread slices; the crusty narrow loaves are easy to hold in the hand, and they taste delicious. Another small loaf called a *petit pain* (little bread), like a narrow hard roll about 8 inches long, makes a good base for a sandwich of pâté or any other cold meat.

Some people think hard rolls are better for sandwiches than soft hamburger or frankfurter buns. There are many kinds of hard rolls on the market, and an especially tasty kind is made with sesame seeds. Poppy-seed hard rolls are old favorites, too.

The frankfurter in a bun is another American favorite, perhaps more often eaten as a snack than for lunch, but it could make a good lunch with some additions. Relish, sliced onions, sauerkraut—all sorts of flavorful foods can be added to the frankfurter in its roll to make it more filling and nutritious.

Any of the cold sliced meats we have mentioned can be diced or chopped to make salads for sandwich fillings; chicken and ham salad are common, but other meats can also make excellent salads. These same meats can be ground and mixed with other ingredients to make spreads; if you prepare a filling ahead of time, concocting a sandwich is the work of a minute.

Hamburgers and frankfurters are not the only meat sandwiches served hot. An open-faced sandwich can be broiled if you omit the lettuce or other greenery; when broiled, a layer of mayonnaise becomes an attractive golden-brown sandwich topping. Another familiar hot sandwich is made with sliced meat heated in gravy, which is spooned over the sandwich before serving. Hot roast beef and turkey sandwiches are the most usual, but, as with most of our sandwich ideas, this preparation is great for other meats too. Grinders are normally heated in an oven and served hot in Connecticut, because heating melts the cheese and blends the flavors. You can also make a sandwich of very thin slices of meat and fry it like French toast. If you get too elaborate with any of these suggestions, they will no longer be true sandwiches, because they will be impossible to eat in the hand and will require a knife and fork.

Eggs with Meat

Eggs mixed with meat serve as well for lunch as for breakfast. Corned-beef hash with poached eggs, a chicken-liver omelet, steak and eggs, scrambled eggs with diced cooked chicken, all described in the preceding chapter, make excellent luncheon dishes. To make eggs Benedict, start with an English muffin half, lightly toasted. On it, place a slice of cooked smoked ham lightly sautéed in butter or oil. Crown the ham with a freshly poached egg, and spoon hollandaise sauce over all. With different meats and sauces, you can produce several variations on the eggs Benedict theme; no part of the preparation takes more than a few minutes, but the final dish looks elegant. For an excellent lunch, serve with a salad or vegetable.

Corned-beef hash without eggs is good, and so is red-flannel hash, a New England specialty often attributed to New Hampshire. To made red-flannel hash, add peeled freshly cooked or canned beets when chopping or grinding the other ingredients. The resulting hash will be a bright beet red.

If your family loves salads, nothing will please them more for lunch than a meat salad. Precooked meats can be used, sliced, diced or slivered. For some occasions, you might want to cook meat for the sole purpose of making a salad. An American favorite is chicken salad.

Chicken for Salad

While good salads can be made from any cooked chicken, the most juicy and flavorful meat will come from a poached bird. For best results, poach the chicken whole. Small chickens are all right, but for more meat and flavor, use a large bird, a fowl of 4½ to 7 pounds, for instance. Wash the bird carefully inside and out, then tie the legs together, and flip the wings under the shoulders so that the chicken will fit in the pot. Start cooking in enough cold water to cover the bird. Add 1 table-spoon of salt and some flavoring vegetables if you like—celery leaves, leeks, onions, fresh parsley, etc. Bring the water to a boil, then reduce to a simmer and poach a 4½- to 5-pound chicken for about 2 hours. Add another 30 minutes for each extra pound. Then remove the pot from the heat, and let the chicken cool in the broth, where it will finish cooking. When the chicken is cold, lift it from the broth, and remove skin and bones. Leave the meat in large pieces until you are ready to make the salad.

With a larger and older bird, start cooking in cold water without flavoring vegetables or seasoning. When the liquid comes to a boil, let it boil for 1 minute; discard liquid and rinse the bird. Then start the poaching again, this time adding the flavoring vegetables and seasoning. If you skip this preliminary step with an old bird, you will need to skim the top of the liquid for the first hour to remove scum.

There are as many chicken-salad recipes as there are cooks. Chicken goes well with all sorts of vegetables; the simple standard salad is made with celery alone, but other recipes call for a dozen vegetables either cooked until just crisp or used raw. Chicken mixes well with fruits too. The salad dressing can be the conventional mayonnaise, a French dressing with fruit juice substituted for vinegar, or simply a mixture of white wine (not too dry—a sauterne is delicious) and a little light olive oil. Any salad green can serve as a bed for the salad bowl or the individual serving; endive, watercress, little round leaves of Boston or Bibb lettuce, long slender leaves of romaine—all are good.

If you are planning a salad luncheon and the day turns cool, you can adapt your menu to the weather by adding a cup of soup; if you make your own stock (see Chapter 10) you will always have soup makings at hand. On a cool day, hot rolls or biscuits can also warm your salad luncheon.

Chicken or other poultry left over from stock making can be used for salad, but letting the bird cool in the broth is what gives you especially good chicken for salad. As the bird cools, it absorbs flavor from the vegetables and juices from the broth.

For a generous chicken salad, allow $^1/_3$ to ½ cup of diced chicken per person, plus $^2/_3$ to 1 cup of the other ingredients. However, a good salad can be made with as little as ¼ cup chicken; just be sure not to dice it too small.

Chef's Salad

One of the most popular salads for lunch is the Chef's Salad, which includes several kinds of meat, various greens and usually cucumbers, tomatoes, hard-cooked eggs and onion rings. This salad is always presented before it is tossed or mixed, with the ingredients arranged in patterns in a salad bowl or on a large serving platter. The meats include ham or tongue and turkey or chicken. These, with Swiss cheese, are cut into very thin long slivers and placed in neat mounds on top of the other ingredients. After everyone has seen the salad, the dressing is added, and the salad tossed. Chef's Salad is a good example of a dish in which a relatively small amount of meat protein reinforces proteins of lesser quality present in the other ingredients. The same idea can be used to make other salads and other kinds of dishes more nutritious. A small amount of meat attractively arranged in large dice, julienne slivers or thin slices can add to the appearance, taste and nutritional value of many preparations.

Soups and Stews

Another excellent lunch, especially in cool weather, is a hearty soup or stew. This can be entirely prepared in advance, and the storage time actually enhances the flavors by giving them a chance to blend. If yours is a hurried lunchtime, you will appreciate the need for only a few minutes of reheating. There are a few examples of soups and stews in Chapter 10, but you can find good recipes in the cookery of most countries.

Since good soups and stews are usually the result of long, slow cooking, they can be made successfully with less-tender cuts of meat, which makes them economical meals. Probably the smallest amount of meat is used in clam chowder—a chunk of salt pork, diced, in which onions and potatoes are cooked. Another good example is using smoked ham hocks in pea soup (p. 163). A similar soup recipe calls for any kind of dried bean (California pea beans, black beans, chick-peas, white marrow beans, lima beans) and ham hocks or the end of a baked ham. Without pork, a good bean soup can be made more nutritious by adding slices or chunks of frankfurters a few minutes before serving, allowing just enough time for the frankfurters to become well heated. Lentil soup served with knackwurst is another nutritious lunch dish of this kind.

Mulligatawny is an Indian chicken soup flavored with curry; basically, it is good chicken stock thickened to a cream soup and served over a mound of rice with diced or slivered chicken—an excellent luncheon with a salad and a good loaf of bread or some hot rolls.

Another type of soup—and this can be quickly prepared—consists of a thin pasta, vermicelli or spaghettini, and tiny meatballs about the size of marbles cooked in some of your own clear stock. The meatballs can be fixed the night before if you are usually in a hurry at lunchtime.

You can make good soups with giblets, rabbit, any of the meats used to make stock, tripe—almost anything you have. Tripe is the chief ingredient in Philadelphia

129

pepper-pot soup, an excellent choice for lunch, but not one of those dishes you can whip up in a hurry; it takes at least a day, assuming that you buy precooked tripe from your butcher. This soup also has a veal knuckle in it, plus vegetables and cayenne and black peppers, which give it its name. Pepper-pot soup is always served with little dumplings made of 1 part chopped beef suet to 2 parts of flour, with seasoning to taste and enough water to make a mix; these are dropped into the soup and cooked for 10 to 12 minutes.

Soup Dumplings

Many Pennsylvania Dutch soups are served with dumplings; one such dumpling, called *rivels* or *rivvels*, is easy to make and can garnish any soup, adding to its appearance and providing further nourishment. Mix 2 well-beaten eggs with 2 tablespoons of softened butter, and stir in 1½ to 2 cups of flour. Mix well with a spoon; then rub the mixture between your fingers until it falls into little crumbs *(rivels)* about the size of lentils or rice kernels. Add these to the soup about 8 minutes before it is done and let the soup simmer until ready to serve. Except for fewer eggs in the batter, *rivels* are like Hungarian *tarhonya*. Another dumpling recipe calls for less flour, about ½ cup, and some minced parsley or chives. Beat the batter thoroughly, and push portions of it into the hot soup from the end of a spoon; the dumplings should be about the size of marbles. For a hot lunch that takes only minutes to prepare, try adding either of these dumplings to your own finished stock.

Gumbo

Another delicious American soup-stew is gumbo, a specialty in the Mississippi delta and other Southern coastal areas. Except for the kind made with vegetables alone, *gumbo z'herbes*, probably a relative of the Provençal vegetable bouillabaisses, gumbo is a mixture of ingredients almost always including shellfish. Ham is often used in gumbo, hard-cured firm Southern-style ham, which makes a delicious combination with shrimps, oysters and crabs. If this taste idea is new to you, do not discard it out of hand. Perhaps you have already tried a similar flavor combination without realizing it in Clams Casino, in which each clam is topped with a tiny spoonful of vegetable mixture and a square of bacon. Chicken or other poultry combined with one or more kinds of shellfish also makes a delicious gumbo. The thickening ingredient in gumbo is sliced fresh or frozen okra or filé powder, which is ground sassafras leaves. To blend the flavors into one deliciously rich taste, all the ingredients in a gumbo are well cooked; even the shellfish are cooked for a much longer time than would be necessary for other preparations. Obviously, gumbo is not the ideal luncheon choice for a home cook who has only a few minutes to assemble a sandwich, and it is most successful when freshly prepared. If you use filé powder as a thickener, it must be added just before serving because it becomes stringy if cooked for any length of time or if boiled. Like mulligatawny, gumbo is always served over a mound of rice. It is a good dish for a supper menu too.

Pasta with meat sauce is another great luncheon dish, and it has the advantage of being quick to prepare. Good sauces need long, slow cooking, but they can be made in advance and stored in the refrigerator. Pasta cooks very quickly. For some sauce ideas, see Chapter 12.

Many of the stuffed vegetables described in Chapter 13 make fine fare for lunch or supper. If you can prepare the stuffing ahead of time, some of these dishes can be whipped up in short order. Stuffing and baking especially tender vegetables like tomatoes and small young summer squashes takes only minutes.

Of course, sliced, cold cooked meat—steak, roast beef, pot roast, roast chicken or turkey, roast pork—makes a nutritious lunch or supper. Accompany it with a raw or cooked vegetable or a salad and some good bread, and finish with fresh or cooked fruit. For this sort of lunch, everything can be ready in advance, including a hot vegetable. Trim and blanch the vegetable the day before, then quickly plunge it into cold water, drain and refrigerate. At serving time reheat it in a tiny bit of butter, or steam it in a little water or meat stock. Blanched vegetables will retain their color even after a second heating.

The luncheon ideas given so far have been tailored to the situation in which the cook has very little time to prepare a meal and the family members have only a short time to eat. But there are other kinds of midday meals: the business lunch, which serves as a conference as well as a meal; the entertaining luncheon, which gives cooks the chance to prepare some *spécialité* of their own, with the expectation that their guests will remain at least several hours; the formal luncheon to honor a special guest; a lunch for a large group, either sit-down or buffet style.

BUSINESS LUNCH

The meal that combines business and nutrition hardly provides ideal conditions for eating. Relaxation, a feeling of being at ease with oneself and others, and a chance to observe and savor the dish before one, are basic prerequisites for good dining and digestion. Nevertheless, the business lunch is a common occurrence today, and it is not always most appropriately eaten in a restaurant. If you must serve this kind of lunch, try to preserve a balance between offering hearty food and providing so much that the diners feel overstuffed. Eating too much in a relatively short time can have a stultifying effect and dull the wits; some people become extremely sleepy. It is best, for such meetings, to serve the meal on individual plates rather than have a buffet or require the diners to help themselves from serving dishes.

Mixed Grill

A good main dish for such a gathering is a mixed grill—any combination of meats that can be broiled. Although this dish can hardly be called a "grill" if cooked another way, you can prepare the same ingredients by sautéing or baking. Since it takes a relatively short time to broil or sauté meats, it is possible to start cooking

VEAL CHOPS

*Loin chop, containing a slice
of the kidney, cut from the loin
portion, called a "kidney chop"*

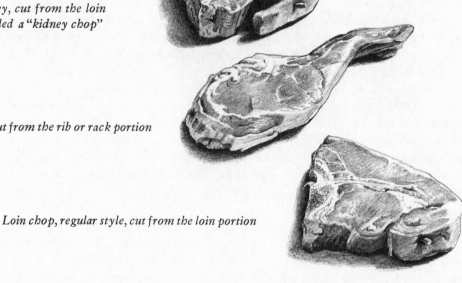

Rib chop, cut from the rib or rack portion

Loin chop, regular style, cut from the loin portion

when all the diners have assembled, so that the dish can be served piping hot and freshly cooked. Even latecomers can be accommodated, because their portions can simply be held aside until they arrive. A mixed grill usually includes a chop—lamb, veal or pork; a variety meat—lamb kidney or chicken liver; a slice of bacon or a link sausage or both, and a large mushroom. The meats are either served on toast or garnished with toast triangles. Mixed grill may also be garnished with a broiled tomato half, a peach half, or a parsley or watercress bouquet. Possible combinations for a mixed grill are many: instead of a chop, an individual small steak or *noisettes* of lamb or veal chops wrapped in bacon; various kinds of sausage or none at all; calf's liver instead of chicken liver, sliced veal kidneys instead of lamb kidneys. With this meal, have a simple first course, nothing filling or elaborate, to keep people occupied while the main course is being prepared.

Individual steaks or double-thick chops are always acceptable for luncheon, as are individual meat pies—chicken, turkey, beef—or that great English standby, steak-and-kidney pie.

Most people love sliced cold ham or tongue and good potato salad. Any meat without a lot of bones, which can be eaten without having to concentrate on the plate, is good for conference luncheons—and this absolutely eliminates broiled chicken.

There are a few classic stews—veal goulash, beef with red wine (*boeuf bourguignon*), French lamb stew with spring vegetables (*navarin d'agneau*)—that are perennial favorites. All of them taste delicious, they are easy to eat, and most of the preparation can be completed ahead of time.

Sauerbraten

Another dish most people seem to like is sauerbraten with potato dumplings (*Kartoffelklösse*). It takes time to make sauerbraten, which means "sour-roasted," but nothing in the preparation is very difficult. Basically, it is marinating carried to the nth degree, and we do not consider it a good way to treat beef because the natural flavor of the meat is entirely lost in the process. A cut of beef suitable for pot-roasting is used. In the classic recipes, the whole piece, 4 to 5 pounds, is marinated in a mixture of wine vinegar, water and spices for 2 or 3 days! The meat is then pot-roasted in the strained marinade. If you soak the meat for a shorter time, it will be less "sour" and less authentic, but you might like it better. As for the potato dumplings, the authentic way to make them is with grated *raw* potatoes, and this sounds much easier than it is. If you do not care much for grated fingers, try a recipe that uses cooked potatoes, or serve the sauerbraten with noodles.

ENTERTAINING LUNCHEON

When giving a luncheon for the sole purpose of entertaining, assume that your guests will notice everything: the table setting, flowers, menu choices and, of course, how the food was cooked. On these occasions appearance is important. If you serve a clear soup as a first course, be sure to include an attractive garnish—a four-leaf clover pattern of watercress leaves, some very tiny soup dumplings or a spoonful of whipped sweet or sour cream sprinkled with slivered almonds or pistachios. If you are having chicken, turkey or veal salad for such a luncheon—excellent choices because they involve no last-minute cooking—serve it in perfect salad leaves or in containers made of scooped-out orange or grapefruit halves or pineapple halves with leaves still attached. Chicken salad made with cubes of avocado and diced pimientos looks very pretty served in an avocado half.

Although usually considered appetizers, pâtés or terrines can make excellent main dishes for party luncheons. So can elaborately constructed open-faced sandwiches.

Veal Scallops

Hot lunches for party occasions can include any of the stuffed individual rolls: veal birds, beef scallops, etc. Unstuffed veal scallops are equally festive and can be prepared in many ways; the Austrians have developed dozens of recipes for the *Schnitzel*, most of which can be adapted to the small scallop. Here are a few examples:

133

1) Dip the flattened scallops into flour, and shake off the excess. Sauté them quickly in a mixture of oil and butter, then serve at once, garnished with thin lemon slices sprinkled with capers.

2) Sauté the flattened scallops very briefly in oil and butter, then pour dry vermouth over them, about 2 tablespoons per scallop. Let it cook over high heat for no more than 2 minutes, then transfer the veal to individual plates. Let the liquid cook for another minute, then spoon about 1 tablespoon of this thin sauce over each scallop. Sprinkle with slivered hazelnuts, and serve with tiny fresh green beans cooked whole.

3) Before you cook the veal, make cream sauce or hollandaise. Sauté sliced fresh mushrooms together with an equal amount of diced cooked ham. Turn the ham and mushrooms into half of the sauce and mix. Sauté the flattened scallops until just done, then transfer them to a shallow baking dish or to individual bakers. Spoon some of the ham and mushrooms on each scallop. Stir whipped cream (2 tablespoons for each ½ cup sauce) into the rest of the cream sauce or hollandaise, and spoon some of this over each scallop. Place under a preheated broiler until the sauce is golden brown on top, and serve at once.

These preparations will require only a little last-minute attention, since the cooking time is so short. The same is true of individual steaks and most chops, which taste best when cooked only to the point of juicy tenderness. If you and your guests prefer such meats well done, you will of course need longer for preparation.

Boneless Chicken Breasts

Another good hot luncheon for company can be made with chicken breasts, with bones or boneless, or *suprêmes* of chicken. The chicken breast with bones and skin can be broiled or deep-fried, but the boneless and skinless breast meat tends to dry out rapidly during cooking if it is not treated with great care. This portion has scarcely any fat. The best way to cook the boneless breast is to sauté it like a veal scallop or to follow a method that is a combination of poaching and sautéing. Put oil and butter in a sauté pan, as though you were going to sauté the chicken, but add some liquid—lemon juice, white wine, stock, whatever suits your recipe. Heat the liquid to simmering, and add the chicken in a single layer. Cover the chicken with a sheet of foil to prevent steaming, and poach the pieces for 5 to 10 minutes on each side, depending on the size. If you like chicken well done, increase the poaching time, but with each extra minute the meat will become drier and stringier. Cream, cream sauce or another delicate sauce can be added to the pan and mixed with the cooking juices to make just enough sauce to nap the cutlets, and minced herbs, sliced nuts, grated cheese, minced sautéed vegetables or mushrooms or tiny dice of lemon pulp mixed with pimientos can be sprinkled on top as a garnish. Garnishes are more important for a party luncheon than for everyday family meals, and these quickly cooked and rather delicate individual meats make excellent foils for beautiful edible garnishes.

A chicken *suprême* can be cooked by any method suitable for chicken breasts. If elegance is your aim, serve the sautéed-poached *suprême* on a slice of sautéed ham, and cover it all with sherry-flavored mushroom sauce.

Both boneless breasts and *suprêmes* are delicious dipped into beaten egg and crumbs and baked. Allow 45 minutes to 1 hour in an oven preheated to 350° F.; the larger the breasts, the longer the baking time. When they are done, the crumb coating should be golden brown. *Suprêmes* cooked like this are sometimes served with a paper frill, like the frill on a Frenched chop bone, on the wing bone.

Other meaty parts of the chicken—legs and thighs—can also be prepared in these interesting ways. The dark meat needs longer cooking, of course.

FORMAL LUNCHEON

Formal lunches call for your most handsome dishes and glassware, plus elegant food. The hero sandwich simply will not do, and neither will a plain broiled steak. If beef is your choice, serve *tournedos* wrapped in bacon, broiled and beautifully garnished or sautéed and served with a spoonful of bordelaise or any red-wine sauce. There are many recipes for *tournedos* in classic French cookery, but the beef is always either broiled or sautéed; the differences are in the garnish. The most famous is *Tournedos Rossini,* in which the meat is crowned with a slice of *pâté de foie gras* and covered with an elaborate sauce made with truffles; a slice of truffle or a mushroom is usually placed on top. Serve *tournedos* with potatoes and an attractive vegetable garnish.

If you have chosen to serve poultry at your formal luncheon, boneless chicken breasts or *suprêmes* in any of their preparations will be equal to the occasion.

Game Birds

If you would rather have game, roasted pheasants, partridges or guinea hens are certainly special. They need care in roasting because they have little fat, so baste them with butter, wine or pan juices. An average pheasant or partridge (2¼ to 3 pounds) will be cooked in about 1 hour in a 350° F. oven. Guinea hens range in size from small babies to birds as large as partridges. For the 2-pound birds, allow 45 to 50 minutes for roasting. Another good way to utilize game birds, since it is difficult to be sure how tender they will be, is to cut off the breasts for *suprêmes* and serve the rest of the birds in a stew or casserole at some less-formal occasion. Treat game *suprêmes* like chicken, but remember that since their meat is drier it will need outer-larding or basting while it cooks.

Breast of Duck

Breast of duck can make a most delicious dish for a formal occasion, but do not try to make a duck *suprême*. The shape of the breast is somewhat different from that of other birds, and after removing the bones and separating the tendons, you will have a much flatter layer of meat than you would with chicken breast. An easier way to prepare duck is to poach the breast quarters until just done, then carefully separate the breast meat. Use the poaching liquid in a sauce, and flavor it with oranges, cherries, peaches or blanched green olives. At serving time, reheat the duck pieces in a little sauce, and serve on a large *croûte* spread with a paste of duck livers with additional chicken livers if needed. To make a beautiful garnish for any bird, make a basket from an orange or a lemon—much easier than it sounds—and fill it with bar-le-duc flavored with cassis or with lingonberry preserves.

Another elegant main dish for a formal luncheon is the *noisette* of lamb or veal—the eye of the loin chops. Broil or sauté *noisettes*, or use a combination of cooking methods. Serve on round *croûtes* with fluted mushrooms, or serve plain and garnish with puff-paste crescents or triangles and watercress.

MANY GUESTS

If you are entertaining a large group for lunch, either sit-down or buffet style, it would be impractical to serve many of the dishes we have already described. Any dish that requires last-minute preparations, like quickly cooked scallops, *suprêmes* or *noisettes*, would be too difficult to cook in large quantities. It is far better to plan on a casserole or stew that can be left in the oven to finish cooking while the guests are being greeted. Chicken or turkey Tetrazzini is a fine company dish that can be served on plates or arranged on the buffet table. Meat baked in loaves or in terrines can be useful for such lunches, and individual meat pies—or large pies for the buffet—are filling and nutritious. Most buffet dishes (see Chapter 21) can be adapted for lunches, and they are especially practical for occasions when guests may arrive over an extended period of time. For hot days, prepare sliced cold meat or cold cuts and meat or poultry salads. Hearty soups are good for cool days, if you have large tureens.

FAMILY LUNCHEON

Beef and barley soup
Cold meat salad with carrot chunks

Pot-roast sandwiches on whole-wheat bread
Mustard pickles
Dandelion salad with crumbled bacon

Cold sliced chicken
Tomato salad with fresh tarragon and slivered red onions

★

Red flannel hash
Boston lettuce with Italian peppers

BUSINESS LUNCH

Mixed grill (lamb chop, lamb kidney, thick bacon)
Mushroom caps
Pickled crab apples
Hashed brown potatoes
Green peas with pearl onions

★

Beef stew with red wine
Broad noodles
Broccoli flowerets
Romaine lettuce with mandarin-orange sections and lime French
dressing

ENTERTAINING LUNCHEON

Vichyssoise
Chicken salad with avocado, in avocado halves
Whole-wheat toast

★

Boneless chicken breasts with sherry sauce
Sautéed mushrooms
Creamed spinach with slivered almonds

FORMAL LUNCHEON

Chicken consommé
Crumb-coated baked chicken suprêmes
Potato puffs
Whole green beans with diced lemon and tomato garnish

Poached duck breasts on toast spread with puréed liver
Orange-flavored sauce
Orange baskets with lingonberries
Brown rice
Fresh asparagus

MANY GUESTS

Cold sliced turkey and cold sliced ham, plain or glazed with aspic
Platter of cooked and raw vegetables at room temperature, with may-
onnaise dressing flavored with lemon and herbs

Curried Lamb and Chestnuts (p. 346)
Red cabbage
Bulgur pilaf

Double or triple the recipe for Curried Lamb and Chestnuts to have enough.

★

Stuffed Boneless Shoulder of Veal (p. 366)
Thin noodles
Broiled tomato halves
Spinach salad

APPETIZERS

Chapter 9

T̲HE F̲RENCH T̲ERM hors-d'oeuvre is often used for all the preparations we will discuss in this chapter, but in its proper meaning it refers only to those dishes we call "first courses." It means, literally, "before the work," that is, the course that precedes the main course. The Italian word antipasto is even more specific; it means "the course that precedes the pasta course." The menu patterns from which these terms developed are still observed rather strictly in France and Italy; for instance, luncheon in France customarily begins with a selection of hors-d'oeuvre, including vegetables, fish and meats. Antipasto is similar; as befits a country that makes so many different delicious sausages, some of these are always included.

The American word, "appetizer," is not very satisfactory either. An appetizer should be a dish that stimulates the appetite, awakening a hunger for the main dishes that follow. The best dish for this purpose is actually a serving of clear soup; the hot liquid starts the digestive processes, and it is not in itself filling enough to dull the appetite. Too often, so-called appetizers are extremely filling.

Cocktail-party food is different; these tidbits must serve as "splashers," and they *should* satisfy the appetite for the duration of the gathering. Snacks fall into this category also: foods eaten on the run or between meals; they should be nutritious and flavorful, filling but not overfilling.

We will discuss meats and poultry used for all these preparations, but first we must define our terms: We will use "first course" to mean a preparation eaten at the table before the main course; "starters," an English term that seems better than "appetizers," to designate tidbits eaten before a meal, with or without drinks, at table or not; and cocktail-party food and snacks, which are self-explanatory.

Many good first courses consist of fish or shellfish, or vegetables alone. Of course, we will not deal with any of these. But do not hesitate to combine meats and poultry. A main course of meat can be preceded by a course of poultry or another kind of meat. A poultry main course can be preceded by a meat, or even by another kind of poultry if it is presented in a different way. And either can precede a fish main course.

Fruits with Prosciutto or Other Ham

Simple dishes that require little preparation can make the most sophisticated beginning. Melon or figs with prosciutto is not an original idea, but it looks pretty and tastes fresh. Usually honeydew melon is used because the taste and color contrast well with the strong taste and red color of the ham. However, you can use any kind of melon. If you serve melon wedges draped with paper-thin slices of the meat, be sure to provide both knife and fork for your guests. To make this dish easier to eat, completely detach the melon from its rind and leave it in place. Then cut the wedge into crosswise slices, and push alternate slices out of alignment, to make them easy to separate. Instead of using whole slices of prosciutto, cut them into strips the size of the melon slices, and arrange them on the melon.

Whole figs, fresh or canned, are hard to eat without utensils. Make it simple for your guests by cutting the figs into quarters and wrapping each quarter in a sliver of prosciutto. Be sure some of the fig shows, because seeing the color contrast is part of the pleasure.

Pineapple is often used to garnish ham. You can reverse this for a different version of fruit with meat. Use a wedge of pineapple with its leaves still in place, and separate the pieces in the same way used for the melon wedge. Place a sliver of cooked ham or a chunk on each crosswise slice.

Dishes like these, with contrast of color, taste and texture, need no garnish; they are complete in themselves.

Another excellent first course is a small serving of cold poached or roasted chicken, which can be made from leftovers. Trim the slices neatly, mask or decorate them with a thin layer of mayonnaise, and sprinkle with minced parsley or a few capers. This dish will be greatly enhanced by an edible garnish like cherry tomatoes or carrot rounds—anything of contrasting color.

Cold meat salads are good first courses too, especially with dinners based on nonmeat dishes like pasta, to which they add necessary protein. If the salad contains contrastingly colored ingredients, no garnish will be necessary. Beef, veal, ham and poultry can be used this way.

When you prepare a first course that seems to need garnishing, be sure each lettuce leaf or parsley sprig—or whatever it may be—is absolutely fresh and crisp. If it is limp or tired-looking, forget it; no garnish would be better in such a case. Do not feel that every meat *hors-d'oeuvre* must rest on lettuce—far from it; but if it does, the lettuce must be attractive and edible.

Antipasto

Antipasto usually includes salami, a vegetable preparation, a fresh-tasting pungent cheese and oil-cured black olives. You can prepare a delicious version of your own, using any kind of spicy sausage that you like and any kind of cheese, or slices of prosciutto or boiled ham. The cheese can be plain or mixed with herbs or peppercorns. As for vegetables, a salad of dried white beans, marinated mushrooms, even plain sliced tomatoes or chunks or slivers of raw fennel. If you like green olives better than black, go to it! Be sure to have the meat cut into very thin slices, and remove any casings or rind before assembling the ingredients.

Aspic

With a little extra effort, you can prepare more elaborate dishes that require no last-minute work. Aspic is a help in such cases (see p. 167 for how to prepare it). If you plan to use aspic, acquire some molds of a size that suits you. Most plates are round, so choose round molds that will hold 6 to 8 ounces of liquid. You do not have to fill them to the brim if you want a shallower layer.

A tomato aspic filled with slivers of chicken can be garnished with watercress sprigs and topped with a dab of mayonnaise or sour cream. Other meats or combinations can be used in the same way.

Many delicious French egg dishes are based on *oeufs mollets*, whole eggs cooked in the shell but only to a very soft stage. The whole egg is carefully peeled. Arrange one in a small mold on a layer of pâté or a slice of ham cut to fit the mold. If you like, place vegetable bits or herb leaves on the bottom, which will be the top when unmolded, as decoration. Fill the mold with a clarified aspic, and chill until set. You can use the same idea without eggs; for a shallower layer, cover a slice of meat with overlapping layers of mushroom slices. If you have fresh, unblemished mushrooms, use them raw.

Although there is a whole chapter on stuffed dishes in this book, it is inevitable to think of them here because they make such attractive first courses. A whole large tomato can be stuffed with chicken, ham or tongue salad. Large mushrooms can be stuffed with countless mixtures. Artichoke bottoms filled with slivers of meat or salad mixtures are delicious and handsome to see. You can brush a little aspic over the top if you prepare such dishes in advance; the aspic will keep the salad and vegetable from drying out.

COLD STUFFED MUSHROOMS

Mushrooms for stuffing can be prepared in various ways. If they are to be first courses, any method will serve. They can be poached until tender, then chilled and stuffed; they can be sautéed in butter or a mixture of oil and butter until tender, then cooled to room temperature and stuffed; they can be marinated raw, then drained and stuffed; they can be broiled or baked. Here is how to marinate them.

4 coriander berries	½ cup Japanese rice vinegar
4 black peppercorns	¼ cup olive oil
¼ teaspoon dehydrated onion flakes	16 large or 24 medium-sized mushrooms

Mash the coriander berries and peppercorns in a mortar and turn into a large plastic bowl with a cover that can be sealed airtight. Add onion flakes, vinegar and oil; cover the bowl and shake thoroughly. Take the stems off the mushrooms (save them for another recipe), and peel the caps; or, if they are very white and fresh, wipe with a damp cloth. Put the caps into the bowl, cover and marinate overnight, shaking the bowl now and then. The remaining marinade can be used for salad dressing or to marinate something else.

VEAL AND SALMON STUFFING

8 to 12 ounces boneless cooked veal
1 green pepper, about 3 ounces
1 small onion, about 1 ounce
1 tablespoon lemon juice

¼ cup dry white wine, or more if needed
1 small can (3¾ ounces) red salmon
salt

Use leftover roast or braised veal. Grind it in a food grinder and set aside. Hold the pepper on a fork over the flame of your stove and char the outside. Then rinse off the skin, using a nylon scrubber if necessary to get rid of all charred particles. Peel the onion. Chop pepper and onion and blanch in boiling water for about 2 minutes; drain. Put the vegetables in the blender container, and add the lemon juice, half of the wine and any liquid from the salmon. Pick over the salmon to eliminate all bones or skin, and add the fish to the other ingredients. Purée to a smooth mixture; if the machine labors, add the rest of the wine and more if needed. Mix the purée with the veal, and add salt to taste. Stuff the mixture into the marinated mushroom caps; this amount will fill about 20 large caps. Sprinkle the tops with minced fresh parsley, or garnish with a tiny onion ring or a crisscross of green-pepper slivers.

If you have less veal than called for, reduce the amount of salmon, because even a little salmon can overpower a small portion of veal.

Pâté

The best-known and most popular first course is pâté, suitable for service by itself or as a part of a selection of *hors-d'oeuvre*. Pâté is a dish that usually includes liver, but other meats can be used either in addition to liver or in place of it. There are so many ways to make this dish that we can only suggest a few of them. Pâté is often made of poultry livers, chicken and goose primarily, but turkey and duck livers can also be used. Meat livers for pâté are beef, calf and steer, and pork. The livers can be chopped or ground; in French pâtés they are usually ground and reground with any other ingredients that make the forcemeat part of the pâté until they are like a paste. Country pâté, on the other hand, which is generally more hearty and less refined in its preparation, often contains chunks of meat within the ground paste; the finely ground portions go down smoothly, but the pieces need chewing.

Liver can be combined with other meats in pâté; pork liver with calf's brains is one established combination. Another incorporates pork meat and fat with liver. Most French recipes for pâté call for fresh pork fat. Elaborate recipes including additional ingredients of contrasting colors or textures (tongue, ham, pistachios, pieces of chicken breast, pitted prunes) are built very carefully, so that each slice of the completed pâté will show a pattern. Game can also be used—in fact, a pâté can make a palatable dish of old game animals that are no longer tender. Everything in a pâté is well cooked.

Depending on the way you prepare and serve it, pâté can be spreadable or firm enough to be sliced. French pâté from Strasbourg, the most familiar type in the United States, comes in tins with a rounded top, small or large according to volume, but always the same shape. Usually directions say to chill and slice. But even this can be spread if it is allowed to soften a little at room temperature.

While pâté can be made of several types of meat, *pâté de foie gras* is made only of the livers of force-fed geese and ducks. *Foie gras* means "fat liver." The birds raised for *pâté de foie gras* are not allowed any exercise, and they are literally stuffed by their keepers. Such a procedure is against the law in the United States, so any pâté made from these livers is imported. To make the pâté even more exquisite, chopped black truffles are added. When these ingredients were less costly than they are today, country inns in Alsace used to put whole truffles in the middle of the pâté so that each serving had a round black truffle slice in the center. Some rather bland canned products, called "purée of *foie gras*" or some other modified name, are made of a small proportion of liver mixed with other ingredients and whipped. Recently the United States has been importing liver pâté from France that is made of a mixture of goose and pork liver plus other ingredients. Even though it comes from Alsace and is good, it is not the true classic *pâté de foie gras*.

Liverwurst is entirely different from pâté; it is usually made of pork liver, but under various names it can contain beef or pork and onion or other seasonings. It is a much coarser article than pâté.

Here is how to make your own pâté from poultry livers.

POULTRY-LIVER PÂTÉ

2 pounds poultry livers	2 eggs
1 pound goose or chicken fat	salt and pepper
1 pound yellow onions	

Cook the livers by broiling, baking, or poaching; poached livers are the easiest for home grinders to handle. Render the fat uncovered over *very low* heat for 3 to 4 hours. If you cannot adjust your heating elements low enough, put an asbestos pad or other device between pot and heat. While this is going on, peel the onions and chop them fine. After 2½ hours, add the onions to the fat and continue cooking. Stir occasionally to keep onions from burning. During the remaining cooking time the onions will drop to the bottom of the pot and begin to brown.

Let the fat cool at room temperature for 2 to 3 hours.

Hard-cook the eggs, let them cool, and peel them. Then put everything—livers, eggs, onions, ½ cup of the rendered fat and 3 tablespoons of the cracklings (the crisp residue of rendered fat)—through the fine blade of a grinder. The mixture will be pasty in the grinder, but its texture will be slightly chunky when finished. Season with salt and pepper to taste, and chill.

If you prefer a smoother texture, strain the onions from the pot, and purée everything in a blender instead of grinding it. To give a French flavor to this pâté, add 1 tablespoon brandy to the whole thing.

This basic method can be used for any kind of liver. For instance, you might try a mixture of melted pork fat, cooked cracklings and chopped fresh pork. Cook it all, then blend and cool. For an extra fillip, make some stock for aspic with pork bones (see p. 167), and spoon a little of the aspic over the finished liver.

If you want a molded pâté, spoon the mixture into a mold, and let it chill until firm. Lining the mold with aspic is an excellent idea. When the pâté is turned out, it will be firm enough to be sliced.

While chopped liver made in this fashion is sometimes found frozen in markets, we advise against freezing pâté because it loses moisture and flavor in the freezer.

To serve a firm pâté as a first course, slice it and arrange one or more slices on a plate. Lettuce underneath is not necessary. You may garnish if you like with black olives, tiny tomatoes or slices of larger ones, sprigs of parsley or watercress, or a mound of minced fresh onion; or you can serve it plain. Melba toast or plain crackers are the usual accompaniment. If you have soft-textured pâté, arrange it in a mound.

Most French-style pâtés are baked, usually in a loaf pan, although any sort of container will do. Country restaurants in France often bake them in stoneware bowls. Some pâtés are baked in terrines, which are rather deep fireproof earthenware or pottery baking dishes with a long narrow shape. Some are baked in metal molds especially designed for pâtés; they are round or oval, hinged so as to separate into two wings, and have no top or bottom. Such molds are designed to be used for *pâté en croûte*, that is, pâté baked in a pastry crust. Bake your pâté in any of these receptacles, or wrap the ingredients in pastry and bake like a flattened loaf without a mold. You can use packaged pastry or your own favorite, but the classic pastry is *pâte brisée*, made of flour, fat, salt and eggs.

Pieces of meat for these preparations can be marinated for added flavor; if you are using game or other meat that is not very tender, marinating will help.

Many recipes for pâté call for fresh pork fatback to line the terrine or the pastry, and some even suggest wrapping pieces of meat for the filling in thin sheets of fatback. For American tastes this is much too fatty, and in some recipes the taste of pork may not be compatible with that of other meats. If you do want to line the mold with pork, try uncured lean bacon or streak lean.

The nonmeat ingredients of a pâté should be mixed with enough fat to make them moist and smooth but not fatty-tasting. Some of the fat will rise to the top and become a firm layer when the pâté is cold. This fatty layer surrounding the meat will keep it in good condition for at least a week. Scrape the fat off the top for serving; if there is a neat layer around the sides of the slices, you may serve it if you like.

Pâté is not confined to the first course, and we will discuss some of its other uses later.

HOT HORS-D'OEUVRE

Even though cooking is involved in the preparation of some of the first-course dishes mentioned so far, they are all served cold or at room temperature. But if you have the time and perhaps a little help in the kitchen, you can prepare countless hot *hors-d'oeuvre*. One of the nicest ways to serve hot pâté is to bake it in individual ramekins or in pastry in small flan rings. You can decorate the top as you would the larger *pâté en croûte*, with pastry cutouts. You can fill the spaces in baked pâtés of any size with aspic, just as English pork pies are filled (p. 237).

Delicious first courses can be served piping hot in their baking dishes. If you like this idea, acquire some individual baking dishes: round pottery or heatproof glass dishes with ears, called "shirred-egg dishes," which come in two sizes; oval *au gratin* dishes; or shallow bakers of tin-lined copper, the most handsome and also the most costly. Ramekins, either pottery or metal, have a smaller circumference than these others but are deeper. Glass or pottery custard cups are good too, especially if you want to turn out the baked contents to serve.

CHAWANMUSHI

One of the most delicate of these baked preparations is a Japanese dish, *chawan-mushi*. This is a custard, baked in individual dishes, with a filling of slivers of white meat of chicken and small shrimps. You can add sliced mushrooms and bits of other Oriental vegetables: blanched snow peas, bamboo shoots, water chestnuts, watercress leaves, blanched shreds of Chinese cabbage and so on. Poach the chicken and shrimps until almost done; they will finish cooking as the custard bakes. Then divide the ingredients among the individual baking dishes, using about 4 tablespoons of the filling for each 6-ounce custard cup. Pour the custard mixture over. Set the cups in a baking pan filled with enough water to come halfway up the sides of the cups. Bake until the custard is just set, about 15 minutes in a 325° F. oven or slightly longer in a cooler oven. The custard mixture can be any that you like, but Japanese recipes usually say to mix the eggs with *dashi*, Japanese soup stock, and flavor with soy sauce. For each custard cup, add 1 whole egg and ½ cup of liquid; use 3 cups of liquid, 4 whole eggs and 2 or 3 egg yolks for 6 servings. Chicken stock with a little white wine makes a good substitute for *dashi*. Serve in the baking dishes while still warm. A simpler version of *chawanmushi*, a timbale (p. 317) made from leftover chicken, can also be used as an appetizer.

Use your little baking dishes to make all sorts of *au gratin* preparations. For instance, in each dish alternate layers of small meat or poultry slices with layers of vegetable slices—tomato, poached artichoke hearts or celery knobs, sautéed eggplant, mushrooms. Spoon a sauce over them—Mornay or other cheese sauces are very good—and sprinkle with crumbs, plain or buttered. Heat until the ingredients are thoroughly hot, the sauce is bubbly and the crumbs are golden brown.

Small versions of chicken divan, with broccoli and Mornay sauce, and other sauced dishes can make very attractive first courses. Such dishes do not require huge amounts of meat and provide excellent uses for leftovers. One of the prettiest consists of slices of ham rolled around asparagus stalks and covered with a velouté made of chicken stock; sprinkle the top with grated Swiss cheese, and heat until melted and golden.

Variety meats can make good first courses. Chicken livers sautéed in butter and finished off with a little sherry or Madeira are quick to prepare; sprinkle with a little parsley before serving. Sweetbreads, braised, broiled or sautéed, look pretty arranged on slices of ham or Canadian bacon; sprinkle with sautéed shallots and chopped green olives. The classic dish brains in black butter makes an excellent first course for people who like brains, but be sure your guests do, because this is an acquired taste. A good accompaniment for any of these dishes is a heaping table-spoon of sautéed potato or cucumber balls, scooped out with a melon-ball cutter.

Baked stuffed mushrooms served hot make an excellent first course. Here is a basic recipe you can vary by following the method and using different stuffing ingredients.

HOT STUFFED MUSHROOMS   8 servings

16 large mushrooms
lemon juice
salt
1 small onion
4 tablespoons oil or butter
1 jar (2½ ounces) brine-packed pitted
   green olives

8 ounces cooked white meat of chicken
4 ounces cooked boneless ham
2 tablespoons all-purpose flour
1 cup chicken stock
½ cup soft fresh bread crumbs
5⅓ tablespoons melted butter

Wipe the mushrooms with a damp cloth. One at a time, hold them cap side down in the palm of your hand, and with the other hand gently twist out the stem; try not to damage the cap. Set the stems aside. Mushrooms can be left unpeeled, or you can peel them if you prefer. (Even though we have suggested not peeling vege-tables for stuffing, the skin of large mushrooms can be very tough.) Then drop the caps into a saucepan of water. Add 1 teaspoon of lemon juice and ¼ teaspoon salt for each cup of water. Gently poach the mushrooms for 8 minutes, then place them, caps up, on a rack to drain. (If you have peeled the mushrooms, save the peelings, and cook them in the poaching liquid to obtain a broth for use in sauce making.)

Peel the mushroom stems and chop them; peel the onion and mince it. Sauté both in 2 tablespoons oil or butter until tender but not browned. Let the mixture cool. Pour the olives into a strainer and discard the brine, then blanch the olives for 5 minutes to remove excess salt. Chop chicken, ham and olives into very small pieces, but do not grind them; if you do, the texture of the filling will not be right. Mix with the mushroom stems and onion. Preheat oven to 375° F. Make a thick velouté sauce with the remaining 2 tablespoons oil or butter, the flour and the stock. (You can use mushroom broth instead of chicken stock if you prefer.) Mix the sauce with the stuffing mixture. Fill the caps, rounding the tops. Cover the filling with 1 to 1½ teaspoons crumbs for each mushroom, and sprinkle 1 teaspoon melted butter on top. Arrange on an oiled baking sheet. Bake in 375° F. oven for about 30 min-utes, until the tops are golden brown. The mushrooms can be tested for doneness with a cake tester; they should be fully cooked—if not, cook a little longer. Serve 2 mushrooms for a first course, plain or on toast. Parsley or watercress garnish is op-tional.

This is only one of hundreds of possible mushroom stuffings. For another, use chicken and walnuts. Creamed chicken and oysters with pimientos is good for an au-tumn day, and so is a mixture of fresh pork, rice, onions and tomatoes. You can experiment with any mixture from the stuffing chapter. If you like, add cheese to the bread crumbs for the topping.

Fritters and croquettes make pretty first courses (see Chapter 19). If they are small, pile them in little pyramids on plates, and garnish with parsley sprigs and lemon twists, or arrange individual servings of sauce in lemon baskets. While the directions for making fritters and croquettes assume you are working with leftover meats or poultry, you can of course cook something especially for this purpose. Brains, sweetbreads and livers are good in fritters, and excellent croquettes can be made with ground cooked chicken, veal or ham.

Quenelles

If you want to work a little harder to produce a delicate dish, try making a veal or chicken *quenelle*. A *quenelle* is like a fluffy meatball but oval or cylindrical in shape. To make these, poultry or veal is pounded and sieved or puréed in an electric blender with whole eggs or egg whites as liquid. All tendons and connective tissues should be removed from the meat, but to be doubly sure none remain, sieve the puréed mixture after blending. Chill the purée, then mix with heavy cream, butter, beef marrow or suet (according to your recipe), and season. *Quenelles* can be flavored with herbs or vegetables too. Shape the *quenelles* with 2 tablespoons, and poach them in stock or plain salted water until they are firm. Drain on a linen towel, and serve with a delicate sauce of an attractive color.

Stuffed pasta, especially cannelloni or shells, and pancakes rolled around filling make excellent beginnings to meals. One large crêpe folded in half over a filling or 2 or 3 small ones rolled around the filling will be ample for a first-course serving.

If you are sure your guests will be ready at the right moment, an exquisite first course can be individual soufflés made with chicken, veal, lamb or ham, served in their own baking dishes hot from the oven. For an especially nice dish, try baking a chicken soufflé in a large tomato shell, or ham and cheese in zucchini halves, or lamb in small eggplant halves. These are not really difficult to make, and even if your first efforts collapse, they will still taste delicious.

Hors-d'Oeuvre Variés

To get back to the *hors-d'oeuvre* that we started with, for some occasions you might want to serve *hors-d'oeuvre variés*, a selection of dishes from which each guest chooses. These are usually served in *raviers*, shallow, rectangular glass or pottery dishes that can be fitted together neatly on a tray or serving table. While restaurants sometimes offer a choice of 30 items, at home 4 to 8 dishes provide an ample selection. There is always at least one meat dish, and often it is a cold beef salad, made from roast or pot-roasted beef. Ideas for salads can be found in other chapters, but you can make this one any way you like: plain meat slivers with vinaigrette and capers; meat cubes mixed with cubes of potato and green and red pepper; round pieces of meat with fluted rounds of carrot and cucumber; whatever combination suits you will make a good dish.

Add slices of tomato, marinated whole or sliced mushrooms, some red radishes with fresh greenery still attached, and you have a beautiful *hors-d'oeuvre*. If you think more is necessary, serve slices of pâté; stuffed hard-cooked eggs, halved or quartered or sliced; cold rice salad; a fish or shellfish dish; or small slices of poultry topped with pieces of chicken liver, both glazed with aspic.

Garnishes are generally omitted from the foods in *raviers*, but good French or Italian bread with fresh butter is a good accompaniment.

STARTERS

Starters are foods that can be eaten in the hand, in a few bites. These make good splashers for drinks, which are often served away from the table. The obvious first-choice starter is the canapé. A canapé is an open-faced sandwich that is only big enough for two bites. Any idea you have for a sandwich can be adapted for a canapé. The chief difference is that a canapé must look attractive, so part of the preparation should include some sort of garnishing.

Canapés

Spreading deviled ham on a cracker may be quick, but it will not really impress a guest. To begin with, it is a mistake to make canapés with crackers. They tend to crack and crumble with the first bite, scattering crumbs all over the guests' best clothes and the carpet. The French word *canapé* means "sofa," so assume the food is served on a tiny sofa—bread certainly makes a better sofa than a cracker does. Another disadvantage of crackers is that they get soggy and lose their distinctive crispness if the topping is at all moist. You can prevent this more easily with bread, by toasting or sautéing it lightly (be sure to drain thoroughly on paper towels after sautéing) or by spreading it with a thin layer of butter before adding anything else. Bread used for canapés can be of any kind, but firm, close-textured bread is easiest to cut and spread. With a cookie cutter or a sharp knife, cut the bread into rounds, strips, triangles, small squares—whatever you like. If possible, wait until just before serving to add the topping. In the meantime, cover the little pieces closely with plastic wrap, and keep them cool.

For canapés, have meat ground or chopped finer than for ordinary sandwiches; it will be easier to spread, and there will not be any little chunks to roll off. Chicken, ham, veal—even hamburger—can make good canapés. To season the meat and make it spreadable, mix it with mayonnaise, butter, a tiny bit of sour cream, a sauce or prepared mushrooms—whatever suits you. Then garnish with a sprinkle of paprika, a small parsley sprig, a slice of olive, etc. Even steak tartare can be used for a canapé; of course, this makes an excellent first course too.

Canapés can also be made of sliced meats, especially if they are tender. Have the slices cut to fit the bread exactly. Top them with dabs of red caviar, or slices of cherry tomato, pickles, anchovies, minced herbs.

Canapés are a lot of work, and they are usually gobbled up quickly. Another disadvantage of serving them is that they are useless if left over; the small portions of food just dry out and lose all savor.

Miniature tarts, pies or turnovers are great splashers. Any meat or poultry tart or pie can be adapted to a splasher-sized version (see Chapter 14); the pieces must be very small, and the pastry must not be buttery or oily to the touch. Some great examples can be found in the cuisine of any country.

An appetizer and snack possibility from south of the border is stuffed tortillas. Use the tiny ones, which are available canned and frozen, and fill with chopped beef or chicken with diced fresh tomato and minced onion and olives. These can be sloppy to eat, so choose them only for informal parties where everyone can reach for an additional paper napkin when needed. The tortillas will be stiff and crisp when you open the package; steam them to make them flexible (directions come with the packages), but do not fry them for appetizers, because they will be too oily to hold.

Stuffed Vegetables

Stuffed dishes in miniature are excellent for starters. Cherry tomatoes, rings of cucumbers, mushrooms, Brussels sprouts, snow peas, ribs of fennel and celery—all these can be used. For these small containers, you need very finely minced or puréed fillings; use only a little mayonnaise or dressing. Blanch the Brussels sprouts, mushrooms and snow peas very briefly; the others are used uncooked. Scoop out the tomatoes and cucumbers, and let them drain before filling them. Good fillings can be made with steak tartare; cooked chicken or chicken mixed with tongue; ham or ham mixed with veal; veal mixed with salmon or tuna, like a miniature version of *vitello tonatto*; lamb mixed with mushrooms or eggplant; any tiny meatball. You can also make little bread cases for these fillings.

After you fill the little hollows, brush the tops with aspic to keep them from drying, especially if they have to wait. Or top the opening with a slice of cucumber, or cover with minced parsley. To cover cherry tomatoes, use some extra tomatoes; with a very sharp knife, cut off all 4 sides, leaving a square, which you may save for something else; use each little rounded slice as a cap for a tomato. If you want to suggest a stem, insert a parsley sprig or a clove in the middle of the cap. To cap other small stuffed vegetables, spread a little mayonnaise over the top and crown with a caper, a tiny twist of lemon rind or whatever makes a pretty contrast.

Most of these vegetables can be filled with a spoon, but you can also use a pastry bag with a plain tube. This is the way to fill the snow peas, but they often separate after blanching and are then easy enough to stuff; it takes only a little filling to make a snow pea look chubby in the middle.

If you are stuffing mushrooms to be eaten cold in the hand, prepare them by marinating only. Sautéed caps are too oily to pick up in the fingers, and poached caps are too soft, tending to lose their cup shape and consequently their filling. Use only perfect little caps, and do not peel them. Try the marinade on page 143, or make one of your own. After marinating, dry the little caps thoroughly on absorbent paper before stuffing them.

Stuffed hard-cooked eggs, halved, make a substantial starter but one that is acceptable to most people. For a really delicious stuffing, add 1 tablespoon of the pâté on page 145 to each cooked yolk; mash, mix and stuff; sprinkle the tops with minced parsley or stick a little sprig in the center.

We have mentioned meatball mixtures in containers, but how about meatballs by themselves? Fine, if they are small and made according to a recipe for firm little meatballs that will not feel oily or wet when you pick them up. Here is an example.

LEON'S HAM AND VEAL HORS-D'OEUVRE BALLS   20 tiny meatballs

¾ pound cooked smoked ham
¾ pound boneless raw veal
1 egg

1 tablespoon honey
1 tablespoon dry bread crumbs

Grind the meats once, then mix with the raw egg, honey and bread crumbs. Shape into small balls, about the size of walnuts or smaller. Arrange on a baking sheet, and bake in a preheated 350° F. oven for 10 minutes. Try one; if it is not cooked to your taste, cook for a few minutes longer. Transfer to a plate covered with absorbent paper, and put a food pick in each one. To prevent crumbling, try not to handle them too much. Transfer to a serving tray. Chinese sauces—plum and hot mustard—are good with these, but only when served at table.

At large parties, it has become stylish to serve meatballs with a container of red sauce. This can be very sloppy, and it is hard to clean that sauce off. Better make your meatballs tasty enough without sauce, or use meatballs with sauce as a starter to eat at table, with individual sauce dishes.

Lambburgers can be made very small; season them well and broil them, then pair them on a food pick with a marinated mushroom cap or a tiny tomato. Or fill a large mushroom cap with the lambburger, serving this on a food pick. Other combinations are ham chunks with pineapple, and chicken with blanched or marinated green-pepper squares.

Saté

Another delicious appetizer on a food pick is *saté*, an Indonesian skewered meat served with peanut sauce. The meat used is pork or chicken, cut into small cubes 1 inch thick or less. Marinate in a mixture of soy sauce and honey with spices—coriander, cuminseed, cardamom, black pepper. Use all of these spices or whichever you prefer, but for best flavor, use whole spices and mash them in a mortar before mixing into the marinade. Let the pork marinate for at least an hour; chicken will be well flavored in half that time. Thread the little cubes onto small skewers about 6 inches long; Indonesians usually use bamboo, but we think steel skewers are safer. Broil chicken *saté* for 8 to 10 minutes, and pork for about 15 minutes; turn them so all sides are grilled. These look pretty served on a long narrow tray or board covered with lemon leaves.

Although it is the most common, peanut-butter sauce is not the only one that can be used. It is made of peanut butter, stock, sautéed onions, garlic, red or green hot chilies and salt. You can add some of the spices used in the marinade or even some of the marinade itself. *Saté* is spicy. Like the meatballs with red sauce, it is not a dish for dressy stand-up occasions, but it can be served at informal parties or as a first course at table, with individual bowls of sauce.

Other delicious preparations that can be served on little skewers or food picks are the reverse of stuffed cases; in these, meat is wrapped around a filling. Chicken livers wrapped in bacon, fastened with a food pick, can be sautéed or broiled. So can ham strips rolled around bread cubes or skewered to make tiny ribbon sandwiches. Other meats can be used in the same way or rolled around cooked chestnuts or water chestnuts; pastrami is especially good for this. Alternate layers of ham and slices of cheese or salami and cheese can be rolled, cut into little slices, and fastened with food picks. Strips of corned beef wrapped around whole small mushrooms make another good combination.

COCKTAIL PARTIES

In planning the menu for cocktail parties you have to take into account that everyone will be standing up. Of course, you may have lots of room with ample space for guests to sit, but very few do. Part of the fun of a cocktail party is the mingling. For a small informal party, you can serve any *hors-d'oeuvre* that can be eaten in the hand, including food on skewers or even food cooked during the party, such as fondue (see Chapter 17 for these). Try to strike a balance between shapes and flavors, just as if you were planning a dinner menu. One dish on skewers or picks is enough; do not have everything stuffed or ground or mixed with olives or made with cheese.

For informal occasions, make soft pâtés or other meat spreads and serve them in mounds, sprinkled with a garnish and surrounded by bread rounds, Melba toast or crackers. In this case, crackers will serve well; guests spread their own just before eating them, and they have no chance to become soggy. Of course, these spreads will not look like much as your party goes on, but they can start out looking impressive. How about a beautiful mound of poultry pâté sprinkled with green pistachios and ringed with very thin rounds of dark rye bread? Or ham pâté sprinkled with a mixture of chopped onion, black olives, parsley and grated lemon rind, with alternate narrow strips of white and whole-wheat bread? Either tastes delicious with any sort of drink and serves as an excellent splasher.

Canapés are good, of course, and so are the tiny bite-sized tarts; bake the tarts in muffin pans of 1-inch diameter. There is no meat pie that cannot be adapted to a one-bite serving, but be sure to use a pastry that is dry to the touch. Cream-cheese pastry is good.

Another favorite today is cocktail frankfurters—Vienna franks—served with bowls of sauce. We have reservations about this because it is messy, but franks without sauce are easy to serve. They are also good rolled in pastry or biscuit dough and baked. Try this idea with any meat mixture; spread it on biscuit dough, roll it into a narrow roll and slice; bake the little slices until the biscuit is done. If you make your own bread, you can use yeast bread dough, risen once, for these roll-ups.

Stuffed mushrooms are especially nice for cocktail parties, and other stuffed vegetables are good too. Even though we said one stuffed dish was enough for any party, you could serve a selection of stuffed vegetables.

If you have someone to help you in the kitchen, try this: Stuff pitted green olives with cheese—Cheddar or Gloucester or whatever you like—and wrap each one with one quarter of a bacon slice (cut them into halves lengthwise and crosswise). Fasten with a wooden food pick, and broil until the bacon is cooked. Do not leave the kitchen while this is going on; they will be done in an instant.

The hot stuffed mushrooms on page 148 can be used too, if you have help in the preparation. You can fill at least 50 little mushrooms with the stuffing in that recipe. Tiny bite-sized mushrooms will be done in 15 to 20 minutes, and they should be served at once.

If you have kitchen help, try serving hot canapés. Instead of the parsley garnish, cover with a thin slice of cheese, a film of mayonnaise or a spoonful of hollandaise sauce; then broil just long enough for the topping to become golden brown.

Miniature pizzas made with meat are good too. You can make your own quarter-sized English muffins, or buy pizza-dough mix and cut into small rounds or squares. Tomato and cheese are not the only fillings; add diced salami or other meat, a spoonful of chopped plum tomatoes, a crisscross of anchovies. This could be your household specialty.

One of the most delicious tidbits is a stuffed grape leaf, a Middle Eastern favorite. These can be served hot or at room temperature. The filling always includes rice, and olive oil and lemon juice are used in cooking them. While lamb is the meat most often used for the stuffing in the Middle East, you can use anything you like. Here is one version of this preparation.

STUFFED GRAPE LEAVES

If you have grape vines, pick some perfect leaves, and wash them thoroughly. Then blanch them for about 1 minute, rinse, and let them cool. You can purchase grape leaves in Italian or Middle Eastern markets, and they usually come packed in vinegar, in 1-pound jars containing 50 or 60 leaves. Carefully unroll them, and blanch them for a few seconds only. The blanching is to soften the leaves, making them easy to roll.

½ cup olive oil	1 to 1¼ cups almost-cooked rice
1 medium-sized onion, minced	1 teaspoon salt
8 ounces boneless raw lamb, ground	1/16 teaspoon ground pepper
2 ounces dried currants	50 grape-vine leaves
3 ounces pine nuts	2 lemons

Heat 2 tablespoons of the oil, and in it sauté the onion until translucent. Then add the ground lamb, and cook over gentle heat until no longer red; do not overcook, and do not let any ingredient get brown. Add the currants and the pine nuts, then the rice. Season; add more seasoning than called for if you like. Carefully spread the leaves on a board, with the upper side of the leaves facing upward. Put 1 teaspoon of the filling in the middle of each leaf, then fold in the sides and roll. If you have small or torn leaves, put several together. Choose a large skillet with a cover, and be sure you have a heavy plate that will just fit into the pan. Pour the rest of the oil into the skillet, and carefully place the leaves in a single layer in the pan. Pour the lemon juice over the top, and add enough water to come almost to the top of the leaves. Put the heavy plate upside down on top of the little bundles, to keep them from unrolling. Cover the pan, and simmer over low heat for 1 hour. Check once to be sure the stuffed leaves are not getting dry. If you are serving the leaves as finger food, let them cool and be sure to pat them dry; they will be a little oily.

If you do not have currants, just omit them; do not substitute raisins—they are too large and too sweet. The rice should be firm, not mushy; Patna or Piedmont rice will do well in this recipe. You can adjust the proportions of the fillings. Other possible filling ingredients are a little tomato purée, chopped parsley and chopped mushrooms; beef can be used instead of lamb.

When it comes to large cocktail parties, skip everything on skewers; they can stab innocent victims, and it is hard to know what to do with the empty skewer once the food is eaten. Also skip the mounds of spreads because, with a mob, it is difficult for everyone to reach them. Have everything ready to pick up and eat without more ado. Unless you have help in the kitchen, do not try to serve hot dishes. To keep cold dishes from drying out, cover them with plastic wrap until you serve them. If your tidbits are suited to it, brush a layer of aspic over the tops to keep them looking fresh and prevent drying.

Zakuska

Recipes for *zakuska* can be well adapted to cocktail parties. This impressive spread of flavorful and attractive tidbits originated as the first course of Russian dinners and as a permanent snack bar. It included pâté, caviar, fish of many kinds, meats, game, vegetable preparations. Russians are particularly fond of mushrooms, so those were always included. Americans can do decorative things with mushrooms too, and although caviar is not so easy for us to use casually, tiny bits of it do make excellent garnishes to blander foods. Barquettes of puff paste, separately baked, can be filled with salad mixtures or even hot mixtures. *Zakuska* usually included whole fish in aspic and great bowls of salad. If you have someone to help serve, you include these too. Also, if your facilities allow room for tables, you can have such impressive pieces as whole smoked turkey or Virginia ham or prosciutto; these can be sliced and served on plates, but they cannot be eaten very well standing up. Serve beaten biscuits with turkey or ham.

Smörgåsbord is too huge a spread to be considered a first course, but some of the individual dishes that are usually part of it can serve well as cocktail party food.

SNACKS

For snacks, you can use any dish mentioned in this chapter, but make the tiny servings bigger. Sandwiches with or without tops are quick and easy. If it is a party occasion, you can make them pretty by rolling the edges in mayonnaise, then in minced parsley or paprika. Large pizzas are a natural; use standard English muffins, or make large pizzas and serve in wedges.

A slice of pâté is a very good snack by itself or in a sandwich. (Incidentally another good way to serve pâté, especially if it is baked in a pastry crust, is as an addition to the meat course in place of a starch.) The mixtures you assemble for *antipasto* and *hors-d'oeuvre variés* make delicious snacks, not too filling or fattening.

Any of the pastry turnovers from Chapter 14 makes a great snack—and a rather large one! And the custard quiches, with any filling, can be served at room temperature; this snack can be ready without any last-minute effort.

Here are some menus to illustrate the uses of some of these first-course dishes.

LUNCHEON

Pâté
Melba toast
Broiled chicken
Green beans with tiny onions
Fresh strawberries in red wine

Chicken and leek quiche
Beef salad with cherry tomatoes
Baked apples with walnuts and raisins

DINNER

Hors-d'oeuvre variés
Roast veal shoulder with herb and marrow stuffing
Watercress
Browned potatoes
Braised endive
Apricot tart

Ham and asparagus rolls au gratin
Broiled steak
Duchess potatoes
Broiled tomato halves with herbs
Hazelnut mousse

SMALL COCKTAIL PARTY

Pâté
Chicken spread
Light and dark bread strips and rounds
Hard-cooked eggs stuffed with ham and green olives
Dilled green beans
Toasted almonds

LARGE COCKTAIL PARTY

Canapés
Broiled stuffed mushrooms
Miniature ham tarts
Black olives
Cherry tomatoes
Turkey and watercress sandwiches
Vatrushki filled with veal and anchovies

STOCKS

AND

SOUPS

Chapter 10

Sᴛᴏᴄᴋ ɪs ᴍᴀᴅᴇ ᴘʀɪᴍᴀʀɪʟʏ for use in cooking. Stock making may seem to be an extra chore when there are bottled, canned and dehydrated products available, but your own stock, if well made, will be superior to any packaged variety. You can make your stock as rich and full-bodied or as delicate as you like, and you can flavor it to suit your particular purposes. Most packaged stocks, bouillons and broths are far too salty for use in cooking. But the chief advantage of homemade stock is that it is far more nutritious than packaged stock. This does not preclude the use of any of the packaged products, however; indeed, they are very handy for emergencies and can be used by themselves as soup. The small packets of granular or dehydrated broth are sometimes useful as seasoning; part of a packet can be used, and the rest can be refolded in its foil wrapping and stored for another time.

STOCKS

Stock can be used in a variety of ways: as the base for gravies and sauces; as the liquid ingredient in pot-roasting; as meat flavoring for salad dressings, particularly for meat salads; as an important ingredient in soups; as a flavoring and moisturizer to brush on meats to be barbecued.

Ingredients

The animal parts to use in stock making are marrowbones; shinbones, knee bones and neck bones, which are rich in gelatin; breast bones, and boiled beef bones. The bones of the breast are fattier than the long bones and are surrounded by cartilage; because breast bones ossify differently from long bones and do not contain such a condensed substance, they release their nutrients more easily during cooking, which makes them more valuable for stock.

For thick jellied stocks, calf's and steer's feet are ideal. Oxtails and ox feet will also yield a good gelatinous stock, but since they are hard and tough, they require much longer cooking than calf's feet, a factor to consider when planning your stock making. As you can see, the gelatin-rich parts of the animals are those with much connective tissue. Gelatin is not present in these parts in the form that we know, but as collagen in the connective tissues and in the bones themselves. It takes a long time for the collagen to melt and be released from the tissues, and this is why a better stock results from long slow cooking.

Besides meat, vegetables and herbs are used to flavor stock. The most suitable vegetables are leeks, onions, scallions, carrots, celery and greens, but actually you can use anything you like. Green peppers and turnips, to name just two others, have a pronounced flavor, but they might be just what you want. For greens, spinach, lettuce and celery leaves are good. The ingredients you use will be restricted only by how you intend to use the stock; for instance, tomatoes will give the liquid a pink color, and you will have to strain it carefully to eliminate seeds and peels; beets will color everything red; likewise, an abundance of greens will impart a distinctive color and flavor to stock.

Unless you want your stock to be flavored with a particular herb, do not add any, because at the end of the long slow cooking the herb flavor will be so concentrated that it may overpower the taste of other ingredients. Thyme and rosemary are two herbs you might want to experiment with when you do intend to have an herb-flavored stock.

If you do plan to make stock, take the trouble to acquire a proper stockpot, one that will hold at least 8 quarts, made of sturdy material—stainless steel, cast aluminum, porcelain enamel over cast iron—*with a cover*. Even if you plan to make only 2 quarts of stock, you will start out with more than 2 quarts of water plus all the other ingredients. The pot should be large enough to allow 5 inches of space between the top of the liquid and the top of the pot. Also, since stock requires long cooking, your pot must be sturdy enough to be able to withstand long hours of cooking.

To make stock, prepare all your ingredients first. Have the meats and bones cracked or cut to suit your purposes. Scrub or peel the vegetables, or do both, and cut them into pieces. Our suggestion is to cut all the vegetables into large pieces so you can retrieve them after the cooking if you do not intend to use them in the stock; for instance, cut carrots lengthwise into halves. If you do plan to use the vegetables as well as the stock for soup, they will be so softened by the long cooking that it will be easy to mash them or purée them in a blender.

Pour a lot of water into your stockpot. How much water is a lot? We could specify how many quarts, but here is an easy rule that applies to all stock making: The water must be 2 inches above the top of the ingredients. If the stock-making process is new to you, first put the ingredients into the empty pot, and note how high they come. Then dump them out, and fill the pot to the right level with water. When you have done this a few times you will be able to gauge the amount of water at a glance. If you end up with too little water after all, simply add more; if you have too much, reduce the liquid by cooking a little longer, until both flavor and amount suit your intentions.

BEEF CUTS FOR BRAISING OR POT ROASTING

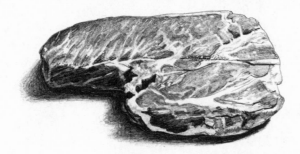

A piece cut from the blade portion of the chuck

A piece cut from the bottom round, a portion of the wholesale round

Basic Method

Bring the water to a boil and add seasoning: salt and cracked peppercorns. If you like, you can add some bouillon granules or crumble some cubes into the water at this point; remember that these include salt, and adjust the amount you add accordingly; most dehydrated bouillon also includes vegetable extract and dehydrated herbs and spices. When measuring the seasoning, remember that it will become concentrated as the stock cooks, so start out with a light hand. A good rule is to use 1 teaspoon salt and 2 cracked peppercorns for every 2 quarts of water. Cook the seasoning in the boiling water for 5 minutes, then add the meat and bones. When the liquid returns to the boil, reduce the heat to a simmer, and let the meat simmer, uncovered, for 45 minutes. After 20 minutes skim the top of the liquid. The grayish scum floating on the top is mostly cooked blood extracted from the meat; it is not harmful and may be left in the stock, but it clouds the liquid and looks unattractive. At the end of the 45 minutes, skim the liquid once again.

At this point, add the vegetables, bring to a boil, cover the pot, and reduce heat once more to a simmer. Simmer for 1 hour, then taste the stock to see if it needs ad-

161

ditional seasoning or flavoring of any kind. Then cook until done, for a total of 3 hours.

You now have a stock and meat that can be eaten. If you used beef shin or neck for the stock, you can lift the meat from the liquid, cut it into bits, and serve it as boiled beef. Boiled beef with horseradish sauce has always been a favorite in New York City.

HORSERADISH SAUCE OR DIP

1 tablespoon prepared white horseradish sauce
1 tablespoon commercial sour cream
½ teaspoon chopped fresh chives

Drain the horseradish briefly if it is very moist. Mix the ingredients well. Increase all the ingredients in the same proportions to make the amount you need.

If you used a whole knuckle of veal for your stock, it can be served as *osso buco*, as can beef shank pieces. Neck of veal can be cut into chunks for serving. The meat on a calf's foot can be removed from the bones and used. Any meat can be chopped or puréed in a blender to be added to soup or a meat sauce, or to be used as a stuffing ingredient.

If you intend to use the stock as an ingredient for something else, first remove all the solid particles, either by lifting them out with a large perforated spoon or by pouring the whole thing, a little at a time, through a large colander into another pot. Then pour through a fine-meshed strainer. To strain even more thoroughly, line the strainer with a double layer of dampened cheesecloth; this process will take some time, since the stock will drip quite slowly through the cheesecloth.

Remember that you are working with a large amount of liquid and ingredients, and the full stockpot will be heavy to hold. Do not try to lift the whole quantity at once to pour; you will find that the stock pours out faster than the strainer can take it, and it is not easy to balance such a heavy, awkward pot. It is better to use a small saucepan with a long handle as a dipper, or spoon out the stock with a large ladle.

Simple Soup

If you plan to make soup, you can use the stock without much further work. Remove bones, and purée everything else in the blender. You will have to purée a portion at a time, of course, because there will be far more liquid than could fit in the average blender. After puréeing, combine the blended portions, and mix well. Reheat to serving temperature, and serve. You may garnish the soup with carrot slices, chopped parsley, croutons or whatever suits you.

Stock can be made with beef as the only meat ingredient. Use several 2-inch slices of beef shin and several pieces of breast flanken or plate flanken. However, a mixture of beef and veal makes a smoother stock. The same parts of veal—shin and flanken—can be used. The shin and flanken bones themselves give a large amount of flavor to the stock. A more delicate stock can be made with veal alone.

If you are using the shanks of veal or beef or both, remember that these pieces need long cooking to extract maximum flavor. It is a slow process, but the results are well worth the effort. Allow an extra hour—for a total of 4—to the total cooking time if you are using shanks.

Lamb is a strong-tasting meat and less adaptable than beef or veal for stock. Certainly you would never use a lamb stock with anything but a lamb preparation.

Because pork has a bland taste unless well seasoned, it is seldom used in Western cookery for stock, but in Oriental preparations pork stock with monosodium glutamate is often used as the basis of other dishes.

Smoked Hocks

Hocks and shanks of smoked ham are familiar as flavoring for pea soup. In the old days, they were cooked with the peas, which required long cooking themselves. If you use precooked peas, it is more practical to make stock from the smoked hock or shank and use it as the cooking liquid for the peas.

Here are some other ideas for using smoked hocks or shanks. Put a smoked ham hock into the liquid you use to cook corned beef or pickled tongue to add extra flavor. Or use a hock to flavor fresh vegetables like green peas—particularly the large peas available late in the growing season—and carrots. Southern cooks often add a chunk of salt pork to their vegetables, especially greens and green beans. Our suggestion for using the smoked ham hock is similar to this idea, but the flavor imparted by the hock is more pronounced, and the cooked vegetables will not have the greasy coating that salt pork gives.

Chicken Stock

Chicken stock is a favorite for all the uses of stock. It can be made with any kind of bird, but the timing is a little different with each type.

If you are working with a pullet, a tender young bird of 4 to 6 pounds, you will need much less time than you would for a fowl, and the broth will be smoother and sweeter. A fowl, an older bird of 4½ to 7 pounds, will require longer cooking but will give you much stronger broth. As a general rule, the older the bird, the stronger the broth. The older birds are more flavorful, but extracting the flavor does take more time.

Put the whole bird, uncut, into cold water; the water should be fully 2 inches above the bird. Add everything else at once; chicken takes a shorter time to cook than veal or beef, and you should add all the flavoring vegetables at the start to give the flavors a chance to blend. Bring the liquid slowly to a boil, then at once reduce to a simmer. Because chicken is delicate, it should be treated like veal. Boiling has a toughening effect on meat fibers, and as the water becomes steam, flavor and juices evaporate with it. This rule against boiling applies to all kinds of stock, however, because you want to retain as much flavor as possible in the final product.

If you are using a pullet, it will be fully cooked in 1¾ to 2 hours, and you can use the meat for any preparation that calls for cooked chicken. It will still be juicy.

The stock can be strained as described on page 162. If you want a more intense flavor, you can reduce the stock by simmering further.

If you are using a fowl, you will need to simmer it for 3½ to 4 hours, and the resulting stock will have a strong flavor. The meat of the fowl is also good to eat, but it will be drier than that of the pullet. It is excellent for chicken salad, also good for chicken fricassee—and you can use some of the stock for the sauce—and just right for Jewish dishes like chicken soup and chicken matzo brai. Also, a fowl has a considerable amount of fat in it, and this can be retrieved from the stock and used for matzo balls.

Here is another idea for the fowl. Start the stock making in the usual way, and simmer the fowl for 2½ hours. Then take the bird out of the water, season it, and roast in the oven for 1 hour. Use it like a roasting chicken. The stock will be good even though not as strong.

Of course, you can make stock with chicken cut into pieces instead of whole. Allow the same amounts of time as for the whole chickens.

Here is a way to use a cut-up fowl for both a chicken dish and stock. Cut the fowl into sections before starting the stock. Then cook in water in the usual way for 2½ hours. Remove the pieces from the stock, and cool them. Pat them dry, bread them, and bake them slowly for 45 minutes.

Do not try to use two cooking methods with pullets, however, because the meat is tender and the whole bird or the pieces would just collapse.

Another way to make stock is to use just the bony portions of chickens. This idea is a money saver, because when cut-up chickens are used for other dishes, the backs, necks and wings, which have relatively little meat on them, sometimes end up being thrown out. In some markets you can buy chicken wings separately; if they are cheaper than other parts, your stock can be relatively inexpensive.

In stock, you can also use the raw carcasses and bones of chickens you have boned for other purposes. If you have only a few pieces, freeze them until you have enough to make stock—at least 2 pounds for about 1 quart of stock. Do not be tempted to use the bones or carcasses of cooked chicken; you might get a little flavor from them, but too many nutrients will have already been cooked away to make it worth the effort.

Despite the long tradition of making soup from the bones of the Thanksgiving turkey, we do not recommend it, for the reason just mentioned. However, raw turkey wings and other bony parts can be used; proceed as you would with chicken.

Here is an easy, good recipe for soup made with raw turkey, including the bony portions. Large old birds can be used for this, and the long cooking will give you tender meat.

TURKEY-VEGETABLE SOUP   8 servings with leftovers

2½ quarts water
2 large onions, cut
12 whole cloves
10 peppercorns
2 bay leaves
4 chicken-bouillon cubes

6 to 8 pounds turkey with bones, cut
    into small sections by a band saw
1 bag (5 to 6 ounces) mixed dried soup
    vegetables
1 teaspoon salt
pinch of ground ginger
½ cup uncooked white rice

Put water in a large kettle, and bring to a boil. Measure a double thickness of cheesecloth about 18 inches square. Put onions, cloves, peppercorns, bay leaves and bouillon cubes in the center; bring the corners of the cheesecloth together to make a sack, and tie it closed with white string. Drop the sack into the kettle, and add turkey, mixed soup vegetables, salt and ginger. Let the water come to a boil again, then reduce heat to a simmer, cover, and cook for 2 hours, stirring occasionally.

Add rice, stir gently, cover, and cook over very low heat for 1½ hours longer; *do not stir!* Turn off heat, and let the soup rest for 15 minutes. Lift out and discard the cheesecloth sack and its contents. Then gently lift out the pieces of turkey—they will be very tender. Serve the soup as a first course and the meat as part of the main course.

Because duck and goose are both fatty and bony, neither bird makes good stock.

Pheasant can be used to make stock or broth; proceed as you would with a pullet, and cook for 1¾ to 2 hours. When the bird is cooked, cut it into quarters, and serve it in a sauce or flaming. Or you can prepare pheasant as you would the half-simmered, half-roasted fowl: Simmer it in liquid for 1 hour, then roast it for 1 hour.

Other small domestic birds and game birds may be used for stock, but we do not recommend it. Small birds will become tender and be done so quickly that stock made from them will have only slight flavor. Or you may not care for the flavor; for example, we do not like the flavor of stock made with squab.

The bones of roasted game birds are sometimes used for stock. Just as with chicken, we do not recommend this because it is not nutritious. If you want to try it, however, cook the bones with a smoked ham hock for added flavor.

Brown Stock

Many cooks recommend browning meats and bones to obtain a brown stock. Put the meat and bones in a shallow heavy pan, uncovered, in a hot oven (400 to 425° F.), and let them roast for 45 minutes to 1 hour, turning them occasionally. Be sure to retrieve any meat juices that have baked onto the sides or bottom of the pan, since these bits will add flavor to the stock.

Another method of browning is to put beef or veal bones in a heavy saucepan containing 5 tablespoons of hot bacon fat. Heat the bones over medium heat for 45 minutes, turning them every 10 minutes. At the end of the time, put the bones on several layers of absorbent kitchen paper, and let them drain. Use the browned bones for stock making, or combine them with ingredients for vegetable soup to add flavor; remove the bones before serving the soup.

Giblets can be prepared the same way and added to the stockpot or to vegetable soup. For soup, trim the giblets, cut them into small pieces, and serve them in the soup.

Bone Stock

Since bones are the most important ingredient in stock making, stock can be made with bones alone. Although it will have less nutritive value than stock made with both meat and bones, it will still be flavorful. Beef bones with flavoring and seasoning can make a good beef broth. The bones should be cracked, as should all bones to be used in stock, to release minerals; more flavor and nutrition will result. Also, especially if you are using the bones of a large animal like beef, it will be much easier to fit the bones into your stockpot if they are cracked. Cook bone stock for about 3 hours. Use the bones browned or unbrowned, according to your own wishes. Reduce the amount of seasoning if you are using bones alone; ½ teaspoon salt and 1 peppercorn, cracked, for each pound of bones is enough to start with. You can adjust this at the end of 2 hours of simmering. Stock made from bones can be used in all the usual ways.

There are many other methods of making stock. Use the one that you like best, because they are equally good. All methods are based on the same principle: long slow cooking to extract the flavors of the ingredients. Do not forget, use a light hand with all seasonings, because they will be concentrated when the stock is done.

Storing Stock

When your stock is finished and you have carefully strained it, you should store whatever portion you do not intend to use immediately. Chill it; during refrigeration the fat released by meats and bones will slowly rise to the surface and become firm. You can usually lift off the fatty layer in meat stocks, but chicken fat will never become firm enough for that; you will have to spoon off the chicken fat. Discard these fats. Transfer the stock to clear plastic containers with tops; use the kind in which you can create a vacuum by pressing on the lid. These containers are better than the glass jars so often recommended in the past; keeping air out also keeps out airborne organisms that might change the taste of the stock. Store the containers in the refrigerator; the stock will keep for 6 to 8 days.

Stock can be frozen, but flavor is lost as a result. Crystals of ice form on top of frozen stock and dilute it as it defrosts. To use chilled stock, heat it very slowly to boiling.

Clarifying Stock

Chilled, defatted, well-strained stock will be tasty but not transparent. To make it clear and sparkling, you must clarify it. You can find directions for this in most cookbooks, and every one will be different. Try one of those procedures, or follow this simple method.

For each 2 to 3 quarts of stock, use 2 egg whites. Break the eggs, and separate them. Use the yolks for something else, but be sure to gather all the whites in a small bowl. Do not discard the egg shells, but crush them in a piece of kitchen paper. With a fork, beat the whites only until they are frothy. Turn the whites and shells into the cold stock in a large pot. Stir, then *very slowly* bring to the boiling point. Reduce the heat at once so the liquid barely shudders, and keep it at this level for about 30 minutes. All the tiny particles suspended in the liquid will be attracted to the egg whites and shells and will float to the top.

To finish the clarifying, lift off the egg-white mass, or gently push it aside, and pour the stock through a fine strainer lined with moistened cheesecloth into another pot; or ladle it into the strainer if the pot is heavy to handle. Do not stir or disturb the stock any more than necessary to transfer it, and do not try to hurry the straining.

CONSOMMÉ DOUBLE

You can use the clear stock as bouillon or consommé just as it is. To make *consommé double*, a richer-tasting and even more nutritious first course, add, with the egg whites, ½ cup chopped raw vegetables and 1 cup chopped raw meat for each quart of stock; use the kind of meat that matches your stock—beef with beef stock, chicken with chicken stock and so on. The usual vegetables are leeks (the white part only), carrots and celery. Proceed as with simple clarifying, but let this mixture shudder for about 1 hour, then strain. The solid parts are all discarded.

Aspic

If the stock is to be used for aspic—and we will talk more about that in Chapter 21—it is especially important to make it with those gelatin-rich cuts of meat mentioned on page 159, so that the finished stock will jell adequately. Add additional flavorings or seasonings before clarifying to keep the stock absolutely clear. Clarify following the basic method, then cool. To test for jelling, pour a little stock onto a small flat plate and refrigerate; it should be firm in 10 minutes. If it is not, add commercial unflavored gelatin in the proportion of 1 envelope to each quart of stock. To jell ordinary liquid you would use 1 envelope to 1 pint, but your stock will already have a lot of gelatin in it from the meats, and too much gelatin makes a tough aspic. Pour some of the cold stock into a separate container, and soften the gelatin in it. Heat the rest of the stock, and stir in the gelatin until it is completely dissolved.

An unclarified meat stock can be used as the basis of countless other soups. However, do not make the mistake of using the same stock for all your soups; you do not want them all to taste alike. This is a common error in professional kitchens, and one of the chief advantages of the home cook is that he or she can make every dish taste distinctive and different.

SOUPS

Here is another way to make a good soup: Fill up the stockpot with all the ingredients for beef stock, including the necessary amount of *cold* water. Store the pot in the refrigerator overnight. The meat will become saturated with the flavors of the other ingredients. In the morning remove the pot from the refrigerator, set it immediately over very low heat, and cover it. Let it cook undisturbed for 5½ hours. Lift out the bones and meat, and serve the rest as a thick vegetable soup; or cut the bits of meat off the bones, return the meat to the pot, and serve as a thick beef-vegetable soup. If you plan to use the meat for a specific purpose other than as part of the soup, lift out the bones and meat from the pot after 3 hours of cooking, cut the meat from the bones, and return the bones to the pot, where they will continue adding flavor to the soup.

You can make chicken-and-vegetable soup in the same way, but for this you must use a fowl. The soup must cook for 5 hours, and a pullet would fall to shreds if cooked so long.

Lamb can be used to make good soups, even though we do not recommend it for stocks. The famous Scotch broth is a soup of lamb with barley and vegetables. Usually neck of lamb is used, and the procedure is just like stock making. Use regular, not precooked, barley, and cook barley and lamb together until the lamb is tender. Then discard the bones, cut the meat into pieces, return the meat to the stockpot, add vegetables and cook until the vegetables are done.

The following recipe provides two courses: soup, and meat for the main course.

LAMB SHANKS AND MINT SOUP   4 servings

6 cups water	4 lamb shanks
2 large onions, whole	½ teaspoon salt
4 celery ribs, without leaves, halved	12 peppercorns, cracked
¾ cup dried split peas	20 wafer-thin slices of cucumber
½ cup leafy sprigs of fresh mint	

Pour the water into a large pot, and add onions, celery and split peas. Let simmer, covered, for 1 hour. Remove onions and celery, and discard. Add mint, lamb shanks and seasonings. Cover the pot, and let the soup simmer for 2 hours, stirring gently occasionally. Add more water if needed; there should be about 4 cups when the soup is done.

Transfer lamb shanks to a baking dish or heatproof serving dish. Keep warm in a 200° F. oven until ready to serve.

Serve the soup first, topping each serving with 5 slices of cucumber. Then serve the lamb shanks on a bed of buttered noodles and mushrooms. Accompany with a hearty salad and a glass of dark beer.

Oxtails

Oxtails make a classic soup, but remember that they require long cooking to become tender. For more about them see page 186, where you will find a double recipe including a soup that we invented. When making the classic soup, proceed as if making stock, using the usual flavoring vegetables, and the tails, cut into pieces, as the meat. Cook for 4½ to 5 hours, then remove the solid ingredients, and strain the stock. For a clear soup, adjust the seasoning, clarify the stock, then pour it a second time through a cloth-lined strainer filled with tiny sprigs or leaves of fresh herbs— rosemary, chervil, tarragon or whatever suits your taste. A dash of sherry or tawny port is good in this. For a thicker, more hearty oxtail soup, strain the finished stock, and add separately cooked vegetables (carrot rounds, little onions, etc.) and the meat from the oxtails just before serving. After such long cooking, vegetables cooked with the stock would be far too mushy to serve.

Stocks are a chief ingredient in many sauces. If you anticipate sauce making or any other procedure that will reduce the stock further, be especially cautious with the seasoning at the start. You can reduce a stock to half its volume by simmering it very slowly to evaporate some of the moisture. A well-reduced stock needs no further thickening to make a sauce; it will be smooth and glossy and will adhere to the food it is served with.

VEGETABLE PILAF

Stock can be used to cook rice and other grains, and is always used for making pilaf and risotto. Here is a trick that will result in a delicious vegetable pilaf. Use the puréed soup stock on page 162 without the meat, in these proportions: 1 cup of stock, ½ cup vegetables, ½ teaspoon butter and a tiny pinch of puréed fresh garlic or a dash of garlic powder. The vegetables can be whole if they are small like peas, or cut into pieces if they are large like carrots or green beans. Bring the stock to a boil, then simmer it with the vegetables over low heat until the vegetables are cooked and the liquid absorbed.

Marrow

Since bones are so important to stocks and soups, we should mention marrow, which is found inside all bones. In young animals the marrow is red, and even in older animals the marrow inside flat bones is red. However, the marrow in the long (leg) bones becomes yellow from the accumulation of fat as the animal ages; and it is the "yellow marrow" that is used as food. Marrow contains nutrients as well as fat, and is valuable in stock making and in other cookery (see Index). Marrow by itself was considered a great delicacy in Victorian and Edwardian times. Pieces of cooked marrowbone were served on linen napkins, and the diners used a long narrow scoop called a "marrow spoon" to extract the marrow and spread it on hot toast. With the current concern about fats in the diet, few people today would find this dish desirable, but marrow can be used in other ways.

Marrow is not sold separately, of course, but the pieces of long bones you buy for stock will have marrow inside. For example, in a slice of the shin you will find a round slice of bone containing its marrow. If you buy large soup bones, you must have them cracked, as you would any other soup bone.

If you want marrow to use in something other than soup, you must buy marrowbones, cook them, and extract the marrow when it is soft. Here is how to do it: First have the butcher cut the bones into crosswise pieces 2 to 3 inches long, and then have him split the bones lengthwise, so the marrow will also be split. Soak the bones in cold water overnight; drain. Wrap the pieces in foil, and place them, split sides up, on a baking sheet. Heat the bones in a preheated 325° F. oven for 45 minutes. The heat loosens the marrow from the bone. When the bones are cool enough to handle, scoop out the marrow with any narrow utensil; the handle of a fork will serve. Turn the marrow into a container, and add to it all the moisture gathered in the foil wrappings. What you now have is "softened" bone marrow, useful in making omelets (see p. 119), adding flavor to stuffings, and for the purposes described in the next paragraph. Marrow can be refrigerated for 6 to 8 days. In a tightly closed container it can be kept frozen for 2 months; after that it will develop freezer burn. Unsoftened raw marrow can be scraped out of the bones for some special uses (see p. 81). Do not try to cook bones in water or panfry them to extract the marrow, because both processes drastically reduce its nutritional value.

The name *bordelaise*, meaning "in the style favored in Bordeaux," usually refers to a sauce or garnish made with minced shallots, red wine, minced parsley and beef marrow. Shallots, parsley and marrow mixed to a spreadable texture make a simple but excellent steak sauce. A spoonful of marrow instead of the more commonly used butter can be added to a finished sauce made with beef stock to provide glossiness and smoothness.

Any clear soup will be enhanced by a delicious garnish. If you retrieve the chicken fat from the stock made from a fowl (p. 164), you can use it in making matzo balls.

MATZO BALLS   12 matzo balls

2 eggs	½ uncooked chicken breast, without skin or bones
2 tablespoons melted chicken fat or oil	
¾ teaspoon salt	3 tablespoons minced parsley
⅛ teaspoon ground white pepper	2 quarts water
½ cup matzo meal	1 teaspoon salt

Separate the eggs, putting the whites in a medium-sized bowl and the yolks in a large bowl. Mix the fat with the yolks. Stir salt and pepper into the matzo meal, and mix with the yolks and fat. Grind the uncooked raw chicken once, stir it and the parsley into the meal, and mix well. Beat the egg whites until stiff, then gently fold them into the other mixture. Cover the bowl, and refrigerate for 1 hour.

Start water boiling, and add salt. Shape the mixture into balls about the size of small walnuts, and drop into boiling water. Reduce heat to a simmer, cover the pot, and cook the balls for 45 minutes to 1 hour. They will rise to the top; turn them over with a skimmer to cook evenly. As they cook, they will swell to the size of golf balls. Serve one or two in each serving of soup. Do not cook them in the soup, because they will cloud the liquid. Onion is not traditional in these, but if you like the flavor, scrape enough fresh onion to make 1 teaspoon of pulp, and add that with the chicken and parsley. Adjust salt and pepper to taste.

ODDS

AND

ENDS

Chapter 11

Y ou read in Chapter 2 that all organ meats except kidneys are removed from meat carcasses and sold separately. One reason for this is that organ meats are perishable and must be cooked promptly; aging does not do anything but spoil them. The most perishable are brains, fresh tongues and sweetbreads.

BRAINS

Of all organ meats, brains are the most delicate in texture and taste. Keep them in your refrigerator no longer than 2 days. If you realize on the second day that you will not be able to cook and serve them, rinse them in fresh water and freeze them without delay. They will keep in a refrigerator freezer for 4 weeks and in a self-contained freezer at − 10° F. for 3 months maximum, if they are carefully wrapped.

There are calf, beef and lamb brains. Calf's brains are the best and naturally the most popular; the average calf's brain weighs about ½ pound. Beef brains are larger, weighing about ¾ pound each; they are somewhat coarser, since the animal is larger and older. Lamb brains are very small, weighing less than 4 ounces, and they are difficult to remove from the head, so they are not often seen for sale except on special holidays.

Blanching Brains

The membrane covering brains is usually shattered in removing them from the bony casing, but small bits of the membrane may remain on the brain. Some blood vessels will also remain, but they are edible. Traces of blood will be removed by the first step in preparing brains for further cooking, and bits of membrane can be removed after this step. This first step may consist of either soaking or blanching (parboiling); you can omit this step, but it is best to use one of these procedures to whiten the brains. Cover the brains with water, and add 1 teaspoon salt and the juice of a quarter of a lemon. Either soak the brains in this mixture for several hours, in the refrigerator, of course, or simmer them gently in it for about 20 minutes, then drain and cover with cold water to stop the cooking. During this process, the soft texture becomes somewhat firmer.

There are many things you can do with brains; their delicate flavor makes them an excellent protein supplement for other dishes. Scramble them with eggs; add color with chives or other herbs. Cut them into small chunks or slices, and sauté in oil with garlic. They make a good main-course salad when mixed with crumbled blue cheese, diced pears or apples, or vegetables. In a salad used for the salad course, brains can be mashed and mixed with the dressing or diced and tossed with tomatoes, cucumbers and other ingredients. Mash brains, and use them to thicken sauces; they add protein, and their flavor will not overpower that of anything else in the sauce.

The classic brains with black butter, a great favorite in New York as well as Paris, is made with blanched brains, sliced. Sauté the slices in butter, then transfer them to heated plates. Continue cooking the butter until it is very dark, then add vinegar and minced herbs or capers, and heat. Quickly pour over the brains and serve. All this takes only a few minutes. Use about 4 teaspoons vinegar—any kind you like—to each ¼ pound of butter; ¼ pound of butter is enough for 2 or 3 calf's brains.

Brains can also be breaded with egg and crumbs or batter and fried; or they can be brushed with seasoned oil and broiled. Here are 2 good brain dishes. The first is excellent as a first course or the main course at a luncheon or supper; the second is a good appetizer or cocktail food.

BRAINS À LA BARBEGAL   6 servings

3 pairs calf's brains	4 to 6 tablespoons black caviar
1 teaspoon salt	1 tablespoon melted butter
½ lemon	1 medium-sized onion (2 ounces), peeled
18 pitted green olives	1 large carrot, scraped

Blanch the brains in water with salt and lemon juice. Blanch the olives in water separately, so they will not be too salty. Dice the brains, and chop the olives to bits about the size of the caviar. Mix brains, olives, caviar and butter—just gently toss together without mashing the brains—and divide among 6 buttered *au gratin* dishes. Grate the raw onion and carrot separately. Bake the brains in a preheated 400° F. oven for 10 minutes. Remove from the oven, and sprinkle some grated onion and carrot around the edges of each dish. Serve at once.

STUFFED CELERY   24 pieces

1 pair calf's brains	2 hard-cooked eggs, shelled
½ teaspoon salt	salt and pepper
2 teaspoons lemon juice	6 large pieces of celery, trimmed
1 small onion (1 ounce), peeled	6 teaspoons black or red caviar

Blanch the brains in water with salt and lemon juice; let them cool completely. Chop brains, mince onion, and mash eggs. Mix all together, and season to taste. Cut each piece of celery into 4 sections, and stuff with 1 tablespoon of the mixture. Sprinkle ¼ teaspoon of caviar on each piece. Keep chilled until ready to serve. If you prefer, you can use the mixture as a spread for canapés.

BEEF CUTS FOR BRAISING OR POT ROASTING

Eye round, a portion of the wholesale round. This cut has been outer-larded for greater juiciness; the larding is tied with butchers' string.

Brisket, cut from the wholesale brisket

TONGUE

There are beef, veal, lamb and pork tongues. Pork tongues are usually ground for various canned products. Lamb tongues are either ground or pickled and sold in jars. Beef tongues are cured (see Chapter 3) or packed in cans and jars, both whole and sliced. Fresh beef tongues are plentiful, veal less so; you should order fresh lamb tongues in advance if you want to be sure of having them.

Beef tongues weigh from 2 to 5 pounds, with an average weight of 3½; veal tongues weigh ½ to 2 pounds; lamb tongues seldom weigh more than 4 ounces. Use fresh tongues within 3 days, smoked tongues within 8 days. Fresh tongues can be kept frozen for up to 6 months; freeze them before cooking, and make sure they are carefully wrapped.

Poaching Fresh Beef Tongue

Parboil fresh tongues in lightly salted water (1 teaspoon salt per quart water) for 20 to 30 minutes, according to size. Drain, and remove the skin, fat and any little bones at the root. It is easier to remove the skin when the tongue is fully cooked, and you can cook it completely at this point if you prefer; however, you will want to use the shorter parboiling and peeling procedure for some preparations. Simmering or poaching a beef tongue takes 3 to 3½ hours, a veal tongue 2¼ hours. If you are cooking fresh tongue completely, add salt (1 teaspoon per quart of water), bay leaf, cracked peppercorns and other flavorings—a carrot, an onion, parsley sprigs, garlic, whole cloves, other spices—whatever suits your taste. If you do not season well, the finished tongue will be too bland.

Tongues can be braised or pot-roasted. Allow 3½ hours for a beef tongue, about 2½ hours for veal tongue and 2 hours for lamb tongue. Braising is a very good method for the smaller tongues. Turn them over in the pot halfway through the braising to be sure they cook evenly. When the tongue is tender—test with a fork and check to see if the tiny bones at the wide end are loose—remove it from the cooking pot, and let it rest on a large plate or a carving board for about 20 minutes. Then remove skin, fat and little bones. Most of the skin can be peeled off like a glove if the tongue is fully cooked. At the tip, you may need to use a knife. Since the very thin tip of the meat can be tough, cut it off and set it aside; chopped or ground, it will be good in salads or stuffings. Return the tongue to the pot to keep it hot until you serve it; or slice it first, and then reheat it.

TONGUE PARMIGIANA

Tongue is not always a favorite with children, in spite of its nutritional value, tenderness and digestibility. Tongue parmigiana is a trick to try. Cook tongue completely by poaching, pot-roasting or braising, and chill it. Cut slices of the cold tongue, and arrange them in a single layer in a baking dish. Spoon tomato, marinara or mushroom sauce over the top, and sprinkle with a thick layer of grated Parmesan cheese. If you like, add a tiny pinch of Italian seasoning and a few drops of olive oil. Bake until the cheese is melted and everything is hot and bubbly. You can vary this by using different sauce, different cheese and different seasoning. Anyone who likes pizza will like this, and tongue will become acceptable.

TONGUE SOUP

This preparation is like some famous European and Oriental dishes that provide several courses from one cooking process. Use beef tongue, and parboil it, but do not skin it at this point. Rinse it, and put it in a large stockpot. Add enough water to reach a level 4 inches above the top of the meat. Add 2 or 3 bay leaves, 1 teaspoon salt and ½ teaspoon cracked peppercorns. You can add other flavoring ingredients, but for this soup do not use bouillon cubes. Also add 4 cups of diced fresh vegetables including onion and celery, and ½ cup dried split green peas. Bring to a boil, then simmer for about 3 hours. Dice one eighth of a head of green cabbage, and add that. Then cook for 1½ hours longer. You can vary the amounts of flavorings and vegetables or use entirely different vegetables; this is a very flexible recipe.

Remove the tongue to a carving board and let it rest until cool enough to handle. Skin it, and remove fat and bones. Adjust the seasoning of the broth. Serve the broth as the soup course, and the sliced tongue as the meat of the main course, with horseradish or mustard horseradish. If you want to keep the tongue hot while serving the soup, return it to the stockpot, or place it in another container and spoon some of the hot broth over it.

Tongue is often used as an ingredient in pâté because of its color; sometimes it is layered in the forcemeat; other recipes use it ground. We call the recipe that follows a meat loaf, but a slice of it can be served, like any baked pâté, for a good first course.

TONGUE AND PORK MEAT LOAF

1 fresh beef tongue, 3½ pounds	½ cup olive oil
3 pounds boneless fresh pork	½ teaspoon black peppercorns
1 large onion	1 teaspoon coarse salt
3 celery ribs	1 jigger (3 tablespoons) Drambuie
1 green pepper	1 cup tomato-vegetable juice
1½ to 2 teaspoons minced fresh herbs (thyme, parsley, basil)	

Parboil the tongue, then skin it, and remove fat and bones. The weight of the skinned tongue should equal that of the pork. Grind both meats, and mix well in a large heatproof bowl. Peel the onion, trim the celery, and remove ribs and seeds from green pepper. Chop the vegetables to very fine bits, and mix with herbs. Heat the oil in a large frying pan. Grind the peppercorns and salt into the oil. Add the vegetables, mix, and simmer over low heat for 20 minutes until everything is tender but not browned; stir occasionally. Add the Drambuie, mix, and heat for a few minutes longer. Add half of the vegetable juice, and let that heat. Remove from the heat, and mix in 3 or 4 large spoonfuls of the ground meat, then turn it all into the bowl of meat, and mix well. Shape into a loaf, and put in a 3-quart loaf pan. Bake in a preheated 325° F. oven for 45 minutes, then pour the rest of the vegetable juice over the loaf, and bake for 45 minutes longer. If you like, you can sprinkle bread crumbs over the top and let them brown before serving. Serve with rice or potatoes.

The vegetable mixture, including the Drambuie, makes a very good sauce for reheating leftover meat. It can also be used as a pan sauce to finish cooking sautéed kidneys and liver.

CALF'S HEAD

Now, you may wonder about the whole head, particularly the calf's head, from which the brains and tongue have come, especially if you are familiar with French specialties like *tête de veau vinaigrette*. Calf's heads are still prepared for sale in several ways, as whole heads or boned, but the likelihood of your finding such an item for sale in a retail market is very small. Heads of all meat animals are carefully examined during the inspection process, and the edible portions of most of them are removed for separate sale. In addition to brains and tongue, there are cheek meat and other bits, which are sold for various ground-meat products. French dishes made with calf's head originally developed out of economic necessity, and only later did they come to have snob appeal. The preparation of a calf's head in the home is neither quick nor easy—really an unpleasant job. Heads of other meat animals are not sold. The meat from pork heads is used to make headcheese, a commercial product flavored with onions, herbs and spices. Headcheese is stuffed into various casings, natural or synthetic, and cooked.

Other organ meats are hearts, kidneys, livers, sweetbreads and tripe. Lungs used to be sold, and lots of Jewish cookbooks have recipes for lung stew, made of beef or calf lung. Today lung is not for sale, even in Kosher markets, because it was discovered that germs were retained in the spongy texture.

HEART

Beef and veal hearts are sold in markets, but other kinds are seldom seen, even though pork and lamb hearts can be cooked and used in the same ways as beef and veal. Heart meat is flavorful and very nutritious, but it is not tender. It must be cooked by a moist method, and braising and pot-roasting will give the best results. Veal heart is tenderer than beef heart, of course, because the animal from which it comes is younger. Keep fresh veal hearts for no longer than 3 days before cooking; frozen, they can be stored for 6 months.

Heart can be cut into dice for stews and used alone or in combination with other meats. Another good idea for heart meat is to grind it with an equal amount of beef chuck for a very nutritious hamburger. Heart can be stuffed for braising also. This can be an economical meat if time is not counted as part of the cost. It will take about 4 hours to cook the average beef heart, 3 hours for smaller ones, and somewhat less time if they are diced or slivered.

A beef heart can weigh up to 5 pounds; a veal heart weighs about 1 pound. Lamb heart weighs 5 to 6 ounces, and pork heart about 8 ounces.

KIDNEY

Kidneys from beef and calf have lobes that give them a somewhat lumpy appearance. Pork and lamb kidneys are smooth. A beef kidney is the largest, of course, and weighs about 1 pound. A veal kidney is far more delicate than beef, paler in color, and it weighs from ⅓ to ½ pound. Veal kidneys are the most popular, although the little lamb kidneys are a favorite with us. Veal kidneys are the only all-purpose kidneys, and they can be prepared by any cooking method. They have the mildest taste of all kidneys; in fact, they are rather sweet in flavor. Pork and lamb kidneys look like giant kidney beans. A pork kidney weighs almost as much as a veal kidney, but it is stronger tasting and is not as good for general use; pork kidneys are often used in ground-meat mixtures, and you can use them in pâté or meat loaf. Lamb kidneys, the quickest to prepare and weighing only 3 ounces, are also very versatile.

Do not buy any kidney that has a disagreeable odor, and after buying kidneys, unwrap them to make sure they are fresh before storing them. You can trim and parboil kidneys at once, to use later, or rewrap them in plastic wrap for a short time before cooking. Although kidneys are not as perishable as brains, they need refrigeration and should be cooked within 2 days of purchase. After cooking, they can be kept for 3 or 4 days. They can also be frozen, but only when they are very fresh; rinse and wrap them with great care in freezer paper. They can be stored in a refrigerator-freezer for 4 to 6 weeks, in a self-contained freezer for 4 months.

Kidneys are covered with a membrane or capsule that is usually removed when they are separated from the carcass. It is simple to remove it, but this is something your butcher should do. Whether the membrane is removed or still in place will have nothing to do with the presence of an odor. Kidneys will naturally release some odor in cooking because their function causes them to contain large amounts of purine. If those you buy are fresh and in good condition, they will not release an objectionable odor during preparation.

Trimming Kidneys

It is best to trim the kidneys just before you cook them. If you find this hard to do, ask your butcher to do it. However, it is not really difficult. For lamb kidneys, cut a circle of ½-inch diameter, and scoop out the hard little center as though you were coring an apple. Do the same even if the kidneys are split. With larger kidneys, veal and beef, cut into the center of the kidney along the fatty line. Then scoop out the hard center from each side, again as if you were coring an apple. You definitely need a sharp knife for this. Remove any extra bits of fat and shreds of membrane.

After trimming, parboil all kidneys before proceeding to any other cooking method. For lamb kidneys, use 1 cup of water with 1 teaspoon salt, and *boil* them for 1 minute. Of course, increase the amounts of water and salt for larger quantities. Boil beef kidneys for 5 minutes, and veal and pork kidneys for 3 minutes.

The primary use of smaller kidneys is in "kidney chops." They are rolled inside the loin, where they are in the carcass, and sliced when the loin chops are cut. Another way to use them is to roll them in a roast. Veal kidneys can be used in a rolled loin or rump, lamb kidneys in a rolled lamb roast, pork kidneys in a rolled loin. Another good way to use lamb kidneys is to sliver them and use them, with seasoning, as a filling inside a boned and rolled rack of lamb. You can probably think of similar uses for a veal kidney.

You can do a lot with the little lamb kidneys. Split them, and sauté in butter and garlic; or split them and broil, basting with seasoned oil. A broiled lamb kidney is a good addition to a mixed grill. They can be slivered to make round slices, like the beef slices for sukiyaki, to be cooked at table.

For an unusual burger, use equal amounts of lamb kidney and fresh pork sausage. Cook the sausage partially, and let it cool; chop the kidney into fine pieces. Mix together, shape into patties, and broil for 6 or 7 minutes on each side; turn them once. These kidneys can be used for stew too.

Veal kidneys must be sliced or diced for cooking since they are too large to be used split. They are good sautéed and then quickly sauced with wine, red, white, sherry or Madeira. They are delicious combined with mushrooms and tiny onions in a quick stew, and they can be braised whole on a bed of vegetables, with lemon slices or anchovy fillets to enhance their flavor. Another good way to cook them is to cut them into large dice and skewer them with small bacon squares; broil or barbecue them outside, basting with seasoned oil; they will cook very quickly—in about 10 minutes. Slices or chunks of lamb or veal kidney can be served in *fritto misto* or in mixtures cooked in boiling stock (Chinese firepot).

Both veal and beef kidneys can be used for inexpensive and nourishing stews, either alone or with other meats. Cut into chunks, they can also be used in soups, according to the recipe for Turkey-Vegetable Soup (p. 165) or Tongue Soup (p. 176) but cooking for less time than specified. To prepare another nice dish with veal kidneys, start by gently poaching them until tender; then grind them and mix with fresh herbs. Add enough of the poaching liquid to make a moist mixture, and spoon it into prebaked tart shells. Sprinkle cheese on top, and heat until the filling is hot and the cheese is melted.

Beef kidneys come from large, mature animals, and consequently they have a more pronounced taste and are less tender than the veal or lamb kidneys. Nevertheless, they can be prepared in most of the ways we have described for the others. They do take a little longer to cook, but not hours; overcooking will toughen them rather than making them tender. A beef kidney from a young animal can be prepared very quickly (see p. 296). If you have a beef kidney that weighs more than 1 pound, assume it came from a larger, and probably older, animal. For such a kidney, braising or stewing is better than sautéing. Beef kidneys are sometimes found frozen in large markets, and they can be a bargain if your family likes them. The steak-and-kidney pie on page 240 can be made with beef kidney, even though we prefer veal or lamb.

LIVER

Liver, like kidney, will have no objectionable odor if it is fresh and in good condition. Calf's liver, the most popular, is odor free; beef liver has a beefy smell; pork liver smells bland, like pork. As you will read in Chapter 22, liver is one of the best sources of iron, vitamin A and riboflavin. If it is properly prepared, it is delicious and digestible.

A whole beef liver weighs 7 to 14 pounds, a calf's liver 2½ to 5 pounds, a lamb liver ¾ to 1½ pounds, and a pork liver ¾ to 1¼ pounds. Lamb liver has a pronounced lamb taste, but it is very tender.

Ideally, your butcher should prepare the liver for you when you buy it. If the butcher does not, however, you should do it as soon as you get home with your purchase, before you store the liver. Remove all cartilage, veins and outer skin; rinse in room-temperature water. Then refrigerate, and cook within 2 days. After cooking, liver can be kept for 3 days, but it is better to purchase and cook only what you will use, because a second heating will dry the liver. Uncooked liver can be kept frozen in a refrigerator freezer for 4 to 6 weeks and in a self-contained freezer for 4 months. However, we do not recommend freezing liver at all, because fresh liver is so much better to eat. As with other organ meats, careful wrapping is essential for freezing.

Liver is ideal for quick stir-frying. Cut it into slivers, and sauté with onions, mushrooms and green-pepper slivers, or choose any vegetable mixture you like. Liver of any kind is good in a mixed grill; for this, broil thick slices just as you would broil a steak. Liver and bacon can be panfried or broiled.

Baked whole calf's liver may be a new idea to you. Here are two ways to prepare it.

BAKED WHOLE CALF'S LIVER   8 to 10 servings

Use a whole calf's liver of about 3 pounds. Remove all membranes. Make a mixture of cracked peppercorns and ground coarse salt, and cover the liver with a thick coating of it. Put the liver in a shallow metal baking pan, and roast in a preheated 400° F. oven for 20 minutes. Then slide the pan under a preheated broiler, and broil for 8 minutes. Turn carefully, to keep the coating intact if possible, and broil for 8 minutes longer. The center of the liver will be rare, the thinner part well done, so the roast can be sliced to serve all tastes. Slice as you would a London broil; each slice should have its flavorful crust in place.

CALF'S LIVER À L'AMIRAL   8 to 10 servings

1 whole calf's liver, about 3 pounds
3 cups dry white wine
1 orange, peeled and sliced
1 sweet Bermuda onion, sliced

1 tablespoon green peppercorns
1 tablespoon coarse salt, ground
1 recipe Pâte Brisée (p. 234)
1 egg mixed with 1 tablespoon water

Trim the liver if necessary, and put it in an earthenware or enamelware vessel that holds it snugly. Pour the wine over it. The liver should be covered; if your vessel is too large, you may need to add more wine. Add orange and onion slices, green peppercorns and salt. Turn the liver over in the pot so that the other ingredients are well distributed over and under it. Cover the pot (use foil if there is no cover), and refrigerate. Let the liver marinate for 12 to 18 hours.

Drain the liver, and roast it, as you would a roast beef, in a preheated 350° F. oven for about 1½ hours. Baste occasionally with some of the marinade. Meanwhile make the pastry, divide it, and roll out each half to a long oval. Remove the baked liver to a platter, and divide it lengthwise into halves. Roll each half in one of the pastry ovals, seal with the egg and water mixture, and turn the pastry over so the seal is on the bottom. If you like, you can decorate the top with scraps of pastry, gluing them on with more of the egg wash. Place the roasts on baking sheets, and return to the oven to bake until the pastry is done, 30 to 40 minutes. You can wrap the whole liver if you prefer, but it is easier to wrap and slice halves. This makes a beautiful presentation.

There are other recipes using livers in the book. You will find them all listed in the Index.

SWEETBREADS

The most adaptable of all organ meats are sweetbreads, the thymus glands of young animals. The most popular are those of veal, and for all practical purposes, they are what you can expect to find for sale in most markets. Young beef sweetbreads are slightly grayish in color, and the membrane is tougher than that of the veal. Lamb sweetbreads are very small and seldom found for sale; you would have to ask your butcher to order them for you, and there is no guarantee your market will have them even then. Veal sweetbreads are generally available, but it is never a mistake to order them in advance to be sure you get just what you want.

Usually you read of a "pair" of sweetbreads; in each animal there are 2 lobes, a heart sweetbread, which is the larger, and a throat sweetbread. This pair is also called a "cluster." The pair in good condition weighs ¾ to 1¼ pounds. Sweetbreads of ¼ to ¾ pound are pieces only; they are smaller, cheaper and less desirable than a whole pair.

Sweetbreads are as perishable as brains. The maximum storage time is 2 days, but it is best to use them or freeze them at once. They can be stored in a self-contained freezer for 6 months.

What to do when you get home with veal sweetbreads? Well, that depends a lot on where you bought the sweetbreads. If your butcher has trimmed them for you, you will not have to soak or parboil (blanch) them, although parboiling is a good first step if you plan to sauté or broil them next. If your sweetbreads still have blood vessels or connective tissues on them, you will do better to soak the sweetbreads in cold water, changing the water if necessary, until the blood is gone. Remove blood vessels, connective tissues and outer skin. Do not remove the delicate inner membrane; it holds the sweetbreads together.

Blanching Sweetbreads

If your recipe dictates blanching next, or if you choose to do it in any case, here is how to proceed. Put the sweetbreads in an enamelware or glass saucepan. Cover with cold water, and add 1 tablespoon of lemon juice or vinegar for each 2 cups water. Bring the sweetbreads *very slowly* to a boil, and let them simmer for 5 to 15 minutes—5 minutes if the next cooking step will be long, up to 15 if it is very quick, like sautéing. The lemon juice or vinegar is for whitening (blanching). Drain, and cover with ice water, or at least very cold water, to stop the cooking.

Many texts, especially French cookery books, advise flattening the blanched sweetbreads under weights. We do not advise it because we think it does nothing for the dish. If you want to, do it as soon as the blanching is finished, and let the sweetbreads stand for 1 hour.

With beef sweetbreads, parboiling is recommended, because they are older and less tender than veal sweetbreads. The membrane on beef breads should be removed because it will be tough.

Beef sweetbreads can be sautéed, and the cooking can be finished in a pan sauce. They can also be braised or cooked in a casserole with vegetables.

Here is an unusual soup made with beef sweetbreads, but you may substitute veal.

GREEN GALLANT SOUP   8 servings

Use a mixture of vegetables, including a lot of greens—leeks, watercress, celery, green beans, spinach, Swiss chard; choose whatever combination you like. If you use spinach, cook it separately because it tends to overpower the soup and lose its color if cooked long enough for the other vegetables to be done. For 1½ quarts of water, use 3 cups of chopped vegetables and ½ tablespoon salt. Cook the vegetables with 1 pair sweetbreads until very tender. Remove sweetbreads, and purée broth and vegetables together; add well-drained cooked spinach at this point if you are using it. Return to the pot, and stir in 1½ cups heavy cream and the sweetbreads, trimmed if necessary and cut into 1-inch cubes or smaller. Slowly reheat to just below boiling.

To make a thicker soup, use 1 carrot and 1 potato, chopped fine, in addition to the other vegetables; or make a *liaison* with 2 egg yolks and part of the cream, let the mixture thicken, stirring all the while, and add the rest of the cream at the end. If you use egg yolks, be sure not to let the mixture boil, or it will curdle.

SWEETBREADS WITH PURÉED FRESH CORN

This is made like the soup, but it is a thicker mixture. Scrape kernels from ears of corn, and poach them with whole sweetbreads, using just enough water to cover and ½ teaspoon salt for each 2 cups water. When both are tender, remove sweetbreads and dice. Purée the corn, using only enough of the broth to keep the mixture from clogging the blender. Reheat the purée with the diced sweetbreads and enough heavy cream to give a thick mixture. Add seasoning to taste, and serve on toast or large *croûtes* of French bread. For 4 servings, use 2 pairs sweetbreads, 6 ears of corn and ½ cup heavy cream.

Another good dish using beef sweetbreads is like a beef Stroganoff. Parboil the sweetbreads for 15 minutes, drain, and let them cool. Then cut into thin slices or slivers, and sauté in butter. Use a skimmer to transfer the slices to a plate, then, in the same butter, sauté sliced onions and mushrooms until tender. Add sour cream and heat; return sweetbreads to mixture, heat and serve. You can flavor the sauce with mustard or horseradish if you like. Garnish with watercress sprigs or sprinkle with paprika. Or use the sauce on page 309, and heat the sautéed slices in it, in the top part of a double boiler over barely simmering water.

Veal sweetbreads can be sautéed in butter with vegetables, to be served in pattie shells or on toast. They are also good broiled. Brush with seasoned melted butter, and cook until golden brown on each side, turning them only once, because they are more fragile than a steak. Sprinkle with chives. Sweetbreads can be creamed or sauced in many ways. They combine successfully with mushrooms, chicken and ham. A veal *blanquette* including sweetbreads would be an elegant dish.

TRIPE

The digestive system of bovines is different from that of humans; it contains more than one stomach. The portions called "rumen" and "reticulum," the first and second stomachs, are prepared as tripe. The rumen gives "plain," or "smooth," tripe; the reticulum gives "honeycomb tripe." These require careful preparation at meat-packing plants to remove the contents and the mucous surface; after the first step is completed, the cleaned paunches are scalded. Tripe is therefore partially cooked when you buy it, but it is called "uncooked" and does need a lot more cooking to become edible.

Tripe must be ordered in advance from most markets. A whole piece weighs about 3 pounds, but it can be bought by the pound.

The famous tripe dishes that have snob appeal today were originally devised, like those calf's-head preparations, because of the need to utilize the least costly parts of meat animals. *Tripes à la mode de Caen* is a stew flavored with apple brandy, baked in a sealed *daube* for hours. A Polish tripe dish is a thick white stew flavored with cheese. For other dishes, simmer the tripe for about 3 hours, then cut it into squares or strips, and finish cooking according to the recipe. Tripe makes excellent

Creole stew—with tomatoes, onions and green peppers—and it is good dipped into a batter and fried in oil. Squares of tripe can be added to oxtail stews for additional protein; the flavor of tripe is so mild that it will not affect the taste of the final dish.

BUTTER-POACHED TRIPE   6 to 8 servings

3 pounds tripe	pinch of dried orégano
¾ pound butter	2 green peppers, trimmed and minced
3 garlic cloves, peeled	1 large onion, peeled and minced
3 tablespoons snipped chives	16 cherry tomatoes, washed and
1 teaspoon salt	stemmed
¼ teaspoon cracked peppercorns	1 cup tomato sauce

Rinse the tripe, and cut it into thin slices like those for beef Stroganoff, about ¼ inch thick. Melt the butter in a heavy pan with a tight-fitting cover. Push the garlic through a press into the butter, and add chives, salt, pepper and orégano. Mix well into butter, then stir in tripe pieces until they are well coated. Cover the pan and butter-poach over low heat for 1½ hours. Remove cover, and add minced green peppers and onion, whole cherry tomatoes and tomato sauce. Stir gently; ingredients should be well mixed, but tomatoes and tripe pieces should remain whole. Cover again, and continue to cook slowly for 2½ hours. Serve over fine noodles.

TRIPE STEW WITH BISCUIT DUMPLINGS   6 to 8 servings

3 pounds tripe	1 teaspoon peppercorns
1 bottle dry white wine (Bordeaux or	1 teaspoon salt
Loire)	3 cups strong chicken stock
2 carrots	4½ tablespoons cornstarch, or 6
2 green peppers	tablespoons all-purpose flour
1 large onion	3 cups prepared biscuit dough
3 large celery ribs	

Rinse the tripe, and cut it into 2- to 3-inch squares. Put the squares in a large earthenware or enamelware vessel, and add wine. Trim or peel vegetables, and cut them into slivers. Add slivers, salt and pepper to the wine, mix, cover, and marinate in refrigerator for 24 hours. Then pour everything into a 3-quart, deep baking dish or casserole, cover tightly, and bake in a preheated 250° F. oven for 2½ hours.

While the tripe is baking, prepare the chicken-stock mixture. The chicken stock should be strong, with good flavor; if it is not, enrich it with 3 bouillon cubes or 3 teaspoons soup granules. Mix the cornstarch or flour with part of the cold stock; slowly heat the rest, and stir in the starch mixture. Continue stirring over low heat until the stock is quite thick. Pour stock over the tripe, mix, cover again, and bake for 2 hours longer.

Increase the oven heat to 400° F., and make the biscuit dough, using your favorite recipe or a prepared mix. Open the baking dish, and drop round balls of the dough on top; make 12 or more, enough to fit them all in a single layer on top of the stew. Cover the pot, and cook for 10 minutes. Uncover, and let the dumplings become golden brown. With a slotted spoon or 2 soup spoons, turn the dumplings over, and cook until they are golden brown on the other side.

If your children have never eaten tripe, you can use this recipe as an introduction with one small change: When you add the chicken stock, add 1 to 2 cups diced boned chicken breast or diced boned veal cut from the shoulder. Both chicken and veal have a more pronounced taste than tripe, and they will add more protein to the dish as well.

The dumpling recipe can be varied by adding minced parsley or other herbs.

The most famous American tripe dish is Philadelphia pepper-pot soup. This soup is alleged by many writers to have been invented for General George Washington during the winter at Valley Forge, when all other provender was exhausted, but we have yet to find a reference to it by any of Washington's contemporaries. A dish called "pepperpot" was recorded as early as 1704; it was a West Indian stew made of meat or dried fish, vegetables, young green okra pods, chilies and cassareep. Cassareep is a flavoring agent made from the juices of the bitter cassava, the same plant from which we get manioc and tapioca; obviously pepperpot was a hot dish! A dish called pepperpot is also recorded in Surinam in Guiana, where it was made in a calabash. Our guess is that the Valley Forge soup, or the Pennsylvania Dutch soup, whichever it was, was modeled on the peppery West Indian stew and made with tripe because that is what was left when the rest of the meat had been used. The American soup is always called by its whole name, "Philadelphia pepper-pot soup," which seems to indicate that other dishes named pepperpot were well known. For more about it, see page 130.

OXTAILS

Maybe in Tudor days they actually used the tails of oxen, but today "oxtail" refers to the tail of a beef animal. Buy fresh oxtails, and use them fresh. They should have a rosy appearance, they should not be aged, and they should have a sweet taste. Small tails can weigh from ¾ to 1½ pounds, and large ones from 1½ to 2 pounds. Your butcher should cut or crack them through the cartilage at the joints. Have all the exterior fat removed. Uncooked oxtails can be kept for 3 days before using; if you are obliged to freeze them, they will keep for 2 months.

Oxtails can be used for soup stock, and they can be braised. If you serve the actual pieces of tail, remember that they will not make fancy party fare; they provide an informal and hearty meal. Each vertebra contains small holes filled with marrow, and to get all the nutrients from the tails, the diner should suck out this marrow. In addition, little pieces of cartilage, like miniature kneecaps, make tails messy to eat. All oxtails require long, slow cooking. Here is an unusual double recipe that takes a long time, but gives delicious results.

TAILS WITH FIRE   6 servings

3 oxtails, about 6 pounds altogether	2 garlic cloves
8 ounces dried green split peas	½ cup olive oil
1 large bay leaf	1 tablespoon (scant) chili powder
½ teaspoon ground peppercorns	½ cup pitted green olives, chopped
1 green pepper	1 cup tomato sauce
1 large onion	1 tablespoon Cognac

Have the oxtails trimmed well and cut apart at the joints. Put them in a large pot, and cover with water. Add peas, bay leaf and peppercorns. Bring to a boil, then reduce to a simmer, and cook for 2 hours. Use a skimmer to transfer the oxtail pieces to a platter. The soup can be cooked longer to concentrate the flavors. It can be served as is or puréed; remove the bay leaf before puréeing. Adjust seasoning to taste.

Trim green pepper, removing seeds and membranes; peel onion and garlic; chop them all. Heat the oil in a large, heavy sauté pan with a tight-fitting cover. Add chopped vegetables, and sauté until almost tender. Add oxtails, chili powder, olives and tomato sauce. Stir to mix, then cover, reduce heat, and let everything simmer for 1½ hours. Check now and then to be sure the liquid has not evaporated; you can add a little water or more tomato sauce if the pan is getting dry. At the end, uncover, stir, and flame with the Cognac. Serve the flamed tails as a first course on white rice; at the same time, serve the soup accompanied with garlic croutons. The soup will be mild in flavor, but the tails will be fiery! The degree of hotness will depend on the chili powder—each brand is different; you can use more or less than specified if you like. Also, you can use more Cognac for flaming if you wish.

CALF'S FEET

Of all odds and ends, calf's feet are the most useful to the serious cook, because they are full of gelatin, which enriches stocks and sauces and can provide the basis for aspic dishes. Do not expect to find calf's feet on the counter at your market; you will have to order them. Have your butcher split them lengthwise, leaving the skin on. If they are clean and well prepared, just rinse them; if not, you may have to scrub them or blanch them in boiling water. Since it takes long slow cooking to release the collagen, which forms gelatin, use calf's feet in stock, soup or other long-cooking dishes like tripe stew.

CALF'S - FOOT JELLY

Calf's-foot jelly, the standard food for invalids 50 years ago, is a good dish for anyone who needs an easily digested nutritious dish that is easy to swallow. To make it, cut each half foot in half again, crosswise, and put the feet in a large stockpot with about 3 cups water for each pound of feet. Add ½ garlic clove, ½ onion, ¼ teaspoon salt and 2 peppercorns for each 3 cups of water. Bring to a boil, then simmer for 4 to 6 hours, until the bones are falling out. Strain the broth into another pot. As soon as the bones are cool enough to handle, separate the meat and discard the bones, gristle and skin. Taste the broth before jelling, and adjust the seasoning. You can make a clear jelly, or jell the meat with the broth, or purée broth and meat to make an opaque jelly.

If you dice the meat and add hard-cooked eggs, you will have the classic jellied dish called *Sulz*, an excellent first course. Cut into squares to serve.

To vary this dish, add other meats to the broth, and make a patterned jelly. Tongue, boned chicken, corned beef, all sliced, are good, and even tuna or cooked fruits can be added—not all in the same dish, of course.

PIG'S FEET, TAILS AND EARS

Pig's feet are available fresh, pickled and smoked. Pickled pig's feet are a popular item for hearty country menus, served with sauerkraut and such. Smoked feet are used most often for flavoring other mixtures, like pea soup. Fresh feet can be used as calf's feet are, to provide gelatin and flavor for long-cooking stews and stocks. To prepare them, have them split lengthwise, as you would calf's feet, and scrub. You can make a jelly with pig's feet too; it takes 4 to 5 hours for them to release their gelatin; add salt toward the end of the cooking. Season the jelly, and use it as a basting sauce for such other pork dishes as loin roasts; basting will prevent the dryness that is often a problem with fresh pork. Because of the gelatin, the liquid will cling to the meat. To make it even more flavorful, add soy sauce to taste and a few tablespoons of any bottled sparerib sauce; this idea is especially good for barbecued pork—it will add flavor and give a glossy coating.

You can chop the meat of cooked pig's feet and mix it with the jelly to get a dish called "Souse." Feet can also be combined with other pork to make jellied headcheese.

You can pickle the feet yourself after they have been cooked until soft. Put them in a stone crock, and cover with spiced vinegar or your favorite pickling solution. It will take several days to pickle them. Pickled or plain cooked feet can be dipped into batter and fried.

A famous French *hors-d'oeuvre* made with unsplit feet is *pieds de porc Sainte-Menehould*, named for a town near Verdun. Cook the feet with flavoring vegetables and herbs and simmer for about 4 hours. Drain, cool, then gently remove the skin. Roll the feet in butter and a thick coating of bread crumbs. Arrange them on a flameproof baking dish, and bake in a preheated 325° F. oven for 25 minutes. Then put them under the broiler, and let them become golden brown on all sides and very hot. Serve with a flavorful sauce; sauce tartare is traditional, but pig's feet are equally good with tomato-flavored mixtures or sauces made with onion or green herbs.

Tails and ears have not absolutely disappeared from the retail market, but they are scarce in most places. Their chief use is to provide gelatin, but sometimes these are pickled.

RAGOUT OF PIGS' EARS

Ears were used for a stew called a "ragoo" in the eighteenth century. If you would like to try this, here is a modern version of the recipe: Boil 12 ears in 2 cups of wine and 2 cups of water until tender. Cut into pieces, roll in ¼ pound butter, then mix in 1 cup or more of brown gravy, 2 tablespoons minced shallots, 2 anchovy fillets, 2 tablespoons prepared mustard and ½ lemon with rind cut into thin slices. Gently stew until all the flavors are blended and the sauce is thick. Season with salt and grated nutmeg to taste.

POULTRY ORGAN MEATS

Poultry also has organ meats, but only the heart, liver and gizzard are sold. These, with the neck, are packed inside any domestic bird you buy, including commercially raised game birds. In addition, you can buy chicken and turkey hearts, gizzards and livers separately. Those of duck and goose can be specially ordered from some shops. These innards of poultry are called "giblets."

Gizzards

The gizzard is the bird's substitute for a stomach; it is actually a thickened portion of the alimentary canal and is used to grind the seeds and grains that form a large part of a bird's diet. It is a rather tough muscle, so it is usually ground or chopped, as is the heart. However, there are some ways to use gizzards whole. Peel off the tough outer membrane, and you will have two little pieces of meat. Simmer them in seasoned water for about 1 hour. After that they can be marinated to be served stuffed in a mushroom or wrapped with a piece of bacon as cocktail party food, or they can be skewered with other ingredients for the barbecue.

Chopped hearts and gizzards are used in the classic giblet gravy and in other sauces; and they are especially suitable for pasta sauces that are cooked for a long time. Gizzards and hearts can be ground and mixed with beef—equal amounts or more beef—to make a nutritious and flavorful hamburger. Ground giblets can be used to make very good dumplings for garnishing soups or stews; poach them until tender, then grind once; sauté, and stir into the dumpling mixture.

Poultry Livers

Chicken and other poultry livers are delicacies that can be used in appetizers, main courses, salads, sauces and gravies. Although they can be frozen before or after you buy them, they are best when purchased and used fresh. Livers are the most perishable of the giblets, but all of them should be used within 3 days. If you freeze them whole, they can be stored for 4 months; if they are chopped or ground before freezing, use them within 6 weeks.

For chopped liver or pâté, see page 145. Other liver preparations include sautéing or poaching and mashing for sandwich filling or canapé spread; poaching, chilling and slicing for salad with sliced tomatoes and chives; sautéing them in butter and finishing with a wine pan sauce; braising with vegetables. A delicious meat pattie can be made by grinding equal parts of chicken livers and beef sirloin together once, seasoning, and broiling or panfrying. Add minced onion and parsley if you like.

Turkey livers can be added to dumplings or used in any of the ways suggested for chicken livers.

Here is a very tasty main course of chicken giblets.

POTTED GIBLETS AND LIVERS   6 servings

2 pounds chicken gizzards and hearts, ground
2 eggs, beaten
¼ cup light cream
¼ cup unseasoned fine dry bread crumbs
¼ teaspoon salt
10 peppercorns, ground through a pepper mill
3 tablespoons oil
½ teaspoon dry mustard
½ teaspoon soy sauce
⅛ teaspoon dried basil
8 whole chicken livers, halved
1 cup fresh tomato sauce, or 1 can (8 ounces)

Mix ground giblets with eggs, cream, bread crumbs, salt and pepper; stir or beat until thoroughly blended and smooth. Refrigerate. Spoon the oil into a skillet, and add mustard, soy sauce and basil; heat until very hot, stirring all the while to mix seasonings with oil. Sauté chicken livers in oil for 2 minutes. Transfer livers to a plate, and let cool. Allow the oil to cool slightly, then add the tomato sauce. Heat and mix over low heat for 2 minutes, then set aside to use later. Preheat oven to 300° F.

Make 16 small balls of the giblet mixture, about as big as golf balls. Make a hole in each ball, and insert one of the liver pieces; reshape the ball to enclose the liver completely. Put the stuffed balls in a baking pan, and cover them with the sauce. Bake for 40 minutes without turning them.

Instead of ending this chapter with the part that went over the fence last, we will conclude with necks—chicken and turkey. They can be cooked with the giblets to make stock for gravy, or they can be stewed to make fricassee. There is quite a bit of meat on a turkey neck. An old-world dish, *helzel*, or stuffed neck, gave us the idea for this dish for children. Use either chicken or turkey necks; carefully pull off the skin and set it aside. Mash a mixture of cooked vegetables, season them, mix with butter, and add partly cooked cornmeal or any other cereal grain; use about 1 tablespoon cornmeal to ½ cup mashed vegetables. Stuff the mixture loosely into the neck skin, and sew closed at both ends. Drop into a stew pot, or add to pot roast, and cook for a maximum of 1½ hours. The filling will expand somewhat. Serve slices of this to youngsters who think they do not like vegetables, and watch them change their minds.

Here are some lunch and dinner menus illustrating the use of odds and ends at different times of the year.

FALL LUNCHEON

Broiled lamb kidneys
Scalloped potatoes
Tomato salad

WINTER LUNCHEON

Butter-Poached Tripe (see p. 185)
Fine noodles
Spinach with nutmeg

SPRING LUNCHEON

Potted Giblets and Livers (see p. 190)
Fresh asparagus on toast

SUMMER LUNCHEON

Sweetbreads with Puréed Fresh Corn (see p. 184)
Croûtes of French bread
Boston lettuce salad with slivered fresh red peppers

FALL DINNER

Baked Whole Calf's Liver (see p. 181)
White rice
Brown mushroom sauce
Baked tomato halves with herbs
Escarole salad

WINTER DINNER

Tongue and Pork Meat Loaf (see p. 177)
Baked potatoes
Broccoli polonaise
Chicory with orange slices and onion rings

SPRING DINNER

Brains à la Barbegal (see p. 174)
Roast chicken
Château potatoes
Green peas à la française

SUMMER DINNER

Sliced tomatoes with lemon and herb dressing
Sautéed veal kidneys with Madeira sauce
Rice timbales
Steamed whole tiny zucchini

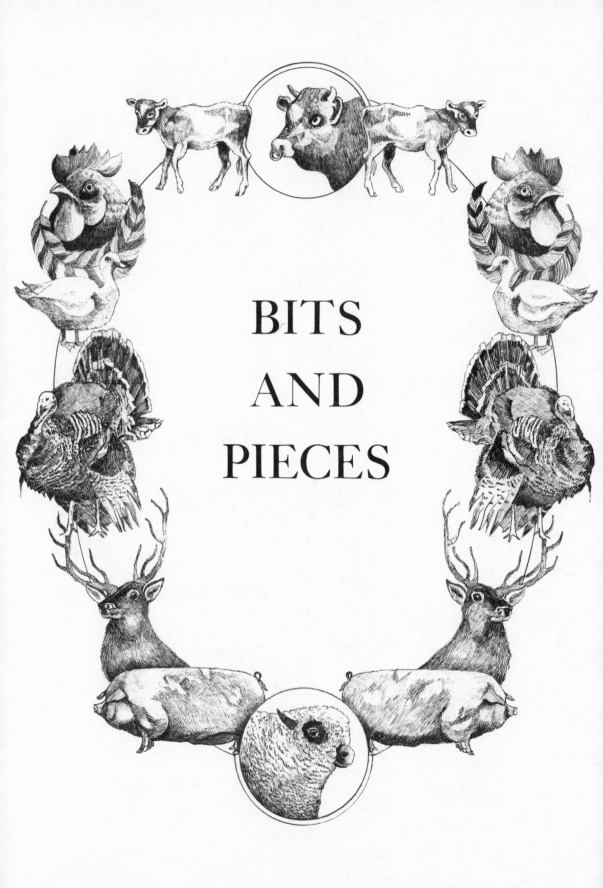

BITS

AND

PIECES

Chapter 12

Even though you think you might enjoy a steady diet of sirloin steaks, roast prime ribs, veal scallops or chicken breasts, you probably cannot, simply because there is a limited number of these very tender cuts in the animal. When, for reasons of economy or gastronomic variety, you turn to some of the less-tender cuts, you will discover that they can be delicious; with careful cooking, such a cut can result in a dish just as good as one made with a higher-priced cut. Very good dishes can also be made with meats cut into small pieces, and with ground or chopped meats. Today, ground or chopped beef, often called "hamburger," is one of the most popular meats in the United States. It is extremely useful because of its versatility: It can be cooked by itself or mixed with other ingredients; it can be used in sauces, in appetizers, in sandwiches. However, ground beef is just the tip of the iceberg as far as ground meat is concerned; there are so many other kinds and so many possible preparations. We hope to give you new ideas about these bits and pieces.

GROUND BEEF

To begin with, the prepackaged ground beef you find in your market is subject to federal regulations, as all meat is. The meat used must come from the sides, hindquarters, or wholesale cuts of recently slaughtered beef carcasses that have been properly chilled. The parts used should be boned within 24 hours of being selected for this use, and should be ground within 4 hours of boning. Various kinds of beef are combined, to mix those that are more flavorful with those that are less so, and to mix lean and fatty parts. After this mixing step, the beef is ground twice. The fat content of the ground meat is analyzed, to make sure it is below 30%. Of course, the meat should be carefully packaged under sanitary conditions and kept properly refrigerated at all times.

Large markets may buy such sizable quantities of beef that they will grind their own hamburger. Reputable markets will follow the federal regulations and present only good meat correctly labeled and packed. However, we must admit that there are markets that do not follow these regulations to a T. Some markets grind scraps left over from butchering various retail cuts; while such meat might be perfectly sanitary, it may not have the right balance of fat and lean, or it may lack good flavor. You must be able to trust your butcher or market, for you have no way of knowing if the meat was freshly ground or properly refrigerated. "Freshly ground" is really important because the many surfaces of ground meat offer far more possibilities for bacterial action than do solid pieces of meat. Some markets indicate on the package that the meat has been "ground fresh daily"; others may date the package. A shop with large turnover is less likely to have ground meat left over; it may even be necessary for them to grind several times a day.

The change in labeling that began to come into use across the United States after the adoption of uniform retail meat identity standards has been significant for the American consumer. Under the new system, the name "hamburger" will not be used; instead, all ground beef will be called "ground beef." While the commercial "hamburger" of the past was made entirely of beef, the new labeling will be more specific about the contents. The difference between one kind of ground beef and another, and the consequent price difference, will be based on the lean-to-fat ratio, but no ground beef will be allowed to be more than 30% fat. To protect the shopper, various devices for determination of fat content will be used by the retailer and the inspection agency.

Some shops and supermarkets have made a practice of labeling packages with the specific cut used—"ground chuck," "ground sirloin," "ground round"—and some markets have used such terms as "diet lean." They may still do this under the new system, but they must also specify the percentage of lean meat in the mixture. This will give the consumer a much better chance to purchase what he really wants. However, even "diet lean" might be fattier than you would like, and any one specific cut might fail to provide your ideal flavor. As you may have guessed, we have been leading up to the suggestion that you buy your ground meat before it is ground. Then you can have exactly what you want for the purpose you have in mind and the cooking method you plan to use.

Steak Tartare

Steak tartare is made of uncooked ground meat. For this dish, buy round steak or sirloin—not top sirloin—depending on your budget, and have it ground four or five times. If you have a food grinder, you can do it at home; if you have a proper chopping block and a good chef's knife, you can chop it. Steak tartare should be in *very fine* bits and should be eaten as soon as possible after grinding or chopping.

The traditional way to serve steak tartare is to make a mound of the raw meat, form a depression in the center, and drop in a raw egg yolk. Surround the meat with whatever garnish suits you; minced raw onion, anchovy fillets, capers and lots of chopped fresh parsley are customary. If you like, add horseradish, mustard or any table sauce: Worcestershire, H. P. Sauce, etc. Mix everything together, and eat on thin slices of good bread, rye or whole wheat, plain or toasted. For a luncheon, steak tartare makes an excellent main dish. Small portions are good appetizers, and you can eat it even for breakfast if you feel like having raw meat at that hour.

We have developed our own version of steak tartare. For this, bake a large potato for each person. When they are done, split them lengthwise and scoop out the insides, leaving a shell about ⅜ inch thick; use the scooped-out potato for something else. Oil the potato shells, and bake for a few minutes longer, until crisp. When they are cool, fill them with steak tartare; you will need 1½ to 2 pounds for 6 servings. Put ½ tablespoon black caviar on top of each potato half, and sprinkle with chopped chives.

Here is a variation: Instead of caviar and chives, use anchovy butter. Chop flat anchovy fillets, and melt them in butter over very low heat. Put 1 teaspoon of the anchovy butter on each potato half, and sprinkle fresh parsley on top.

You might like to know one version of the origin of steak tartare. Tatary was the name given to a huge area between the Dnieper River, in European U.S.S.R., and the Chinese coast on the Sea of Japan. The boundaries were vague because Tatary was inhabited mostly by nomadic people. The story goes that when the Tatars engaged in wars against more settled communities, they would slaughter the village cows. A horseman would put a chunk of the cow under his saddle and ride off on his next marauding jaunt. By the end of the day, the meat would have become minced under the saddle, and it was then eaten raw.

And what could have been the origin of the hamburger? There is an old story about a man who had heard of hamburger steak for so long that he finally went to Hamburg to try it. But when he asked for hamburger steak, the waiters all looked blank. He said, "Very well then, just give me steak!" and what do you think they brought him? Hamburger steak, of course.

Actually, the hamburger is a descendant of steak tartare. The taste for ground or chopped raw meat was spread by Tatary's nomadic horsemen throughout the area known today as Russia. Before World War I, Hamburg was the second largest city in the German empire and the largest seaport on the European continent. Because Hamburg was part of the Hanseatic League, a sort of commercial union founded in the thirteenth century, the city had special trading privileges in various Russian ports. The German seamen who traveled to Russia brought home a taste for minced beef. It was only centuries later that anybody thought of cooking it.

Hamburgers

If you plan to cook your ground meat, the type of meat you should use will depend on the cooking method. For hamburgers that are to be broiled, use a mixture of equal amounts of chuck and sirloin. For 2 pounds of meat, add ½ cup of milk, and include whatever seasonings you like.

For hamburgers that are to be panfried, use ground top sirloin; it is flavorful and lean yet juicy. Since sirloin is only about 2% fat, you can add a little more, to help keep the meat moist. Use steak fat, and grind it with the meat. Shape the meat into flattened patties ½ to ⅜ inch thick. Without adding any fat or oil, heat the pan until very hot, and sprinkle it with salt and cracked peppercorns. When the little pieces of pepper start to bounce up and down, put in the patties. For patties that are rare in the middle, cook for 60 seconds on each side. For well-done patties, cook longer, but do not let them dry out. Because the meat of round steak is dry, never use it for panfried hamburgers.

Here is a good dish made with hamburger, a cooked version of the steak tartare in potatoes. Scrub large Idaho potatoes, bake them, halve them lengthwise, and scoop out the potato, leaving a shell ½ inch thick. Spread butter inside each shell, about 1 pat per potato. Then stuff the halves with seasoned hamburger, put the halves together again, and wrap in foil. Bake in a preheated 350° F. oven for 45 to 55 minutes.

Another good hamburger meat is ground chuck alone. Butcher's, or hanging, tenderloin, alone or mixed with chuck, is another good choice. For barbecuing hamburgers, see Chapter 16.

Ground beef can be stretched by adding rolled oats, cracked wheat, or egg and cracker or bread crumbs, and it can be flavored with grated or minced onion, green pepper, garlic, parsley or other herbs, or combinations of these. If you do add bread or cracker crumbs, you will need to add extra liquid—water, milk, sour cream—or a moist vegetable like onion.

MEATBALLS

The mixture you use for meatballs should be different from the one you prepare for hamburgers. Usually a meatball includes beef and another meat. For the beef part, use chuck. The fat in chuck helps bind the meatballs and any sauce cooked or served with them, and the flavor enhances the sauce.

Our discussion has not exhausted the possibilities of using ground beef, but while we are talking about meatballs, let's consider meatballs made of other meats.

In Scandinavia, veal is popular for meatballs. If you plan to use it, remember to add some oil to the mixture to keep it from drying; start with 2 tablespoons to 1 pound of meat, and adjust to your taste if you think more is needed. Because it is sinewy, veal must be ground several times. The best cuts to use are shoulder, neck and shank; they are flavorful and—a valid consideration for the shopper—any other cut would too expensive to use this way.

Veal balls can be potted and cooked with a sauce that includes sour cream. If you add minced fresh or dry dill, you will have a truly Scandinavian taste.

Grinding Pork

Swedish cooks also use pork, and there are beef and pork meatballs in Danish cookery. Meatballs that include pork do require care in preparation. Because of the grinding, there are many surfaces subject to spoilage. If a mixture containing pork is not properly cooked, the dish could be spoiled. A butcher who grinds pork usually keeps a separate machine for it. If you grind the mixture at home, be sure to scrub and scald your grinder, and be careful to refrigerate pork before and after grinding. A good meatball mixture is half beef and half pork. The pork is best cut from the shoulder, and for this mixture the beef should be sirloin or top round; these drier, less fatty cuts will compensate for the abundance of fat in the pork.

Meatballs are an integral ingredient in many Italian pasta dishes, especially in those tomato-flavored sauces from the southern end of the peninsula. The mixture for these can be all beef, half beef and half pork, or a mixture of beef, veal and pork, either equal amounts of each or half beef. For Italian meatballs, the meats should be ground several times to make a very smooth mixture. They are usually seasoned and often contain fresh parsley and some garlic or onion. Other ingredients vary according to the particular recipe. The mixture is shaped into round balls. If the meatballs are to be served by themselves or in a sauce, they should be about 2 inches in diameter before cooking; if cooked in a sauce, they will swell a little. For meatballs to be served as part of a sauce or in a dish like lasagna, make them smaller, no wider than an inch. Several delicious traditional soups are enriched by the addition of very tiny meatballs, and you can use this idea to add nutrition to many other soups. If you plan to cook meatballs in a soup, be sure to add an egg to the mixture to bind it well; otherwise, the meatballs may tend to crumble during cooking. Any vegetable soup—either a mixture like a minestrone or a simple soup like escarole soup—tastes better with the addition of little meatballs. They are excellent in clear soups too (see p. 129).

Sausage meatballs, shaped from bulk sausage, are another possibility. Of course, bulk sausage can be shaped into flattened patties too. Both are good for breakfast (see p. 116) and in sauces and baked dishes as well. You can even mix some sausage with other meats. Use 25% sausage with either beef or veal to perk up the flavor.

Potted Meatballs

Another good combination for potted meatballs is equal amounts of leftover cooked smoked ham and fresh veal ground together. You will not need to season this because the ham is well flavored. Add an egg to bind the mixture, and brown the balls on all sides in oil. Then transfer them to a casserole that will just hold them, add some stock—beef, veal, chicken or a mixture—and bake them in a preheated 350° F. oven for about 45 minutes.

Some classic, world-famous dishes are nothing more than meatballs or patties. Hamburger steak is the perfect example. Others are *fricadelles de veau*, which are simply veal patties; *frikadeller*, which are Danish meatballs, the mixture we described on page 198; *albóndigas*, meatballs made in the Spanish-speaking countries of South America; *köttbullar*, Swedish meatballs; lion's head, a large Chinese pork ball made of fresh pork and Chinese cabbage, a simple recipe but absolutely delicious; and *Königsberger Klops*, meatballs as they were made in Königsberg, formerly the chief city of East Prussia, now part of the U.S.S.R. These last are made of a mixture very like a basic meat loaf with the addition of minced anchovies, and served in a sauce flavored with anchovies and capers. With all those possibilities, can you be satisfied with a plain old hamburger?

Although lamb is often barbecued, lamb meatballs and patties can also be broiled. The shoulder is the best cut to use, because the proportion of lean to fat in the shoulder is just right.

Another delicious meat pattie can be made from a mixture of chicken and veal ground together. The resulting delicately flavored pattie should be mildly seasoned so as not to overpower its natural taste. Use white meat of chicken, or a mixture of white and dark, and veal cut from the shoulder (remember to grind the veal several times). Sauté these gently in a mixture of oil and butter.

If you belong to a hunting family, you will want to know what to do with small chunks of game left over after cutting the animal into the larger sections. Venison, bear and elk can be used for meatballs. Remember that game animals generally have lean meat, so you will have to add some oil to the mixture. If you have fattier game—bear can be fatty—grind a little of the fat with the meat.

For grinding, you may think it would save a lot of trouble to buy fat meat to begin with, but do not be tempted to do this. Buy lean meat—it is better for you— and add a little oil if necessary. Old cookbooks may advise grinding beef suet into hamburger or meatball mixtures. But today, because of growing concern for weight maintenance and serum cholesterol levels, the addition of suet is not recommended. In fact, commercial ground beef with the highest legally acceptable ratio of fat to lean is too fat for anyone with a dietary problem, and it is not economic, because the fat extracted in cooking is discarded, leaving you with only about 75% of your original purchase.

MEAT LOAF

Another familiar use for ground meat is in meat loaf. This dish, often made the subject of jokes, is delicious if well made. You cannot make a good meat loaf from leftovers; use fresh meat, and, just as with meat patties, it is best to get the right cut for your particular purpose. We emphasize that refrigeration of ground meats is very important, and that your grinding equipment must be scrupulously clean.

There are endless combinations for meat loaf. You can make a loaf of just one kind of meat, or you can combine beef and veal, beef and lamb, beef and veal and pork. Choose a mixture your family likes best.

Beef: The juiciest and fattiest beef comes from the forequarter, the chuck. Next best for juiciness and fat is the round. The best cut in our opinion is the sirloin; it has less fat than the other two cuts but even more juicy flavor. Use any one of these cuts for meat loaf.

Veal: Use shanks or neck, and be sure to grind veal three times because of the sinews.

Lamb: Use the shoulder.

Fresh pork: Use the shank end of the ham or the blade portion or pork chops. As you have already read on page 91, there is no need to worry about using fresh pork in these mixtures. If your meat loaf is properly cooked, it will be much hotter than the degree necessary to destroy the parasites of trichina.

Cured pork: The meat of most smoked pork is juicy because it has been pumped full of moisture. It thus adds not only flavor but also moisture to mixtures. However, drier cured pork products—prosciutto, for instance—and fattier products—bacon—can also be used for flavor in various mixtures. Diced Canadian bacon can be a good addition too.

Some good combinations: ⅔ beef (chuck, sirloin or top round) and ⅓ veal (shanks or neck); ⅓ beef, ⅓ veal and ⅓ pork; ½ beef, ¼ veal, ¼ pork or lamb. Have the meats mixed in grinding or hand knead them to blend. If the meats are juicy to begin with, they will not lose their juiciness; nevertheless do not handle the mixture too much. When you are through it will look pasty, but it will cook well.

BASIC MEAT LOAF   8 servings, with leftovers

3 pounds meat, ground	2 eggs
1 whole onion, peeled	½ cup half-and-half
¼ head of garlic, separated into cloves and peeled	½ tablespoon salt
	10 peppercorns, cracked

Put the meat into a large bowl; if it has not been mixed in grinding, knead it to mix. Grate onion and garlic over the meat, or put garlic through a press if you prefer. Add the raw eggs, half-and-half, salt and pepper; then mix all together, stirring with a wooden spatula or kneading by hand. Shape into a loaf and put in a loaf pan or a shallow baking dish. Bake in a preheated 325° F. oven for 1 hour. The loaf is self-basting so you do not need to open the oven to do it.

Red wine is a good addition to the mixture if you like it. You can substitute minced fresh parsley for the garlic. You can also vary the flavor with other herbs, seasonings and vegetables. You can even shape this into individual loaves if you like; bake them for about 45 minutes. The mixture can be patted into a round loaf, like a giant pattie, to be baked in a pie pan, or it can be baked in a ring mold or a pan of any shape. You may need to adjust the time by a few minutes for any of these variations.

For a veal loaf, which can be very delicate and different, use meat from the shoulder. The same portion is good for a lamb loaf. It is a good thing to remember that when you choose any meat for grinding you should choose a juicier cut because it will have better consistency when ground.

LAMB LOAF WITH MINT JELLY

Here is a trick with lamb that will give you a delicious taste as well as surprise your family: shape half of the meat into a flattened loaf, then spread it almost to the edge with a layer of mint jelly; add the rest of the meat. Be sure the meat is sealed all around because you do not want the jelly to ooze out in cooking; it should be a delicious surprise when the loaf is sliced.

Liver

Liver is not usually used for meat loaves, even though it is so often used for pâté (see Chapter 9). The reasons are three: the consistency is poor when used raw—it almost liquefies in grinding; the taste is so pronounced that it may overwhelm the taste of any other meat mixed with it; it cooks so quickly that it will be completely done before the rest of the ingredients are finished. A way to solve these problems may be a boon to you if there is someone in your house who cannot stand liver plain and who may need it for nutritional reasons.

To solve the first problem, poach the liver in water or stock for about 2 minutes, then let it cool enough to handle and remove the membrane and any veins or hard bits. It will be easy to grind but the texture of the partly cooked meat is rather dry and crumbly so you have to mix it with just the right other ingredients. As for the flavor, well, you just need to overwhelm the liver by using sausage, or onions, or tomato, or crumbled cooked bacon in the mixture. If you do not use sausage or bacon, add some oil to overcome the dryness. Also be sure to add eggs to help the mixture stick together. As for its being cooked quickly, yes it will be very well done when the loaf is finished, so if you like your liver sautéed briefly and still juicy, do not try this. This is a suggestion for that family which despises liver. Use beef or calf's liver; frozen liver, which is sometimes less expensive, can be used for this.

LIVER AND SAUSAGE LOAF

1 cup uncooked white or brown rice	½ pound fresh sausage meat
1 teaspoon salt	2 eggs
1 pound liver	1 cup chopped and drained canned
½ to 1 cup beef stock or water	tomatoes
1 onion, peeled	¼ cup chopped parsley, or more
1 green pepper, trimmed of seeds and membranes	

Cook the rice in 3 cups water with 1 teaspoon salt (add a dash of lemon juice and 1 teaspoon oil if you like) until almost done but still somewhat chewy. There should be only a little water left; drain it off, and set the rice aside. Poach the liver in enough water or stock to cover for 2 minutes, then cool, and remove membranes and veins. Grind liver, onion and green pepper together, then mix with the sausage. Add the rice, eggs, tomatoes and parsley (you can use more parsley if you like). Mix everything together, and put it into a loaf pan or 2-quart casserole. A standard bread pan (9 by 5 by 3 inches) will be nearly filled to the brim. Smooth the top. Bake in a preheated 350° F. oven for about 1 hour. When this loaf is hot, it is somewhat crumbly and hard to serve in perfect slices, so do not try to turn it out whole, but use a serving spoon or pie server to transfer slices to plates. It can be sliced easily when cold.

Poultry makes good loaves—at least chicken and turkey do. We do not recommend using duck or goose, because there is so little meat on the carcasses. For a turkey loaf, use the meat from a whole bird, add some oil and season well.

BEEF AND CHICKEN LOAF WITH RED CABBAGE   6 servings

1 pound beef chuck
1 pound beef sirloin
¼ pound veal shoulder
¾ pound raw chicken breast, skin and
    bones removed
¾ pound mushrooms, peeled and sliced
10 slices of bacon, cooked crisp and
    pulverized

½ cup crumbled unsalted crackers
1 cup milk
1 egg
1 teaspoon dehydrated onion
4 pinches of finely ground peppercorns
¾ teaspoon salt
¼ teaspoon dried thyme

Have chuck, sirloin and veal ground together 3 times. Cut the chicken into cubes. Preheat oven to 350° F. Put ground meats in a large bowl, and add all the other ingredients. Mix thoroughly but gently, then pat into a loaf, and put the loaf in a greased large loaf pan. Bake for 1 hour.

Transfer the loaf to a serving platter, and spoon red cabbage (recipe follows) over the top. Slice the loaf to serve. Or, if you prefer, serve the meat loaf plain and the cabbage separately as a vegetable dish.

RED CABBAGE WITH ORANGE

1 orange
1 small red cabbage, shredded
1 medium-sized red onion, minced

pinch of grated nutmeg
½ cup raisin wine

Wash the orange, and cut it, peel and all, into wafer-thin slices. Put orange slices, cabbage, onion and nutmeg into a deep casserole or heavy saucepan, and cook covered over low heat for 30 minutes. Add the raisin wine, and continue to simmer for 45 minutes longer. Spoon this over meat loaf or serve separately. This is also good with roast duck and chicken.

Headcheese and Scrapple

Headcheese is a type of meat loaf usually served cold. Unless you live in the country and raise your own porkers, you will probably never make the genuine article, but you can make a similar dish. Headcheese is made of the head of the pig, along with leftover scraps and the feet. The meat is cooked until falling off the bones, then separated from the bones and cartilage, and chopped. It is flavored, usually with sage and summer savory, and seasoned with salt and pepper. With some of the strained cooking liquid, which is very gelatinous, it is pressed into a mold and chilled. Calf's feet cooked in the same way make *Sulz*, a dish with a similar texture (see p. 188). You can use any small bits of meat in jellied loaves, but unless you have calf's or pig's feet, you will have to add extra gelatin.

Scrapple is made in the same way, with fresh pork scraps, traditionally including the head. Discard bones and cartilage, chop the meat, and return it to the strained, defatted cooking liquid. Bring the liquid to a boil, and slowly stir in

203

cornmeal. Cook the mixture over low heat, stirring occasionally, until the cornmeal is cooked and the mixture is very thick. Then turn the scrapple into loaf pans and cool. To serve, turn it out, slice it, and sauté the slices until browned. Scrapple is a good dish for breakfast, lunch or supper.

HASH

Hash has almost as negative a reputation as meat loaf, as shown by the use of the derogatory term "hash house" for an unimpressive restaurant. In addition, hash is often thought to be made only of leftovers, but this is not necessarily so. Hash is simply meat that has been cut into small pieces. The word comes from the French word for "battle-axe," *hache*, so as you wield your cleaver on the chopping block, you can imagine yourself doing battle against the foe. *Hachis*, "minced meat," is not a dish of last ends but can be good fare; however, hash is usually made of already cooked meat. While meat for hash is often ground, it should be chopped into small pieces. If you grind the meat, you will have a smoother, more pasty hash, but it will tend to lose juices during cooking. Meat that is chopped or cut into little cubes can be juicier, and its taste is more pronounced, because it is chewed longer.

One very famous hash is the elegant chicken hash invented by Louis Diat for the old New York Ritz. It was made with poached white meat of chicken, cooked slowly with cream, then mixed with a little cream sauce. It was put in a baking-serving dish, then covered with more cream sauce enriched with egg and whipped cream. Finally it was glazed under the broiler; the whipped cream made the sauce beautifully golden.

This sounds rich for today's tastes, but you could easily make a simplified version. Use both white and dark meat of poached chicken or turkey. Be sure to chop the meat instead of grinding it. Make a thick cream sauce or béchamel, or a velouté with chicken stock. Mix about 2 cups sauce with 4 cups chopped poultry, and spoon a shallow layer of the mixture into a baking dish. Cover the dish with foil, and bake in a preheated 350° F. oven for 30 to 40 minutes, until the sauce is bubbling. Remove the foil, and sprinkle the top with bread crumbs, fresh or dry, mixed with a little melted butter. If you like, mix in some grated Romano cheese and a little grated lemon rind. Put the dish back in the oven until the topping is browned.

If you want to be fancy, add mushrooms to the poultry, or follow another pretty trick of Mr. Diat's—pipe a purée of green peas around the edge of the dish before the last baking. Other vegetable purées will also work; they will hold their shape well if mixed with 1 egg yolk to each cup of purée, like duchess potatoes.

Corned-Beef Hash

The chicken hash made in the Ritz, suitable for any company meal, is a far cry from the old standby, corned-beef hash. Nevertheless, this "homely" dish is the absolute favorite of many, and it is every bit as good tasting as the chicken and cream mixture. We do not consider this a leftover, although you can use leftovers to make it. Many people buy corned beef just to make hash. You can grind the meat or chop it according to your preference. If you grind it, grind with it whatever onions you are putting in the hash. Parboil potatoes in their jackets until barely done; they should not be mushy. Cool them enough to handle, then peel them and dice or chop. Mix the meat and onions with the potato dice. Heat a heavy skillet and add a little oil (corn, peanut, olive—whatever you like). If you want a crusty brown outside on the hash, the pan has to be quite hot to start with. Turn the hash into the pan and let it cook till well browned on the bottom. Use a pancake turner to turn it over, or, if you want a smooth unbroken crust, flip the whole thing over into a second pan, also heated and coated with oil. Serve plain, or with poached eggs, or with ketchup or tomato sauce, or with mustard or horseradish. You do not have to serve cabbage with it; use any green vegetable.

The proportions of the ingredients for hash can be varied in any way you like. Actually, it is a good way to make a small amount of meat stretch. However, for really good corned-beef hash, use about equal amounts of corned beef and potatoes, with about 1 large onion for each 8 ounces of meat. Corned-beef hash can also be baked.

Ham hash can be made in the same way as corned beef. If you want to decorate this, you can glaze the top just as you would glaze a ham, or even arrange pieces of pineapple or other fruits on top to be glazed as the hash cooks.

Good hashes can also be made with lamb. Grind or chop the lamb, season it well, and mix with cooked green peas and slivers of raw potato or mashed cooked potatoes. Bake it, or sauté it.

Here is another delicious hash made with lamb and eggplant; it may remind you of a *moussaka*, a Balkan dish of layered meat and vegetables.

BAKED LAMB AND EGGPLANT HASH   6 servings

2 pounds boneless raw lamb, *or* 1 pound
   lamb and 1 pound chicken
½ pound butter (2 sticks)
1 large eggplant
1 teaspoon salt

10 peppercorns, crushed
dash of cayenne
2 garlic cloves, put through a press
2 cups tomato sauce

Grind the lamb, or the mixed lamb and chicken. Sauté the mixture in 4 tablespoons of the butter until about half done. Line a baking dish, about 2-quart size, with half of the meat. Peel the eggplant, and cut it into ¾-inch cubes. Melt the rest of the butter over low heat; season the butter with salt, black pepper and cayenne, and add the garlic. Sauté the eggplant cubes in the butter, turning them with wooden spoons (or chopsticks) to cook them on all sides; cook each cube for about 5 minutes; do them in batches if they do not all fit in the pan. Arrange the browned eggplant on top of the lamb in the baking dish, then cover with the rest of the lamb, making a loaf about 2½ inches high. Cover the whole loaf with tomato sauce. Spoon any butter left in the sauté pan over the top; do not mix it in. Bake in a 350° F. oven for about 40 minutes. Serve with rice or noodles.

Two other famous dishes made with minced meat can be considered relatives of the hamburger because of their Russian origin. These are *bitoques* and *pojarski*, both made of chopped meat stirred to a very smooth mixture, almost a paste; the paste is patted into the shape of a large chop, dipped into egg and crumbs, and sautéed in butter. The process may remind you of a vegetarian specialty, a nut cutlet, but it is an elegant preparation that requires care to be just right. The difference between the two is that *bitoques* are made of beef and *pojarski* of white meats—chicken or veal. The meat has to be chopped very fine, but it is best not to grind it. Cream is usually mixed into the meat.

There are lots more dishes in Russian cookery made with minced meat, as you can imagine, since Russia is the home of steak tartare and hamburger.

Here is a little trick to use if you want a very smooth mixture that will hold together in cooking. Use it in making meat loaf, hash, meatballs or patties. Add moistened bread crumbs as one of the ingredients; they can be fresh or several days old, from rolls, bread slices, unsalted soda crackers or matzo. Discard any crust, and tear the rest into little pieces; soak them in liquid—water, milk, cream, whatever suits the recipe best. Squeeze out any excess liquid. For a very smooth paste, whirl the crumbs in a blender or use an electric mixer to combine them with the other ingredients. How much to use depends on your recipe, but the crumbs from 1 roll or 2 pieces of bread will have a good binding effect on 2 pounds of meat. Use more bread if you want to stretch a small amount of meat.

GROUND MEAT CASSEROLES

Countless casseroles can be made with ground meat; there are delicious examples in the cookery of every country. Italian dishes use crumbled browned meat or meatballs with pasta—lasagna is a typical example. Lasagna is not an economical dish because it requires a lot of cheese and really good tomato sauce, homemade preferred, and there are a lot of steps needed to prepare all the different ingredients. However, other dishes based on meat with pasta can be economical; a relatively small amount of meat can serve quite a few people and you can prepare the whole main course, vegetables included, in one casserole. If you are an imaginative cook, you can do something different each time, and the family will never tire of your menus.

Chile con Carne

In addition to tamale pie (p. 241), many other Mexican and Southwestern dishes use ground meat. A great favorite across the United States is chile con carne with beans. It takes time to make this dish because the dried beans used in it must be soaked and cooked, but in other ways it is an easy dish. It can be made in large quantities to feed crowds, probably one of the reasons why it is so popular in roadside restaurants. You need not make it overspicy; if seasoned and cooked properly, chile can be delicious. If some members of your family like it very hot, let them add crushed red pepper to their own servings.

In addition to pasta and beans, rice, barley, cracked wheat or kasha can be mixed with bits of meat to make casseroles. Some of these dishes can be very elegant, fit for the most exacting guest, and most of them can be prepared ahead to eliminate a lot of last-minute work.

Moussaka

Moussaka, mentioned on page 205, can be made with vegetables other than eggplant, but the meat is usually lamb, the most popular meat in the Middle East. Instead of having the vegetable in the middle of the lamb, as the eggplant is in the hash recipe, the lamb is usually in the middle, surrounded by the vegetables.

Here is one way to make it. Sauté all the ingredients in olive oil until delicately browned. Then layer them in a casserole such as a lasagna dish. Use slices of zucchini or yellow summer squash, thin slices of yellow onion and slices of red or green tomatoes. Mix sautéed ground or diced lamb with minced green Italian peppers and Greek black olives. Spread some of the meat over each vegetable layer, ending with a layer of zucchini. You can vary the proportions to suit your taste, and you can use different vegetables if you prefer. Mushrooms, little artichokes and eggplant are good. Bake the casserole in a 350° F. oven for about 45 minutes. Then pour a custard made of eggs and light cream into it, filling all the spaces. Bake long enough to cook the custard; the top should be golden brown.

A more spectacular *moussaka* is one baked in a mold, with purple eggplant skins on the outside. Choose perfect, long eggplants; you will need 4 or 5 for a 2-quart casserole or mold. Split them, and scoop out the pulp without breaking the skins. Drop all the pieces into cold water until you are ready to use them, to prevent discoloration. Poach the shells for 2 to 4 minutes, just long enough to make them limp. Then use them to line the oiled casserole; the ends should hang over the edge. Combine the eggplant pulp, sautéed in oil; ground or diced lamb, also sautéed; minced onions, mushrooms and parsley; and lightly beaten eggs. If you like, add puréed garlic, minced fresh basil leaves or both. Season with salt and pepper. Turn the mixture into the eggplant-lined dish, turn the eggplant ends over to cover the filling, and press a sheet of foil over the top. Bake the *moussaka* like a pudding, set in a larger container of water, in a 350° F. oven, for 1 to 1¼ hours.

You can vary this by adding cooked rice or bulgur, chopped drained tomatoes or other flavoring ingredients to the lamb. If you are using the oven for another dish, the cooking temperature and time for the *moussaka* can be varied without harming it.

MEAT SAUCES

Meat sauces offer another way to add nutrition and flavor with a relatively small amount of meat. If you think we are just referring to tomato sauce with hamburger, stop right there! Meat sauces need not be made with ground beef and they don't need to be made with tomato. While ground meat of any kind can be used, for even more flavor use thin chunks of meat; these release their juices differently and are more flavorful than ground meat; the meat juices will help to thicken the sauce. As for sauces made with ground or chopped meat, the meat can be anything—diced ham, chopped chicken or veal, even giblets; each kind will flavor the sauce differently. The sauces can be made of any vegetable purée—eggplant, squash, onion, and so on—or from any good meat stock thickened with a starch or bread crumbs or a puréed ingredient. Pasta is delicious with sauces that are delicately flavored, and sauces can be served also with rice or various vegetables or stuffing mixtures. If you want a ground meat sauce that is closer to the traditional spaghetti sauce, the mixture for meat loaf is excellent to use.

STEWS

Stews are made of pieces rather than bits, and some of the most delicious dishes of any country's cookery are these seemingly homely preparations. Aside from the fact that one would not want to waste tender steaks or ribs of beef by cooking them this way, any kind of meat and poultry can be made into a stew, with or without extra ingredients. Generally, stews are best prepared by long slow cooking. This cooking can be done when the oven is being used for other preparations and the heat does not need to be adjusted to the stew, but the stew can adjust to the right heat for the other dish. Also, because of the long cooking time and the liquid used in stews, they do not require much attention during cooking. And best of all, *most* stews are greatly improved by being made in advance so that the flavors will be well blended. The exceptions are kidney stew, which should be served as soon as ready because kidneys toughen when reheated, and chicken stews, because chicken loses flavor and becomes overcooked and dry in texture when reheated.

As was stated in Chapter 8 some stews are so delicious and well known that they can serve for company occasions. The French beef stew with red wine, *boeuf bourguignon*, is a great favorite and can be made more elegant by adding little fresh mushrooms and fresh peas toward the end of the cooking. The cuts to use for this are chuck, cross-rib or top sirloin. While the usual size of the pieces is 1½-inch cubes, you can cut them to suit yourself. Smaller pieces will soak up more of the flavors in the sauce.

Gulyás (goulash), the Hungarian national dish, is a stew of beef and onions flavored with caraway; potatoes are often added. Chuck is the preferred cut, but any cut suitable for *boeuf bourguignon* can be used. *Gulyás* can be made moister or drier according to your taste.

Veal is especially good in white stews, fricassee and *blanquette*, but it is also used by Hungarian cooks for a paprika-flavored stew called *pörkölt*. Veal shoulder is the best cut to use for any of these. A brown veal stew with vegetables is especially good with dumplings cooked in the stew at the last minute.

Lamb Stews

Irish stew in Ireland is made of mutton, but oddly enough it was once made of spareribs. We usually use lamb. This stew always contains potatoes and onions, but there is disagreement about whether the vegetables should be sliced or whole. Even when sliced, they will not fall to mush if you bake the stew or cook it under boiling temperature. English and Irish recipes usually call for the neck or upper end of the rib, what we call the middle chuck, but we think the shoulder or leg is better—the shoulder because it is flavorful, the leg because it is lean. While the basic recipe does not call for any seasoning but salt and pepper, you can add whatever you like; caraway and dill are good with lamb.

Another famous lamb stew is the French *navarin d'agneau*. For this, shoulder is used, and small vegetables are added toward the end of the cooking. The conventional additions—potatoes, onions, carrots—are used, but this stew is distinctive in including little white turnips, either halved or cut into small ovals, and fresh green peas and beans. If you cannot get small potatoes and carrots, cut large ones into small rounds, but the taste is enhanced by the use of new potatoes and whole young carrots. The first early vegetables distinguish this delicious dish.

Chicken Stews

There are countless stews made with chicken. Chicken gumbo, *coq au vin*, chicken Marengo, chicken fricassee, Country Captain, all sorts of curries. You can invent your own because the delicate flavor of chicken is adaptable to all sorts of vegetables and herbs and wines. A *blanquette* of chicken and a fricassee are pale in color, but brown chicken stews are equally good. The wine used in *coq au vin* is always red, and the original recipe calls for a young cockerel, but it can be used for any kind of chicken; young cockerels are not available in our markets.

Chicken *paprikás* is a Hungarian chicken stew flavored with paprika and finished with cream or sour cream. Since chicken cooks in a relatively short time, all sorts of quickly prepared dishes are available even for the cook who gets home late from work.

Veal Stews

Veal stew made with white wine and flavored with tarragon is a delicate French dish, and veal stewed with tomatoes is another. The cut often used in France for veal stews is the *tendron*, the part cut from between the end of the ribs next to the

Chunk of veal shin containing a slice of the marrowbone, cut from the leg portion of the veal round. It is this cut which is used for osso buco (hollow bone). Slices of beef shank can be prepared in the same way.

flank, also called *côtelettes parisiennes*. This cut is tough and gelatinous and needs slow cooking to be good.

The Northern Italian dish called *osso buco* is made with chunks of the veal shin cooked with tomatoes and always served with rice, either plain or as a risotto. In Milan the mixture called *gremolata* (minced parsley and garlic and grated lemon rind, all mixed) is always sprinkled over the top when the dish is ready to serve. The same kind of preparation can be made with slices of beef shank, and you can alter the other ingredients of the stew to suit your own wishes. If you're not trying to be authentically Lombard, you could serve this with pasta instead of rice, or even with barley. White wine is used in cooking the veal, but for beef red wine is preferred. Incidentally, these two Italian words *osso buco* mean "hollow bone" or marrowbone. Either stew is rich in nutritive values because all the minerals in the marrow and in the bones are retained in the stew.

Oxtail Stew

Oxtails seem to be made for stew. They need long slow cooking to become tender, and long slow cooking is just what a good stew needs for perfect blending of flavors. Have them cut into sections, roll them in seasoned flour, and brown them in oil. Add whatever flavoring vegetables you like; the most usual with oxtails are onions, carrots and tomatoes, but you can use white turnips, parsnips, celery knobs, leeks, and so on—some or all of them. To add more color and flavor, the vegetables too can be browned before mixing into the stewpot. A good beef stock and a little red wine will enrich the sauce, but plain water can be used. Cook for 3 to 4 hours, until the oxtails are tender when pierced with a fork. For a perfect presentation, let the stew cool overnight. Lift off and discard the fat on top, then heat the stew enough to separate the oxtails. Set them aside, and purée the sauce and vegetables in a blender or a food mill. Return the purée to the kettle and reheat the oxtails in the puréed sauce. If you want to serve whole vegetables with the stew, cook them separately, choosing some of the same kind as in the purée.

Pork Stews

The best-known pork stew is *Székelygulyás*, made with diced lean pork, sauerkraut and, of course, paprika and caraway seeds. It is really a country dish, and very hearty. You can vary this by adding onions, tomatoes, sour cream.

Another pork stew, less well known, is the Portuguese dish made with pork and little clams. No matter how fantastic this sounds, it is delicious. Diced fresh pork is stewed with onions, tomatoes and herbs; sometimes spicy pork sausage or dry-cured ham or both are used instead of fresh pork. Just before the stew is done the well-scrubbed clams are added to cook just until they are steamed open.

There are countless recipes for stews, but the same basic rules can be applied to most ingredients. Have your meat cut in pieces—small dice, large cubes, sections—whatever suits the meat and the recipe. Roll the pieces in flour; shake off any excess. If the pieces are cubes or larger, sauté them in oil or butter or a mixture; if the pieces are smaller than 1-inch cubes, do not sauté them because they will be too cooked by the time the stew is finished. Let the larger pieces brown; or sauté them enough to sear them, to keep in juices during the rest of the cooking; or brown them to release excess fat. Transfer the meat to a heavy pot or kettle or casserole or baking dish. Add the liquid for the stew, at room temperature. Bring the liquid to a boil, then reduce to a simmer and cook, covered, on top of the stove or in the oven. Vegetables or other ingredients are added at the start or later on depending on what they are and how long they need to cook. And you can vary all these steps to suit your own tastes. The liquid can be anything you like, but your own stock with a little wine will be delicious.

For hunters, stews are a good solution if you are not sure about the tenderness of your game. Venison can be stewed following any recipe for beef, but it should be marinated first unless you know it is young and tender. Red wine, juniper berries and peppercorns are most often used in venison stews.

Rabbit Stews

Although rabbit is used infrequently in this country, it is a great favorite in Europe, especially in France and Italy. There are many stews based on rabbit, which is raised as a domestic animal in France and considered part of the poultry supplies, and based on hare, a much larger animal usually shot or trapped as game. The hare presents the same problems as other game—one does not easily know how old it is and there is no way to guess how it was fed. The frozen rabbit in our markets is generally tender, but if you catch your own or have any doubt about the rabbit you buy, stewing is the method for best use of the rabbit. Rabbit is often marinated before cooking, in wine and oil or in wine vinegar and oil, but there is an Italian recipe that uses lemon juice for marinating which might remind you of Moroccan cooking. The pieces of rabbit or hare are browned in oil, then stewed with some wine or with the wine marinade (do not cook with the lemon juice—it would make the rabbit too sour). A little sweetening is not amiss with these preparations; either use a slightly sweet wine or add a little sugar (2 tablespoons per rabbit if you are using a dry wine). For a good French-style preparation using frozen rabbit, see page 63.

LUNCHEON

Baked potatoes stuffed with steak tartare
Anchovy butter
Asparagus salad with mimosa dressing

Chicken hash
with puréed sweet potatoes
Belgian endive salad

Broiled Hamburgers (see p. 100)
Potato salad with diced salami
Sliced tomatoes with chive dressing

DINNER

Veal balls with sour-cream sauce
Steamed new potatoes with chives
Chopped fresh spinach with chopped fresh beets

Melon balls with lime juice and fresh mint leaves
Liver and Sausage Loaf (see p. 202)
Mixed salad greens with slivers of raw zucchini and cucumber slices

Beef and Chicken Loaf (see p. 203)
Red Cabbage with Orange (see p. 203)
Toasted garlic bread
Hearty tossed salad topped with slivers of water chestnuts

Veal osso buco
Risotto milanese
Sautéed mushrooms, cherry tomatoes and pearl onions
Arugula salad with Italian dressing

Whole artichokes vinaigrette
Moussaka of yellow summer squash and lamb with custard
Steamed cracked wheat

Whole tomatoes stuffed with vegetable salad
Rabbit with Mustard-Cream Sauce (see p. 63)
Thin noodles
Carrot ovals with seedless green grapes
Watercress

MEATS
AND
POULTRY
FOR
STUFFING

Chapter 13

STUFFING MEATS AND POULTRY and using meats and poultry to stuff vegetables and fruits were probably some of the first elaborations on basic cooking techniques. The Romans are said to have enjoyed stuffed dormice—they fattened them and then filled them with other dormice cut into pieces and mixed with spices and nuts, or with honey and poppy seeds. In eighteenth-century cookbooks, there are recipes for stuffing breast of mutton and breast of veal that sound quite appropriate for today. One recipe for slices of veal as thin as what we would label "scallops" calls for stuffing them with marrow, sweetbreads and lambstones (*animelles*) mixed with egg yolks: "Put it into your pockets, as if you were filling a pincushion; then sew up the top with fine thread"—a workable directive even now. Probably the most astonishing stuffed preparation is described by Abd-allatif, an Arab physician from Baghdad, in his *Account of Egypt*. This dish was served during the sultanate of the great Saladin. It was a pie filled with three lambs stuffed with pounded veal, pistachios and spices; in the spaces between were twenty fowls, twenty chickens and fifty smaller birds, some stuffed with eggs, some with meat, some with fruits. This chapter will not tell you how to do anything so elaborate.

The simplest stuffing procedure is to use thin slices of meat, in some cases flattened further with a mallet or the flat side of a cleaver, and to roll them around a stuffing. Some familiar examples are veal birds or *paupiettes de veau* or *involtini*, beef rolls or *Rouladen*, pork rolls or *braciole* or *braciolette*.

SCALLOPS

Veal is very successful prepared this way and because of its delicate flavor it can be stuffed with quite a variety of ingredients. For these little *paupiettes* use the slices called *scaloppini* or *escalopes* or scallops. These are cut from the leg, but for Kosher cooks such slices must be cut from the shoulder.

The leg of veal is dissected and skinned, and all membranes are removed. While other segments of the leg can be used for scallops, the round steak is ideal because it has an even smooth surface with no fat. The round has a wide surface at the end nearer to the hip. The wider portion is used for veal cutlet and is cut into

The veal round dissected from the leg and prepared for slicing into scallops (scaloppini). The slices will be flattened to make very thin smooth scallops.

slices thicker than one would use for scallops. Regardless of the name, when the slice is thicker than a scallop, it needs a different method of cooking.

For scallops the meat is sliced quite thin—⅛ to ¹/₁₆ inch or even thinner. When cut thicker than ⅛ inch, it is a cutlet and not a scallop. The slices are cut at an angle of 30 degrees. Put each slice between 2 pieces of paper (wax paper or polyethylene-coated so the surface is smooth and will not stick) and pound it lightly, not to make the scallop bigger, although pounding does spread it out a little, but to give a smooth and even surface.

To make beef rolls you need good cuts. Depending on the elegance of the occasion choose shell, or top sirloin, or top round. Shell is first choice. Have these cut into thin slices too, maximum ½ inch. Flatten them to ¼ inch.

For pork scallops, use the loin or the leg, but the loin is far better. The leg meat is too coarse for the best scallops. Bone the loin, keeping the bones for baby spareribs, remove all outer membranes, and cut the meat into boneless scallops. Flatten them just as you would the veal. To have a larger surface to work with, cut a double width and split it, leaving it attached along one side, to make a boneless butterfly chop. Flatten this in the same way to a circle 6 to 8 inches across.

The procedure for stuffing all these is the same. Place a mound of stuffing near one end of the scallop, leaving a bare edge of meat beyond it. Fold that little edge over the stuffing; then roll the stuffed portion over until you reach the other end. Do not try to tuck in the ends, but sort of pinch them together. You do not want them to be really sealed because part of the attractiveness of these little rolls when cooked is the appearance of the stuffing at each end. If you like, fasten the ends with a wooden food pick or a metal poultry pin, but it is best to fasten the meat with one pin at the center of the roll.

Stuffings for scallops can include vegetables, mushrooms, marrow, cheese and other meats. Usually some bread crumbs are added to make each roll swell somewhat as it cooks, which gives it a plump and attractive appearance at serving time. Do not use any ingredient that takes long to cook, because the thin slices of meat will be cooked in a matter of minutes. The texture of the mixed stuffing should be like a heavy thick sauce or moist paste.

To cook stuffed scallops, sauté them in butter, oil or a mixture of butter and oil until browned on all sides. Then pour over them a small quantity of stock or wine, and simmer them very gently until done. The length of time depends on the meat you are using and the thickness of the slice—the thinner the slice, the quicker the cooking. Veal scallops will cook in 10 to 20 minutes, beef scallops in about 20, and pork scallops in about 30.

Scallops can also be baked or braised, which will take longer than sautéing. Veal birds usually need 45 minutes to 1 hour for braising, beef rolls 1 to 1½ hours and pork rolls 1½ to 2 hours. Serve 2 small rolls per person.

If it is more convenient, you can cook stuffed scallops until three-quarters done and freeze them. When you plan to serve them, defrost them overnight in the refrigerator, and finish cooking just before serving.

BEEF SCALOPPINE STUFFED WITH CHICKEN   6 servings

6 beef scallops, cut from Delmonico steaks	3 garlic cloves, chopped
1 uncooked boneless chicken breast	¼ teaspoon salt
6 slices of bacon	10 peppercorns, cracked
5 tablespoons olive oil	¼ cup all-purpose flour
3 tablespoons chopped onion	3 tablespoons Drambuie
1 tablespoon chopped fresh chives	6 squares (5 by 5 inches) of prepared Basic Pastry (p. 231)

Place the steaks between sheets of wax paper, and flatten them, or have your butcher do this. The flattened scallops should be 6 by 4 inches. Cut the chicken breast into ½-inch dice. Cook the bacon until crisp, then pat dry and crumble.

Heat 3 tablespoons of the oil in a large saucepan or skillet. Add the onion, and cook over low heat until transparent. Add chives and garlic, and cook for 5 minutes. Add chicken dice, bacon crumbles, salt and pepper. Mix all together with a wooden spoon, cover, and cook over low heat for 20 minutes. Stir occasionally to mix and to prevent sticking. Let the mixture cool, then stir in the flour, and mix well.

Dip each beef scallop on one side into Drambuie, then arrange them on your work surface with the moistened side up. Divide the stuffing among the scallops. Roll up the scallops so the stuffing does not ooze out and tie each little roll with a single string around the middle.

Heat remaining 2 tablespoons oil in a skillet and quickly brown the beef rolls. When they are browned on all sides, remove from skillet, pat dry, and cut off the strings. Wrap each roll in a square of pastry and moisten the edges to seal the dough completely around the roll, including the ends. Place the dough-wrapped rolls on an oiled baking sheet and bake in a preheated 350° F. oven for 5 minutes. Reduce oven heat to 325° F. and bake for about 15 minutes longer, or until the crust is golden brown.

■

217

You can also make scallops from boneless chicken breasts; see page 333 for boning, or have your butcher prepare them. Flatten each piece gently—you do not want to shred it. Chicken differs from veal and the other meats—it is difficult to roll around a filling. It is better to find the pocket in the larger chicken fillet and stuff the pocket—not too full. You do not need to seal the opening because the natural protein released in cooking will serve as a sealer. These boneless pieces are very tender and delicate. It is best to sauté them, whether stuffed or unstuffed, in butter or clarified butter or oil or a mixture. Cook over moderate heat—too high heat has a tendency to shrivel the meat and toughen it—for 6 to 10 minutes, depending on the size of the piece. Turn it once during the cooking so it is delicately browned on both sides. If you prefer, you can brown it quickly and finish cooking with wine or stock as the veal birds are cooked. Stuffed chicken breasts can be poached without browning for some recipes.

STUFFED LARGE PIECES OF MEAT

Chops

Other stuffed preparations for individual serving can be made with thicker pieces of meat with pockets. Pork and veal chops are excellent for this, but don't use lamb because it cooks too quickly and the meat would be dried and overdone before the filling was cooked. Use rib chops of pork or veal, the center portion. Shoulder chops are sinewy, with more muscle, and drier, and not as delicate looking. Use double chops, 2 inches thick. Single chops are too thin and the meat dries out too fast. Keep the bones in to help retain the juices.

While it is perfectly possible for the home cook to make a pocket in a chop, and we describe the process on page 328, it is far better to have your butcher do it. He can make a pocket with a very small hole on the outside and a relatively large space inside. When done this way, the normal protein will seal the opening during cooking so that the stuffing and meat juices cannot escape. With a larger opening the stuffing tends to escape in cooking. You can skewer such an opening to close it, but when the pocket has been professionally made, this is not necessary. Stuffed double chops like this are most delicious when braised. Allow 1 to 1½ hours.

London Broil

Following the same basic methods as for the little rolls, you can stuff larger pieces of meat for more servings. London broil is good for this. A London broil can be made from any steak sliced on the bias. It is often made from flank steak, but can be made from the first cut of the top round, from top sirloin or boneless sirloin. Flank steak is normally too thick to roll or to butterfly, so let us consider that later.

With the other cuts, have slices cut just as thin as for individual rolls—no thicker than ½ inch. Pound the meat between sheets of paper to flatten it and enlarge it. Arrange the stuffing near one end and carefully roll up. These larger rolls can be fastened with wooden skewers or poultry pins, but it is easier to tie them with butchers' string at intervals of 1½ inches. Don't tie the string too tightly because the stuffing will swell in cooking. Braise these larger stuffed rolls, or brown them in a heavy saucepan or kettle and finish cooking by simmering in liquid in the saucepan. The top-of-the-stove method will take about 1 hour, the braising in the oven about 1½ hours. Leave the strings in place when you serve the roll and snip them off as you reach them. To serve cut the roll into slices between the strings.

Round of Veal

The same kind of large roll can be made with thick pieces from the top end of the round of veal. Cut the slices ¼ inch thick and pound them between sheets of paper until they are doubled in size. To make an even larger piece, cut 2 slices, leaving them joined along one side to make a butterfly, and pound these until they are triple the size of one slice. Then proceed with the stuffing and rolling.

Flank Steak

The flank steak can be stuffed by having a pocket cut into it. This cut is not as tender as the other cuts used for London broil, therefore it should be first marinated, not for flavor but for tenderizing. Use oil, vinegar, salt, pepper and garlic, and marinate the meat overnight, or longer if you like, but remember the longer you marinate, the less of the original meat flavor will be left. After marinating, pat the meat dry, lay it flat on your work surface, and cut a pocket in it. Fill the pocket with stuffing and skewer it closed at 1-inch intervals. You can bake or braise the whole roll for 2 hours. Another method is to cut the steak into slices between the skewers—leave the skewers in place to hold the edges together—and broil these little stuffed pieces for about 5 minutes on each side, or bake them in a preheated 350° F. oven for 35 to 40 minutes. They can be sautéed also, but that isn't the preferred way because the stuffing tends to fall out.

You can also make pockets in any cut of beef that can be broiled or roasted. A double shell steak with a pocket will make 2 portions, and a 2-inch sirloin with a pocket will make 4 portions. Beef pockets can be made at home because the large size of the animal makes the meat relatively easy to work with, but you will probably have a better pocket if you have it cut professionally. Top round and top sirloin are also good for pockets.

Carpetbag Steak

One of the most delicious preparations with beef is the "carpetbag steak," made with a sirloin steak. The stuffing is simply fresh raw oysters. Use small ones, 16 to 20 for a 2-inch sirloin, and drain them in a strainer for a few minutes. Then turn them onto absorbent kitchen paper and pat gently to absorb a little more moisture. Season with salt and peppercorns ground fine and stuff them into the pocket. Skewer the edges. Use a double length of string to braid around the skewers to help keep the stuffing inside. (You can use this braiding trick with any stuffed meat fastened with skewers, but it is necessary when the stuffing is as moist and slippery as oysters.) Broil the steak in the usual manner, allowing 20 minutes on each side for medium.

You might be interested to know that Mrs. Charles Dickens served leg of mutton stuffed with oysters over 100 years ago.

Many other meats can have pockets cut in them. A whole loin of pork can be prepared by boning (see p. 331); save the little bones for baby spareribs. Make a pocket 2 inches deep from one end to the other, leaving 1 inch at each end uncut. Spread the meat apart, stuff it, fasten with string, and roast it in a preheated oven, 300 to 325° F., for 30 to 35 minutes per pound. Leave the strings on to serve, and slice the roast at the table, snipping off the strings as you come to them.

Veal shoulder makes a delicious stuffed roast. Be sure to use something flavorful as contrast to the bland veal taste and be sure to outer-lard this cut or baste often with oil to keep it moist during cooking. For a holiday version see page 366.

Boned Meats

Any meat that has had interior bones removed, such as a fresh or smoked ham, a leg of veal, a beef sirloin roast or arm roast, leg of lamb, and so on, can have stuffing inserted in place of the missing bones. This will add flavor to the meat, will give an attractive appearance, and of course the meat will be easier to carve without its bones. For these preparations, do not use the kind of stuffing that swells in cooking, because there will be no room for it to swell. You can use other meats of contrasting color, pâté of various kinds, herb mixtures, even nuts and fruits. For instance, the Scandinavians like to stuff boned pork with cooked prunes, and an old Polish favorite is boned veal with a stuffing of egg yolks, butter, crumbs and fresh dill.

Breast of veal is an excellent choice for stuffing. Have your butcher make a pocket and crack the breast bone between the ribs to simplify serving later. Use a dry and firm rather than moist stuffing. Insert the stuffing loosely because it will swell to double the size from the moisture in cooking. Sew with a larding needle and white butchers' cord. If you have no larding needle, use a large heavy-duty needle; if the eye of your needle is too small to insert the butchers' cord, use dental floss instead. Another way is to skewer the opening closed with small wooden or metal

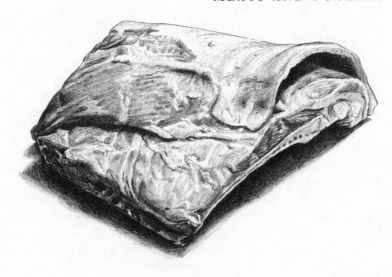

Breast of veal, with a pocket prepared for stuffing

skewers or poultry pins. If you like, you can braid string around the pins as described on page 220. This is excellent braised; allow about 2 hours for a 3-pound piece. Or roast in a low oven (300 to 325° F.) for about 2 hours.

Crown Roast

Another handsome stuffed presentation is the crown roast. The usual crowns are lamb and pork. These are made of the entire rack of the animal. The smallest crowns are made of 12 chops, which is the smallest number that can make a circle, but 16 chops is more usual. With pork 16 chops are necessary because the meat is bulgier and fatter, and more are needed to make the circle.

First make a mark 1½ to 2 inches above the eye of the chops and draw a line with the knife blade across the covering of the rib bones at that level. French the chops to that line, that is, trim off the meat all around the rib bones so you have bare bones. Have the ends of the bones sawed off so they are evenly trimmed to about 1½ inches above the line you cut for Frenching. Fix both racks to match exactly and then sew them together. With a roast-beef tier sew a length of cord through the spinal column to join the racks in one long piece, and tie. Sew again at the end of the chop, and tie. With the rib bones on the outside, bring the two racks together in a circle and sew the opposite ends together in the same way. The rack is slit between the chops to make it easier to bend it into a circle, but these slits should not be too deep. If they are too deep, the separation will be too wide and that portion will overcook and become dry. If the separation between the chops is larger than 1 inch, press in a piece of foil to protect the meat, because that is the most tender portion of the chop.

Wrap the ends of the chop bones in foil. Your butcher will usually have them tipped with frills of paper or foil. Take these off and save them for serving. The foil wrapping will keep the bones from charring.

The stuffing of these crowns offers many possibilities to the cook. Lamb can be stuffed with a mixture of ground lamb and ground beef (lamb alone would be too strong-tasting). Another possibility is a rice stuffing. Pork crowns taste best with a fruit stuffing, because the fruit keeps the meat moist. You may prefer to cook the crown without stuffing and serve it filled with vegetables that have been separately cooked, or large bouquets of parsley or watercress. It is not necessary to put a utensil inside the bones if you omit stuffing. The bones will be adequate to keep the crown in shape. If you do cook stuffing inside the crown, cover it with foil for at least half of the time and uncover at that point to let the top brown. However, for the ideal preparation, it is probably better to cook stuffing and crown separately. To illustrate, the lamb crown will be adequately roasted (rare) in a 350° F. oven in 45 minutes to 1 hour but the stuffing needs longer cooking if it is the mixture of ground meats. Cook the stuffing until it is about three-quarters done, then turn it into the crown to finish cooking as the racks cook. The stuffing will fall into shape automatically. The top of the stuffing should be rounded within the bones.

A veal crown is about the same size as a pork crown. If you intend to stuff it with veal, use lamb and veal ground together to add juiciness. To cook a pork or veal crown, start in a moderate oven (350° F.) and after 30 minutes reduce heat to 325° F. Continue to cook for 25 minutes per pound until the roast is done.

To serve a crown roast, slice between the chops to the center to give everyone a chop with some stuffing. Allow 2 chops per serving for lamb, pork or veal crowns.

A stuffed whole meat animal would be rare today in the United States, although in some other countries a whole stuffed lamb or small pig might be prepared for festivals. The only example here would be the suckling pig or piglet. If you can find one (see p. 271), stuff the cavity just as you would stuff poultry.

Poultry

All sorts of poultry are stuffed in the body cavity, and in large turkeys the neck cavity too is stuffed. With fatty birds such as ducks and geese you will do well to cook the stuffing separately so that it does not become too fatty. Or fill the cavity with a very dry stuffing that can absorb the fat; do not add any extra fat to the stuffing. For game birds, prepare stuffing separately.

The most popular stuffing is made with cubes or crumbs of bread and chopped onions, seasoned with thyme or sage, and moistened with butter and a little stock made with the giblets of the bird. Sometimes the giblets are chopped and added, even extra giblets. Instead of bread, you can use rice, wild rice, cracked wheat, buckwheat groats, potatoes, corn bread. To add texture and flavor, you can add nuts—almonds, chestnuts, pine nuts, etc.—and fruits such as dried currants, chopped apples and other dried fruits. Other vegetables such as celery, green peppers, mushrooms, can be used. A great American tradition calls for stuffing birds with oysters, especially turkeys and quails. (If you get any quails, there is room inside one for about 1 large oyster.) Sausage is another American favorite. While this might seem to add a lot of extra fat to the stuffing, a little goes a long way. For an 18- to 20-pound turkey, use 1 pound of fresh pork sausage. It will add some extra fat, and you must allow for the excess in the balance of the stuffing ingredients. Sausage is added chiefly for its flavor.

For turkeys, allow about 1 cup of stuffing for each pound of the bird. If you have some left over, bake it separately. The same rule applies to capons, but chickens may need a little more stuffing. Cook the vegetables in butter, and toss them with the dry ingredients. If you use nuts, be sure they are blanched (almonds), or cooked and peeled (chestnuts). Cook rice, wild rice, groats, etc., before adding to the vegetables. Oysters can be added raw, either whole or chopped, or they can be poached for a few minutes. Giblets should be cooked until tender, and sausage should be partly cooked for a large bird and almost completely cooked for a chicken. Dried fruits should be soaked or parboiled for a few minutes. Toss all the ingredients together so the stuffing is light but well blended. If it seems too dry, add a little stock, wine, fruit juice or even water, depending on the other ingredients.

LOBELS' ALL-PURPOSE STUFFING   6 to 8 cups

1 pound skinned and boned raw chicken, including dark and light meat	4 tablespoons chicken fat
2 large onions, peeled	2 tablespoons Cognac
¾ pound fresh mushrooms, peeled	1 pound packaged seasoned stuffing cubes
10 chestnuts, shelled, cooked and peeled	½ cup light cream

Chop the chicken; mince the onions; chop the mushrooms; pulverize the chestnuts. Melt chicken fat, and cook the onions in it until transparent. Add chicken, and stir well; cook and stir over low heat for 15 minutes. Still over heat, add chestnut powder, and mix well; add mushrooms, and mix well. Add Cognac, stir in, and remove from heat; cool. Put stuffing cubes in a large bowl, and add the cooled chicken mixture. Last, add the cream and mix thoroughly. Use to stuff poultry, vegetables, other meats.

Do not stuff a bird until you are ready to cook it; if you make the stuffing ahead of time, refrigerate it separately from the bird. However, do not stuff the bird with cold stuffing, because this will slow the cooking too much. Let bird and stuffing reach room temperature.

Stuff the bird lightly; do not ever pack it tightly, because any stuffing containing bread or other dry ingredient will swell during cooking. Sew the vent closed, or skewer it with poultry pins, or skewer and braid around the pins with white string. If you have a large turkey, stuff the neck too. Bring the neck skin over to the back, and skewer or sew it. If your birds have arrived at the market with little skin remaining at the end of the body cavity, making it difficult to cover the stuffing, try this trick: Rub a piece of firm bread with butter on both sides and insert it in the cavity over the stuffing; it will help hold the stuffing in place and prevent loss of flavor. Pin the bird on each side and stretch the braid of string across the bread to close the cavity. Truss the bird (see p. 83), and you are ready to roast (see p. 94).

For bread crumbs and cubes, many recipes call for "stale" bread. What they really mean is bread that is several days old and not fresh from the baker. However, if you use a firm loaf, you can make good stuffing with very fresh bread. While stuffing cubes can be purchased, it is easy to make your own. Simply place the bread on a board and, with a chef's knife or a bread knife, cut it into strips, then into cubes. About 2 pieces of bread will give 1 cup of cubes. To make fresh soft crumbs or dry crumbs, you can use a hand grater—much easier than it sounds—or an electric blender.

Galantine and Ballottine

Some other complicated stuffed meats or poultry are the *galantine* and *ballottine*. We are going to tell you what they are, but we are not going to tell you how to do either, because we think they are much too complicated for the home kitchen.

A *galantine* starts with a chicken, capon, duck or turkey, which is boned without damaging the skin, which should be all in one flat piece. The meat is also removed, and the large pieces are cut into symmetrical strips. The rest is ground and mixed with other stuffing ingredients and seasonings. On the inside of the skin are arranged in layers the pieces of the bird, the stuffing, other pieces of meat such as tongue or ham, maybe some pistachios or truffles or olives, more layers, etc. The skin is folded around the stuffing and sewed up. It is then rolled and tied in cloth, then poached in a stock made from the bones that were removed. When done, it is cooled and pressed with a weight. Meantime, make aspic from the stock. When the *galantine* is cold, the cloth is removed, and the roll is glazed with aspic and garnished. Just describing this makes us tired, and it will use most of the kitchen equipment you own!

A *ballottine* is made in the same way, but it is served hot. Sometimes small birds like squabs or just the legs of larger birds are made into *ballottines*, and in France hares or large rabbits are also treated to this very elaborate preparation.

The name *galantine* is also given nowadays to boned stuffed meats that are served cold and coated with aspic. These are made in the same way, but since there is no skin to wrap them in, they are more often roasted or braised instead of poached.

STUFFED VEGETABLES

Meats can be stuffed, but they can be used in stuffings as well. Anything with a natural hollow has been stuffed by somebody at some time, and you can make a hollow in almost anything—from a cherry tomato to a watermelon—that does not have one. A meat stuffing is probably not appropriate for watermelon, but all members of the tomato family are excellent stuffed with meat. So are green peppers, eggplant, squashes of all kinds, mushrooms, onions and potatoes. A delicious Hungarian dish is prepared by stuffing halves of large cucumber pickles with ground pork and veal; after stuffing, the pickle halves are tied together and braised. Stuffed hard-cooked eggs are the most popular picnic fare. Pineapple halves, apples, figs and other fruits can have meat or poultry stuffings. A new favorite in the United States is stuffed grape leaves. Pasta, both the tubular kind and the flat pieces that are rolled around a filling, and pancakes and bread cases and pastry turnovers—all these can be stuffed.

As for what meats and poultry to use, almost anything will do. A basic all-meat stuffing could be similar to a meat-loaf mixture—half beef, a quarter veal, a quarter pork. For those who do not eat pork, substitute one quarter lamb. Have the meats ground together to mix them well. Fresh sausage meat is another flavorful choice, alone or mixed with other ingredients. Ground beef and ground lamb can be used alone too, of course.

For stuffings with a different texture, chicken livers, calf's brains and sweetbreads can be used, and veal kidneys, which are odorless in themselves and also odorless in cooking, are also good in stuffings.

Various cured meats and sausages are excellent for flavor, including salami, liverwurst, knackwurst, frankfurters, bacon, corned beef. Tongue, because of its color as well as texture, is a fine ingredient where appearance matters.

Potatoes, both white and sweet, can be mixed with meats to achieve a soft texture or to give a particular color to a stuffing.

Leftover cooked meats and poultry are fine for stuffings; they should be soft and are usually ground.

All stuffings should be well flavored, since they will need to flavor their containers too, so spices and herbs can be added to the usual salt and cracked peppercorns used for other preparations.

To proceed with vegetables, prepare the hollow, either by removing the seeds and strings from natural hollows (acorn squash) or scooping out the interior portions with a melon-ball scoop (tomatoes, summer squashes, eggplants). With peppers, it is important to trim out the little membranes and shake or rinse out all the seeds, because these parts are very "peppery" in flavor. Onions and potatoes are usually cooked before stuffing—onions parboiled and potatoes most often fully baked. To make a hollow in a mushroom, you need only break out the stem. Do not peel vegetables for stuffing, because the skin helps hold them together. Be sure when scooping to leave enough of the vegetable all around to make a reasonably stable container, and do not cut slices from the bases or stuffing will leak out.

Very wet vegetables like tomatoes are usually improved by being drained upside down on a rack, so that excessive moisture will not make the stuffing mushy. Peppers to be stuffed and baked can be parboiled briefly—they can be tough-skinned—if you like. The portions removed from the centers of most vegetables can be used for part of the stuffing. Chop or mince these bits, and drain them if they are very wet. Try to discard most of the tomato seeds, which can be bitter when cooked.

Stuff the cases, rounding the filling, and finish off in whatever way best suits the recipe: Sprinkle with crumbs, crumbs and cheese, paprika or minced nuts; or dot with butter or oil; or cover with the top cut off to make the hollow—the latter works well with tomatoes and peppers. Sometimes it is a good idea to cover the vegetables with foil until they are partly cooked, then uncover to let the topping brown. Since these are flexible dishes and can cook for a short time in a hot oven or a longer time in a low oven, it is easy to accommodate them to other dishes that must be baked at a specific temperature.

When preparing a stuffing for vegetables, adjust your method to the vegetable you are working with. Tender, quickly cooked tomatoes should have stuffing that is nearly all cooked; the necessary baking time is so short that it serves only to blend flavors and heat everything. With larger pieces, such as halves of eggplants, which might bake for 40 or 50 minutes, the stuffing will have longer to cook, but even with these it is best to cook the meat halfway or even three-quarters done before mixing it into the other stuffing ingredients. Flavoring vegetables should usually be sautéed briefly, not to be sure they are cooked, but to help release their special flavors at the outset so that everything will be tasty.

PORK-STUFFED GREEN PEPPERS   6 servings

3 pounds boneless loin of pork
6 short fat green peppers (about 7 ounces each)
1 tablespoon honey
1 tablespoon orange juice
12 small white onions (silverskins), peeled
¾ pound mushrooms, peeled
1 canned pineapple ring

4 tablespoons oil
½ teaspoon salt
¼ teaspoon ground white pepper
pinch of dried thyme
6 slices of bacon, cooked crisp and crumbled
1 cup dry bread crumbs
1 tablespoon grated orange rind

Have butcher bone the pork (before weighing) and remove all fat and nerves. Cut the meat into ¼-inch cubes. Cut a slice from the stem end of each pepper to make an opening about 3 inches across; remove seeds and membranes. Mix honey and orange juice, and brush all over the outsides of the peppers; refrigerate the peppers. Chop the onions into fine pieces, and chop the mushrooms and pineapple to ¼-inch dice.

Heat the oil in a large skillet; when hot, cook the onions over low heat for 10 minutes. Add salt, white pepper and thyme, and mix. Add pork cubes and crumbled bacon, and mix again. Cover the skillet, and let the mixture cook over low heat for 30 minutes. Stir occasionally to mix well and keep from sticking. Add the mushrooms and pineapple, and mix well. Preheat oven to 400° F.

Remove the peppers from refrigerator and arrange in a baking pan. Spoon the stuffing into the hollows, rounding the tops and smoothing them. (If there is any stuffing remaining, bake it separately, or use it to stuff another vegetable.) Put the peppers in the oven, and immediately reduce heat to 325° F. Bake for 20 minutes. Mix bread crumbs and orange rind, and spoon the mixture on top of the peppers. Return them to the oven, and increase heat to 350° F. Bake for 15 minutes longer, then serve.

BEEF AND CABBAGE ROLLS   6 servings

4 pounds beef cross-rib (shoulder)
1 small green cabbage
1 cup all-purpose flour
½ pound butter (2 sticks)
8 garlic cloves, crushed
1 large onion, minced
½ pound mushrooms, peeled and chopped

¼ teaspoon curry powder
½ teaspoon salt
1 cup tomato sauce
⅓ cup dry red wine
4 carrots, scraped and sliced
2 large onions, sliced
2 green peppers, diced

Have butcher trim all fat from the beef and cut it into chunks 1 by 3 inches. Remove the core of the cabbage. Put the cabbage in a deep saucepan, cover with boiling water, and let stand for 8 to 10 minutes. Drain the cabbage, and carefully separate the leaves.

Roll the chunks of meat in flour. Melt the butter in a saucepan; put in garlic and minced onion, and cook over low heat for 30 minutes. Add mushrooms, curry powder and salt, and mix well. Roll the meat chunks in the mixture, and place each chunk on a cabbage leaf. When all the pieces are arranged, divide the remaining mushroom mixture evenly among them, spooning it over the pieces of meat. Roll up the cabbage leaves, and fasten with wooden food picks or poultry pins.

Preheat oven to 350° F. Pour tomato sauce and wine into a baking pan large enough to hold the rolls, and add carrots, sliced onions and green peppers; mix well, and spread evenly over the bottom of the pan. Arrange the cabbage rolls over this bed, in a single layer or in several layers, and cover the pan (use foil if there is no cover). Bake for 1½ hours. Turn off oven heat, and let the pan remain in the oven for 15 minutes longer.

Not all stuffed vegetables must be baked. Some are excellent with cold stuffings. Chicken or veal salad in tomatoes is delicious; other vegetables can be poached until tender but still firm, chilled and stuffed with minced tongue, ham or steak tartare. Hard-cooked eggs stuffed with minced poultry, chicken livers, pâté, dried beef, deviled ham, all served cold, make good appetizer or luncheon dishes. Pineapple halves or quarters can be filled with cold mixtures of various meats, and they seem well suited to Oriental combinations of pork and shellfish, chicken and pork, and so on.

STUFFED PASTA AND PANCAKES

As for stuffing pasta, pancakes and turnovers, the sky is the limit! Seasoned and well-sauced variety meats are especially good fillings for any of these. The classic Bolognese stuffing for *tortellini* is made with fresh pork and veal, ham, capon, mortadella sausage and calf's brains. *Cappelletti* for Christmas Eve in Perugia are stuffed with a mixture of veal, pork, ham and brains. Chicken livers make a good stuffing for any pasta, and sweetbreads with spinach are another fine choice.

Any good pasta stuffing can be used for pancakes and turnovers by adjusting the liquid content. Pancakes stuffed with creamed chicken, sauced and briefly browned under the broiler, are beautiful to look at as well as delicious to eat. Pancakes can be made ahead of time and refrigerated or frozen, each one separated from the next by a sheet of freezer paper. When you are ready to stuff the pancakes, defrost them until they are flexible enough to fold, and then either heat them in the oven before filling or heat them in a sauce after filling.

LUNCHEON

Baked tomatoes with lamb and rice stuffing
Sautéed okra

Chicken consommé
Pancakes stuffed with creamed sweetbreads and mushrooms

Pork-Stuffed Green Peppers (see p. 226)
Cucumber and mushroom salad

DINNER

Beef Scaloppine Stuffed with Chicken (see p. 217)
Sweet potatoes duchess style
Snow peas and water chestnuts

Veal scallops with mushroom stuffing
Jerusalem artichokes with lemon and egg sauce
Rice salad with pimientos and dried currants
White-wine dressing

Carpetbag steak (sirloin stuffed with oysters)
French fried potatoes
Broccoli with lemon

Roast stuffed chicken
Fried parsley
Sautéed new potatoes
Creamed onions with chopped peanuts

Pasta shells stuffed with chicken and grated cheese
Spinach sauce
Roast veal round
Baked potatoes
Leeks braised in red wine

Cream of tomato soup
Stuffed breast of veal
Buttered parsnips
Curried green peppers with yogurt

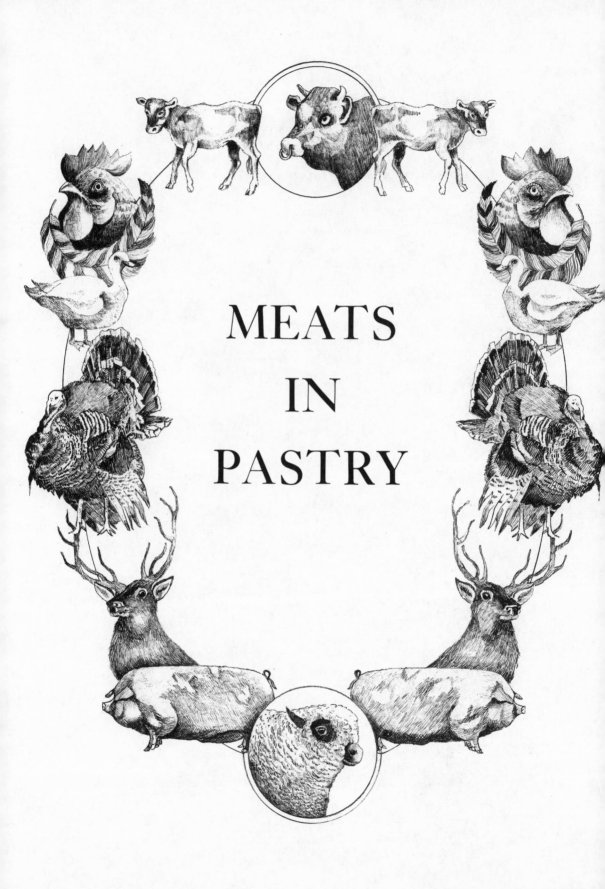

MEATS
IN
PASTRY

Not only can pastry-wrapped meats and poultry fit into every course of the meal, but they can also be used for snacks, picnics and cocktail parties. Even for dessert? Yes, even for dessert, if you like the true mince pie made with beef!

Since this is not a pastry cookbook, we are going to provide only a few basic pastry recipes; you can substitute favorite recipes of your own or use packaged or frozen pastries. If you remember to use a light touch, you will have good results with very simple means.

QUICHES

Tarts are pretty to start a meal. *Quiche lorraine*, a custard tart made with cream and filled with bacon, is the most familiar for first-course serving. It is usually baked in an 8-inch tart pan and cut into 4 to 6 pieces to serve while still warm. This preparation has become almost a cliché; why not make a similar dish with something a little different? The meat can be Canadian bacon or ham, cut into slivers, and you can add various kinds of cheese. Or try a filling of onion and diced veal or fresh pork mixed with the custard, or dark meat of poultry with sliced artichoke hearts or leeks. The possible fillings for these open tarts are endless.

For an elegant serving, bake individual quiches in shirred-egg dishes or in flan rings, metal rings with no bottoms. The pastry is fitted into the ring on a baking sheet, but you must be careful to keep the top edge of the pastry within the rim of the ring so that it will be easy to remove the metal ring when ready to serve. Flan rings come in various sizes; 4-inch muffin rings, just right for individual flans, are also available.

BASIC PASTRY FOR PIES AND TARTS

Use all-purpose flour, hydrogenated vegetable shortening (or half shortening and half butter), and very cold water, iced if possible. Sift the flour, and measure 2 cups. Sift again with 1 teaspoon salt. Dump ⅔ cup cold shortening into the flour, and, with a pastry blender or two knives, chop the shortening in the flour, making little crumbs about the size of lentils. Add 2 tablespoons cold water, and with a fork mix all together. Add up to 2 more tablespoons of water, but only enough to make a soft mass that holds together in a loose ball. It should not be sticky or stiff. Turn out on a *lightly* floured surface—a pastry cloth is easiest to work on if you are new at this. Cool your hands with cold water and dry thoroughly. With fingers mix the dough for about 1 minute. Pat into a ball, roll in wax paper, and chill in the refrigerator for 1 hour.

Turn out again on the floured surface, and pat into a flattened oval. Cut into pieces for whatever you plan to make: halves for a large 2-crust pie; 3 pieces for 1-crust 8-inch pies; 8 to 10 pieces for individual tarts. Roll out each piece, from the center to the edges, to a circle of the right size. Lift each piece on the rolling pin, and place over the pan or ring, then fit it in loosely.

Some general pointers:

Use only the lightest sprinkle of flour on the pastry cloth or board; some of it is absorbed by the dough, and too much can make the dough tough.

It will be much easier to serve the pie or tart if you oil the pan or ring; use a little tasteless oil, and rub it on with a sheet of absorbent kitchen paper.

Do not handle the dough too much; this will make it tough.

A bottom crust for a pie should be about 1½ inches larger in diameter than the top edge of the pan; when the sheet of dough has been fitted, you will have about ½ inch left all around. For a 1-crust pie, fold over the extra ½ inch, and pinch it to give it a firmer edge. For a 2-crust pie, fold the bottom edge over the top edge to seal the pie.

For flan rings, fold the extra edge down inside the ring, and pinch to seal.

To bake tarts and pies before they are filled, line the dough with foil, and fill the foil with dried beans or rice; or use metal pellets especially devised for blind baking. Bake in a preheated 425° F. oven for 15 minutes, or until the pastry is brown enough to suit you. If you like, you can remove the foil and beans or pellets after 10 minutes and let the pastry finish baking. (You can use those beans or rice for other pies or to eat; they will just need a little soaking because they will be quite hard.)

These shells can be partly baked if that suits your recipe better.

Custard tarts are always baked in one crust, without a top. A trick to make them look beautiful as you serve them is to add the egg whites, beaten until stiff, to the custard at the last minute; the filling will puff up like a little soufflé. Do this only when guests are ready to eat, because, as with any soufflé, the filling will sink if the tarts are kept waiting.

SMALL TURNOVERS

Other pastries are baked without pans or rings—turnovers, little rolls and so on. The Egyptian *sambousek* is a turnover filled with minced raw meat or cooked meat and minced onion cooked in a little oil. While the Egyptian pastry is made from flour, butter and a leavening like baking powder, you can use any pastry. Be sure to season the meat well, and seal the edges with a little egg. If you like, brush the top with egg to give it a glaze, and sprinkle with ground cuminseed, whole cuminseeds slightly crushed in a mortar, caraway or poppy seeds. Bake the little turnovers in a 400° F. oven until the pastry is golden brown.

Pirozhki, the small versions of the *pirog* (p. 237), are made in almost the same way as the *sambousek*. Use a raised dough (p. 238), or any standard pastry. The filling can be beef and onions seasoned with dill, or liver and onions, or veal and anchovies, or any meat combination you like. For a very smooth texture, sauté the minced meat in butter or oil, then grind it again with the other ingredients. You can make turnover shapes or log shapes like miniatures of the larger *pirog*. Seal well, then bake in a 400° F. oven for about 30 minutes, until the pastry is golden. If you use a raised dough, the *pirozhki* will swell up to very fat little turnovers.

Vatrushki, also Russian, are usually filled with pot cheese, but you can substitute a meat or poultry filling. Cut the pastry into rounds; put the filling in the middle, and lift the sides up around the filling to make a boat-shaped container. Be sure the edges are well crimped together. Bake them like the *pirozhki*, but for a shorter time if you make them smaller.

Empanadas are little turnovers from South American countries. Any standard pastry and any of the fillings already mentioned will do. The main difference between *empanadas* and the turnovers we have discussed so far is that the *empanadas* are fried in deep fat heated to 375° F. instead of being baked. To make them taste Latin, add minced green chilies to the filling. Cheese is a great favorite in South American countries, and it makes a good *empanada* filling when mixed with ham. Tomato paste and puréed spinach are also pretty additions to the filling mixture.

Tiny versions of any of these small turnovers are perfect for cocktail parties; bake them in tiny muffin pans, or sandwich the filling between two 2-inch rounds of pastry.

MEATS WRAPPED IN PASTRY

Beef Wellington is the most common dish in which a large piece of meat is wrapped in pastry. Oddly enough, the idea has not been developed, although there are so many other possibilities. For the classic recipe, see page 378, and for a similar preparation, see Calf's Liver à l'Amiral (p. 181). Here are some other ideas.

LAMB LA CORUÑA

Use the eye of the rib or loin of lamb. Have the butcher bone it and strip it, as in preparing a beef filet. Melt butter in a large heavy frying pan; use about 3 tablespoons for each lamb eye. Add seasoning (salt, pepper, an herb of your choice) to the butter, and let the butter bubble. Then butter-fry each piece of lamb separately, turning to cook all sides, for 5 minutes, without browning. Lift the meat to a flat

233

surface, with the butter still on it, and refrigerate; the butter will become firm. Make the pastry, and let it chill, for 1 hour if possible.

Roll out pastry for each piece of lamb; make an oval large enough to cover the meat completely. There are two ways to proceed; the simplest method—and a very good one—is to roll up the meat without any other ingredients; trim the pastry at the edges so that the overlapping layer of pastry is as small as possible, and seal at the overlap with egg wash (1 egg yolk mixed with 1 tablespoon water). Brush the top with more of the egg wash. Bake in a preheated 350° F. oven until the top is golden brown; roll over, and let the bottom brown also. Serve with the best-looking side up; each lamb eye will make 3 or 4 servings.

For a more elaborate preparation, spread the pastry oval with chopped un-cooked mushrooms, sprinkle with some of the melted butter left from cooking the meat, and scatter chopped cooked chicken breast over the butter. Add the lamb, roll, seal and bake.

You can use packaged pastry, the basic pastry on page 231, or *pâte brisée* with egg; the egg gives the pastry stretchiness and helps keep the moisture inside the package.

PÂTE BRISÉE

2 cups all-purpose flour	¼ pound butter (1 stick), or margarine
1 teaspoon salt	2 egg yolks
1 teaspoon sugar	2 tablespoons light cream

Measure the flour before sifting it, then sift together with the salt and sugar into a large bowl. (You can omit sugar, but it helps to give good color to the pastry and it will not make it taste sweet.) Cut in the butter until the mixture looks like lumpy cornmeal. Turn out on a pastry board and make a well in the center. Mix egg yolks and cream with a fork, and pour into the well. Little by little, mix the dry ingredients into the well, until the whole mixture is moistened. Some flours absorb more liquid than others; if yours is quite absorbent, add a little more cream or a few drops of cold water. "Break" the dough with the heel of the hand, as if kneading a bread dough, until it is smooth. Wrap in wax paper, and chill for 1 hour. When you are ready to use the dough, roll it out as you would the basic pastry.

There are recipes for whole hams and legs of lamb wrapped in pastry. We do not think such dishes are practical, because they are too hard to carve. Boned ham, pork loin or lamb would work better, but the larger the piece of meat, the more dif-ficult it is to adjust the cooking to insure that the meat will be cooked just enough in the first stage so that it will be perfectly done when the pastry is done.

FRUIT-STUFFED PORK IN PASTRY

Have your butcher bone a 6- to 10-inch center-cut loin of pork; have all but a ⅛- to ¼-inch-thick layer of fat trimmed away. Score the fat in diamonds down to the meat. Cut a pocket in the center of the meat. Brush the inside of the meat with fruit-flavored brandy, matching the brandy to the fruit you use in the stuffing. Make the stuffing with bread crumbs or cubes, herbs, chopped dried apricots or prunes or chopped fresh apples, mild seasoning and a little oil. Fold the pork over the stuffing, tie well, put on a rack and roast in a preheated 325° F. oven for 1 hour and 15 minutes. Increase the heat to 400° F., and roast for 15 minutes longer; the fatty crust should be golden brown. Let the meat cool. Make the pastry, whatever kind you like, and chill it.

Roll out the pastry to a large oval, and brush with a mixture of melted butter and fruit-flavored brandy. Place the pork in the center, roll up, and seal the edges with egg wash. Mix more butter and brandy with egg yolk and brush all over the top of the pastry. Bake in a preheated 350° F. oven until the top is golden. Turn over, and brush the side now uppermost with more butter, brandy and egg yolk. Bake until the rest of the pastry is golden.

Veal can also be cooked in pastry. Use the filet of veal, which has a small circumference. The eye of the veal chop is larger and takes too long to cook. Follow the recipe for Lamb La Coruña (see p. 233).

For a special occasion, try the following recipe, which combines the ideas of two great French dishes, *coq en pâte* (chicken in pastry) and *poularde demi-deuil* (chicken in half mourning).

BLACK AND WHITE CHICKEN

Have a chicken of 4 to 5 pounds boned completely when you buy it. (Take all the bones home for stock.) Thumb open the skin over the meat wherever it is possible without tearing the skin. Insert thin slices of peeled truffle; 1 large truffle will be enough. Turn the bird over, and rub the inside with a mixture of 1½ tablespoons melted chicken fat and 2 tablespoons butter. Mix brandy with the butter if you like. Sprinkle with salt and pepper, celery seasoning, and minced herbs—your choice, but use a light hand. Fold the bird, and tie it into a cylindrical shape. Put on a rack, and roast in a preheated 350° F. oven for 1 hour; turn over, and roast for 45 minutes longer. Remove from the oven, and cool.

Make the pastry, and roll it out into a rather thick rectangular sheet. Remove strings from the cooled chicken, and roll the bird in the pastry; seal the edges with egg wash. Brush more egg wash all over the top and sides, and sprinkle with poppy seeds. Bake in a preheated 350° F. oven until pastry is golden brown; turn over, brush the part now on top with more egg wash, and sprinkle with poppy seeds. Finish baking until golden brown all over.

Individual servings of black and white chicken in pastry packages can be prepared in the same way. Use whole chicken breasts (both sides) of small chickens; the whole breasts should weigh about 1 pound each. Bone the breasts, leaving the skin on, add the truffles, butter the insides and fold each breast closed. Bake for about 20 minutes, 10 minutes on each side—or for longer if the pieces weigh more than a pound. Cool. Wrap in pastry, and bake until golden. This is a nice dish for a party.

Hamburgers in Pastry

You can make other individual pastries like miniature beef Wellingtons or double-sized rolls. Make hamburgers or lambburgers, being sure to use meat with very little fat. Season well. Pat into any shape you like. Bake in a preheated 400° F. oven for 5 minutes. Take out, roll in seasoned flour, put on a baking sheet and cool. Wrap in pastry, brush with egg yolk, sprinkle with poppy seeds, and bake until golden brown.

Many variations of the recipe on page 217 can be prepared for individual servings. Make boneless beef scallops from the first cut of the sirloin or from shell steaks. Have them cut ½ inch thick, and flatten them to ¼ inch. Roll out dough to very thin rounds about ½ inch larger in diameter than the flattened scallops. Brush the dough with oil, and sprinkle with crumbled dried thyme. Put a beef scallop on the pastry; brush with Cognac or other brandy if you like. Add your choice of other ingredients; thin slices of Canadian bacon and a melting cheese is one possibility; another is cooked sausage meat mashed to little crumbs. Add more seasoning if you like (sausage needs very little). Roll up, seal the ends, flour the rolls lightly, and place them on a baking sheet. Bake in a preheated 350° F. oven for 10 minutes; turn over, and bake for 6 minutes longer.

MEAT PIES AND PASTRIES

The cookery of every country includes preparations of pastry filled with snippets of meat. Some of the pastries are bite-sized, and others are large enough for a sizable snack, a lunch or even the main course of a dinner. Some of these turnovers are like sandwiches with pastry outsides instead of bread.

Cornish Pasties

One of the most famous of these pastries started out as a fish turnover—the Cornish pasty. This was originally the lunch of tin miners—a whole fish baked in a pastry coating. The shape of this turnover still faintly suggests the fish—it is a large, slightly curved half-moon. Today the pasty is usually filled with lamb, potatoes and onions, but other meats are sometimes used. The filling is different from most others because it is not mixed together, but sliced into the pastry one ingredient at a time. The meat is not ground, but sliced into small pieces. The pastry is thick, and all Cornish cooks have their secret ways with it. The pasty is large—a good size for a hearty lunch—and can be eaten hot or cold. How about this for a novel picnic or lunchbox item?

Pork Pies

Another English speciality is the Melton Mowbray pie. Pork pies are made everywhere pigs are raised, but the true Melton Mowbray pie is made only in Leicestershire, and although the details of the recipe are secret, here is a close approximation. The pies are about 4 inches across, flat on the bottom and straight sided. The thick, sturdy pastry, made with lard, holds its shape; in spite of being so different from the thin, flaky crusts so popular today, it is a digestible and delicious container. The container is shaped around a mold and then filled; it is baked, not in a pan, but on a baking sheet. Inside there is nothing but chopped fresh pork and seasoning. When the pie has been filled, a pastry lid with a hole in the top is fitted in place. The pies are baked for a long time—2 hours in a 325° F. oven. While they bake, a gelatin-rich stock is made by cooking the bones and cartilage from the pork. After it has cooled, this aspic is poured into the cooled pie through the hole in the top. One of these pies makes a huge lunch. For a special occasion, make a large pie with pastry leaves and decorations on the top. Make small versions for people with less sturdy appetites. These pork pies also make good picnic and lunchbox fare. In England, they are never refrigerated, but it is just as well to keep them in a cold place.

Pirog

A Russian dish based on chopped meat in pastry is the *pirog*. The standard pastry for the *pirog* is a buttery yeast dough, like a bread dough, containing eggs, but you can use cream-cheese pastry or an unsweetened tart pastry made with half lard, half butter, and egg. The pastry must be stretchy and smooth, not flaky like a delicate dessert pastry. A *pirog* can be shaped like a big turnover or like a loaf of bread. The meat can be chopped beef or a mixture of beef and veal. The filling is usually flavored with minced onion, and a traditional *pirog* includes chopped hard-cooked eggs. The onion and meat are cooked in butter, then minced again or ground, to blend completely. Chopped eggs are then added along with any flavoring the cook likes; dill is a favorite in Russia as well as in Scandinavia. Roll out the dough into a circle for a turnover shape or into a rectangle, pile the filling on it, and fold the pastry over to cover completely. If you use the bread-loaf shape, roll it over on the baking sheet so the seam is on the bottom. Make a few holes in the top to let steam escape. Start baking in a preheated 400° F. oven. After 10 minutes, reduce heat to 350° F., and bake for about 20 minutes longer, until the pastry is done.

Cabbage and other vegetable fillings for *pirog* are great favorites in Russia. You can mix other vegetables with the meat for variations. Some fish and meat mixtures also taste good; try veal with either tuna or salmon.

CREAM-CHEESE PASTRY

¾ pound salted butter, at room temperature
¾ pound cream cheese, at room temperature

3 cups all-purpose flour
light cream, if needed

Fill an earthenware bowl with very hot water, then pour it out and dry the bowl. Put butter and cream cheese in the warmed bowl, and mash with a wooden spoon or blend with an electric mixer until completely mixed, creamy and fluffy but not melted. Add flour, and mix until you have a smooth dough. Add a few drops of cream if the dough is too stiff. Knead for ½ minute, until you can roll into a ball, then chill for at least several hours—overnight if you have enough time. If the dough has been chilled overnight, let it rest at room temperature for about 1 hour before rolling it. This pastry is stickier than most, and you will need a pastry cloth and a stockinette cover for your roller. If you do not have these, roll between sheets of wax paper. All pastries can be frozen, but this one is so successful for freezing that it is worth making a large amount.

Coulibiac

Another Russian dish is the *coulibiac*, a hot fish pie. It is made as the bread-shaped *pirog* is, but the dough is brioche dough. The filling includes chopped hard-cooked eggs and a grain. While the classic dish is made of fish, most often salmon fillets, this preparation could be made with a meat filling as well, ground meat or meat cut into thin slivers. As with the filling for *pirog*, all the ingredients are cooked before they are layered onto the dough, so the final cooking is just long enough to bake the brioche and blend the flavors. This is a more complicated dish than the relatively simple *pirog*, and may well include more costly ingredients. Fresh mushrooms are a good addition, and an elegant filling can be made of chicken and lobster or either of the veal-and-fish mixtures suggested for *pirog*. The grain can be rice, but kasha (buckwheat groats) or bulgur (cracked wheat) can also be used. For *coulibiac* the ingredients are arranged in layers instead of being mixed together. A sauce of lemon butter, fresh horseradish and butter, or dill butter is usually served as accompaniment. It was Escoffier who introduced this dish to French cookery when he was chef in the Grand Hotel of Monte Carlo, which was a favorite haunt of Russian noblemen and had a regular season of Russian ballet.

BRIOCHE DOUGH

2 packages active dry yeast	3 tablespoons sugar
½ cup water (about 110° F.)	4 eggs
6 cups all-purpose flour	½ pound unsalted butter, softened
2 teaspoons salt	

Dissolve the yeast in the water in a large bowl. Sift in 1 cup of the flour, and knead into a ball in the bowl. Cover with water at 85° F. Sift the rest of the flour with the salt and sugar, and place on a pastry board. When the ball of dough (the sponge) expands and rises to the surface of the water, lift it out with a skimmer. Make a well in the center of the flour mixture, and add the eggs, the sponge and half of the butter. Gradually mix the flour into the moist ingredients in the center, and knead the dough for 10 minutes, until smooth and elastic. Add the rest of the butter, 1 tablespoon at a time, and continue kneading until the dough is no longer sticky. Turn into a buttered bowl, roll over to coat with butter on all sides, and cover the bowl with a damp towel. Let the dough rise in a warm place (75° to 85° F.) until doubled in bulk. Punch it down, turn it over, and let it rise again until doubled. Punch dough down again, cover, and let rest for 10 minutes.

Turn out the dough, cut off as much as you need (this is enough for a very large *coulibiac* or 2 smaller ones), and roll out to a thin sheet. Any remaining dough can be refrigerated. The filled dough should be allowed to rise for 30 minutes. Brush with beaten egg yolk mixed with water or cream. Bake in a preheated 400° F. oven for about 30 minutes, until the dough is baked and golden. A *coulibiac* can be baked in a deep pottery dish if you prefer, although the bread shape is traditional.

Little pies made of chopped chicken breast, mushrooms, rice and hard-cooked eggs are called *petits coulibiacs*, but they are actually more like turnovers and the pastry used is puff paste. This idea can be adapted for any meat filling. Since all the ingredients are cooked before being layered, these little pies do not require hours of cooking, only enough time to bake the pastry. However, puff paste is a tricky pastry. It is usually suggested for beef Wellington and often used for other wrapped meats and poultry. You will notice we have not suggested it for anything before this. When this pastry dough is ready to bake, it is composed of hundreds of layers of dough and hundreds of layers of butter, each in sheets as thin as onion skin. As the pastry bakes, the moisture in the butter layers acts as leavening and causes the layers to rise, giving a delicate, light pastry with a rather crackly texture. Unfortunately, in a dish like a Wellington, the weight of the meat or poultry prevents the rising of the pastry layer underneath; even if you turned the meat over partway through cooking, it would be too late for that layer to rise as puff paste should. That is why the pastry-wrapped masterpieces in many an elegant restaurant are soggy on the bottom. With smaller turnovers, the puff paste has a better chance to bake properly. The best use for puff paste is to make pattie shells or containers for timbales or *vol-au-vent*, which are fully baked separately and filled later. Although puff paste has so few ingredients, it does require dexterity and time; it freezes well, so you can make a large amount while you're at it. You may find frozen puff paste available in shops. If you cannot buy it and do not have the time to make it, use another kind of pastry. If you are on a restricted diet that excludes butter, choose another pastry. Puff paste can be made with margarine, but it does not taste as good as if made with butter.

PUFF PASTE

1½ pounds unsalted butter (6 sticks)	2 teaspoons salt
6 cups instantized flour	2 to 2½ cups ice water

Unwrap the butter and squeeze together to make one lump. Knead the butter in a large bowl of cold water, to extract any milky liquid remaining in the butter, until it is very smooth. Press into a large flat cake, dry with a kitchen paper towel, wrap and refrigerate. Dump the flour on a large board, and make a well in the center. Put the salt in the well, and add ½ cup of the water. Dissolve the salt, then start mixing the flour into the water. When the water is completely absorbed and lumps of dough have formed, add more of the water, about 2 tablespoons at a time, until all the flour and water forms a dough that holds together. Wrap the dough ball, and refrigerate for 30 minutes.

Roll out the flour paste to a rectangle slightly less than ½ inch thick. Place the butter on one half, and fold the other flap over; press together. With a rolling pin roll the dough from the center to the outer edge; turn the package around and roll the other half in the same way; do not roll over the edges, because this pushes out air and butter. Fold the top third of the dough toward the center, then fold up the bottom third over that. Turn the package at right angles, so an open end is toward you. Then roll again just as before. Fold in thirds again, wrap and refrigerate. After 20 minutes roll and fold twice more, and refrigerate for 20 more minutes. Once more, roll, fold twice and refrigerate for 20 minutes.

PATTIE SHELLS

Cut off as much dough as you need, and roll it out into a sheet not quite ½ inch thick. Cut out circles with a doughnut cutter for tiny shells, or with a large coffeepot cover for larger shells. With a smaller cutter, mark a circle in the center of half of the rounds, but do not remove the circles. Moisten the edges of the solid rounds, and place the others on top. Put the shells on a buttered baking sheet, and bake in a preheated 450° F. oven for 15 minutes; reduce heat to 350° F., and bake until golden brown. Let the shells cool, then carefully lift out the circles on the tops, and scoop out the uncooked dough in the center. Let the shells dry completely. Fill with any mixture—creamed chicken and mushrooms, sweetbreads and so on.

A *vol-au-vent* is simply a large pattie shell, and you make it in the same way as the smaller shells. Roll the dough into a slightly thicker sheet, at least ½ inch thick, and cut the rounds about 8 inches across. Bake for about 5 minutes longer.

If this sounds like too much work, use frozen pattie shells.

Steak and Kidney Pie

Conventional meat pies baked in standard pie pans or deep-dish containers are made of cubes, slices or chunks of meat. The most famous example is the English favorite, steak and kidney pie. The best choice for the steak is center-cut chuck, because it is quite juicy, although sirloin is sometimes used. Because of their delicate flavor, veal or lamb kidneys are best to use. Remove membranes and tough centers of the kidneys (see p. 179), then parboil them with a dash of salt for about 5 minutes. Drain well, and dice. Cut the beef into small chunks. Mix the meats with fresh vegetables of your choice, add some brandy or wine, and turn into a pastry-lined deep pie dish. Use the basic pastry on page 231 or a packaged mix. Cover the pie with a top crust, make some vents for steam to escape, and decorate with leaves or other designs made of pastry scraps. Bake the pie in a preheated 450° F. oven for 10 minutes, then reduce heat to 350° F., and bake for 50 to 60 minutes longer. If you are in doubt about the meat, test it for doneness by sticking a skewer through the vents in the crust. To make your pie more English, put pastry only on the top. (An English pie always has a top crust; it may or may not have a bottom crust.) Another English idea is to brown the meats, sprinkle with flour, then poach them with the other ingredients in stock for 45 minutes to 1 hour. Pour the mixture, with any remaining liquid, which will be thickened like a gravy, into the pastry, and bake at 450° F. for 20 minutes, until the pastry is golden.

Individual pies can be made in prepared pattie shells—beef pies and other kinds. You can also make pies with basic pastry in tart pans for individual servings. These pies can be frozen if you omit potatoes, which do not freeze well.

Chicken Pie

Chicken pies can be made of all white meat or a mixture of white and dark meat. You can use raw chicken, but by the time it is cooked, you might have over-cooked pastry. It is easier to use cooked chicken; it can be baked, barbecued or poached, but poached chicken will give you the juiciest results. Use a large chicken, and do not overcook it. Cool, remove skin and bones, and cut into large dice. You can add any vegetables you like—green peas, sliced carrots and celery, slivered cabbage, sliced leeks, little white onions. Use a combination of vegetables, season them lightly, and sauté them in butter with a few pinches of a good curry powder until they are not quite done but still a little crunchy; to make sure the vegetables are evenly cooked, sauté the ones that need the longest cooking first. Mix with diced chicken. Turn into a pastry-lined deep baking dish. Cover the filling with button mushrooms, and top with pastry. The vegetables usually provide enough moisture, but a thickened velouté made with well-flavored chicken stock can be added. Make vents in the top to allow steam to escape. Bake in a preheated 400° F. oven for 45 minutes, or until the pastry is golden. If the edges brown too fast, cover them with foil.

You can make pies with other poultry and meats following the same basic recipe. Turkey requires longer cooking than chicken, so be sure to poach or roast the meat first. Use white meat for best results. Lamb pies are good; use the leg because it is leanest. Dice the meat, or cut it into chunks. Veal and pork can also be used for pies.

If the filling ingredients for your pies are completely or nearly cooked, bake them at brisk heat (400 to 450° F.) until everything is hot and the crust fully cooked. If the filling is still raw, start the pie at high heat to crisp the crust bottom, then finish at lower heat (350° F.) for enough time to cook the filling; the amount of time will vary according to the meat you use. Test through the steam vent with a skewer or two-tined fork if in doubt.

Another possibility is to bake the filling with a biscuit topping instead of a pastry crust.

Other dishes called "pies," although not made of pastry, can be made with potato crust or grains. Liver, diced and mixed with onions and mushrooms, makes a good dish baked in a mashed-potato crust or in a shell of rice.

Another example is the tamale pie. In this, the "crust" is made of cornmeal mush and the filling of ground beef mixed with onion, tomatoes and chili powder, plus any additional seasonings or flavorings you like.

PASTRY LASAGNA

Here is an experimental dish we call "pastry lasagna." Use a lasagna dish, and line just the bottom with a sheet of pastry cut to fit it. Bake in a preheated 375° F. oven for 10 minutes. Remove from the oven, and sprinkle the pastry with a delicate coating of flour. Spread an inch-thick layer of diced or ground meat mixed with diced vegetables over the pastry. Season the layer, and cover with a second layer of pastry cut to fit the dish. Sprinkle with a delicate coating of flour and then add a *thin* layer (¼ inch thick) of the meat and vegetable mixture. Cover with slices of cheese, and sprinkle the cheese with seasoning. Top with another pastry layer, and brush the top with melted butter or oil. Bake at 275° F. for 30 minutes, then raise heat to 325° F., and continue baking until the pastry is brown.

You can use basic pastry for this, but another good choice is strudel dough, which is available frozen.

Leftovers are discussed in Chapter 19, but we would like to make a few suggestions here for using pastry for leftovers. Corned beef, roast beef and pot-roasted beef can be diced or ground and used in small tarts or larger pies, and they are very good in the pastry lasagna dish.

Roly-Poly

Another good way of using leftover meat is to make a roly-poly of it. Make basic pastry (p. 231) or cream-cheese pastry (p. 237), and roll it out to a long rectangle. Chop or grind your leftover meat with some onions, season, moisten with a little gravy or tomato sauce, and spread on the pastry. Starting at one of the narrow ends, roll the pastry; seal the end, and turn the roll over, placing the seam underneath. Bake in a preheated 400° F. oven until the pastry is done. Slice across, and serve with a sauce or gravy.

If you feel ambitious, you can make the same kind of roll with bread dough. When the dough has risen, you can bake the roll whole, or slice it and bake the slices lying flat on a baking sheet. Brioche dough, twice risen (p. 238), and biscuit dough can be used in the same way.

Another good trick with leftovers is to make fried pies. You can also bake the pies, but the quick cooking of deep-frying is good for meat that is already cooked. Roll out the pastry, and cut it into squares or rounds. Put a mound of chopped or ground leftover meat on one side, fold the pastry over, and seal to make rectangles or half-rounds. Fry in oil heated to 375 to 385° F. until the pastry is puffed and golden—only a few minutes. Lard pastry and suet pastry are good for meat pies, but packaged pastry will do. Lard pastry can be made following the basic pastry recipe (p. 231); use lard instead of the shortening and butter mixture, and add 1 teaspoon sugar with the salt.

You can make good little turnovers with leftover stews and other cooked mixtures. Cut up any large pieces of meat or poultry, and season with a little barbecue spice or curry powder. Spoon about 2 tablespoons on a 5-inch round or square, and sprinkle with grated cheese or add a slice of cheese. Fold the pastry over, crimp the edges, and bake at 400° F. until the pastry is puffed and brown.

We will add one more pastry for those who cannot eat the usual fats. This uses vegetable oil, which will enable those on low-cholesterol diets to eat pastry.

OIL PASTRY

Measure 3 cups all-purpose flour, and sift it with ½ tablespoon salt into a large bowl. Pour ¾ cup safflower oil (or other polyunsaturated oil) and the same amount of water into a small bowl, and stir with a fork until emulsified. Pour at once into the flour, and continue to stir with the fork until well mixed. It is easiest to roll this dough between sheets of wax paper, and, since it is a moist dough, you will have to flour your hands. This recipe will make enough for both crusts of a 10-inch pie or a deep-dish pie.

Some people still make mincemeat with minced meat, a more robust dish than the apple and raisin product that is most common today. In 1920, a mixture without meat was called "mock mincemeat." Here is a modernized version of a 1900 recipe.

MINCEMEAT

2 pounds lean fresh beef
4 pounds tart green apples, pared and
  cored
½ pound beef suet
¼ pound citron
1½ pounds seedless raisins, rinsed
1 pound dried currants, rinsed
½ pound dark brown sugar
2 cups molasses
2 tablespoons ground cinnamon

1 tablespoon grated nutmeg
½ tablespoon grated mace
½ tablespoon ground allspice
½ tablespoon ground cloves
½ tablespoon salt
½ tablespoon ground black pepper
5 cups apple cider
1 cup brandy
2 cups Madeira

Poach the beef, as if making boiled beef, in enough water to cover; cook until the liquid has almost evaporated and the meat is tender. Remove bones and gristle, then chop the meat fine, and moisten it with the remaining cooking liquid. Chop apples, suet and citron; add raisins, currants and chopped beef. Put everything in a large kettle, and add brown sugar, molasses, all the spices, salt, pepper and cider. Stir until the sugar has dissolved and everything is well mixed, then cook over low heat, stirring occasionally, until almost boiling. Remove the mincemeat from heat, let it cool, then add the brandy and Madeira. Put in a crock or in quart jars, and keep in the refrigerator; or turn into preserving jars, and proceed as if canning fruit.

To make pie, line a pie dish with basic pastry (p. 231) or cream-cheese pastry (p. 237), fill with mincemeat, cover with a top crust and make vents in the top for steam to escape. Bake in a preheated 450° F. oven for 10 minutes, then reduce heat to 400° F., and bake about 35 minutes longer, until the pastry is golden.

LUNCHEON

Beef and barley soup
Leek and Canadian bacon quiche
Sliced tomato salad

Chicken-liver tarts baked in flan rings
Chef's salad

Cantaloupe balls with green grapes
Creamed veal and mushrooms in pattie shells
Endive salad

DINNER

Tomato and watercress soup
Lamb La Coruña (see p. 233)
Baked Bermuda onions filled with creamed spinach

Celery consommé with marrow dumplings
Black and White Chicken (see p. 235)
Individual molds of currant jelly
Fresh green beans
Steamed wedges of yellow squash

PICNIC

Cornish pasties
Beer in cans
Whole small tomatoes
Belgian endives
Carrot and cucumber strips
Fresh pears

Chopped leftover beef and cheese turnovers
Chicken sandwiches
Beet and celery salad
Apples and cookies

SUPPER

Pirogi filled with chopped beef, onion and hard-cooked eggs
Dill sauce
Romaine salad with garlic croutons

Chicken pie
Fruit salad with lime dressing

SUMMER
COOKING

Chapter 15

YOU MAY THINK ALL SUMMER DISHES should be cold. In temperate climates, however, air-conditioning has become so common that many people's dining areas are as cool in summer as they are in winter. If this is your situation, you may not have to prepare food specially for a warm season. But those of you who are attuned to the weather outdoors will probably want to plan menus around the seasons.

Summer foods should be light and easy to digest, particularly when it is very hot. Also, whether you are cooking for yourself or have a cook in the kitchen, no one wants to spend hours over a hot stove when it is hot everywhere else too. And the less time you have to spend cooking, the more time you have to be outside enjoying all the delightful things that summer offers.

Since everyone has refrigeration today, fresh meats and poultry can be kept just as well in summer as in winter. Actually, humidity speeds deterioration of meats and poultry even more significantly than heat, so refrigerate promptly, and be sure your equipment is in good working order. Decades ago, pork and turkey, for instance, would not have been generally available during summer months, but now you can buy most meats all year round. However, the refrigerator has to work harder to keep things cold in the summer, and it is probably being opened far more often for cold drinks and ice cubes. Plan, therefore, to use perishable items promptly. Leftovers should be planned carefully too. If you find you cannot use within a short time all of a large piece of meat you have prepared, freeze the remainder without delay.

The oven heats up a kitchen more than any other cooking device, so the first thing to avoid is roasting large pieces of meat or large birds. On the other hand, heating the oven for one day to roast something that can be served cold on several occasions may be more practical for you. Long slow cooking on top of the stove does not produce as much heat in the kitchen, but it will produce much more steam. If the weather is extremely humid, you may find the steam more unbearable than the heat of the oven. Generally speaking, eliminate dishes, such as pot roast or boiled beef, that require hours of cooking. On the other hand, pot roast cooked according to the classic French method of *boeuf à la mode* can be turned into a superb cold dish and can even be jellied; whether cold or jellied, it is a great summer dish. It is impossible to make universal rules; with today's insulated equipment, exhaust fans and air conditioning, you may find no impediments to cooking anything.

Even if you can cook comfortably with any method during summer, you will probably not choose to spend the time doing it. The quicker methods will serve better—sautéing, short-term poaching, broiling, barbecuing.

Beef

Steaks are good summer fare because they cook quickly; broil or barbecue them. Thinner minute steaks can be sautéed; if they are cut at least 1 inch thick, they can also be used for a quick barbecue. Ground beef is a natural, either raw, as steak tartare, or in any of the ways suggested in Chapter 12. If you are cooking outdoors, braising over coals is a good technique. Use beef flanken or rump, and place it in heavy-duty foil; add fresh tomatoes cut into slices or wedges; season the meat, and wrap it well. Or use a cast-iron Dutch oven for outdoor braising.

Veal

Veal chops can be rubbed with oil and dipped into crumbs to be sautéed or quick-baked in a high oven. If they are of good quality and thick enough, they can be broiled. Another beautiful veal dish is Stuffed Boneless Shoulder of Veal (p. 366); this takes time to prepare, and it does require the oven, but it can be served at room temperature, without gravy, and is just as delicious as when it is served hot. The same is true of stuffed breast of veal. Plain or stuffed veal scallops are fine in summer because they cook so quickly.

The most famous veal dish for summer is *vitello tonnato*, veal with tuna fish. Use a boneless piece of veal from the leg, rump or shoulder; tie if necessary. Stud it with small pieces of anchovy fillets, and place it in a large heavy kettle with flavoring vegetables, more anchovies and a 7-ounce can of oil-packed tuna for 5 pounds of meat. Add dry white wine and light veal stock or water to half fill the kettle, and simmer the meat until tender—1½ to 2 hours. When the meat is cold, remove any fat from the cooking liquid. Make a smooth sauce with mayonnaise and some of the cooking liquid, and adjust the flavor with lemon juice and more anchovies if needed. The sliced veal, covered with sauce, is usually garnished with capers, but parsley and wafer-thin slices of lemon are good too. This dish is served cold.

Lamb

Spring lamb is sold through the summer months and until October, so you can be sure of having tender, easy-to-cook lamb for summer meals. Good choices are the quick-cooking chops, for broiling; the rack, for quick roasting; ground lamb, for indoor patties or outdoor ground kebabs. A butterflied leg of lamb can be roasted quickly or broiled, and it is excellent barbecued. Lamb shish kebab is fine for summer meals, especially outdoors, and another good choice is lamb spareribs cut from the breast. Breast of lamb can be stuffed and baked or braised; while it does require long cooking, it can be served at room temperature like the stuffed veal shoulder. You can also barbecue the breast whole instead of carving it into spareribs first.

Pork

Pork can be delicious served cold. Use a boned loin of pork, well seasoned with herbs, and garlic if you like, or a piece of the leg similarly treated. Add a little water, white wine or apple juice to the roasting pan, because pork needs extra moisture because of its close texture. Cover the roasting pan for about three quarters of the time, and cook for about 35 minutes per pound. If there is any liquid left in the roasting pan pour it off; it will jell, and you can lift off the fat; serve the jelly with the meat, and accompany it with fruits in season.

A loin of pork can be boned and rolled with its kidneys inside, as is often done with a loin of veal. Add extra kidneys if necessary. This is another dish that requires lengthy cooking, but it can all be done in advance, and the meat can be served cold or at room temperature.

Pork spareribs, a natural for the barbecue, can also be cooked under the indoor broiler. As you will note in Chapter 16, it is a good idea to precook spareribs, and this is especially helpful in the summer; the actual barbecuing or broiling will then take less time.

Cured meats are good for summer meals. Most of them require little if any cooking, and the salt they contain is useful in hot weather to replace salt lost by the body through evaporation. They also keep well. Regular ham and delicious dry-cured hams like prosciutto, Canadian bacon and smoked pork chops are all good summer choices.

For a party occasion, even for a buffet, you could use a crown of pork made with smoked loins. Roast it as you would cured ham; use a 325° F. oven, and allow about 1¼ hours. As the crown cooks, baste it occasionally with white or rosé wine or with a fruit juice. Let it cool, then serve with a filling of fruits sprinkled with a mixture of orange and lime juice. For a delicate all-green salad, use grapefruit sections, honeydew melon and seedless grapes. A mixture of several kinds of melons and blander fruits like pears and apples is good too, but you can use your favorite recipe. Do not use a conventional salad dressing, and skip the lettuce. Instead of paper frills, top each chop bone with a piece of fruit.

Corned beef and pastrami, though both require long cooking, are good served cold.

Eggs with Meats

An excellent quick summer meal can be made with eggs and slivered cured meats; almost any kind will do. Make individual omelets, filled with a mixture of ham, salami or pastrami slivers and sautéed mushrooms, onions or whatever vegetable you prefer. For a company occasion, try this version: Cut the meat slices into neat rounds, and sauté them in a little oil until lightly browned; make tiny omelets

PORK CHOPS

Butterfly chop, prepared from two loin chops, split almost through and flattened

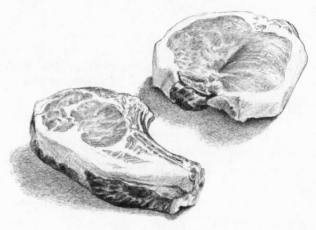

Blade chop, cut from the blade portion of the loin

Rib chop, cut from the center loin

Sirloin chop, cut from the sirloin portion of the loin

Loin chop, also cut from the center loin, but toward the sirloin so that it includes a portion of the tenderloin next to the T-bone

about the size of a small pancake—slightly smaller than the round of meat. Serve each meat slice topped with a miniature omelet, and garnish with a spoonful of a sautéed vegetable or serve with an appropriate sauce: parsley, mustard, tomato, etc. This can be a perfect luncheon or supper, and it can be dressed up for a dinner.

Tongue is very good cooked with scrambled eggs. To add more color contrast, toss in some chopped black olives or chopped fresh parsley.

Although cold dishes are practical and refreshing in summer, a menu of all cold food is not nearly as good for you or as appetizing as a meal with at least one hot dish. Some summer meals may be all cold, for instance most picnics and other outdoor meals. And a cold buffet like the one described in Chapter 21 will seldom include hot dishes if any of the cold items are aspic preparations. For other meals, consider at least one hot dish. There are so many possibilities for quick cooking that this need not add too much work. Your freezer can be a help with lengthy preparations; cook them on a cool day, and freeze them for later use. Even rather elaborate dishes like soufflés can be prepared and frozen *before* baking (see Chapter 24). Soufflés made of ham, veal or chicken are so light and delicate that they are perfect for summer meals.

Broiled Sandwiches

One simple hot lunch for summer is the broiled sandwich. This takes only a few minutes and does not heat up the kitchen. Spread bread or muffins with mustard butter, add a slice of ham cut to fit the bread, and sprinkle with a thick layer of grated cheese—Cheddar, Parmesan or your choice. Broil until the cheese is melted. For variations, substitute other flavored butters, other meats and other cheeses.

Here is another version: Use English muffins; split them, and cover each half with a slice of tongue trimmed to fit. Add a slice of mozzarella cheese and spoon a little marinara sauce over all. Sprinkle with orégano. Put under the broiler until the top is brown and the cheese melted.

You may also cut slices of tongue and slices of ham slightly smaller than a slice of bread. Place a slice of dill pickle across the center, and roll a tongue slice and a ham slice together, then wrap in a slice of bread with the crusts cut off. If you want bigger rolls, get unsliced bread and adjust the size of all the slices accordingly. Fasten the bread slice with a food pick, and bake in a hot oven until the bread is crisp. You can use pastry dough instead of bread; prepare it ahead of time—you can even roll it out and cut it into squares; just separate the squares with sheets of wax paper and refrigerate until ready to use them.

Meat pancakes are quick to cook. You can add slivered or chopped meat to standard pancake batter or make a separate recipe.

HAM AND CRUMB PANCAKES   about 16 small pancakes

4 to 6 ounces cooked ham (1½ cups ground)

2 apples, cored but not peeled

1 to 1½ cups dry bread crumbs

1 cup scalded milk

2 eggs, beaten

1 tablespoon baking powder

clarified butter or peanut oil for cooking

Grind ham and apples together through a food grinder. Soak 1 cup of crumbs in the milk, then stir in eggs and baking powder, mixing thoroughly. Fold in the ham and apples. If the mixture is too wet, add more of the remaining ½ cup of crumbs. Drop by small spoonfuls onto an oiled heated griddle. Turn only once, and do it carefully, because these pancakes are fragile.

Another idea for a summer lunch is to assemble a meal like an informal buffet, of first courses and starters. If you have all cold dishes, add hot rolls or herb-buttered hot French bread. Any of the dishes in Chapter 9 can be adapted for this, and you can augment your selections with packaged fish dishes (sardines, tuna) and various vegetables.

Variety Meats

In addition to tongue, which we have mentioned already, other variety meats are practical summer dishes because they cook quickly. However, they are perishable, so buy them when you know you are going to use them. Calf and steer liver, veal and lamb kidneys, sweetbreads and brains are all good choices. Because beef liver and kidneys and heart and tripe require long cooking, they are less suited to summer meals. Pork variety meats are strong tasting and are not served to good advantage by themselves; they are usually used in other preparations. Chicken livers are great for summer meals; they cook in minutes and are delicate in flavor, easily digestible, and adaptable to many ways of serving.

Sweetbreads and kidneys of lamb and veal can be cubed and cooked on skewers, by themselves or with small mushrooms and pieces of onion or parboiled whole small onions. Baste with a mixture of oil and wine with seasonings. Any of these meats can be sautéed or broiled. Sweetbreads and brains can be cooked in sauces, and both can be completely cooked by poaching, to be used cold in salads. (See Chapter 11 for basic preparations.)

Chicken

Chicken is a perfect food for summer use. It cooks quickly, and it is probably the most versatile meat. Young birds are excellent broiled, either plain or with a basting sauce. You can serve them hot immediately after cooking or let them cool and serve them cold. Cold chicken is always tasty, and it is also good finger food, fine for picnics and other outdoor meals. As you will read in Chapter 16, chicken is great barbecued. For an economy barbecue, adapt the precooked chicken on page

267; it is economical because the precooking saves on barbecue fuel and time. Split small birds or quarter larger ones; parboil the pieces for 10 minutes—you can do this early in the day. Put the pieces on a hot grill, and cook them on the bone side for 10 minutes, on the skin side for 5 minutes. Baste the pieces constantly with a smooth oil or a barbecue sauce.

Deep-frying is also a quick method. Cut chickens into 8 pieces suitable for serving—2 legs, 2 thighs, 2 half-breasts, 2 wings. The remaining bits, the ends of the wings and the back bones and any scraps, can be used to make stock. Freeze them, if you have only a few, until there are enough for stock making. Trim each piece so it has a projecting bone for a handle—easy to do on legs and wings; on thighs, the white cartilage can be scraped off the bone, and the bone can be contoured to form a little handle. In the breast pieces, scrape off the bone at the shoulder. Dip the pieces into batter; deep-fry them in oil heated to 370° F.; use a frying thermometer. Let the pieces drain in the frying basket for a minute, then with tongs transfer them to absorbent paper towels. Put a frill on each protruding bone to serve. These taste great with salads of fresh vegetables.

If you are deep-frying parboiled chicken pieces, use much hotter oil, 385 to 400° F., and fry only until the batter is golden all over.

Baked Chicken

Here is another quick recipe that is great in the summer but good all year long. It does use the oven, but for only a short time. Cut a frying chicken into serving pieces. Mix 4 tablespoons olive oil and 2 tablespoons soy sauce in a soup bowl. On a sheet of wax paper, put ⅔ cup dry bread crumbs, 1 teaspoon Italian seasoning, ½ teaspoon ground cuminseed and ¼ teaspoon ground black pepper. Grind 2 ounces of Parmesan cheese over this mixture; freshly ground cheese is far more flavorful than packaged cheese. Mix the cheese and crumbs together. Dip the chicken pieces into the oil-soy mixture, then roll them in the crumbs, coating all sides. Arrange the pieces in a single layer in oiled baking dishes—lasagna pans are good for this. Cover the pans with foil, and bake the chicken in a preheated 375° F. for 30 minutes. If the legs are not quite tender, leave them in a few minutes longer. The coating will be delicately browned, and the chicken very good. Serve hot at once or later at room temperature.

Turkeys of all sizes can be found in summer months; if your market does not carry fresh birds, ask about them. Small birds can be cut up and broiled. Larger ones require lengthy cooking, but you will have a lot of meat to use, freshly cooked or in leftovers.

Poached duck and other poached poultry can be served cold—plain or in salads—at room temperature or hot. Freshly and simply cooked poultry tastes delicious with orange and currant sauce. You can glaze poached or almost-baked chicken or duck pieces in the oven by letting them bake at 350° F. for about 10 minutes after brushing on the following glaze.

ORANGE AND CURRANT SAUCE FOR DUCK   about 3 cups

6 ounces frozen orange-juice concentrate	½ tablespoon honey
1 cup currant jelly	½ teaspoon dry mustard
6 tablespoons sherry	¼ teaspoon Tabasco
1 tablespoon peach nectar	

Heat all ingredients together, stirring until well mixed. Pour over duck before serving, or use as a dip for pieces of duck or other poultry.

Salads

Salad seems like the perfect summer dish, so it does belong in this chapter, but do not think summer is the only salad season. Today, as people become conscious of the importance of nutrition and the value of maintaining a normal weight, salads are becoming more and more popular all year round. A variety of foods can be included in a salad platter to form a well-balanced meal. Include plenty of lettuce, shredded cabbage, endive, chicory or raw spinach, or mix several greens to your liking.

When leafy vegetables are not in season, root vegetables can be a good substitute. Beets, carrots, turnips and potatoes can be used in slices or chunks; or, for interesting texture and added crispness, grate these vegetables raw. Onions are available all year long, but they are especially good in the winter, when seasonal summer vegetables are scarce. Nuts provide salads with excellent protein as well as crunchy texture. Tomatoes are a good source of vitamin C, especially those picked at the height of the true tomato season, late summer and early fall, but even winter tomatoes provide some vitamins. Other good salad vegetables to use raw are cucumbers, celery, cauliflower, green peas, green peppers and radishes; all of these add crispness and flavor, and since they do not require cooking, it is simple to use them. Fruits can also be added to salads, and they go well with meats and poultry. Just use your imagination!

Always wash salad vegetables well; when preparing greens of any sort, lift them out of the washing water and shake off as much water as possible. Then get them reasonbly dry by shaking in a cloth or salad basket. Shred soft greens, especially lettuce, by hand, to prevent discoloration of the leaves.

Although unpeeled tomatoes can be used, peeling them contributes more elegance to the preparation. It is easy to pull the skin off a fully ripe tomato, but the following method works for any tomato: Dip it into near-boiling water for a few seconds; the skin will burst, and you can pull it off easily.

Such firm vegetables as radishes, carrots and turnips can be cut to make attractive garnishes. Radishes are especially good because of their rosy exterior and white interior. To make radish "roses," cut ¼-inch slices all around the outside of each radish, leaving the slices attached at the bottom. Chill the radishes in ice water for about 30 minutes to crisp them and make the little slices curl outward.

Meats are splendid additions to many salads. Though you might on some occasion prepare meat just for salad, it is more probable that you would use cold meat left over from an earlier preparation. We suggest roast or poached chicken, duck or turkey; ham, corned beef or corned tongue; roast beef or pot roast; pork roast, veal roast or leg of lamb. Cooked bacon is also a good addition. For salads, it is best not to use meat from stew, meat loaves or meatballs.

Cold meats for salads can be cut into dice, shoestrings, cubes or slices. Trim off any bones or fat. Here is a recipe for a salad using four kinds of meat, with a dressing to accompany it.

FAVORITE SALAD   6 servings

½ head of lettuce
¾ pound uncooked fresh spinach, washed
20 slices of bacon, cooked crisp and crumbled into bits
1 cup diced cooked chicken
½ cup diced cooked veal

½ cup sliced cooked corned beef
¼ cup uncooked fresh green peas
¼ cup diced uncooked fresh green beans
¾ cup sliced uncooked fresh mushrooms
½ cup chopped green pepper
10 radishes, cut into thin slices
Orange and Garlic Dressing (recipe follows)

Tear lettuce and spinach by hand into bite-sized pieces. Add all other ingredients, and toss together in a large salad bowl. Pour the dressing over, and toss again to mix well.

ORANGE AND GARLIC DRESSING   about 2 cups

1½ cups plus 3 tablespoons olive oil
10 garlic cloves, peeled and minced
½ teaspoon coarsely ground peppercorns

¼ teaspoon salt
¼ cup grated orange rind
2 tablespoons orange brandy

Pour 1½ cups oil into a heatproof mixing bowl. Pour 3 tablespoons oil into a frying pan, and heat well. Add garlic, pepper and salt, and cook over low heat, stirring often, for 20 minutes. Turn off the heat, and add the grated orange rind to the pan. Stir together quickly, and pour contents of the pan into the bowl of oil; mix well. Heat the orange brandy in a ladle, ignite it, then pour while still flaming into the oil mixture. Use the ladle to mix the brandy well into the rest of the dressing. Use for meat salads.

Terrines

Since it takes time to prepare and bake a terrine, you may think it impractical for a summer menu. However, terrines can be frozen successfully—whereas pastry-wrapped pâté cannot—so you might consider baking one or several on a cool day. Then, on a day when you do not want to cook at all, serve a terrine, either in the baking dish or turned out. Remember, you can make a terrine with poultry, rabbit, liver, pork, veal, ham or combinations. You can bake poultry and rabbits in large pieces, even with bones if space is not an important consideration. These dishes taste better served at room temperature than ice cold.

■

This is not a book about vegetables, so we will not go into details of how to prepare and cook them, but consider this: One of the most delightful aspects of summer is the availability of fresh produce and herbs in their due season. Even though some vegetables are sold all year round, at least in the markets of large population centers, no vegetable transported for a thousand miles, or picked before it is completely ripe, or stored in refrigerated trucks or railroad cars, will be as good as local produce picked when it is just ripe and sold on the same day. The difference between winter tomatoes raised under glass or hydroponically and the delicious red jewels of late summer grown in the good earth is obvious. The difference is less obvious with green beans, peas and cauliflower, but it does exist. A single fresh basil leaf is a world apart from the dried herb. Your meat and poultry dishes will taste all the better if seasoned with fresh herbs and accompanied by fresh vegetables and fruits. Save frozen, canned and dried produce for winter.

PICNICS

Deviled eggs, potato salad and ham sandwiches used to be the routine picnic menu. If you have not enjoyed this combination lately you might find it delicious, but why not try something really different? If you are picnicking someplace where you can cook, almost any dish from the barbecue chapter can be used for a picnic meal. Be sure to take charcoal briquettes with you; some recreation areas do provide fuel, but it may be damp or not suitable for what you plan to cook. Have the meat ready to cook and well packed in foil or heavy-duty plastic bags. If you leave home with meat straight from the refrigerator, it will probably be at "room temperature" by the time you reach your picnic site. If you must travel some distance, put the wrapped cold meat in insulated bags or in a portable ice chest filled with canned ice. Take the meat out of the ice chest when you start your fire, and it will be ready to cook when the fire has burned down to coals. Barbecue or basting sauces can be carried in leakproof plastic containers or in Thermos jugs. Be sure to carry tongs for turning, and carving tools if you are cooking a large piece of meat.

If cooking at the picnic is not part of your plan, you can still eat something other than sandwiches. Cold chicken—fried, baked or poached—is great for finger food in the outdoors. Try cold sliced meats in individual packets, individual meat pies or a good meat salad. That terrine we talked about earlier can be carried to the picnic in its own baking dish. In fact, pâté is a good picnic choice, either by itself or in sandwiches.

If you have always had hot dogs, surprise your family by filling the hot dog rolls with something different. Make long kebabs from ground meat, and cook them on peeled sticks over your fire, or fry them in an iron frying pan you take along. These make-believe dogs can be made of any kind of meat; bind them with raw egg, and season to your taste. Or make them round, as substitutes for the too common hamburger.

If sandwiches suit you better, glance at Chapter 8 for the ideas there. Even the standard ham sandwich tastes different spread with curry butter (2 tablespoons curry powder mixed with ¼ pound softened butter—or adjust to taste) or pepper butter (sauté ¼ cup minced red or green peppers in 2 teaspoons oil and 2 teaspoons butter until tender but not browned; let the peppers cool, then beat into ¼ pound softened butter). Another good idea is to take the bread and sandwich spread or filling to the picnic separately; pâté slices are great for this, and so are potted meats. These can be taken to the picnic in their own little jars, and you can even have several kinds. Ham, tongue, chicken, veal—all are good as potted meat, and your own seasoning will make them special.

You can make your own deviled ham too; it is just a special version of potted meat. For a really different egg sandwich, mix deviled ham and dill pickles with chopped hard-cooked eggs; use 1 tablespoon deviled ham for each egg, and add enough mayonnaise to make a spread. Spread on hard rolls or rye bread.

Try this idea for a surprise: Cut off both ends of a loaf of French or Italian bread, and scoop out the soft interior (if you let these soft portions dry, you can make bread crumbs later). Stuff the loaf with a good meat filling—a baked meat-loaf mixture, one of the potted meats, softened pâté, whatever you like. Slice the loaf when you get to the picnic; be sure to take a sharp knife. The slices will be thicker than those of standard sliced bread, so count on about 14 slices from a 1-pound loaf.

About those stuffed eggs—they are certainly traditional for picnics, but you can do different things with them. Add minced chicken or ham to the deviled yolk, or cover with steak tartare. Potato salad can be improved with some slivers of ham or salami, or you can try another kind of salad.

Picnics, like other summer meals, can be bettered with one hot dish—soup in a Thermos if the day is even a little cool. Potted meatballs and Potted Giblets and Livers (p. 190) can be carried to a picnic in a chunky Thermos or in their own baking dish, to be served hot, warm or cold. Even on the hottest day, most people like hot coffee or tea as a final touch.

Summer food no longer needs to be as special as it was a few generations ago, but it is nice to make it special so you do not get bored eating the same thing at all seasons. The basic idea is to choose a meat or poultry that will keep well, can be cooked quickly, and can be served hot or cold with a fresh vegetable.

SUMMER LUNCH

Sautéed Canadian bacon slices topped with tiny omelets
Mustard and mushroom sauce
Cucumber balls and cherry tomatoes
Fresh peaches

Cold watercress soup
Sliced ham or prosciutto
Melon-ball salad
Almond cookies

257

SUMMER SUPPER

Jellied chicken consommé
Ham cornucopias filled with scrambled eggs and mushrooms
Sautéed cucumbers
Sesame bread sticks

Favorite Salad (see p. 255) with Orange and Garlic Dressing
(see p. 255)
Cheeses
Toasted garlic French bread
White wine

SUMMER DINNER

Chicken with Orange-Soy Marinade (see p. 75)
Rice
Green and yellow beans vinaigrette
Chocolate and orange mousse

COOKING OUTDOORS

Overnight Steak (see p. 75)
Potatoes baked on the grill
Stewed tomatoes with mushrooms, or
cold sliced tomatoes and mushrooms with lemon dressing
Crisp green salad
Husky red wine

PICNIC

Chicken sandwiches on whole-wheat bread spread with Pepper Butter
(see p. 257)
Potato salad with bologna slivers
Salad greens, cherry tomatoes, black olives
A whole fresh pineapple

Pâté-stuffed French loaf
Hard-cooked eggs stuffed with deviled ham
Whole tomatoes filled with green-pepper slaw
Miniature fruit tarts

BARBECUE

Chapter 16

ALTHOUGH WEBSTER GIVES SEVERAL POSSIBLE MEANINGS for the word "barbecue," in this book it means only one thing: to grill meat or poultry over an open fire of glowing coals. Do not look here for a dish prepared in a frying pan and covered with a spicy sauce; such preparations are not true barbecues. It is possible that the word comes from *barbacoa*, the Spanish-American name for a device of green wood sticks suspended over a firepit, used by the Indians to cook meat. Webster suggests that the word originates from Taino, an extinct language of the Arawak Indians, while Spanish authorities suggest a Mexican origin. Probably all early people in the Americas and elsewhere cooked meat in this fashion. Another version of the origin of the word, now regarded as somewhat of a joke, is that it derived from two French words, *barbe*, "beard" or "whiskers," and *cue*, or, more correctly, *queue*, "tail," thus suggesting the roasting of whole large animals. People do barbecue whole animals today, but usually only small ones—Rock Cornish game birds or chickens or, for some special occasion, a suckling pig. The ox roast for the wedding feast so lovingly described in Zilahy's novel *The Dukays* and the roasting deer perfuming Sherwood forest in the days of Robin Hood were even then prepared only on special occasions. Before the development of refrigeration, an animal had to be cooked and eaten soon after slaughtering, so life in those days was literally feast or famine.

Making a Fireplace

It is possible for cooks living in the country to dig pits for fire making or to construct fireplaces. Suburban and city dwellers must use fixed or portable metal grills, or stone or brick constructions. Some basic rules apply to all these circumstances.

There should be a clear space all around and over the fire, so that no accident can result from flying sparks or simply from the heat. If you are a country dweller or camper, this means you must not build a fire under or near trees. It is necessary to think about what is under your outdoor grill as well as what is above it; in any ground-level or below-ground construction, there should be a foundation that will keep heat from damaging what lies beneath it. If you are cooking in the country, be sure to locate your pit or fireplace where the soil is free of roots or bark that could carry a fire underground and spread it.

When choosing stones for fireplaces, avoid slate or any other stone likely to split when heated; chips of these can fly off and injure the cook. The best kind of stone to use is quartzite; it is hard and tough and has no fractures. Even very hard stones like granite can suffer exfoliation. Hunt for stones that look fresh, that are not scraggly, and that have not been used in fires previously. If in doubt about the stones you have, tap them with a hammer; if chips or clumps separate easily with the blow of a hammer, choose other specimens.

Whether you are using an elaborate masonry construction, a circular steel grill, a hibachi, or a ring of stones you assembled yourself, never start an open fire without first providing the means to put it out: a pail of water, a bucket of sand, a spray extinguisher or maybe all of these. If you use water, you may be able to retrieve the food from a conflagration, but you will cause ash, food and grease to fly all over. Using a proper extinguisher is the safest method.

Fuel

If you plan to get the glowing coals needed for barbecue by means of a wood fire, use only hard wood: maple, oak, hickory, etc. Soft woods will quickly turn to ash instead of making coals. Resinous woods like pine do not make long-lasting coals, and the strong-flavored smoke may impart an undesirable flavor to the food. When working with wood, start with the conventional tepee fire and slowly add pieces of hard wood in a crisscross pattern. Make a fire just large enough for the food you plan to cook, but remember that it takes a fair amount of wood to provide a good bed of coals. You should not waste fuel of any kind, and besides, if your fire is too large for your needs, you will have that much more cleaning up to do when you are through cooking. Here is some advice about what to do when you have finished cooking: Whether you have used hard wood, or charcoal, or briquettes, let the fuel burn out naturally, either in the open air or in a sheltered spot with plenty of ventilation. If you have planned your fire carefully, there should not be a huge amount of fuel left. Do not try to douse the fire with water; this will make the ashes fly out in a cloud, and you will have a much worse mess to clean up.

If you are cooking in city or suburb, the best possible choice of fuel is hard charcoal briquettes. Since there are several kinds of briquettes—and some burn with an unpleasant odor—you may have to try a few before you find the one you prefer. Charcoal is a good fuel, of course, but is not as long-lasting as briquettes, because the latter have been pressed during manufacturing and are therefore more dense. Briquettes are essential if you plan to cook a large piece of meat, or do any spit-roasting.

Starting the Fire

The best way to start a charcoal fire is with an electric automatic starter. Do not be tempted to use starter fluids on briquettes; a chemical taste is transferred by smoke to the food, and it alters the natural flavor of meat and poultry. Charcoal or briquettes can, of course, be started with a tepee of wood tinder and kindling, or with paper rolled into cigar shapes or little balls, but the automatic starter is quick and will always work.

There are also gas-operated and electric grills with so-called "permanent" briquettes. These become radiant when the gas is ignited or the electricity switched on; the briquettes should be replaced annually.

No matter which method you use, it is important to remember that it takes time for wood or charcoal to burn down to coals. The larger the piece of meat and the longer you must cook it, the more wood or charcoal you will need to get an adequate supply of heat. The time to start your fire, therefore, is related to the size of the pieces of food. To make a bed of coals adequate to cook a thick steak, you should start your fire at least an hour before you plan to cook. Outdoor cooking should never be done over a roaring blaze or flames, but over the *controlled intense heat of the glowing coals.* In daylight, the coals will look white. If you blow gently on them, dislodging the thin layer of ash, you will see red underneath. In the dark, you can see the glow more easily.

If you find your fire dying down but your food still has some time to cook, add a few pieces of fuel at the edge of the glowing coals. When the new pieces ignite, they will burst into flame; push them in toward the center as they become reduced to coals. Remember, flames are not for cooking, but are just a stage in the production of coals.

Foil

People often use foil in outdoor cooking, and, although it can be a useful tool, food cooked in foil is not barbecued but, rather, steamed or braised. Wrapping food in foil actually defeats the purpose of barbecuing. One important use of foil in outdoor cooking is to cover the bottom of the grill before putting in the charcoal. This will help reflect more intense heat from the firebed onto the food, as well as greatly simplifying the cleanup.

The elaborate device called a "covered barbecue" can be useful for outdoor cooking, but the meat prepared in it will be more like steamed or steam-roasted, because this appliance does not operate on the barbecue principle. It will, however, give the meat a charcoal flavor.

When devising your own barbecue system, remember to include a means of adjusting the distance between grill or spit and fire. The thickness of the piece you are grilling will determine how close to the heat it should be placed, and sometimes you might want to adjust the distance during the cooking. Even if you have a setup like the original *barbacoa,* make notches on the uprights or fasten forked twigs to them at various levels on which you can rest the crosspiece or grid.

INDOOR BARBECUE

So far, everything we have said concerns outdoor barbecuing, but we would also like to discuss barbecuing indoors. Yes, that is possible. You can use a hibachi, which can have a grill as small as 6 inches square or as large as four times that size; or an electric-operated barbecue with permanent charcoals, which we have already mentioned; or a fireplace barbecue, if you have a fireplace with a large enough opening and a fireproof hearth. If you are going to barbecue indoors, be sure to turn on your exhaust fan before you start cooking, unless you are using a fireplace where the chimney will draw out the smoke.

On some occasion you might start to cook outside and be surprised by rain or wind. If you have a portable grill, you can wheel it under cover—onto a porch or into a garage—as long as there is ample ventilation. (Leave the garage doors open.) This will be safe if your fire has reached the stage of coals, but be sure there is nothing flammable over the grill.

There are some notable differences between indoor and outdoor barbecuing, and we will mention these as we describe the barbecuing process.

What can be barbecued? Obviously, barbecuing is a good method for short-order items—steaks, chops, anything that does not require long cooking. For barbecuing, it is possible to use Choice meat rather than Prime and still get good results, but, as in all meat cookery, the better the meat the better the dish. For example, if you are using Prime beef, it will have superior flavor, and you will not have to marinate it or add garlic or salt; the delicious flavor of the beef alone will be enough. On the other hand, the cheaper the meat, the more advance preparation is required to make it tender and suitable for this cooking method. However, the longer a meat is marinated, the less of its natural flavor will be retained in the finished dish.

For outdoor barbecuing it is not necessary to grease the grill if the coals are white hot and the meat properly prepared. Grease of any kind spread on the grill might fall into the fire and flare up, so for safety's sake avoid this practice. As for oil, it evaporates over the intense heat of the coals and does not serve any purpose. Instead, prepare the meat itself to prevent sticking. Here is what to do: If you are dealing with beef, rub the surface of the meat with a piece of beef fat; it will provide added flavor as well as preventing sticking. Lamb and veal should be brushed with olive oil. This is necessary for veal because the meat is so tender that it will dry too quickly without an oily coating. Olive oil is good for lamb because it helps to temper the meat's strong flavor. Despite the large amount of fat in pork, the meat itself is dry because its tight texture allows no room for fat to seep in. Therefore it is good to brush olive oil on pork as well, in this case for added moisture. After these preparatory steps, put the meat or poultry on a heated grill over a white-hot fire, and leave it for at least 1 minute. The meat will be seared by that time, and you will be able to lift it and turn it without sticking.

If you are barbecuing indoors, you must proceed a little differently to insure safety. For instance, cook only pieces of meat with a minimum of outside fat, to prevent flare-ups; and, for the same reason, do not grease or oil the meats. Because your fire will be smaller, you must cook thinner pieces of meat—nothing over 2 inches thick. Cooking in a fireplace is an exception to this rule; because of the chimney, you can have a larger fire, with more coals, and therefore you can cook larger pieces of meat. With thinner, less fatty pieces of meat, greasing the grill is necessary. Rub the indoor grill with a piece of beef suet, which will mellow the iron and prepare it for the meat; or rub it with a cut lemon, which will make it easy to lift or turn the meat early in the cooking, a necessity with very thin pieces. In addition, use the same trick we recommended for indoor broiling: Rub lemon on the fatty edges of steaks and chops; the acid on the fat prevents flare-ups.

Steak

The first barbecue choice for festive occasions is steak. The delicious flavor of good beef makes fussy preparation unnecessary, and it is easy to carve and serve the cooked meat. Allow the meat to reach room temperature before starting to barbecue by leaving it on a kitchen countertop for 2 to 3 hours. This will insure that the meat will have a uniform temperature throughout, which, in turn, will guarantee that it cooks evenly. Season the steak when you remove it from the refrigerator. When we talk about seasoning for the barbecue, we mean salt, black peppercorns freshly ground to coarse pieces, and garlic or onion powder if you like the taste of either.

The thicker your steak, the more often you will have to turn it during cooking. If the meat cooks too long on one side, that side will be too crisp and the middle will not get done.

Thickness in inches	Turns	Minutes each side	Minutes total
1	4	3	12
2	8	3¾	30
3	8	7½	60

For cooking large pieces of meat, use a proper grill, not a small hibachi. For a really thick piece—say, 3 inches—keep the grill as high as possible from the coals—at least 7 inches.

Do not plan to barbecue a steak thicker than 3 inches. If you need to feed a large number of people, get two 2-inch steaks for speedier cooking.

Leg of Lamb

Another good meat for a large group is leg of lamb. To cook it on the grill, have the leg boned and opened or butterflied. The flavor of lamb depends on the season. In the spring, young tender lamb has good flavor, but later in the year, when the flavor is stronger, lamb is better if marinated. Marinate it overnight or, if you are doing a last-minute job, baste it with a marinade or basting sauce during cooking. If you are cooking winter lamb, marinate it for 24 to 48 hours, mainly to tenderize it.

Chops

Chops—lamb, pork and veal—are good for the barbecue. Brush them with a thin coating of olive oil. Remember, veal needs this especially, because it will dry quickly without it. Turn the chops to inspect the progress of the cooking—frequently if the grill is close to the coals. A 1-inch spring lamb chop will cook in about 12 minutes. Chops from older lamb will take a little longer.

Spareribs

Pork spareribs are a superb cut for the barbecue. Drop the ribs into boiling water, and boil them for 15 minutes. Barbecue over medium heat for 45 minutes, turning the ribs to cook twice on each side. Baste them constantly with a sparerib sauce of your choice or with a good sweet and pungent sauce. Here is our recipe for this.

SWEET AND PUNGENT SAUCE (for spareribs or loin of pork)   about 4½ cups

¾ cup apple juice
¾ cup honey
1 can (10¾ ounces) condensed onion
   soup
½ cup wine vinegar
½ cup light brown sugar

½ cup ketchup
¼ cup prepared dark mustard
½ teaspoon chili powder
3 tablespoons cornstarch
6 tablespoons (2 jiggers) Southern
   Comfort

Mix everything except cornstarch and Southern Comfort in a saucepan, and simmer over low heat, stirring occasionally, for 10 to 15 minutes. Mix cornstarch thoroughly into cold Southern Comfort, then stir *gently* into the simmering sauce as the sauce thickens. Simmer for 10 minutes longer, continuing to stir gently from the bottom.

Loin of Pork

Another excellent pork cut is the loin. Precook this by baking it in advance. Season the meat, then put it in a plastic oven bag (see p. 109), wrap it in foil, or put it in a covered roasting pan. Bake it in a preheated 300° F. oven; a 5-pound loin will be adequately *precooked* in 45 minutes. Then complete the cooking on the barbecue. Place it bone side down on the grill, and arrange the grill 7 to 8 inches above the fire. The barbecuing will take 1¼ hours, and you should turn the meat about 4 times. If you omit the precooking with this cut, the outside will become quite hard before the center is cooked.

Fresh ham is not suitable for the barbecue because it needs too much time for proper cooking. On the other hand, *precooked smoked ham* can be heated on the barbecue to make a delicious dish. Cut 1-inch ham slices, and grill for 5 minutes on each side. Glaze the slices if you like.

Sweetbreads

While most variety meats are best cooked by other methods, sweetbreads are good cooked over coals. Steer or young beef sweetbreads are even better than veal sweetbreads for this purpose. Blanch them (see p. 183), then lay them on the grill. If you like them crisp, cook them plain. If you prefer them softer, brush them with oil before grilling. Turn them often as they cook. Sweetbreads will be cooked in 30 to 40 minutes, depending on the size. The smaller lobe will be cooked in less time, of course.

Chicken

Poultry prepared on the barbecue makes fine fare. If you have limited time for the actual barbecuing, a good trick is to precook the chicken in some other way, then to reheat it on the barbecue grill with a flavorful sauce as basting liquid. For example, bake broiler halves in a preheated 325° F. oven for 30 minutes; this precooking can be done early in the day or the day before or a week before. If you do it the week before, of course, you will need to freeze it. When you plan to finish the cooking, defrost the chicken. Place the chicken pieces on the grill, with the bone side down at first. Keep the skin side as moist as possible with chicken fat or olive oil. Do not use beef fat on chicken. As with meats, it is not necessary to grease the grill, but you should let the chicken pieces cook for at least 1 minute before trying to turn them over. To avoid breaking the pieces, do not turn the chicken too often. Remember that poultry burns quickly, so cook it over low heat. Cook on the bone side for 5 minutes, then turn, placing the skin side down over the coals. Baste the bone side. After 4 minutes, turn again, putting the bone side down, and baste the skin side. After 5 more minutes, repeat the process. Inspect the chicken at 1-minute intervals, but give it only 4 turns, basting at each turn. A precooked 2½-pound broiler-fryer will be barbecued in 15 to 20 minutes.

Chicken can also be barbecued without precooking. For this, use smaller birds—1¾ to 2 pounds. Cut them into halves or quarters. Sever the whole wings from the breast quarters, and barbecue them separately. Since the breast piece can now lie flat on the grill, it will cook more evenly. When the wings are left on the uncooked quarters, they tend to burn, because they stick up as the tendons shrink from the heat. Before barbecuing, bring the chicken to room temperature. Season the pieces at this point, or brush them with sauce as you turn them. Cook for a total of about 40 minutes, 30 minutes on the bone side and 10 minutes on the skin side.

Turkey

Barbecuing uncooked turkey is not such a simple process. It would take a long time to cook, and to keep it from becoming burned on the outside before the inside was done, it would have to be turned many times. Even the most patient cook would find tending such a turkey a tiresome process. However, precooked turkey—

roasted or partly cooked in a low broiler—can be reheated on the barbecue just like precooked chicken. After the pieces of roast turkey have come to room temperature, brush them all over with poultry barbecue sauce. Cook the pieces over moderately low coals for 15 minutes on each side; just one turn is enough.

ONION AND BACON BARBECUE SAUCE (for poultry)   about 2 cups

¼ pound butter (1 stick)
8 slices of bacon, chopped
2 large onions, chopped
2 celery ribs, chopped
6 garlic cloves, minced
12 peppercorns
¼ teaspoon dried thyme
¼ teaspoon crushed red pepper

1 cup chicken stock (your own or canned)
2 chicken bouillon cubes
1½ tablespoons Cognac
6 walnuts, shelled and pulverized
3 tablespoons all-purpose flour, approximately

Melt butter in a sturdy saucepan. Add bacon and onion pieces, celery, garlic, peppercorns, thyme and red pepper. Simmer over very low heat for 1 hour. Cool, then push through a strainer or food mill. Return the strained portion to the saucepan, and add the stock, bouillon cubes, Cognac and walnuts. Mix well. Mix the flour with just a little water, and stir into the sauce; use less than the measured amount if the sauce is already thick, but do add some, because a little flour is needed to make the sauce stick to poultry when brushed on. Cook the sauce over very low heat until the flour is cooked and the sauce thickened.

Brush sauce on fresh chicken and let it rest in the refrigerator overnight; or brush on chicken and cook the same day. As the chicken cooks, brush it with more of the sauce.

This is also good on spit-roasted chickens and Rock Cornish game hens.

Although it is possible to grill ducks and geese, we do not recommend it. These birds are very fatty, and the escaping fat can cause the fire to flare to such an extent that you might have a safety problem. If you do want to barbecue these birds, it is better to spit-roast them so that fat can escape more easily; the finished bird will be more digestible.

SPIT-ROASTING

Spit-roasting is a kind of barbecuing particularly suited to large pieces of meat. You must have some means, electrical or mechanical, of turning the spit at a steady rate. Turning devices were used in Tudor kitchens, and they can be constructed by anyone with a mechanical bent. Battery-operated spits can be used anywhere; electrical spits are fine if you have an outlet convenient to your barbecue.

Spit rods are square in cross section so that the meat cannot swivel on them. You will also need prongs to fasten the meat at either end and to keep it centered on the rod. Commercial spits come equipped with these.

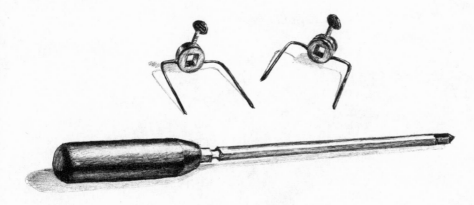

Spit rod and prongs

Meats and poultry to be spit-roasted must be skewered or trussed to make them as compact as possible and to insure that they can be well balanced on the spit. In addition to cooking unevenly, a lopsided roast will cause the turning mechanism to labor. Although you should not use string to tie meats that are cooked on a grill, it is safe to use it for meats to be spit-roasted. Since meat on a spit is constantly turning, and since spit-roasted meats and poultry are usually cooked farther from the heat source, the string will not get hot enough to burn. With electric equipment, a chicken will be about 12 inches from the coils.

Trussing on a Spit

The prongs used to fasten the meat to the spit may be all you need to truss a chicken; the following method will work for all kinds of poultry. Flip the wing tips behind the shoulder joint. Push the drumsticks toward the breast, making the body more compact. When trussing poultry in this way, do not preheat the spit. Put one set of prongs on the spit, and insert the spit through the cavity. Arrange the prongs so that they pass beneath the wing tips and rest on the backbone. Put the other set of prongs on the spit, and slide them over the drumstick bones and into the thighs. Fasten the screws so the prongs cannot move.

Turkeys, ducks, Rock Cornish game hens, and small and large chickens can be trussed on the spit in this fashion, and the finished birds will show very few marks of trussing.

Fatty meats are excellent for spit-roasting. As the spit turns, the fat melts gradually over the heat of the fire, constantly basting the meat and adding flavor to it.

Beef

When choosing beef cuts to spit-roast, remember that boneless roasts and less-tender cuts are best cooked in the oven. Oven-roasting is also better even for a fattier cut like prime ribs because none of the juices will be lost. Even if the spit is

TRUSSING A BIRD ON A SPIT

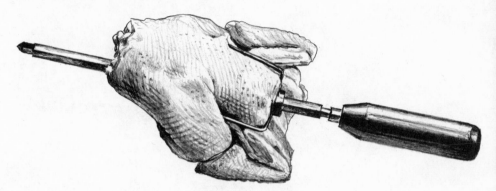

The back of the bird: let the prongs pass beneath the wing tips and rest on the backbone.

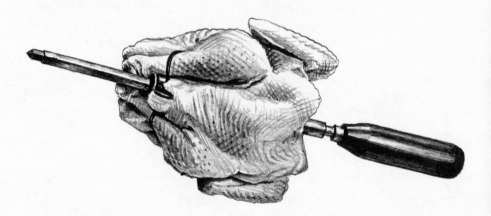

The breast of the bird: slide the prongs over the drumstick bones and into the thighs.

heated, searing and sealing the meat to some extent, beef will lose a considerable amount of juice. Nevertheless, if you prefer to roast prime ribs on a spit, it can be done successfully. For the best flavor, spit-roast prime ribs with the bones in. If your spit is long enough, you can cook a roast with up to 7 bones in it.

Remove the beef from the refrigerator, and season it; add onion or garlic powder or both. Let the beef come to room temperature. Heat the spit, and slide one set of prongs over it. Then insert the hot spit, not through the center of the meat, but about 1 inch from the bones, to make sure the weight of the meat is balanced. There are two reasons for heating the spit: It is easier to insert a hot spit, and, as already noted, the heat sears the meat, preventing excessive loss of juices. Add the second set of prongs, and fasten the prongs at either end. Place the spit over the glowing coals, and start the turning mechanism. A 7-bone rib roast will take 3½ to 4 hours to cook. A 3-rib roast weighing about 5½ pounds will cook in 1½ hours.

Pork

Loin of pork is an excellent choice for spit-roasting. Crack the chops so they will be easy to serve, and season the meat. Tie the meat, and fasten it on the spit in the same fashion as described for a beef roast, with the spit off center, closer to the bones, so that the weight is balanced. As it turns, baste the pork constantly with olive oil, Sweet and Pungent Sauce (p. 266), or a mixture of both.

A precooked smoked ham can be heated on a spit. Glaze the outside with a mixture of brown sugar, honey and cloves. Heat the ham on the spit for 1 to 1¼ hours.

Suckling pig, formerly very popular for spit-roasting, is not in great demand today and is almost unavailable because pigs are no longer slaughtered at such an early age. Whole small animals—pig, lamb, goat—are popular, and possibly practical, dishes in some cultures, but not in the United States. Such a project would be merely a *tour de force* for an American cook.

Poultry

Whole chickens and the smaller birds—squabs and Rock Cornish game hens—are delicious spit-roasted. We have already described how to spit and truss them in one step (see p. 269). A whole broiler-fryer will cook in 1½ to 1¾ hours, the smaller birds in about 45 minutes. Baste these birds constantly as they turn.

Whole turkeys can also be cooked on the spit, but be sure to baste them often. A 15-pound turkey spit-roasted over low to moderate heat (300 to 325° F.) should be cooked in 2¾ to 3 hours. A mixture of melted butter and wine, with herbs if you like them, is good for basting turkey.

Ducks and geese can be successfully spit-roasted. It might seem like a contradiction to say that it is not safe to cook them on the grill but appropriate to spit-roast them, but this can be explained by the difference in the cooking method and in the degree of heat. When food is cooked on a grill over charcoal, the heat is intense, and the food is only a few inches from the fire. Under these circumstances, fat is extracted quickly, falls into the fire, and flares up. In spit-roasting, the meat is much farther from the heat source, and the fat is extracted very slowly.

However, it is better to treat these fatty birds specially even when spit-roasting. First, bring the bird to room temperature, and prick the entire surface with a pin. Then put it in a large pot. Quarter 1 lemon and 2 oranges, and add them to the pot. Cover with boiling water and *boil* together; allow 1 hour for a duck, 1½ hours for a goose. The citrus fruits will draw out a large portion of the fat that would cause flare-ups. Remove your bird from the boiling liquid, and let it become cool enough to handle. Just as with chicken, this precooking can be done in advance. Put the bird on the spit, trussing it with the prongs. Cook duck for 45 minutes and goose for 1½ hours.

If you prepare fatty birds in the manner just described, you can barbecue pieces on the grill, but only on the outside grill. Cook them over moderately low heat, turning them every 10 to 15 minutes, according to the thickness of the pieces

271

and the distance of the meat from the coals. On the outdoor grill, these poultry pieces will be done in 45 minutes to 1 hour.

Game

Game is generally so lean that it becomes unappetizingly dry on the barbecue. However, game birds can be spit-roasted if they are well outer-larded. Skewer or tie the larding fat to the bird. Put the bird on the spit, and truss it with the prongs, as you would chicken. Guinea hen, pheasant, partridge and mallard duck can be cooked in this manner. Since wild ducks are not as fatty as domestic ducks, they will need as much larding as other game birds.

Rabbit is not an easy meat to barbecue. It takes a long time to cook and needs constant basting, so we recommend cooking it by another method.

Venison can be barbecued, but it must be marinated, well outer-larded, and basted constantly during cooking.

We cannot give general suggestions for timing game, because there can be such variation in weight; since the feed of game is unknown, its tenderness is a subject for speculation; and the age of the catch can also make a huge difference. If you know you have older birds or animals, it is best to avoid the barbecue method and cook them with moist heat instead.

If you have an arrangement that permits it, use a basket grill with the turning device to cook small pieces of meat and poultry. A basket grill can also be used without a turning device, with you doing the turning, as you would for chicken halves or chops. However, all the pieces fastened in the basket grill must be of about the same size and thickness; if they are not, thinner pieces will be overdone before the larger ones are properly cooked.

Kebabs

Another popular barbecue preparation is the kebab. Whether it is called "kebab," "kabob," "shish kabab," or "shashlik," it is a small piece of meat roasted on a skewer. The word "shish," meaning "skewer," derives from the Turkish word *şiş*. The Russian word *shashlik*, or *shashlyk*, is of Turkic or Tatar origin. Food quickly cooked was a necessity to these nomadic peoples, and of course small chunks of food cook more quickly than large pieces. The meat of the nomads was lamb or goat, and lamb is still the ideal meat for kebabs. This style of cooking became popular all over the Middle East and wherever the civilization of Islam was carried—west to North Africa, east to India, north to Russia. As a result there are countless recipes for kebabs, sauces to baste and serve them with, accompaniments of all sorts. You can apply any of these ideas to the basic kebab and have endless variations.

The meat for kebabs must be cut from a tender portion of good quality. For beef kebabs, use the filet, or heart, of the sirloin—the best cut. For veal, use the top round (leg); for pork, the loin (the pork-chop portion); and for lamb, the leg. Have

Skewer meat chunks for kebabs with the longer axis perpendicular to the skewer; add vegetables, whole or in pieces, if you like.

the meat cut into chunks of 1 inch by 1 inch by 2 inches, or in these proportions if you have larger or smaller pieces. There should be no fat or membranes on the chunks of meat for a kebab.

Usually, skewered meat is arranged on individual skewers, with the portion for one serving on each. The meat can be arranged in any fashion you like, but preparing individual skewers does make it easy to serve. Use only metal skewers, preferably steel. Never use plastic—it would melt or burn over a fire—and do not use wood, because it too can burn and has an odor that can be picked up by the food.

You can grill the skewered meat alone or add pieces of flavorful vegetables to the skewers in any order you like. The usual vegetables, all popular in Middle Eastern cookery, are tomatoes, onions, eggplant, mushrooms and green peppers; use any combination of them. Mushrooms and cherry tomatoes can be skewered whole, but the other vegetables should be cut into pieces of about the same size as the meat.

Season the meat, and let it reach room temperature. Insert the skewer through the short axis of the meat chunks, with the longer axis perpendicular to the skewer. Place the kebabs from 15 to 18 inches away from the grill. Some grills are equipped to rotate skewers as they would a spit, but you can cook kebabs successfully without such a device. Just turn them often as they cook, and baste them as well, unless you have already marinated them. Kebabs will be done in 15 to 20 minutes, depending on the size of the pieces of meat.

Another trick with these fat-free pieces of meat is to wrap them in pieces of bacon. Placing some bacon around the long axis of each meat chunk will keep the meat moist and add flavor too.

Small kebabs can be cooked on a small stove like a hibachi, which needs only a little fuel to give intense heat (see Chapter 17).

Ground-Meat Patties

Probably the most popular meat for the backyard barbecue is the hamburger. You can buy ground beef from your butcher's case, but you will enjoy a juicier, more flavorful barbecue if you have the meat specially ground for the purpose. The best cut to use is the hanging, or butcher's, tenderloin. This cut is not normally sold in meat markets, but it makes a super hamburger to fry, broil or barbecue. The hanging tenderloin, which is between the rib cage and the loin cage, is shaped like the tenderloin of pork but has a more irregular appearance; it is much larger than the pork tenderloin, and has excellent flavor. If you can't get hanger at your market, here are two other good combinations: half sirloin and half chuck; half lamb shoulder and half beef round. Grind three times to mix well and blend the flavors.

Lambburgers and vealburgers are good too. The lamb should be ground from shoulder, neck, shank or a mixture of these, and lambburgers should be seasoned but not oiled. Vealburgers should be ground from shank (shin), neck or shoulder; the meat in these cuts is moist with sweet flavor, not dry. Be sure to have veal ground three times, because it is sinewy. Brush veal patties with oil for barbecuing.

Any pattie can be cooked simply, with just the seasoning you add before you shape it. You can also mix in other ingredients—minced onion or puréed garlic, crumbled bacon, chopped mushrooms, even eggs and milk. Evolve your own favorite combination of flavors.

To make any kind of burger, put the meat in a large bowl, and allow it to reach room temperature. Then add the seasoning and any other ingredients, and mix lightly; overmixing can toughen the patties, and some of the juices can be lost. Then moisten your hands, and shape the meat into patties. The patties can be of any size, but if they are too small and thin they will become dry during cooking.

For the barbecue, allow 1 pound of beef for 3 patties about 1 inch thick. For rare hamburgers, grill on one side for about 6 minutes, then turn carefully and grill on the other side for about 5 minutes. If you like them less rare, cook them longer. Do not turn them over and over or they may crumble before they are done.

One pound of ground lamb will give you about 4 lambburgers. Mix finely chopped raw onion and coarsely chopped raw mushrooms with your choice of herbs into the ground lamb; use amounts that suit your taste. Then, for each pound of meat add ¼ cup milk. This will make the meat fluffy and give you a delicious lambburger. You can add milk in the same proportions to beef, but do not use it with veal. Pack the mixture together well, then roll the patties in bread crumbs to keep the juices from escaping as they cook. For medium lambburgers, grill the patties for a total of 12 minutes.

Shape 4 veal patties from 1 pound of ground meat, and cook them as you would lamb patties. For very good vealburgers, mix olive oil or melted seasoned butter into the meat.

A common complaint of the home barbecuer is that hamburgers flop through the grill or cook or burn onto it; they are hard to remove, and part of each pattie is lost. Hamburgers and all other patties for outdoor grilling should be firmer than the kind you would sauté or broil indoors. When shaping patties for the barbecue, press them together firmly; add a few bread crumbs to the mixture if they still seem too soft. Be sure your fire is ready to cook; if a pattie begins to cook as soon as it hits the grill, it will not normally stick to the bars. If in doubt, brush the pattie with oil.

Another idea for ground meat is to shape it into round balls and cook it on a spit like a kebab. Mix cornmeal or bread crumbs into the meat to give it a firm consistency. Make the balls twice the size of a small tomato, and skewer them through the center. Put several on a skewer, and add vegetables if you like. Lamb is the best meat for these preparations.

Flavored Oils

As you have read, many meats must be brushed with oil or fat for barbecuing, because this cooking technique tends to dry meat. Although it is possible to use any sort of oil, we recommend olive oil; it cooks easily and does not burn or spatter. All cooking oils can be flavored in various ways by the addition of an herb or spice. For a delicate garlic flavor that does not overpower the taste of the oil itself, crush peeled raw whole garlic cloves, put them into the oil, and store it for a few days before using. Add more oil when the original amount is gone. Oils prepared in this way can be kept for months without losing their flavor. If olive oil is inadvisable for dietary reasons, substitute corn oil or whatever is safe to use.

Here is how to prepare another flavored oil: Measure 1 tablespoon of black peppercorns; wash and trim 4 scallions, and pat them dry; peel the cloves from 1 whole head of garlic. Crush or chop the peppercorns, and chop the scallions, including most of the green part. Crush the garlic. Stir all this into 1 pint of olive oil. Store in the refrigerator, where it will keep for at least 1 week, but bring it to room temperature before using it. When the oil is gone, discard any remaining vegetable bits.

Uncooked marinade used on the meat before cooking can be saved and utilized for basting in some cases. But, to avoid dampening the fire and getting the meat too wet, be careful when basting with a marinade.

Good meat carefully cooked will taste delicious without adornments, but you may want to serve sauces or other accompaniments. Any sauce suitable for *fondue bourguignonne* would be good with barbecued meat. Horseradish sauce and olive sauce are particularly harmonious with chicken, since they complement its rather bland flavor. Mustard sauce and mushroom sauce are especially good with beef, and curry sauce and caper sauce go well with lamb.

If you intend to prepare foods by the barbecue method, you will have to give a little thought to equipment. First, buy or construct the kind of firebox that suits your locality and habits. Do not have something that is too small; it is easy to make a tiny fire within a large enclosure but difficult to cook a lot of food over a very small grill. If you buy sturdy equipment, it will serve you well for a long time. Become familiar with what you have, and learn how to use it. If you buy a commercial barbecue, it will come with directions; read and remember them early on, because in no time at all such little scraps of paper can get lost. Then, very important: Treat your barbecue utensils as you would your best kitchen tools. Keep grids, spits and skewers scrupulously clean, and be sure they are absolutely dry before you put them away. If they are not, they will rust and you will have to clean them before using them again. It is not necessary to oil these utensils, but it is essential that they be dry.

Here are some barbecue menus we like.

Barbecued butterflied leg of lamb
Lebanese flat bread
Ratatouille
Garden lettuce with garlic and basil
Mint juleps

Barbecued spareribs
Sweet and Pungent Sauce (see p. 266)
Potatoes, carrots and parsnips peeled and baked in foil on the grill
Green-bean and red-onion salad
Beer

Barbecued chicken quarters
Onion and Bacon Barbecue Sauce (see p. 268)
Spaghettini with chives
Stewed okra, tomatoes and onions
Rosé wine

Spit-roasted loin of pork
Prunes and chestnuts cooked in Madeira
Italian bread
Baked Bermuda onions stuffed with green peas
Romaine salad with lemon dressing
Italian white wine

★

Lamb kebabs with onions and mushrooms
Steamed rice
Whole large tomatoes filled with
cucumber salad with yogurt dressing
Red wine or ouzo

Vealburgers
Hard rolls with seeds
Red cabbage slaw with chopped apples
Potato salad
Iced tea and beer

★

Grilled ham steaks
Mango chutney
Foil-baked acorn squash
Curried green beans
Raw cauliflower and green-pepper salad
Beer and cider

Spit-roasted small chickens
Tomato marmalade
Eggplant fritters
Raw mushroom salad
Italian white wine

COOKING

AT

TABLE

Chapter 17

For INFORMAL OCCASIONS, nothing beats the fun of cooking with friends and eating the results "hot off the griddle." A few generations ago the chafing dish was quite the thing. When sports enthusiasts began to flock to the Alps for winter skiing, they discovered an old Swiss specialty, the fondue; it was introduced everywhere, along with other dishes based on the sturdy cheeses of Switzerland. After that, it was open season for togetherness.

Table cookery is for small groups, but with fondue this simply means there should be a small group for each fondue pot. If cooking at the table is your favorite way to entertain large groups, you may have more than one pot and cooker, each to be used by a separate group. The ideal number is 4 people per pot, but 6 people are possible. Do not consider entertaining more than 6 unless you have more than one setup.

OIL COOKING

Fondue bourguignonne, in spite of its name, is not a dish of melted anything; it is, rather, beef cooked in hot oil. Any tender meat can be cooked using the same device.

The pot for oil cooking should be a chunky metal pan with sloping sides—the top should be smaller than the bottom—to prevent spattering. A thermostatically controlled electric heating unit is the easiest to operate. Alcohol, butane or canned heat can be used, but you must have some way to control the burner; most alcohol and butane cookers have such controls, but you may need to improvise for canned heat. For safety, place a sizable metal tray under the equipment.

Use any cooking oil you would use for deep-frying—hydrogenated vegetable oils and peanut oil are the best choices. Do not use butter or margarine, because they burn; or olive oil, because the odor would be overpowering; or meat fats, because they too have a strong smell. The pot should be half to three-quarters full of oil, no more than that. If your heating element is slow, it is best to heat the oil in the kitchen, then transfer the pot *with great care* to your table heater. Electric and butane heaters work as fast as a conventional stove, so you can put the oil directly over them. Opinions differ as to how hot the oil should be, but the deciding factor will be what you are cooking. If you are cooking chunks of beef, the oil must be very hot—425 to 450° F. Beef pieces must be seared all over quickly. At lower temperatures the meat takes too long to cook, and it will taste greasy. If your oil is as hot as this, you must be careful to prevent spattering so that no one gets burned. The oil should not be smoking, and you must adjust the control so it does not get hotter and hotter as the amount is reduced during cooking.

If you are cooking a more delicate meat like chicken, the optimum temperature is the usual 375° F. for deep-frying. It is a good idea to heat the oil and cook one piece of meat or poultry to find out how it suits your taste; then adjust the temperature if necessary.

Provide a long fondue fork for each person and an ordinary table fork as well (the fondue fork would be much too hot to use for eating). For easiest serving, arrange a small bowl of each sauce or condiment for each person—a custard cup is a good size. Or allow your guests to spoon some onto their own plates from larger serving bowls.

Because this cooking method is so quick, the beef cut must be tender. Serve the first cut of the shell or *filet mignon* or, for many people, the flat-bone sirloin.

Other good meats for fondue are the eye of the lamb chop—the *noisette*—or cubes cut from the leg; stuffed or plain chicken livers; and plain calf's-liver cubes. No matter what kind of meat you are using, cut it into small cubes of about 1 inch; the smallest practical size is ¾ inch; anything smaller can become overcooked while you are thinking about it. Meatballs can be cooked in oil too, and they can be made of less-expensive cuts. Beef, veal, lamb and chicken meatballs are suitable. Grind the meat coarsely, and mix with egg and cracker crumbs to make a firm ball about the size of a large walnut. You may stuff the meatballs with bits of cheese, bacon or mushroom. Sausage can be served alone, but it is a mistake to cook it with other ingredients, because the fats in sausage melt into the oil in the pot, completely changing the flavor. Also the pronounced seasoning of most sausages will make the oil smell extremely pungent within a few minutes. Cubes of chicken breast and calf's liver are good dipped into batter before being cooked in oil.

For fondue, just as for other cooking methods, meats should be at room temperature, but with this technique it is especially important, because cold meat reduces the oil temperature. Dry the meats. Dip the fondue fork into some cool oil before picking up each piece of meat; otherwise it will be hard to push the cooked meat off the fork. At 425° F., a cube of meat will cook in 1 to 1½ minutes; the outside will be seared, the inside will remain rare.

For oil cooking, meat should not be preseasoned; all spicy and pungent flavors will be provided by sauces or dips. The usual sauces are described in many cookbooks, but you can use anything that appeals to you, including minced or slivered fresh vegetables, plain mustard, fresh tomato sauce and so on.

For an appetizer serving, allow 2 ounces of meat; for a main dish allow at least 4 ounces. Add a big serving of vegetable salad and some good French or Italian bread.

Here is a flavoring idea. Put 1 tablespoon of brandy in a ladle, ignite it and add it flaming to the oil before you start cooking.

Fritto Misto

Fritto misto, which we described on page 105, can also be cooked in an oil fondue pot at table. Use any kind of meat that suits you, but include a variety meat and an assortment of vegetables. Although Italian cooks use olive oil for this dish, we think peanut oil is better at such a high temperature. In some versions of *fritto misto*, small slices or cubes of mozzarella are also dipped into the oil. If you like, you can dip the ingredients into batter, coat them with egg and bread crumbs, or dust them lightly with flour. Try eggplant, zucchini and ripe red peppers as vegetables. The secret of success of this dish is to serve it at once; cooking at table is the best possible way to prepare it. In Italy, the crisp bits are served simply, with wedges of lemon. This is good, but you can use any of the fondue sauces or tartar sauce; mayonnaise made with lemon juice and spiked with capers is good too.

Tempura

Tempura also can be cooked at the table. Special electrically controlled pans are available for this purpose; they have a rack around the oil pan on which the cooked pieces can drain. However, you can use your regular oil pot for *tempura;* just provide a draining rack, and do the same for *fritto misto* if you use a batter. Batter is easy to make, but if you are in a hurry, use pancake mix thinned a little with stock or wine. In a *tempura*, be sure to use seafoods as well as meat; any vegetable can be served, even such unlikely ones as fresh green beans, leaves of spinach and sprigs of watercress.

Appetizers

The oil fondue pot can be used just for appetizers at table and at a *small* cocktail party. Some good appetizers are cubes of cheese wrapped in prosciutto, to be done very quickly; tiny meatballs stuffed with mushrooms; raw mushrooms or shrimps wrapped in thin pieces of ham, prosciutto, uncooked white meat of chicken, or veal scallop; flatten the chicken or veal to make it easier to work with. At such a party, you can also use slices of salami or another firm sausage, but keep a separate pot of oil for these unless you want everything to taste of salami. It might make an unusual cocktail party to provide a separate oil pot for every 4 guests.

The oil can be reused if you are careful with it. To begin with, do not plan to reuse it if salami or any other pungent meat was cooked in it. If you used it for beef cubes or any other unseasoned meat, fry a heel of rye bread or some thick slices of raw potato in it until browned, then filter the oil through a coffee filter or a double layer of muslin. Let it cool, then refrigerate until you need to use it again.

Cheese fondue was the original inspiration for the meat fondues; the classic recipe included melted Swiss Gruyère and Emmental, with additions of Swiss white wine and Kirsch. The true fondue pot is a rather shallow pottery casserole, a *caquelin*, different in shape from the oil pot; but you can use an oil pot for cheese too.

What does cheese fondue have to do with a meat book? Well, in addition to the usual cubes of bread, you can dip meat into the cheese, making an ideal informal supper meal. Pieces of cooked Smithfield ham, or any good ham, pieces of cooked chicken—whatever is harmonious with your cheese can be used. Serve vegetables that can be eaten raw, because they will not cook in the cheese—whole cherry tomatoes, flowerets of cauliflower or broccoli, green-pepper squares and so on.

For a different and delicious flavor, make your fondue with Muenster, Emmental and a medium-dry white wine. Spread melted marrow on toasted cubes of bread, and dip these into the fondue. Vary the fondue by crumbling cooked bacon into the cheese. Another idea: Shred roast chicken, and add to the fondue mixture with grated orange rind; mix well. Or mix deviled ham into the cheese.

The bread you use should be firm, and each piece should have an edge of crust, so it will not fall off the fork. Plain bread, toasted cubes, garlic bread, whole-wheat, rye—all can be used. Try rubbing the cubes with bacon.

Serve the same kind of wine to drink that you mixed with the melted cheese.

There is also a Danish fondue made with Danish cheeses and beer. You can try all sorts of variations on this dish too, and, of course, serve beer to accompany it. It is great with slices of knackwurst and other hearty foods.

Sauces for Dips

Another way to use your fondue pot is to heat sauces in it, as dips for already cooked meats. For this purpose the temperature need not be high; the sauce must be kept hot, but it does not have to cook further. Serve wine-flavored sauces like bordelaise to accompany chicken or beef; make sure to remove the skin from the pieces of chicken beforehand. Sauces made of puréed vegetables—eggplant, squash, onion, tomato—are good served this way.

STOCK COOKING

The Chinese firepot is used for another kind of table cookery. Stock is used instead of oil, so the cooking method is poaching rather than frying. The Japanese have similar preparations. The classic pot is heated with charcoal; it has a chimney in the center and a doughnut-shaped basin around the chimney containing the stock; it may remind you of a samovar. These cooking devices were designed to make the most of limited fuel, and to warm the guests as well as cooking their food. But you can cook in stock in any table cooker you may have; the oil fondue pot is perfect for it. In the Orient the cooking broth is served after the meats and vegetables are finished. Use beef, veal or chicken stock, perked up with wine and seasonings if you like; the broth should be kept just below the boiling point. The guests may cook their own food, as with oil cooking, or the host can put food into the broth for everyone, starting with the ingredient that needs the longest cooking; the guests can remove the food when it's cooked to taste.

Since the stock is much less hot than the oil (about 212° F. instead of 375 to 425° F.), you must choose foods that cook very quickly. As for oil fondue, use the most tender cuts of beef, boneless white meat of chicken, or lamb *noisettes*, but cut them into thinner pieces than you would for fondue. Obviously seafood is a good choice, so you can experiment with combinations. Beef, shrimps, snow peas, zucchini chunks and squares of red peppers make a good mixture. Another is chicken with mushrooms and tiny white onions. As with oil-cooked meats, suitable flavorful sauces should be prepared to accompany the poached foods. For even quicker preparation, you can use already cooked, or almost cooked, meats; the stock cooking will be just enough to finish them. You may need tongs instead of forks for this.

HIBACHI

Two other Japanese cooking devices have become very popular recently. One is the hibachi, the other is the dining table with the cooking surface built into the middle. The hibachi is a cast-iron stove, a miniature of an old-fashioned coal stove, with a damper on the bottom and a grill on the top. Even the smallest models are heavy, but as a result they are very sturdy. Hibachis are often carried on boats, where they are usually set in a metal box filled with sand. A sandbox is not practical for the table, but a heavy metal tray, which is a must under all table cookery devices, will serve the purpose. The smallest hibachi has a very small surface, but larger models are available. All the barbecue information in Chapter 16 applies to hibachi cooking. The best fuel is charcoal briquettes, and they must be reduced to coals before you start to cook. Appetizers on skewers can be fun to prepare on the small stoves, and the larger stoves can be used to cook anything. If your cooking facilities are limited, you can use the hibachi as a conventional stove; you do need sturdy pots—a wok is good—for cooking over charcoal. The hibachi can also be fitted with a steel plate that you can use like a griddle.

Some good choices for broiling on the hibachi are little ribs of lamb, various kinds of steak and pieces of chicken. If you are using a wok or another type of pot, you can prepare anything you would cook over any other heat source.

The table with the griddle in the middle is not often found in homes, but it is popular in Japanese restaurants. You can arrange something like it with the griddle-topped hibachi, but the cooking surface at table level is easier to work on. Good meats to use on the griddle are the first cut of round steak, the sirloin, and completely deveined leg of lamb. All should be sliced fairly thin, as the slices for beef Stroganoff are. You can cook sliced seafood and vegetables on the griddle too.

CHAFING DISH

The chafing dish your mother or grandmother received for a wedding present in 1915 or thereabouts may be stored in the attic. Take it out and use it! The fuel for chafing dishes is denatured alcohol or canned heat. These devices have a blazer pan and a lower pan, to be used like the water bath of a double boiler. You can utilize either as a fondue pan (not for oil fondue—too shallow), and you can cook anything in either pan that requires short-term cooking over moderate heat. With the water bath in place, the chafing dish can be used to keep already-cooked foods at serving temperature.

Scrambled eggs with meats are good cooked in the chafing dish, as are omelets with meat fillings. In fact, the chafing dish is an ideal device in which to cook an omelet, because it enables you to serve it at its puffed-up best, with no chance for it to collapse on the way from the kitchen. Try the Provençal dish of eggs and peppers for a wonderful breakfast or lunch or supper, a perfect early-fall dish. And for an elegant dinner, try butterflied *filets mignons* with a sauce made in the chafing dish. Here are recipes for both.

PIPÉRADE 　　4 to 6 servings

1 green pepper
1 red pepper
2 tomatoes
¼ pound mushrooms
2 garlic cloves
2 fresh basil leaves

8 ounces cooked ham, prosciutto, Westphalian ham or Smithfield ham
6 eggs
3 tablespoons olive oil
¼ teaspoon minced fresh savory
black pepper

Prepare all the vegetables: Remove stems, membranes and seeds from the peppers, and cut them into thick slivers. Peel the tomatoes, chop them, and set them in a strainer to drain (without draining they make the dish too wet). Peel and slice the mushrooms. Peel the garlic, and with kitchen scissors snip the basil leaves to bits. Dice the ham. Beat the eggs thoroughly. Arrange the vegetables separately on a platter, and bring them, the bowl of eggs and the ham to the table. Use only the lower pan on the chafing dish, and ignite the burner. Heat the oil, and add the peppers; let them cook for 5 to 8 minutes, then push the garlic through a press into the pan. In a few more minutes add the drained tomatoes, and cook until they are almost mushy. Then add the snipped basil and savory, and grind some black pepper over all. Mix well, then push to one side of the pan, and add the ham. When it begins to sizzle, add the mushrooms. As soon as they begin to wilt, mix everything together, and add the beaten eggs. Cook and stir until the eggs are scrambled to your taste.

You can adjust the herbs and vegetables to taste; mushrooms are not often used in Provence, but they are delicious with ham. Salt is usually not needed, since there is enough in the meat.

FILET MIGNON ON TOAST WITH BUTTERFLY SAUCE   8 servings

8 slices of toast	16 egg yolks
unsalted butter	2 cups heavy cream
8 butterflied filets mignons,	salt and pepper
each 1 inch thick	2 tablespoons minced fresh chives

Make the toast, and butter each slice on one side. Broil the unseasoned *filets mignons* for 4 minutes on each side. Place one *filet mignon* on the buttered side of each piece of toast. Meanwhile, lightly beat the egg yolks and cream together, and pour into the heated blazer pan of a chafing dish; make sure the pan is just *hot*, not sizzling. Stir the mixture constantly with a wooden spoon until the eggs are set. Add dashes of salt and pepper and the chives—more or less than specified, according to your wishes. Spoon over the *filets mignons* and serve at once.

Good meats for the chafing dish are chicken livers, small meatballs, cooked or raw chicken, sweetbreads and veal kidney. The most famous preparation is chicken à la king, diced cooked chicken heated in a cream sauce that includes diced pimientos and mushrooms and sometimes also green peas. The same recipe can be used for turkey or duck, even for ham.

VEAL STRIPS À LA KING

Veal strips à la king are elegant enough for your fussiest guest. Cut raw veal from the leg, the tenderest part, into slender strips. For 1½ cups of veal strips, measure ½ cup of chopped peeled raw shrimps. Sauté the veal in butter in the chafing dish; when the veal is almost done, add the shrimps and any vegetables you like. When tender, sprinkle flour over them, let the mixture cook until thickened, then finish with light cream. Sherry or dry Madeira is optional.

ELECTRIC SKILLET

The electric frying pan or skillet is the perfect device for all sorts of table cookery, except oil fondues for which the pan is too shallow to be safe. Cooking in an electric skillet is the best way to prepare *sukiyaki*. The beef for this dish should be cut from the filet, the center cut of the cross-rib, the boneless sirloin or the round. The meat can be cut into strips or round slices, which are more attractive. All the ingredients are arranged on a large platter: beef, slices of large round onions, sliced large mushrooms, neat bundles of Chinese cabbage, spinach leaves and whatever else you like. When the skillet is hot, rub it with beef suet or add peanut oil, and sauté the meat, then the vegetables. Push each ingredient to the side as it is finished. At the end, add beef stock flavored with soy sauce and Chinese bead molasses. Let everything cook long enough for the flavors to blend—a few minutes only. Serve with rice.

Steak with Brown Sauce

Tournedos and *filets mignons* can be cooked in an electric frying pan according to any recipe you choose. Other tender beef cuts are good too. Use boneless sirloin or boneless shell; flatten the shell steaks slightly. Make a thick sauce based on brown stock and flavored with minced onions if you like. In a minimum amount of oil or clarified butter, sauté the steaks in the electric frying pan, then add the brown sauce. As soon as the sauce is hot, ignite brandy in a ladle (1 tablespoon per steak), and pour it flaming into the sauce, stirring and mixing until the flames die out. Let the steaks cook in the sauce until done to taste.

Here is another way to prepare steaks with brown sauce: Make the sauce, then mash or slice peeled raw mushrooms into it. Flavor the sauce with brandy. Heat the sauce in the electric frying pan until bubbling. Put in the meat, let it cook for 1 minute, turn it over; add additional ignited brandy in a ladle. Stir until the flames die out, turn the steak over once again, then serve. Preparing the entire recipe, except for the sauce, takes about 5 minutes. Only tender meats can be used for this.

Pepper steak, that is, steak and green peppers, a Chinese dish, is great for table cookery. Here is our version.

CHINESE PEPPER STEAK   6 servings

2½ pounds boneless beef	12 cherry tomatoes
2 green peppers	2 tablespoons peanut oil
2 medium-sized onions	2 tablespoons lichee nuts
½ pound mushrooms	½ to ¾ tablespoon soy sauce
½ package (6-ounce size) frozen snow peas, defrosted enough to separate peas	½ tablespoon arrowroot or cornstarch (optional)

The beef should be cut from boneless sirloin; round steak is often used, but it is a little too dry. Cut into strips about ¼ inch thick; or use 1- to 2-inch rounds of beef. Cut green peppers into thick strips, and onions into slices. Peel mushrooms, and dice or slice. Separate snow peas, and wash cherry tomatoes. Sauté onion slices and pepper strips in oil, then add the beef, and sauté only until browned. Add the mushrooms, snow peas and lichee nuts. Sprinkle in the soy sauce, stir, then put the little tomatoes on top. Cover the pan, and let the mixture cook for 10 minutes. If you like, thicken the juices with arrowroot or cornstarch stirred into a little cold water. Serve over rice, with Chinese fried noodles sprinkled on top.

Steak with Peppercorns

Another kind of pepper steak, steak with black peppercorns, is perfect prepared at table. It is always done at tableside when served in restaurants. Press cracked black peppercorns into both sides of the steak, then sauté it in oil on both sides. Pour brandy into the pan and ignite it. When flames die out, serve the steak with pan juices spooned over it.

A third kind of pepper steak, this one made with green peppercorns, may be new to you. Use ½ tablespoon drained green peppercorns and ½ tablespoon capers, 2 medium-sized onions and ½ pound sweet sausage (sweet chorizo). Mash the peppercorns and capers. Sauté minced onions in oil until translucent; add the sausage, peeled and chopped into ¼-inch pieces, and sauté together until the sausage bits are browned. Stir in the mashed peppercorns and capers, mix well, and cool. With a fork, rub the mixture well into all sides of pieces of steak tender enough to cook at table, or use a single large steak. Let the meat stand until you are ready to serve it. Then heat the electric skillet, add olive oil, and quickly sauté the steaks on both sides. Serve at once. You can use the flavoring mixture for beef strips too, but with less of the spicy peppercorns and capers.

Steak Diane is sautéed until done, then flamed with Cognac. The pan is deglazed with a carefully prepared brown sauce flavored with minced flavoring vegetables and wine. The sauce is spooned over the steaks before serving. Other versions of this celebrated dish use thin herb-flavored mixtures instead of brown sauce. For this elegant preparation, made of steaks cut from the filet, skip all substitutes or commercially prepared ingredients; it deserves the best.

Veal scallops, chicken breasts, tender chops, chicken livers, calf's liver, sweetbreads—and anything suitable for chafing-dish cooking—can be prepared in the electric skillet. You can also use the electric frying pan for many recipes that require longer cooking, but for table cookery, stick to quicker dishes. The recipe that follows is simple and can be adapted to other ingredients.

VEAL WITH MUSHROOMS   4 servings

3 tablespoons clarified butter
4 veal chops
1 cup sliced fresh mushrooms (about ¼ pound)

salt and white pepper
½ cup dry Madeira
1 cup heavy cream

Heat the electric skillet, and add the butter. Sauté the chops quickly on both sides until delicately brown. Add mushrooms, and let them cook until they start to brown; stir occasionally. Sprinkle the chops with salt and pepper to taste on both sides, then add the wine, and cook until it starts to bubble. Add the cream, and mix it well with mushrooms and pan juices. Just when the mixture is about to boil, turn off the skillet, and serve at once. The cooking will take 20 to 25 minutes, depending on the thickness of the chops.

You can use veal scallops for this, which will take at most 15 minutes, or boneless chicken breasts, or turkey scallops. Instead of Madeira use sherry, a table wine, or even stock. Instead of cream use puréed fresh tomato sauce or béchamel mixed with *soubise* (onion purée).

Here are some menus for table cookery.

DINNER
This dinner, for a winter evening, is a mixed grill cooked at the table.

Lamb noisettes, lamb kidneys, chicken livers,
peeled whole mushrooms, zucchini chunks and
cauliflowerets cooked in oil fondue pot
Mint sauce, plum sauce with chutney
Italian bread
Salad of Belgian endives, watercress, Italian peppers
Apple pie

For this dinner the potatoes and braised vegetables can be prepared a little in advance and kept hot in covered casseroles so the hostess will not need to leave her guests.

Pepper steak with black peppercorns
Whipped potatoes
Braised white onions with cherry tomatoes and almonds
Cold broccoli vinaigrette
Peaches and meringues with ice-cream sauce

SUPPER

Danish cheese fondue made with beer
Squares of cooked ham, cooked dark meat of chicken,
chunks of knackwurst, pieces of French bread
Beer
Coleslaw with diced red apples

For this supper use the recipe on page 287; substitute béchamel with *soubise* for the cream, and sweetbreads for the veal chops.

Sweetbreads with soubise sauce
Spinach salad
Bread and butter
Cheese with fruit

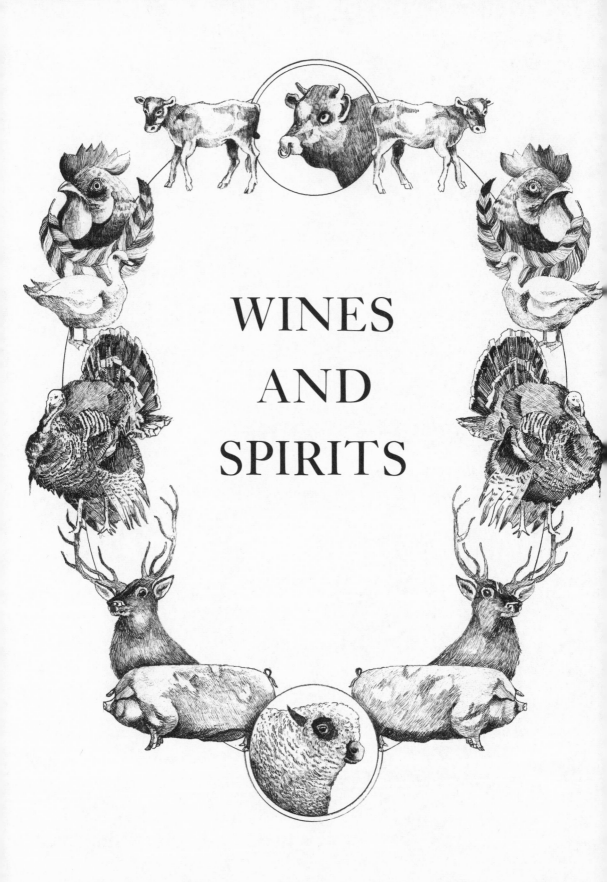

WINES

AND

SPIRITS

Chapter 18

Iᶠ ʏᴏᴜ ᴅᴏ ɴᴏᴛ ᴄᴀʀᴇ ꜰᴏʀ ᴡɪɴᴇꜱ in cooking or as an accompaniment to foods, skip this chapter. Although wine does enhance the flavor of foods and has specific uses because of its chemistry, it is perfectly possible to have good flavor without wine and to make reasonably adequate substitutes for it when flavor is not the primary concern. We will mention some of the substitutes as we go along. You can also skip this chapter if you regularly drink wine and use it in cooking, because you probably know more already than we can fit into one chapter.

Wines and spirits are used in many of the recipes in this book. Do not skip a recipe for that reason, however; just skip the ingredients you do not like. Remember that wine is liquid; when omitting it, substitute an equal amount of another liquid. The flavor of any dish can be changed to suit your taste; you may like less of a wine flavor or prefer a different wine. No recipe is more than a pattern, and patterns can be altered to fit.

The ideal accompaniment for any meal is a glass of wine. Wine acts as a diges-tive while accentuating the flavors of foods. It is both relaxing and stimulating. Fi-nally, its beautiful appearance helps make even a simple at-home meal a happy oc-casion. There are no hard and fast rules about which wines to serve with meats and poultry; there are only customs and traditions. You can drink whatever you like, even white wine with beefsteak, but that would do a disservice to both. Wine should enhance meat or poultry, not overpower it; by the same token, the meat or poultry should not make the wine seem insignificant. Good wine is made all over the world, and some is imported to the United States from most of the countries that produce it, not just France and Italy, but Japan, Hungary, Yugoslavia, Chile, Argentina, Portugal, Spain, Germany, Austria and other countries as well. The United States also produces large amounts of wine, most of it in California. They drink most of it in California too, but if you hunt you can find good bottles in a wide price range.

TENDERIZING

Now let's go to cooking. One of the chief uses of wine is in marinating. It plays the role of an acid in softening the fibers of meat or poultry to allow seasonings to penetrate. You can use any table wine you like, but generally red wine is used for beef and lamb, and white wine for veal, pork and poultry. The reason for this is that red wine would actually discolor the white meats while sinking into the tissues. When is wine indicated instead of another acid? This is up to you, but as far as the degree of acidity is concerned, wine falls far down on the list of acids you could use. It is more delicate than vinegar and citrus juices but more acid than apple juice. The flavor of each ingredient will affect the taste of the marinade and will ultimately make a subtle difference in the finished dish. Acidity can be adjusted by adding more or less wine, or substituting for part of it some more or less acid ingredient. Because it is so much stronger than wine, vinegar has a more pronounced tenderizing effect, but it also seems to extract juices from the exterior of the meat, giving the outer surface a sawdusty taste and making it a little slimy. Wine does not do any of these things. Dry (unsweet) wines are best to use for marinating. If in doubt, taste the wine first. Sweet wines are less acid, and the additional sugar in them will change the taste of the meat in a way that is probably not desirable. However, it is your taste.

If you do not want to use wine at all, try a mixture of vinegar and water, a citrus juice and water, or apple juice or cider mixed with a little lemon juice.

FLAVORING

Wine can also be used to flavor stocks. The way you plan to use the stock will determine whether or not to add wine. Since stocks are cooked for hours and all the flavors are greatly concentrated, a light hand is needed with the wine. Of course, the alcohol content, which is volatile, will be released in cooking, leaving only the flavor and the liquid in its concentrated form.

If you want to add a delicate bloom to a completed consommé or any other finished soup, add 2 to 4 tablespoons of a fortified wine to each quart of liquid just before serving. Sherry is customary with oxtail soup, but port or Madeira could be used as well. Madeira is excellent with consommés, and makes a good accompaniment to a soup course too, along with cheese straws.

When we talk about adding wine at the last minute, we do not mean red, white or rosé table wines. Although these wines are delicious to drink, they have a raw taste in foods if they are not cooked. With soups, stews and braised dishes flavored with table wines, add the wine with the other liquids used in cooking, so that the alcohol can evaporate and the flavor be concentrated.

Another fine use of wine is in preparing stock for aspics. The wine will add jewellike color and good flavor. Cook it with the other ingredients in the basic cooking process, or add it to the completed stock before you clarify it; during clarifying, the wine will cook as much as is necessary.

In baked pâtés, wine is often used to marinate the ground ingredients. This step is not so much for tenderizing, since everything is ground, usually twice, as it is for flavoring and helping to blend seasonings and meat. Wine, Cognac or other brandies are sometimes used alone in pâtés, particularly when unground pieces of meat or poultry are layered in the forcemeat. It takes only a little wine—perhaps ½ cup to every 4 cups of ground meat and just a few tablespoons for unground pieces—but a small amount will make a great difference in the flavor of the completed pâté.

Wine is used in all sorts of moist-cooking procedures, from braising to poaching. Stews are often enriched with wine. *Boeuf à la bourguignonne* is a typical example, a beef stew with red wine used as part of the cooking liquid. You might think the wine for this dish should always be a red Burgundy, but even in France other reds are used. White wine is used in several beef dishes, improbable though it may seem. Lamb is usually enhanced with red wine. With veal and pork, white wines are most common. However, if the white meat for a stew is seared or browned before any liquid is added, the addition of red wine will not discolor the meat. Red wine in marinades is contraindicated only because the meat in its raw state absorbs the pigment.

When choosing the wine for any of these dishes, consider the length of the cooking time, the character of the dish you are preparing—delicate or robust—the other ingredients to be used in the recipe, and the degree of sweetness desired. When you are strolling through the market, you may see a shelf of so-called cooking wines. Will they serve? Yes, they will serve, but the fact that they are so labeled and that they are so inexpensive indicates that their quality is lower than that of table wine. Another serious disadvantage of many cooking wines is that they are already salted and seasoned. Taste the cooking wine; if it is pleasing to the tongue, it will add to the dish; if it is flat or too vinegary or too sweet to the taste, it will detract from it. Inexpensive drinking wine is as readily available, and if you use it, you can serve the same kind of wine with the dish that you used in preparing it.

Do not drown meat or poultry with wine; the sauce that results from braising or pot-roasting or stewing should enhance the chief ingredient, not overwhelm it. Wine by itself is used only rarely in recipes; more often a mixture of wine and stock is called for. If your recipe requires hours of cooking, add the wine, not at the beginning, but partway through the cooking, so that its flavor does not become completely cooked out. The stew recipe that follows will illustrate what we mean. This is an excellent party dish, especially good for a buffet.

LEMON AND CRANBERRY BEEF STEW   6 servings

6 tablespoons oil
4 pounds beef chuck, cross-rib, or sirloin, cut into 2-inch cubes
15 wafer-thin slices of unpeeled lemon
24 cranberries
½ cup chopped green pepper
1 cup chopped green onions (scallions), both green and white parts

3 large uncooked fresh beets, each peeled and cut into 8 pieces
6 garlic cloves, peeled and quartered
½ teaspoon salt
15 peppercorns, cracked
¾ cup sweet red Burgundy wine

Heat the oil in a Dutch oven, and brown the beef cubes. Remove beef and place it on layers of absorbent kitchen paper to absorb the oil. Discard oil in the Dutch oven, and pat oven dry with kitchen paper. Arrange lemon slices on the bottom, then add cranberries, green pepper, green onions, beef cubes, beet pieces, garlic, salt and pepper. Cover the pot, and cook over low heat for 1 hour. (Or bake in a preheated 350° F. oven if you prefer.) Add wine and stir well. Cover the pot again, and cook over low heat for 2½ hours longer, stirring occasionally.

You will notice that the recipe specifies sweet wine. Most people are likely to think only of dry wines when wine cookery is mentioned, but the sugar in sweet wines has color and flavor that can enhance many dishes. A little sweetness seems to develop flavor in some meats—rabbit, for instance—and it helps smooth mixtures of flavors used in many recipes. Sometimes a telling difference can be accomplished by the addition of so small an amount as 2 tablespoons of a fortified wine like Madeira. There are dishes that do require dry wines only; when meats are combined with fish or shellfish, dry wines are usually preferred.

After you have marinated meat or poultry, do not discard the marinade. Strain it, and use it in the cooking that follows. You may not need all of it; perhaps only a few tablespoons will be sufficient to provide the necessary moisture and flavor; remember that the marinade will have some extracted meat juices in it. The next recipe will illustrate what we mean.

RED-WINE AND MUSHROOM MARINADE

2½ cups red Burgundy wine
¼ cup red-wine vinegar
1 cup olive oil
1½ pounds medium-sized fresh mushrooms, peeled
2 large yellow onions, sliced thin
2 large carrots, scraped and sliced thin

3 garlic cloves, chopped
12 peppercorns, cracked
2 sprigs of fresh mint, or ½ teaspoon dried
1 sprig of fresh thyme, or ¼ teaspoon dried
¼ teaspoon grated nutmeg

Mix everything together and use as an all-purpose marinade. Here is how to use it with lamb—it is especially good with the leg.

ROAST MARINATED LAMB WITH MUSHROOMS   6 to 8 servings

Put a trimmed leg of lamb, 6 to 7 pounds, in a large glass, pottery or enamel-ware container, and cover with the marinade. Let the lamb marinate for 2 days, turning several times a day.

Preheat oven to 350° F. Lift the lamb out of the marinade, and place it on a rack. Retrieve the mushrooms from the marinade and put them in a bowl in the refrigerator. With a slotted spoon lift all solid pieces out of the marinade, and place them in the bottom of a baking pan. Strain the marinade, and measure ¾ cup of it; set the rest aside. Set the lamb in the pan, and roast for 1 hour and 15 minutes. Baste the lamb as it cooks with the ¾ cup marinade. About 30 minutes before the lamb is done, melt 2 tablespoons butter in a medium-sized saucepan. Add the mushrooms from the marinade, cover, and simmer over low heat for 25 minutes.

Transfer the roast to a heated platter, and keep it hot. Stir the liquid and pieces in the roasting pan, then purée the contents of the pan in a blender, or push it through a food mill or sieve, or just strain out the large pieces. For each cup of liquid, mix 1½ tablespoons all-purpose flour with an equal amount of water. Stir into the liquid, and cook over low heat until the sauce is thickened. Add more of the reserved marinade if the sauce is too thick, or add a little more flour if it is too thin. Serve the lamb with the sauce and the sautéed mushrooms.

Although we have stated that white wines should be used in marinating and cooking pork, you must do both with caution. Since wine has a tendency to toughen pork, it is safe to use only with pork that is to be stewed or cooked by another slow procedure. Do not use wine to baste pork to be oven-roasted. If moisture is needed, use another liquid. Wine can be brushed over the fat of pork, to help crisp the fat and add flavor. (The suggestion on page 80 is an exception; because of the marinating, the texture of the meat is softer.)

Ham Basted with Wine

Ham differs from other pork in that it has been cured or smoked or water has been added to it. Because of these differences, ham can be basted with wine during cooking to good advantage. Champagne and Madeira are particularly good with ham. Either wine can be used to soak the ham before cooking; you do not need a great deal, because the ham can be turned over in the wine every few hours. Let the ham soak for 24 hours. Lift it out, pat it dry, and place in a baking pan. Make a glaze with honey, brown sugar, orange juice, a pinch or two of ground cinnamon and a pinch of dry mustard. Mix into a paste; if additional liquid is needed for easy spreading, use some of the wine used for soaking. Let the ham bake until the glaze is shiny, using wine as basting liquid. We are talking about conventional ham in this description. For hard-cured hams (Smithfield, etc.), this soaking and glazing would begin only after a lengthy poaching step.

Wine can be added to the liquid used for poaching, but we must emphasize that it should be only part of the liquid; the balance should be water or stock. Veal and poultry are the meats most often prepared this way. To make a fricassee or *blan-*

quette, use some of the cooking liquid in the velouté sauce. The sauce and the dish will be even more delicious if you have used some good white wine in the poaching liquid.

PAN SAUCES

Wine—straight or mixed with stock or another liquid—can also be used for pan sauces. There are several examples in the preceding chapters, but here is another. This is a simple, quick way to prepare kidneys in which wine makes all the difference.

BEEF KIDNEY WITH WINE PAN SAUCE

Use a fresh beef kidney, about 1 pound. Wash and pat dry with absorbent kitchen paper. With a small knife, cut out the fat and hard core. (Or prepare as described on p. 179.) Cut the kidney into thin slices. Heat 2 tablespoons olive oil in a large sauté pan, and sauté the slices over brisk heat until they are no longer red, about 4 minutes on each side. Sprinkle with salt and pepper. Add ½ teaspoon dehydrated onion flakes, 1 teaspoon snipped chives (fresh or defrosted frozen), 1 fresh basil leaf cut into bits, 1 tablespoon prepared Dijon mustard and ⅓ cup dry red wine. Stir to mix, and let the sauce and kidneys cook together for about 4 minutes. The sauce will thicken slightly. The whole thing will take 12 minutes. For this, use a simple California wine, no famous vintage. This recipe is enough for 2 people who like kidneys; or for 3 or 4 people who are less enthusiastic. You can cook the more delicate veal kidneys in the same way.

You can also make more complicated sauces with wine. As you can see from both recipes in this section, sauce need not be cooked separately from meat or poultry; on the contrary, it is often cooked with the meat. In the recipe that follows, the wine serves to blend the other sauce ingredients.

SCALOPPINE WITH PEAR AND CARROT SAUCE   6 to 8 servings

8 carrots, scraped and cut into chunks
3 pears, peeled, cored and cut into
  chunks
2 tablespoons peach jam
½ cup smooth-tasting white wine or
  applejack

3 tablespoons all-purpose flour
12 scaloppine, veal, beef, pork, turkey
  or chicken
¼ pound unsalted butter (1 stick)

Half-fill a blender container with cold water, and add the carrot chunks. Turn blender to CHOP or HIGH (according to your machine), and reduce carrots to bits. Pour water and carrots through a fine strainer, and return the carrot bits to the blender container. Add the pears, jam, wine or applejack, and flour. Turn blender to PURÉE or LOW, and reduce everything to a smooth sauce. Preheat oven to 275° F.

Place the *scaloppine* between 2 sheets of wax paper, and flatten them. Heat the butter in a large skillet until it sizzles. Sauté the scallops for 3 or 4 minutes on each side. Pat the scallops quickly with absorbent kitchen paper, and place in a single layer on a large baking sheet with sides. Pour the puréed sauce into the butter remaining in the skillet, and heat and stir for 3 or 4 minutes. Brush a thick layer of the sauce over each scallop. Heat in the oven for 15 minutes.

Note: This puréed sauce can be used for roasting poultry too. Brush the inside and outside of chickens, capons or baby turkeys. Roast them in a 350° F. oven, brushing them as they roast with remaining sauce.

Here is another idea for wine with chicken. Rub the entire uncooked chicken with white wine, inside and out. Wrap the bird snugly in plastic wrap or foil, and refrigerate overnight. Next day, unwrap the chicken and season in the usual way; let it reach room temperature, then roast.

Wine for Salads

Wine is excellent as part of the dressing for meat or poultry salads, in place of vinegar or lemon juice. Sauterne is particularly good with chicken salad. White wine is preferred to red for most salads, the chief exception being one made with beef. If you do not use wine, use a fruit juice instead: lemon, lime, orange or apple flavored with lemon.

You might try this trick with vegetables: Cook fresh vegetables slowly in a delicate wine marinade until they are tender but still a little crisp. They will not taste winey, just extra good. This is a fine accompaniment to any plain roasted meat.

Vermouth

Some cookbooks state that dry vermouth can be used in place of white wine, but we do not recommend it. Though the alcoholic content of the two is almost the same, the taste is extremely different. Vermouth is made with at least 10 herbs and spices, which give it its characteristic taste. Although you might sometimes want the taste of vermouth, it is not a good substitute for a delicate white wine. Since sweet vermouth is far sweeter than most sweet wines and has such a pronounced flavor, it is seldom used with meats, but it might provide just the right taste accent for particular dishes.

Here is an example of a dish that uses vermouth to perk up the rather bland flavor of chicken. Cut up broiler-fryers and prepare for sautéing. Use 1 lemon for each chicken, and squeeze it over both sides of the pieces; if some of the oil from the rind gets on the bird, so much the better. Sprinkle the pieces with a fine mince of fresh parsley, dill and celery leaves, and grind peppercorns over them. Sauté the pieces, skin side down, in a mixture of oil and butter. When they are golden brown and partly cooked, turn them over and sauté on the bone side for the same length of time. Pour dry vermouth over them to half-cover the pieces; let the vermouth come to a boil, then reduce to a simmer and let it cook until the chicken is done to taste and the vermouth somewhat reduced. Serve each piece with a little of the pan liquid spooned over it. This is quick to prepare.

Wine used for basting, a few tablespoons at a time, will help to crisp the skin and fat of various meats, and the grape sugar in the wine will impart a brown coloring and a glaze to the outside of the meat. However, we are not suggesting that you should baste every dish with wine. Sometimes a little fruit juice will serve the same purpose, and the pan drippings may be best of all.

Sparkling Wines

Champagne and other sparkling wines are sometimes used in cooking and sauce making. You might think this extravagant, because the bubbles are evaporated in any cooking process. True, but as they evaporate, they help the wine penetrate the meat. The completed sauce will have a tangy quality, and, of course, the flavor will be delicious.

Beer

Beer belongs in this chapter also. It can be used in most of the ways that wine is used, but the flavor will be different. Everyone knows about Belgian *carbonnades de boeuf*, a beef stew that uses beer and stock for liquid. But you can also use beer with lamb, ham, fresh pork, veal, chicken and variety meats. Beer is good to use for poaching sausages, as is wine, especially white wine. A delicious Cuban chicken stew made with beer tastes like a wine-flavored stew when the cooking is completed.

Gin and Vodka

Gin and vodka can play a role in dishes seasoned with certain herbs and spices. Gin, which is flavored with juniper berries, has a pronounced flavor; it is a mistaken notion that vodka is tasteless—it too has a distinctive taste and varies greatly from one brand to another. What these spirits do in cooking is accentuate the flavor of caraway seeds, juniper berries or any other flavoring seeds you may use in a dish, making almost an alcoholic extract from them and heightening their effect in the finished dish. It takes only a few tablespoons of either to make a distinct taste difference.

Herb Infusions

If you want to accentuate the flavor of a particular leaf herb in a dish, especially if you are using dried herbs, let the leaves steep in a little wine, preferably white, for about an hour before you need to use the herb. This will act as gin or vodka does on seeds; the dried leaves will uncurl and release more of their flavor. The herbs can be added to stew or pot-roast or braise with the wine, or they can be strained out and the flavored wine can be used alone.

Rum

Scotch, Bourbon, rum and various brandies and liqueurs can be found among the ingredients in many recipes. Only a little of any spirit is necessary. If using a sweet brandy or liqueur, be sure that it is harmonious with the dish. For instance, applejack is quite a bit sweeter than Cognac. The fruit-flavored brandies are sweeter than colorless *eaux-de-vie*, like slivovitz or framboise. Rum might seem unlikely, but it is good with pork and cured ham as part of a glaze, and, because of the sugar in it, it adds color and crispness to the exterior of these meats. Rum can also give excellent flavor to meat stews; use it in place of wine, but less rum and more stock.

FLAMING

In Chapter 24 you will find several ways of preparing meats in advance that employ the trick of flaming meat or poultry midway in the cooking. Even if you are completing a recipe all at one go, you can use this idea. Flaming sears the exterior of the meat, the flavor sinks into it, and the sugar in the liqueur will give good color, a sort of caramelization, to the outside. By some mysterious chemical process, stale tastes are also eliminated by flaming. The same trick is often used earlier in cooking with foods that are sautéed first and finished in a sauce. Immediately after the sautéing is completed, flame the poultry, game or meat with brandy or a liqueur. When the flames die out, the sauce ingredients are added, and the cooking is completed. The delicious flavor of the liqueur is in the meat as well as the sauce. Your guests will not see this, but it will make a greater difference to the taste than the more spectacular flaming at table. You can also flame meat or poultry—in a roast or stew, for instance—about 30 minutes before serving. Any remaining liquid will be used in the finished dish. More of the brandy taste will remain from using it this late in cooking.

Serving a meat or poultry dish while still burning is fun for parties, and the possibilities are enormous since there are so many possible liqueurs to use. To make this work, the liqueur must be heated. Take care when adding it to the dish; pour from the bottle into a smaller container—a small pitcher or sauceboat—to avoid an accident.

The following recipe, basically very simple, will give you a beautiful-looking dish that can be served for any party occasion. If you have more than 6 guests, you can double the recipe, provided there is enough room in the oven.

BAKED APRICOT CHICKEN   6 servings

2 broiler-fryer chickens, 2¼ pounds each	4 cups cornflakes, or 1 cup prepared
½ cup honey	cornflake crumbs
½ cup apricot jam	½ cup apricot brandy

Preheat oven to 325° F. Cut the chickens into quarters; wash and pat dry. (Save giblets for another recipe.) Mix honey and apricot jam. Crush the cornflakes with a rolling pin to make about 1 cup of fine crumbs. Dip chicken pieces first into the honey mixture, then into cornflakes; they should be coated on all sides. Arrange them in a single layer in a greased baking pan (or use several pans if needed). Bake for 20 minutes, then turn the pieces over with a spatula or tongs. Bake for 20 to 25 minutes longer. Transfer to heatproof plates to serve; heat the apricot brandy, and flame the pieces as you serve them.

Brandy is good for flaming duck; it helps counteract any greasy taste. Game birds and other poultry can also be served flaming. Rock Cornish game hens, which are usually served one to a person, can be flamed on the individual plates; prepare everything, and flame all the birds at the last moment, with plain or flavored brandy.

Another interesting touch is to use rose petals. For 1 pound of meat, use 10 rose petals. Wash them, and trim off the white edges at the base; they can be bitter. Sprinkle the petals over the meat or poultry just before flaming. They will add a surprising flavor; serve them with the meat or in the sauce.

Liqueurs can be used in other ways than flaming. They can be part of marinades, used for basting, or added to sauces. Mint is good with lamb, and it does not have to be green—there is white crème de menthe too. Have you ever tried baked ham with red-eye gravy? This is simply hot coffee, poured over the ham at the end of cooking—delicious and not at all easy to recognize. In addition to coffee, you could add some coffee liqueur for a luscious taste. Cherry sauce for tongue or ham can be flavored with cherry liqueur, and duck and goose prepared with apples are glorified by the addition of applejack. Some very sweet liqueurs have an unsweet effect when the cooking is completed. Here is an example. It is impossible to detect the Chartreuse in the completed dish—it just tastes very good.

CHARTREUSE CHICKEN   8 servings

8 whole chicken breasts	1 pound mushrooms
salt	juice of ½ lemon
4 large leeks	½ cup sliced almonds
4 scallions	6 tablespoons lime juice
5 tablespoons water	1 cup (8 ounces) yellow Chartreuse
3 tablespoons butter	2 tablespoons grated lime rind

This recipe is a little fussy, but all the fussy parts can be done in advance. Split the chicken breasts into halves, remove all the bones and skin, and carefully peel out the little sinew. Put each half between sheets of wax paper, and flatten with a cleaver. Your butcher can do this for you; if you do it yourself, use the bits you remove to make stock. Sprinkle the inside (the bone side) of each flattened piece with about ¼ teaspoon salt.

Trim the leeks, and wash them carefully. Cover with cold water, and bring to a boil; let boil for 2 minutes, then, with a skimmer, transfer the leeks to a colander and rinse with clear water. (The pot will have sand in the bottom; discard the water and sand.) Trim and wash the scallions. Put them and the drained leeks into a large pot with 3 tablespoons of the water and 2 tablespoons of the butter. Bring the water to a boil, then reduce the heat, cover, and steam the vegetables until tender but still green. Purée everything in an electric blender. (If you do not have a blender, put the leeks through a food mill, but it is a lot of work.) Meanwhile, peel the mushrooms and slice them. Cook them with 2 tablespoons water and the lemon juice until tender. Purée mushrooms in the blender. Season both purées with salt to taste. Use the remaining tablespoon of butter for the bottom of the baking dishes.

Divide the leek purée among the chicken pieces—about 1½ tablespoons for each piece; then spoon some mushroom purée on top. Sprinkle ½ tablespoon almond slices on top of the purée. Fold the chicken over the filling; use wax paper to help if necessary. Place the rolls, folded side down, in a single layer in the baking dishes. (You can do this much in advance if you like; cover the pans and refrigerate if you do it more than 1 hour ahead of time.) Over each little roll, spoon 1 teaspoon lime juice, 1 tablespoon Chartreuse and ¼ teaspoon grated lime rind. Cover the pans with foil, but make a tiny hole in the foil for steam to escape. Bake the chicken in a preheated 350° F. oven for 20 to 25 minutes. Use less time if the chicken breasts are very small, and more time if you like your chicken well done. It tastes best when still moist and juicy; the green lime rind and the pale-green leek purée visible at the ends make this a pretty dish. There will be a little thin juice in the pan; spoon some over each serving.

If you use this as part of a buffet in which there are other foods, it will make 16 servings.

DEGLAZING

We mentioned pan sauces using wine earlier in this chapter. Wines and liqueurs are also used in making more elaborate sauces and gravies. Various ways to make gravy are described on pages 314 and 315. Wine—red, white, rosé, dry or sweet— and liqueurs can be used for deglazing the pan in which you have roasted, sautéed or panbroiled meat or poultry. Use only a few tablespoons of liqueurs or very sweet wines, more of the others. Whether you use sweet or dry depends on the taste you want in the sauce or gravy. If you do not want to use any liquor, choose the other alternatives: fruit juices, stock, vegetable broth, even cold tea or water. The mixture of liquid and meat juices is usually strained into the other ingredients of the sauce.

Many fine sauces for meats and poultry are cooked separately from the meat. Among them are bordelaise, made with red wine and beef marrow; Madeira sauce, plain or with mushrooms; poivrade sauce for venison, made with game stock and wine marinade; both red-wine and white-wine sauces; and butters, which can be used alone or added to other sauces. Chateaubriand butter, made with veal gravy, white wine and butter, and *marchand de vins* butter, made with shallots, red wine and butter are examples of the latter.

Here are some menus that illustrate some of the uses of liquor in cooking.

Roast Marinated Lamb with Mushrooms (see p. 295)
Bulgur pilaf
Brussels sprouts with browned butter
Red wine
Belgian endive salad
Baked apples

Coq au vin (chicken stew with red wine,
onions and mushrooms)
Browned potato balls
Red wine
Shredded Savoy cabbage vinaigrette
Pear pie

This menu has a harmony of related flavors from beginning to end. If you want more contrast, serve green beans with mushrooms, and caramel custard or chocolate mousse for dessert.

Scaloppine with Pear and Carrot Sauce (see p. 296)
White rice pilaf
Buttered carrots and mushrooms
White wine, not too dry
Stewed pears

This menu can be used for a summer dinner or can be expanded for a buffet party.

Braised beef in red-wine aspic
Potato and cucumber salad
French bread
Caerphilly cheese
Red wine
Blueberries with brown sugar and sour cream

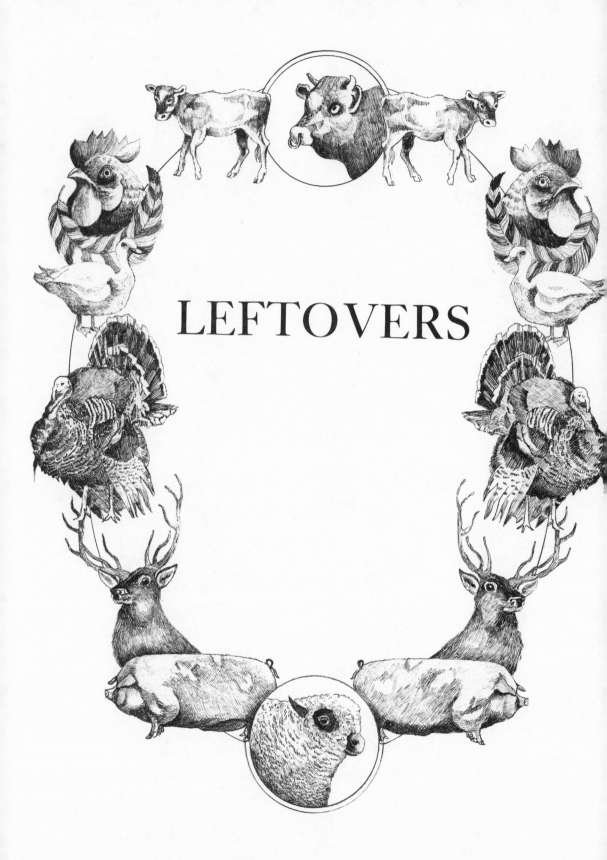

LEFTOVERS

Chapter 19

FOOD IS UNEVENLY DISTRIBUTED to the humans who inhabit this planet; some have more than enough, others barely enough to sustain life. The United States is often called a "land of plenty," yet even here there are people who are hungry all their lives. It is important that those people who do have enough food not waste it. No edible food should be discarded. Everything can be used if you plan well. If you do plan, food is not expensive; if you are casual about it and waste even a small amount, it can be very costly in relation to the nutrition it has supplied.

If your cookery is mostly of the "short-order" variety, with each meal based on a specific amount of meat for a specific number of servings, you may seldom or never have any leftovers. But most families do not choose to eat exclusively in this fashion; indeed most families could not afford to. For variety and maximum nutrition in diet, it is best to eat all sorts of meat and poultry, not just chops and steaks. If you eat in this way it is inevitable that at some meals there will be amounts of food—small or large—that remain uneaten. What should you do with these portions?

To begin with, you may have purchased a large roast or meat for a large quantity of stew, planning to use part of it on a second or third occasion, either served as it was initially or in a different fashion. Even if you have not decided at shopping time what to do with your leftovers, start thinking about it as soon as it becomes apparent that there will be some uneaten meat to be stored.

Storage

First, consider the meat or poultry that remains on your sideboard or in the kitchen. Cool it as quickly as possible; if your refrigerator has ample space and quick cold recovery, the cooked food can be put directly into the refrigerator even while still hot. Most people do not find it convenient to do this, because the heat of the cooked food raises the temperature of the refrigerator to a level unsafe for the other foods stored in it. The hot food also adds excess moisture to the box. If you do not refrigerate it at once, at least remove it from the stove and let it reach room temperature in a well-ventilated area. If you live in a hot apartment or if it is summer, you may find it practical to set the container in a larger vessel filled with ice cubes, to speed cooling and prevent spoilage. How soon the meat will reach a temperature suitable for the refrigerator depends on the temperature of your room. The hotter your kitchen, the more slowly the food will cool.

When the food is cool, transfer it to a suitable refrigerator container, or wrap it in plastic wrap or foil. Cooked meat and poultry have been dried considerably by cooking, and refrigeration can dry and harden them further if they are left uncovered. Wrap them in packages as airtight as possible.

Freezing

If you have such a large amount of food left over that you plan to freeze it, then do so as soon as it is cooled. If you wait a few days before freezing, the quality will deteriorate. To make the most economical use of your freezer, freeze only leftovers in very good condition. Never freeze cooked hamburger or liver; the meat is too dry, and freezing dries it further, leaving an aftertaste.

If your meat or poultry was originally frozen, you may doubt the wisdom of freezing it a second time. If the frozen meat has been fully cooked after defrosting, you can refreeze it. You must wrap cooked meats very carefully for freezing. Such meats cannot be stored in the freezer for as long as fresh uncooked meat. A chunk of meat in one piece can be stored for 3 months; pieces of meat still in their liquid, like those in stews, will be safe in frozen storage for a maximum of 2 months.

Refrigerating

Refrigerator storage may present problems of space for large roasts. If you know how you plan to use the meat, you may want to separate it into portions that suit your purposes. Cut or slice against the grain of meat. Also, it is sometimes practical to remove bones before wrapping to store. Poultry presents problems because of the bulk of the carcass. It is best to section whole birds, unless your refrigerator is large. Of course, remove any stuffing from the cavity, and refrigerate it separately; this will help cool the bird and prevent spoilage in the cavity.

How long can you expect to keep cooked food in the refrigerator? If you have a very cold refrigerator that is not opened often, the food will keep longer than it would under other circumstances. If you are able to cool the food quickly and store it without delay, you can also hope for longer storage. In general, cooked food can be stored in the refrigerator for longer than raw food, because the enzymes and microorganisms have been destroyed. You can expect to keep a large piece of cooked meat or poultry for at least 5 days after cooking. After that, subtle changes will take place, slowly at first, then more rapidly. There are an infinite number of molds and other invisible organisms in the air that attack all food. If you do keep a piece of meat long enough to notice changes, the first sign of deterioration will be a smeariness of the surface texture; later you will detect a slightly odd smell and perhaps some change in the appearance of the meat; finally you will perceive a definite odor of spoilage, a softening of the texture, and obvious changes in appearance.

When you discern the smeariness on the surface, discard the meat. Even though you see evidence on the surface only, there will be changes inside as well.

If your meat is in small portions, or if it is chopped or ground, it must be used sooner than large pieces. Cooked ground or chopped meats will start to spoil after 4 days, because there are so many surfaces to be attacked by microorganisms. It is far better to plan to use such leftovers within 2 days. Meats cooked with liquids and stored in the liquid—pot roast, chicken in broth, beef stew—can be safely stored for 3 more days, because the liquids keep air from getting at the meat and prevent drying.

Roast Beef

Portions of large roasts are frequently left over. Do not be tempted to reheat these in the oven to serve a second time. Reheating will dry out the meat and harden the edges, no matter what kind of roast you have. However, they will not taste best cold from the refrigerator either. Give the roast time to come back to room temperature. Roast beef, for instance, will be juicier and more flavorful if it is not served ice cold. However, try to deal only with the portion that you plan to serve at one time. Fluctuations from hot to cold speed spoilage, and changing the temperature of the same piece of meat several times will result in a noticeable loss of flavor.

If you have leftover roast beef, whether rib roast or boneless, that you do not intend to serve again in the same way, here are some ideas. Roast beef is great for sandwiches or as a cold sliced meat. For these uses, slice it while cold, because it is easier than slicing it while hot. Cold roast beef is superb in salads; slice it a little thicker than for a cold cut, and then cut it into smaller chunks or slivers. There are dozens of salad possibilities.

Another delicious use is in roast-beef hash; you have already read something about hash in Chapter 12; this hash is based on a leftover, but the procedure is similar to that used for corned-beef hash; you can grind or chop the meat. Poached eggs are good on top if you like them, and homemade pickles—mustard pickles, cauliflower pickles—are a perfect accompaniment.

Here is another idea. Dice the leftover beef. Scramble eggs until half done, add the diced beef, and scramble together to finish cooking the eggs and heat the beef. You can use this same idea with leftover chicken. Even frankfurters and salami can be mixed with scrambled eggs; dice either and sauté in a little oil first; add the eggs directly to the sauté pan, and scramble together until the eggs are done to your taste.

Pot Roast

Pot-roasted beef, which has been cooked by a moist method, is excellent reheated. Store it in the gravy that resulted from the cooking process; if you freeze it, freeze it in the gravy; the liquid prevents freezer burn. In either case, reheat it very slowly. You can make good sandwiches for the school lunchbox from leftover pot roast, and pot roast can be diced to use in salads with vegetables.

BEEF AND CAULIFLOWER SALAD   4 servings

1 whole cauliflower, cooked but still crisp
1 pound mushrooms, peeled and sliced
3 tablespoons butter
dash of grated nutmeg
2 cups diced beef from pot roast or boiled beef

½ cup wafer-thin slices of Bermuda onion
½ cup wafer-thin slices of green pepper
½ cup wafer-thin slices of cucumber
Herb Salad Dressing (recipe follows)
¼ cup (or more to taste) crumbled blue cheese (Gorgonzola, Roquefort, Stilton, etc.)

Divide the cauliflower into flowerets. Sauté the mushrooms in butter in a skillet for 10 minutes; season mushrooms with nutmeg. Gently mix beef, cauliflowerets, mushrooms and their cooking juices, and wafer-thin slices of raw vegetables in a large serving bowl. Add the dressing and toss together. Sprinkle the cheese on top. This is an excellent lunch or supper; serve with French bread, and fresh fruits for dessert.

HERB SALAD DRESSING   about 1 cup

1 cup olive oil
½ teaspoon crushed garlic
½ teaspoon salt
pinch of minced fresh dill

¼ teaspoon minced fresh or dried orégano
1 teaspoon mixed chopped olives and capers
½ teaspoon minced fresh or dried savory

Mix all ingredients together, and use for meat salads.

STEAK AND RICE CASSEROLE

It hardly seems possible that there could be leftover steak, since steak is always so delicious and popular, but imagine that you have planned to serve 8 people and half of them cannot come for some reason. Here is a basic idea that you can adjust with different seasonings: Slice the steak, and cut the slices into chunks. Measure the chunks; for each cupful use 1½ to 2 cups cooked rice; you could use even more rice if you are trying to stretch the dish. If you are not at ease with rice cookery, here is a hint: 1 cup of uncooked rice is usually enough for 6 servings. If you cook it in a covered pot over low heat, use 3 cups water to 1 cup raw rice, and you will have 3 cups of rice with no water to drain off and all nutrients preserved. To make it taste even better, add ½ teaspoon salt, 1 teaspoon lemon juice and 1 teaspoon olive oil as soon as the water comes to a boil; stir once with a wooden spoon, then cover and let it cook over very low heat until all the water is absorbed, about 20 minutes. Stir a little olive oil mixed with puréed garlic into the cooked rice; use 1 teaspoon oil for each 1½ cups rice, or more to your taste, and push as much garlic as you like through a press. Stir well to mix, then gently mix in the steak chunks, and put the mixture in a casserole dish with a cover. Heat in a preheated 275° F. oven for 30 to 35 minutes.

Even leftover hamburger or meat loaf can be used cold, sliced in sandwiches, or diced and mixed with other ingredients, or crumbled into stewed tomatoes, etc., to make spaghetti sauce. Here is another idea: Cut the meat into dice, and stir it into hot mashed or whipped potatoes, with butter and milk or cream added. Put the mixture into a shallow baking dish. Cook in a preheated 300° F. oven for 30 minutes, or until the top has a good crust.

Veal roasts make useful leftovers. Cooked veal is good sliced and served cold. If you need a hot dish, make sour-cream sauce, and heat the veal slices in the sauce; use low heat, and allow only enough time to heat the meat—do not let the sauce boil.

SOUR-CREAM SAUCE   2½ cups

1 small onion (1 ounce)	white pepper (optional)
4 large mushrooms (4 ounces)	veal stock (if needed)
2 tablespoons butter	3 tablespoons minced fresh parsley or
4 egg yolks	dill, or 1 tablespoon medium
2 cups sour cream	Hungarian paprika
salt	

Mince the onion; peel the mushrooms, both caps and stems, and mince them. Melt the butter in the top part of a double boiler over direct low heat, and cook the minced ingredients until they are tender but not browned; the liquids should be almost evaporated. Meanwhile, fill the bottom part of the double boiler with water, and put it over heat so it reaches a point just below boiling by the time the first step is completed. Set the top pan over the hot water, and adjust the heat so it stays at just that level until the sauce is done. Mix egg yolks and sour cream together with a wooden spoon or wire whisk, and turn the mixture into the top pan. Mix everything together well, and cook for about 30 minutes, stirring often and scraping the sides and bottom of the top pan. (You can do this more quickly over simmering or boiling water, but the texture will not be as good. This is a custardlike mixture, and the eggs need slow cooking.) When the sauce is thick, season with salt (about ¼ teaspoon if you used salted butter) and a little white pepper if you like. If the sauce is too thick for your use, thin it with warmed white veal stock, 1 tablespoon at a time. Add a little cold water to the lower pan to stop the cooking. The sauce will keep warm in the top pan for at least 30 minutes. Just before serving, stir in the parsley, dill or paprika if the addition is suitable for the rest of the dish.

This sauce can be stored in the refrigerator for 5 days; reheat in the double boiler over simmering water. It can also be frozen. Let it defrost overnight in the refrigerator, then reheat and use at once.

Cold roast veal or pot-roasted veal can be sliced for sandwiches. And veal is very good diced or chopped for salads.

If you have little slivers of any kind of cooked meat left over, do not reheat them or cook them further, because this would just dry out the meat and make it leathery. If you have veal scallops, try not to have any left over; if there are any, eat them cold.

Lamb

Lamb chops do not make good leftovers; order to your specific needs. Other cooked lamb can make excellent dishes. If you have leftover roasts, dice the meat onto a bed of chopped fresh vegetables, either cooked or raw, in a baking dish. Make a curry sauce, and spoon it over the lamb and vegetables. Cover the baking dish, and bake in a preheated 350° F. oven for 20 minutes (40 minutes if the vegetables are raw), until the vegetables are cooked and the sauce bubbly. If you like, you can serve this with a topping of mashed or duchess potatoes or cooked rice.

Shepherd's pie is a well-known English country dish made of leftover lamb, but the same idea can be used for any meat. Use a deep-dish pie pan or any baking pan of a suitable size, either square or round. Chop or dice the meat, and layer it in the pan with cooked vegetables, especially such winter vegetables as turnips, parsnips, potatoes, carrots and onions. The vegetables can be sliced or cut into chunks. Season each layer with a little salt and pepper, and add a little water. Cover everything with mashed potatoes, and bake in a hot oven (400 to 425° F.) until the top is browned. You can vary this by using different vegetables and seasonings. Sweet potatoes make a good topping too. Here is a version we have developed.

LAMB AND POTATO PIE   6 to 8 servings

8 medium-sized potatoes, scrubbed and peeled	pinch of dried rosemary
2 teaspoons salt	pinch of dried thyme
4 tablespoons butter	3 cups diced leftover lamb
⅓ to ½ cup milk	1 package (10 ounces) frozen peas, defrosted
2 medium-sized onions, chopped	3 large carrots, scraped and grated
2 tablespoons olive oil	½ pound fresh mushrooms, peeled and sliced
15 peppercorns, cracked	

Boil the potatoes in water with 1 teaspoon of the salt, or steam them until very tender. Drain them, let them dry over heat for a minute, then mash them. Add the butter, and continue to mash until the butter is entirely melted and mixed in. Add just enough of the milk to make a rather firm mixture. If you add too much, let the potatoes dry over low heat while stirring; they must not be too soft or moist. Oil a 2-quart deep pie dish or casserole and line it with most of the potatoes, setting aside about 1½ cups to use later. Let the potato crust cool and get a little firm.

Sauté the onions in oil until tender and translucent; do not let them brown. Season onions with the rest of the salt, the peppercorns and herbs. Stir in the lamb, and sauté and blend for 5 minutes. (If you are using uncooked lamb for this, sauté for 20 minutes.) Blot the frozen peas, to absorb excess moisture, and add them and the grated raw carrots to the lamb and onions. Mix all together, and turn into the potato crust. Over the top, spread the sliced mushrooms. Cover with the rest of the mashed potatoes, Bake the pie in a preheated 325° F. oven for 30 minutes, until the potato on top is golden brown.

You can use fresh peas—cook them first—or other vegetables; the herbs can be of your choice. You can cut the recipe in half and bake it in a standard 9-inch (1 quart) pie pan.

Leftovers can be used for all sorts of pies made with pastry. For some examples see Chapter 14. They are also good in small dumplings for garnishes, and larger dumplings for main-course servings. Here is an example.

POTATO-MEAT DUMPLINGS   4 servings

1 pound potatoes (about 4), peeled	1 medium-sized onion
1 teaspoon salt	2 canned pimientos
2 tablespoons butter	2 pinches of ground sage
½ cup flour, plus additional flour for rolling	¼ teaspoon ground cuminseed
	⅛ teaspoon ground black pepper
2 eggs	½ cup dry bread crumbs, approximately
6 ounces leftover cooked meat	

Cook the potatoes in water to cover with the salt until tender. Drain thoroughly, then mash with the butter. Beat in ½ cup flour and 1 egg, well beaten. Meanwhile grind the meat, onion and pimientos together; add the sage and spices, and mix well. Taste; if salt is needed, add to taste; this will depend on the saltiness of the cooked meat. If the mixture is very dry, add 1 to 2 tablespoons stock.

Pat out the potato dough on a well-floured pastry cloth or board, sprinkle with flour, and roll out. You may need to do this half at a time, and you definitely will need to flour everything well, because the dough is fragile. Cut into squares or rounds; there will be enough for about 16 dumplings. Put 1 heaping tablespoon of the meat mixture in the center of each piece of dough, and fold up the edges to enclose the filling. Beat the second egg with 1 tablespoon water. Dip each little package into egg, then roll in crumbs. Fry them, a few at a time, in oil heated to 375° F. until golden brown and slightly puffed. They can also be panfried, but the sides of the dumplings will not be browned by panfrying. You can also bake them or steam them.

Pork

Pork is at its best when served freshly cooked. If you have some left over, serve it cold, sliced thin for sandwiches or slivered or cubed for salads.

Here is one idea to try with pork. Cut it into very thin slices, and combine them with slices of cheese, like a *saltimbocca*. You can make a double layer of the sandwich, or add an herb or a seasoning—*saltimbocca* usually has a leaf of fresh sage with each little sandwich. Arrange the little sandwiches on a baking sheet, and heat in the oven (350° F.) until the cheese melts. Serve without delay.

Pork cut into tiny slivers or diced can be used in Chinese-style dishes. Just be sure to add the cooked pork at the last moment of cooking so it is not overcooked and dried out. Here are two ideas.

Cook chopped onions, celery and green pepper in a little oil in a wok (see p.

104). When the pieces are tender but still crunchy, add the diced pork. After 1 minute, add the necessary liquid—a little sherry and stock seasoned with soy sauce—and keep it over heat just long enough to blend and heat everything. You can thicken the liquid if you like; use 2 teaspoons cornstarch stirred into 2 tablespoons cold water for each cup of liquid.

Egg Rolls

The best-known Chinese-style dish is probably not chop suey or chow mein but egg roll. These have grown in popularity since they have been available frozen, and they make great snacks, appetizers, main dishes at lunch and accompaniments to other dishes. The containers, called "egg-roll skins" or "spring-roll skins" can be purchased ready made in Chinese grocery stores. You can make your own if you like; for each 2 cups flour, add 1 beaten egg, ½ teaspoon salt and ½ cup very cold water. Mix all together to make a dough, then knead until smooth and elastic. Divide the dough into pieces, and roll out each piece to make a very thin round; this will make about 12 long rolls or 24 little ones. Put 1 to 2 tablespoons of filling— depending on the size of the dough pieces—on the dough, and fold the dough over, sealing it with some beaten egg, to make a little package.

To make the filling, mix small dice of cooked pork, chopped raw shrimps, thin slices of scallions, chopped mushrooms, bean sprouts, minced raw cucumbers, minced water chestnuts—whatever vegetables and whatever combinations and proportions suit you. Fry the little packages in a deep-fryer—heat the oil to 375° F.—or in a smaller amount of hot oil in a wok.

Pancakes

The same kind of filling, made with pork or other leftover meat, can be used to fill pancakes. If you make the pancakes with eggs, like crêpes, so they are very thin, they can be rolled up, and heated by frying or by baking in a gratin dish. Crêpes can be made ahead of time and can even be frozen, so this can be a much quicker dish than you might think.

Ham

Leftover ham has so many different uses that some people buy a large piece of ham just to be able to serve all the delicious possibilities. Some you have already read about—ham hocks in pea soup, for instance. Leftover ham is good sliced cold. It is also delicious reheated in sauces, especially Madeira sauce, raisin sauce and other fruit sauces. Tongue is good fixed this way too. For a delicious baked sandwich, arrange ham sandwiches, spread with mustard or pickles or whatever you like, in a shallow baking dish, and cover the whole thing with cheese sauce. Bake until the cheese is bubbly. Serve with a pancake turner, to be eaten with a knife and fork.

Slivers or cubes of ham can be used in salads; ham slivers are always a part of chef's salad. They are also good in scrambled eggs, mixed with rice, stirred into all sorts of vegetable mixtures, and mixed with other ingredients to make stuffings. Try stuffing hard-cooked eggs or baked potatoes with ground ham. Of course, ground ham can be mixed with mayonnaise and chopped pickles to make a delicious sandwich spread.

Here is an idea for a ham loaf that looks and tastes delicious. You can serve this to company, and nobody will ever label it a leftover.

HAM LOAF

Bone the end of a cooked smoked ham. Grind the meat once, and mix it with honey and slivers of onion. Use 2 tablespoons honey and 4 tablespoons raw onion slivers for each cup of ground ham, or adjust the proportions to your taste. Pat the mixture into a flattened loaf shape, and put it in a loaf pan. Cover the top with thin slices of orange, including the rind but with any pits removed, arranged in a single layer or overlapping or in a pattern. Drizzle a little more honey on top. Bake the ham loaf in a preheated 325° F. oven for 30 minutes, just long enough to heat it thoroughly and glaze the top.

Poultry

Poultry, except for duck and goose, is drier after cooking than most meats, so it needs care to be successful as a leftover. Moist-cooked poultry—a poached bird, for instance—can be stored in the poaching liquid; use just enough to cover the meat. Be sure to use that liquid in your sauce making, since it will be full of nutrients. Do not leave your chicken stored in liquid for very long; use it within 3 days.

Dry-cooked poultry will be much drier than moist-cooked. If you think it is too dry, cover the pieces with matching poultry stock, and let them rest in the refrigerator for about 2 hours. Do this before you slice or dice the pieces. This way, even roast chicken can be used for salad.

When you roast chicken, capon or turkey, save all the drippings in the roasting pan. Pour them off into a small narrow container, let them cool, and then refrigerate. When you are ready to use your leftover roast poultry, lift the fat off the top of the drippings; you will then have a small amount of jellied meat stock, like a thin sour gravy. The jellied stock will keep for about 6 weeks. If you prefer, you can lift off the fat as soon as it is firm and freeze the stock. Slice the cold poultry, and reheat it in the thin gravy. The gravy will have a concentrated poultry flavor, and the meat will pick it up and be very flavorful.

Gravy

You can use this method for conventional gravy for any roasted meat, not just leftover poultry, but we are including it here because gravy is so delicious with reheated sliced leftover meat.

If you intend to serve gravy with freshly roasted meat, transfer the roast to another pan or to a warmed heatproof platter, and return the roast to the turned-off oven for its resting period before carving; this will give you time to make gravy. Pour off all the liquid in the roasting pan into a smaller container, such as a heatproof 16-ounce measuring cup or bowl. Set this in your freezer to speed the cooling; the fat will rise to the top more quickly. If your roaster is very large and heavy, transferring the liquid may not be easy to do; in that case, spoon the liquid into the other container. Do not risk pouring hot fat onto your feet or the floor; even if you do not burn yourself, it is hard to clean up. Set the emptied roaster over direct heat, and add ½ to 1 cup of stock (matching the meat or poultry you roasted), or wine or apple juice or even plain water. Bring the liquid to a boil, and, as you do, scrape the bottom of the pan with a wooden spatula to free the residue of meat juices; this is called "deglazing." Pour or spoon the liquid through a strainer into a saucepan. Now take the measuring cup out of the freezer, and with a bulb baster transfer the liquid beneath the fat to the saucepan containing the deglazing liquid. Mix together, and season with salt, pepper, onion juice, herbs, wine or whatever you like. If the gravy needs thickening, stir into the hot liquid 1½ tablespoons *instantized* flour for each cup of liquid; it will dissolve at once; stir over low heat until the gravy is thickened to taste and is smooth and hot. Do not try this with regular flour, because it will form lumps.

Roux

Here is another method. Chill the drippings, as described above, and deglaze the roaster. For each cup of defatted liquid, put 2 tablespoons of the fat from the drippings in a saucepan. Heat it; then, off the heat, stir in 2 tablespoons *regular* flour—all-purpose, unbleached, or whole wheat. This mixture is called a *roux*. Return the pan to medium-to-low heat, and let the *roux* cook, stirring all the while, to swell the starch granules and cook them. Heat the deglazing liquid and the nonfat portion of the drippings, then strain them into the *roux*, about half to begin with, then the rest, little by little, until the gravy is as thick as you like it. Stir all the while to make the gravy smooth.

The longer you cook the *roux*, the darker it will become. For brown gravy for beef or lamb, you will want the *roux* to be brown, but for paler gravy for chicken or veal, it is better to cook the *roux* only until pale or very light brown.

All these directions may sound incredibly complicated, but once you have followed them you will see how simple it is and what a short time it takes. The only part that is delicate is cooking the *roux* to just the right point.

Other techniques for making gravy have been suggested in countless cookbooks—for instance, blotting excess fat from the drippings with absorbent paper towels; using paper towels wrapped around ice cubes to speed the chilling; withdrawing the nonfat portion from the roaster itself with a bulb baster. None of these methods is as successful as chilling all the drippings.

If you are not planning to serve gravy with your roast, you can pour off the drippings and deglaze the roaster later, and store the whole mixture together. Later, follow either of the methods for thickening.

If your gravy lumps in spite of all your efforts, do not fret. First try stirring; if that does not work, beat the gravy with a wire whisk or an egg beater. You can strain the gravy but, if all the thickening has lumped, what remains may be too thin. If you use a whisk to stir the gravy as it thickens, it will not usually lump.

Cornstarch

Gravy or sauce can also be thickened with cornstarch. Use 1 to 2 tablespoons cornstarch for each cup of defatted liquid, according to how thick you want the sauce; it will be very thick with the larger amount. Dissolve the cornstarch in cold liquid; water will do, but you can also use wine, soy sauce, chilled pan drippings or stock; try to match the liquid to the sauce you are making. Pour the dissolved starch and the cold liquid into the hot liquid mixture, stirring gently all the time. The gravy or sauce will thicken almost at once. A cornstarch-thickened liquid is not as opaque as one thickened with flour; it will have a shiny, almost translucent look, typical of Chinese thickened sauces. Serve as soon as possible, for these sauces become stiff if they stand for any length of time, or sometimes they liquefy, reversing the whole process. Arrowroot and potato starch can be used also, but with these, half the amount of the starch will be enough.

With a little imagination, any gravy can be made to taste distinctive. Add minced onions or mushrooms, uncooked or sautéed, or slivers of blanched orange or lemon rinds, or minced chutney, or melted currant jelly or chopped fresh mint.

To get back to leftover poultry, when you reheat poultry in gravy, it is best to discard the skin because it will lose all its crispness in the process.

Game Stews

A good way to reheat roasted game birds is in gravy; in fact, this is the only way to reheat breast meat successfully. However, legs and wings and other bits can be made into game stews. Stews made of already cooked game birds are called *salmis*. Make a wine-flavored gravy or sauce, and cook the leftover portions with mushrooms, onions or whatever you like. Since these portions of game birds are often tougher than the breast meat, further cooking actually improves them. Game stews are good served with hominy grits, polenta or kasha.

If you have no gravy, you can make a sauce—curry, mushroom, creole, sour cream—and reheat the sliced poultry in it.

Diced cooked poultry can be mixed with cream sauce or cheese sauce and placed in *au gratin* dishes; sprinkle the top with bread crumbs or little bread cubes, and with grated cheese if you like. Heat the dish in the oven; if the top is not brown enough, finish under the broiler; do not cook too long in the oven though, or the poultry will dry out.

Of course, poultry can also be sliced for sandwiches, diced or slivered for salads, and ground and mixed with mayonnaise for spreads.

Croquettes and Fritters

All the suggestions we have made are relatively simple to implement, and most of them take only a few minutes. There are more complicated preparations, and you can make something that looks really fancy if you want to spend a little more time.

Croquettes and fritters can be made with leftover meats and poultry, and even a small amount of meat can make quite a lot of either. Make a *very thick* sauce; use 2 tablespoons oil or butter and 4 tablespoons flour for each cup of liquid. The liquid can be part milk, part poultry stock. Stir into the sauce the ground or chopped meat or poultry and any other ingredients you want; try chopped mushrooms or summer squash, or grated carrots or parsnips, or minced parsley or green pepper. Season the mixture well, and be sure it is well mixed. Spread the whole thing in a dish or pan, and let it chill for easy handling. There is no one way to shape croquettes. You can cut them into flat rounds, like *gnocchi;* into cones with rounded ends, like Sapsago cheese; into rounds or ovals; into pear shapes (make blossom ends with cloves, stems with short pieces of macaroni); into chop shapes; into the shapes of chicken legs— anything at all! When the croquettes are shaped, sprinkle them with flour or roll them in flour—whichever is easier for the shape you have chosen. They can then be cooked as they are, or you can dip them into beaten egg and crumbs first. If you egg and crumb them, be sure they are evenly coated all over. After they are shaped and coated, let them rest until the coating dries a little, but do not refrigerate them before deep-frying, because they will cool the oil too much. Fry them, a few at a time, in oil heated to 385° F. until they are golden brown. Test the first one to be sure it is cooked enough.

Fritters are slightly different from croquettes. Usually a fritter contains a single chunk of meat surrounded by a batter, but it can consist of a croquette mixture dipped into batter. Any good recipe for fritter batter can be used. Follow the same procedure as for frying croquettes, making sure to test your first fritter.

Drain either croquettes or fritters on paper towels, and keep them hot in a low oven (200 to 225° F.) until all are cooked. Then, for an elegant service, mound them in a pyramid on a serving dish lined with a linen cloth or a paper doily. Garnish with parsley or watercress sprigs, and serve with tomato or onion sauce.

If deep-frying is not for you, here is another way to cook croquettes. Shape them into cones or chops, and arrange them on a baking sheet. Spoon 1 tablespoon of melted butter over each croquette, and bake in a 400° F. oven for 10 to 15 minutes, until brown and crisp.

You can also make a croquette mixture by stirring ground leftover meat into stiff mashed potatoes. Be sure to season these well.

Timbales

Delicate-tasting timbales can be made with leftover chicken, capon or turkey. Make a custard with 1 cup of milk and 3 egg yolks, or use your favorite recipe. Stir in 1 cup of chopped or ground poultry and ¼ cup minced mushrooms. Add 1 cup cooked rice. Season well. Pour the mixture into buttered timbale molds or custard cups, and set them in a deep baking pan with an inch of hot water in it. Bake in a preheated 325° F. oven for about 30 minutes, or until a silver knife blade inserted comes out clean. Remove them from the oven, let them rest for a few minutes, then unmold them. Spoon a little sauce over each, and garnish. Parsley sauce, paprika sauce, creole sauce, tomato sauce—any of these will be good.

Soufflés

Soufflés, which are probably the most complicated preparation, can be made with leftover poultry or ham. Make 2 cups of white sauce for 2 cups of chopped chicken or ham. Either make the white sauce quite thick, or add ½ cup of white bread crumbs without any crust. Fold in the meat, and season well. Beat 4 egg yolks only until well mixed, and stir them into the sauce; if the sauce is still hot, let it cool; the eggs should not cook at this point. Beat 5 egg whites until stiff but not dry, and fold them into the *fully cooled* sauce mixture with a rubber spatula. Gently turn the mixture into a 6-cup soufflé dish. Butter only the bottom of the dish, not the sides. Bake in a preheated 375° F. oven for about 1 hour, until the soufflé is puffed up and golden brown on top. It will rise above the edge of the dish.

Soufflés are part of egg cookery; since this is not a book about eggs, we will not go into this any further, but if you are interested in experimenting with soufflés, you will find a lot about them in many good cookbooks. You can experiment with the ingredients; you can half fill the dish, sprinkle the layer with mushrooms or a contrasting meat, then pour in the rest of the filling; you can even proceed in an entirely different way by making the soufflé base in an electric blender. Consult any good general cookbook for these other ways to prepare a soufflé.

Add bits of leftover meat to vegetable soups. Chop or grind them to add to shirred eggs. Add them to soup dumplings. Mix them with macaroni or spaghetti. Purée them with stock to make sauces. Use them for appetizers. Make omelet fillings. Coat them with aspic. An imaginative cook never needs to serve leftovers the same way twice, but keep a record of your discoveries—they may be so good your family will ask for them again.

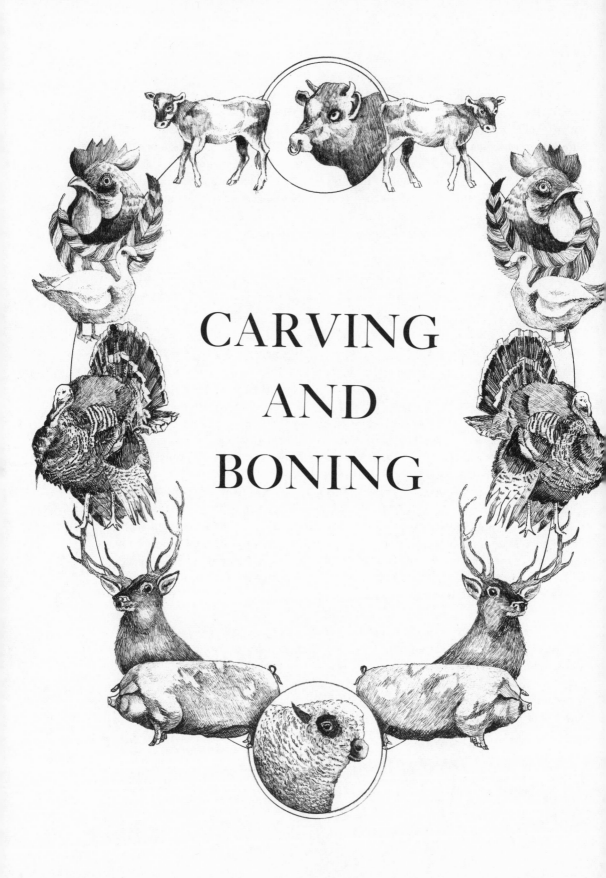

CARVING

AND

BONING

No MATTER HOW MUCH your butcher does for you, some bones will remain in many of the meat cuts you carry home. It is possible to carve and serve everything in the kitchen or pantry, but this deprives the diners of the pleasure of seeing the completed golden-brown roast, and meat usually stays hotter if it is carved at table. However, if you are unskilled and nervous about carving, you may do better with no one watching. An unskilled carver may proceed so slowly that the meat cools off before anyone has had a bite. If this is your problem, it is far better to serve meat differently or select a piece that presents few problems. Carving can be made easier with good tools and some other aids.

PLATTERS AND CARVING BOARDS

If you use platters, be sure they are sturdy enough to stay in place on the table and large enough to hold the meat with adequate space to work. For some roasts, a carving board with prongs may be the best solution, and for beginning carvers these utensils are a great help. Carving platters made of wood and shaped for gathering juices are available; they are handsome and easier to carve on than most platters. However, an experienced carver can work on any surface of adequate size.

You may have a roast that is elegantly garnished—there are some ideas for garnishing in Chapter 25. Though garnished meats are certainly attractive to serve, especially for dinner parties and other special occasions, they present booby traps for the carver. Either the garnish must be transferred to an adjacent serving plate, or the finished presentation should be returned to the kitchen or sideboard after everyone has seen it, to have everything but the meat removed.

For most carving, it is efficient to arrange the carved meat slices or portions of poultry at one end of the carving platter or board; but for some occasions it may be helpful to have an adjacent small platter or a dinner plate to which you can transfer the carved pieces. However you do it, try to reduce the time between presenting the roast and serving the individual portions, so that each portion is served hot. It is helpful to warm platters and plates; if you do not have a warming oven, rinse the plates with *very* hot water, and dry them quickly just before serving.

KNIVES

Carving tools should be of good quality; they need not look fancy or be part of glamorous sets; but they do need good blades and sturdy handles. Many culinary writers claim that knives of carbon steel are the best or only choice. These are very hard to get today, when most knives are made of stainless steel. If you choose the right stainless knife of the right size, you can do a good job. Knives should be honed on stone, with a last-minute freshening on steel just before carving. If you cannot hone them yourself, ask your butcher; after all, he sharpens his knives all day long, and nobody knows how to do it better. If you plan to carve large roasts, be sure the blade of your knife is long enough (11 to 12 inches) to extend 2 inches on each side of the meat; as you move the blade in carving, it must be long enough to allow for a sawing motion, especially important in carving a meat like roast beef. A sharpening steel must be long enough (14 to 16 inches) to let you draw the whole blade along it, and it must have a hand guard, like the medieval sword guard, at the base of the blade; it can be oval or round in cross-section, with ridges all over. The fork, with two tines, should have a guard to keep it steady, and to protect your hand if the knife slips.

For carving small or thin pieces of meat, like steaks, a shorter knife will be adequate. The slicer, a long flexible blade with rounded end, is found less often today than a decade ago, but it is useful for boneless meats and others carved only in slices. Poultry shears are essential for poultry.

We would like to say a word about electric knives. We think the carver has better control with hand power. Also, the heat of a roast tends to dull any knife during carving; if a conventional blade must be sharpened in the middle of a job, you can do it quickly with a sharpening steel, but electric knives need professional sharpening. In addition, the powerful electric blade can cut right through cartilage and softer bones, and you may serve your guests bone chips and slivers of cartilage without knowing it. Electric knives are good for boneless roasts.

Carving knives and individual steak knives require a little extra care after use. Do not put them in the dishwasher, and do not use detergent on them. Wash them in warm water with mild soap, rinse and dry immediately. Store knives so that the edges are protected.

We will describe a few boning operations in this chapter. You may tackle anything you like, but not with our blessing. Boning uncooked meats is difficult for nonprofessionals; it takes a long time and may leave your meat unrefrigerated for too long; if you are not experienced, the meat may be shredded or torn. Ask your butcher to bone the meat for your special occasions; he will be glad to do it if you ask him in time, and he will do it in seconds or minutes and give you a handsome piece of meat. If you do plan to do your own boning, be sure to have a proper boning knife, with a blade 6 to 7 inches long.

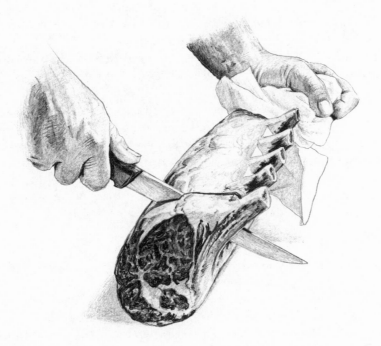

Carving roast prime ribs of beef. The short-rib bones have been "Frenched" and the roast is resting on the chine bones.

Do not forget, cartilage removed in boning contains collagen, a nutritious protein released in moist cooking. Save bits of cartilage for stock making. Most bones are good for stock too, but do not use them if the meat has been aged, because old bones can spoil the taste of stock.

BEEF

Roasts with Bones

Roast prime ribs of beef. Almost all carving illustrations for this cut depict the meat on one face with the bones at the left. We would like to suggest another way. Place the roast on the rib bones, using them as a sort of rack or base to cut against. We are assuming that this roast has been "Frenched," that is, the short-rib bones have been trimmed like chop bones. Do not insert a fork into the meat, because that releases too much blood and juice. Instead, grab the ends of the bones with a table napkin in your left hand; or insert the fork at the edge of the roast, at the bones. Slice vertically down to the bone, using a slightly sawing motion—in doing this, you can see why the knife blade must be longer than the roast is wide. When you reach the bone, tilt the blade to the right, to detach the slice from the bone and lift off the slice. Continue in this fashion until you come to the point of separation between the bones; cut through and separate the bone. If you want to serve all the slices boneless, lay that slice flat, and cut off the bone.

Other beef roasts with bones, like *arm roasts and blade roasts*, are usually braised or pot-roasted; the bones of these will be easier to deal with because of the moist-cooking method. With a small knife, remove the bones—from one side at a time if you want—and separate the portion of meat you plan to serve first. Turn the meat on the platter so the slices can be carved across the grain.

If you have a good-quality blade roast that has been oven-roasted or barbecued, proceed in the same way, but removing the bones will be a little harder. It is better to ask your butcher, when you purchase the meat, to loosen the blade bone and the spine bone, leaving them attached to the meat in only a few places. After roasting, it will be easy to separate the bones in these places.

Boneless Roasts

Roasts without bones include cross-rib roast, boneless rib roast (also called a rib eye roast), roast filet (whole or half), boneless shell roast, top sirloin roast, boneless hip roast, eye of the round (roast or braised), top round roast, rolled rump roast. With these, basically, all you do is carve slices from top to bottom, cutting across the grain. Boneless ribs, a roast with the separated bones tied on the bottom, are placed on the carving board just like the same cut with bones, but snip the strings and remove the bones first. Some of these roasts have a flattened or oval shape, and carving them is simple.

Rolled roasts and those with a more nearly round shape present more difficulty— they are not easy to hold steady. The ideal solution is to use a carving board with prongs, which will hold the rolled meat steady without making deep holes in the meat. To keep the meat firm, leave strings tying rolled meats in place. As you reach each string, snip it or cut it with the tip of the carving knife, loosen it with the fork, and remove it. Without such a carving board, you will need to hold the meat with a carving fork, a carver's helper or a salad grip. The salad grip is best; try to squeeze the meat to hold it steady rather than puncturing it. However, we will be honest— this is not easy for a nonprofessional. The carver's helper or a fork will make some holes in the roast; just try to insert either utensil in a place that will release as little juice as possible, and a place that will serve for as much of the carving as possible so you will not need to make more holes. If the meat is wrapped with a layer of fat, insert your fork in the fatty edge.

Some special problems: If your meat is tough in spite of your efforts, cut the slices as thin as possible, and be sure to cut across the grain. If the meat is very rare, you may want to cook it a little more, because very rare meat is harder to slice. (Or save that portion for another meal; rare meat tastes good cold.) Otherwise you will need to cut thick slices to avoid hacking the meat. Well-done meat should be sliced very thin. Properly cooked meat is easier to carve.

Pot Roasts and Braises

Pot roasts and braises can be steadied with a fork, because they will not lose juices as quickly as oven roasts. There has been an exchange of juices between meat and other ingredients in these cooking processes that alters the meat texture. Do not try to cut these roasts straight from the pot, because they will just fall into shreds. They are much easier to carve when a little cooler. In fact, it is easiest to let the meat cool completely, then carve it and reheat it in the gravy. Carve into ¼- to ½-inch slices, across the grain of course. The knife you use for pot-roasted meat must be *sharp*. Another method is to slice the pot roast in advance of cooking, put the slices together to reshape the piece, tie it, then cook. For this, of course, remove all the strings before serving, and arrange the slices overlapping on a platter.

Steaks

Steaks are not difficult if you understand something about the cut you are using. It is important to give everyone part of the most tender portion. If you are serving portions of the filet—*a Chateaubriand or small sirloin steaks*—just remember to cut very thin slices. There will be a lot of juice; use a carving board or platter with a well at one end, so you can retain the juice and add some to each portion.

With thick steaks, like *double or triple shells* or other steaks from high Choice or Prime beef, you can cut with or against the grain. Put the steak on its face. If there is a bone, insert your fork as close as possible to the bone; if there is no bone, use a salad grip. Remove all fat if you want to, but some people enjoy a few bits of crisp fat. Start slicing at the side farthest from the bone; just slice up and down in a way that is most handy for you.

Steaks like *T-bone and porterhouse* must have their bones removed with as little tearing of the meat as possible; the bone should be practically bare. Then carve the steak into diagonal slices on each side of the space where the bone was, making a chevron pattern. Each serving can include a piece of the top loin and a piece of the tenderloin. If the flank (tail) is on any of these steaks, be sure to cut that portion across the grain, because it is less tender. Often the flank portion is removed; sometimes it is ground, tucked between bone and tenderloin and tied in place; it is then broiled with the steak. A *sirloin steak* can be cut from any portion of the sirloin; the portion closest to the hind will be a wedge-bone sirloin; next, a flat-bone sirloin; then a pin-bone sirloin. Even though these look different from the T-bone or porterhouse, follow the same procedure: Remove the bone, and cut slices diagonally; give everyone a portion of the tenderest part. In a high Choice or Prime steak, all the meat will be tender.

Carving a steak. Remove the bone with as little tearing of the meat as possible, and carve the freed piece of meat into slices diagonal to the line of the bone.

Carving a London broil. Cut at a 45-degree angle, directing the blade away from the main portion of the meat, and making thin slices.

Boneless Meat

Slice boneless meat—*flank steak*, *London broil* made of top round, or any other boneless piece that has been broiled or baked, quite thin, cutting at a 45-degree angle and directing the blade away from yourself. Since these cuts are not so spectacular served whole at table, they can be carved on a board in the kitchen, and the slices can be arranged on a platter for service.

Boning Ribs and Shell

There are two cuts of beef you can bone at home, prime ribs of beef and shell roast, although both can be boned quickly for you when you buy the meat. For the *ribs*, have your butcher cut off the spine bone. Then cut the ribs from the meat, pressing the blade of the knife against the bones, and working on one section at a time. Follow the same pattern we describe on page 331 for boning a loin of pork. If the bones are in good condition, not overaged, fit the meat and bones together, using the bones as a rack for roasting. If you do not use the bones, the roast can be rolled for roasting.

A *shell roast* should always be boned for best serving of the cut. With bones still in, it is difficult to carve without losing a lot of the juices. Remove each bone separately, running the knife under the bone, keeping the blade parallel and as close to the bone as possible, cutting toward the spine. Holding the blade close to the bone, scoop over the ledge where the bones join. With the flat of the knife against the back formation, cut straight down. Fit the bones back, and use as a rack for roasting if you like.

VEAL

Veal cannot be carved as beef is, because the smaller size of the animal makes all the cuts different. The usual *veal roasts* are from the shoulder, leg, rack and loin. You can buy them with bones in, but it would be a mistake; because of the problems in carving, you would have difficulty serving even slices. Ask your butcher to bone, roll and tie veal *shoulder and leg*. Carve them in slices as you would a rolled beef rump roast.

Another way to prepare a veal *shoulder* is to open it like a butterflied leg of lamb. Then slice like a London broil. Other cuts made from the leg are *osso buco* and *veal steak*. The slices of leg for *osso buco* are cut 1½ to 2 inches thick, each slice with a tiny slice of the marrow bone in the center; they should be tied to keep the round of meat in shape. To carve these, simply insert the fork into the center of the bone, and slice the meat. A veal steak is a thick slice of the leg. Insert the fork into the hollow of the little round bone (like the bone in *osso buco*), and carve the steak in diagonal slices.

The *rack and loin* can be prepared in several ways. The rack can be completely boned (see p. 331), following each indentation carefully; then fit the meat and bones together, and tie, using the bones as a roasting rack. To serve, remove the bones, and carve through the chops at suitable intervals. This method has many advantages other than the simplicity of carving. The meat can be seasoned on the inner side, the side next to the bone rack, and none of the seasoning will be lost in roasting. If you use a stuffing, it can be put between meat and bone, eliminating the need to make incisions in the meat itself. This method helps retain meat juices and stuffing flavor. And, of course, the ease of carving will eliminate the loss of juices.

Another way is to have the butcher remove the lower part of the chine bone and crack the bones at the joints. When you serve the roast, slice straight through the chops, giving each person a whole chop. However, this method presents its own little problem: The roast looks best on the serving platter if it is resting on the bones, but if the meat is arranged this way, the carver cannot see where the joints are. It may not look as pretty to rest the roast on the top edge or on the fatty portion, but it will be much easier for the carver. If the rib bones are Frenched, the carver can use them as a handle.

The loin can be prepared like the rack (first method), resting on the detached bones for roasting. It is even better to bone and roll the veal loin around the kidneys or another stuffing.

Breast of veal can be prepared in several ways, and it does need some advance preparation because it is very bony. If it is cut into chunks and used for stew, it will be easy for each person to cut, because of the moist cooking. If it is cooked whole, it should be boned, rolled and roasted; boned, stuffed in a pocket and roasted; or the bones can be left in, but they must be cracked. Prepared this last way, it can be stuffed also. Boned roasts can be sliced easily; the roast with the cracked bones can be cut through the bones at the cracked places.

The *saddle of veal* is both loins roasted together. Most directions for carving this are wrong, in our opinion. First, it is possible, though difficult, to bone the saddle, leaving a single bony framework shaped like an upside-down T. If this has been done, serve the whole saddle resting on the bones, but remove half at a time to carve it. Slice the rack vertically, as though cutting the meat into boneless chops. However, this kind of boning is seldom done. If you are working with a saddle with all its bones intact, first cut down next to the backbone to separate meat from bone. Next, use a thin-bladed knife and, holding it at a very slight diagonal, cut across the loosened side from eye to eye, lengthwise across the top, making slices about ¼ inch thick. Vertical lengthwise slicing, often suggested, is more difficult and gives fewer slices. It is a mistake to try to cut choplike slices from an unboned saddle; it is so difficult that the meat gets shredded or torn. When one side is finished, carve the other side in the same way. You can use this method for an unboned rack also.

The *rump of veal* shows only a small bone at the face, but inside are the hip and pelvic bones, a large and complicated bone structure that makes this cut difficult to carve. Have the bone cracked before roasting; or cut it out after roasting, then section the meat, and slice one section at a time. Actually, there are too many bones in this cut for most amateurs, and it is easier to manage if you have your butcher bone it.

LOIN OF VEAL

Section of the loin for roasting

The meat boned completely, following each indentation of the bones. Fit meat and bones together and tie for roasting. Seasoning or stuffing can be put between meat and bones before reassembling for roasting.

Arm and neck roasts with bones are sliced like a ham, but they can be boned too. Remember to season these roasts before rolling or outer-larding.

Veal chops for stuffing can be prepared by your butcher, but this is one job you can do easily at home. For this dish, use the rib of veal instead of the loin, which has less fat and is therefore drier. Have the chine bone removed by machine at the shop. At home, cut off the rib bones, one section at a time, pressing the knife against the bony layer. Cut the meat into chops 1½ to 2 inches thick, including 1 or 2 feather bones alternately, according to where your measured thickness falls. Rest the chop on the side where the rib bone was cut off. Center the knife between the two flat sides, and insert it about 2 inches from the base. Make only a small hole, but carefully work the knife to make an incision 2½ to 3 inches deep and ¼ to ½ inch below the top of the chop. Work the blade like a saw to enlarge the hole, but do not pierce the bottom. The entrance hole should be no larger than 2 diameters of the knife. All the bones you cut off should be saved for stock. (Veal stock, because of its delicacy of flavor, can be useful for a variety of purposes.) Pork chops for stuffing can be prepared in the same way. Of course, either kind of chop can be stuffed without being boned.

LAMB

The most familiar cut of lamb, the *leg*, can be carved in various ways, according to how it was prepared. If the leg was boned and rolled, carve it like a boneless sirloin roast. Hold steady with a fork.

For the whole leg that still retains its bones, do this before roasting: crack the first two or three chops at the sirloin end; leave the shank bone in place, but French it for gripping. At serving time place the roasted leg on a carving board or platter, with the shank bone to the left and the meatier side upward. The shank bone can be covered with a large paper frill, but it is easier to use a table napkin to grip the bone in your left hand. Do not cut a slice off the bottom to make the roast lie steady; you lose too much juice that way. Since the leg is not perfectly round, it can be steadied well enough without that trick. Remove the chops—for some people, these are the best part of the roast. Then cut downward on the meaty side, toward the bone, slanting the blade toward the shank end. As you continue toward the sirloin end, the slices will get larger. When this side is carved, turn the roast over, and cut the smaller side, beginning near the sirloin end but still slanting the knife toward the shank. Another, but we think less handy, way to carve the leg is to hold the whole roast up on end, resting it on the place where the chops were cut off. When one side is carved, swivel the roast, bringing the other side to the right position for carving.

For a nonprofessional, it is much easier to have the hip and pelvic bones removed by the butcher. You can still use the shank bone as a grip, but the main portion of the leg will be carved like a boneless roast.

A butterflied leg that has been barbecued, roasted or broiled can be carved like a beef sirloin roast.

The *rack, loin and saddle of lamb* can be carved like the same cuts of veal. Of

Carving a leg of lamb that has had the hip and pelvic bones removed before roasting. Use the shank bone as a grip, and carve the meat like a boneless roast.

Rack of lamb with chine bone removed and bones cracked at the joints. The roast is resting on the fatty portion to make it easier for the carver to see where to separate the chops.

course, the lamb cuts are smaller. The saddle requires careful handling, because the layer of meat in a saddle of lamb is small. Two racks put together to form a crown may appear hard to carve, but they are not. To make the crown, the entire backbone has been cracked, so just slice down between the rib bones to serve, giving each person a portion of the stuffing if there is one. Veal and pork crowns are carved in the same way.

A *baron* is the leg and loin roasted together, either one side or both. Of course, a double baron is a large roast, served only on special occasions. In Henry VIII's time, people regularly served barons of beef! When serving these, flame at the table before carving. Separate the leg from the loin, and carve each portion separately, according to the amount you need. This roast is so large you will probably have to carve it on a sideboard, so serve the slices on a platter.

Breast of lamb, usually the least expensive cut, also has the most waste, about 25% fat, which is high in cholesterol. We do not recommend serving the breast whole; instead, have it trimmed well and cut into riblets, and braise with cabbage and caraway seeds. For an interesting variation, add small lamb meatballs to this dish.

The lamb cuts most often boned are the rack and leg. Ask your butcher to bone these cuts; there will be no additional charge. The leg is much too difficult to bone at home. The rack can be boned more easily, but the layer of meat is small, and a butcher can prepare it with a minimum of meat loss.

PORK

Like leg of lamb, the *leg of fresh pork*, also called "fresh ham," is carved according to the way it is prepared. A whole leg with all its bones is hard to carve. Serve the roast on a large platter or board; if you do not have one large enough, provide an auxiliary platter. Insert a fork at one end of the leg, and cut down just inside the shank joint to the leg bone; then cut straight across on top of the leg bone, removing the entire top layer of meat. If your platter is small, transfer the whole piece to the auxiliary platter. Slice it like a London broil, at a 45-degree angle, cutting away from yourself. Next, loosen the leg bone on both sides and at the ends, lift it up and cut it off at the shank end. Then cut the lower part of the roast like any boneless meat, carving straight down. Leave the shank end in place for balance. Use the meat from that end another day, as cold pork in salads and the like, or for Chinese dishes.

The leg can be completely boned—a job for a professional; the butcher should remove the entire hip and pelvic bone, leg bone and shank bone. Whether it has been seasoned only or seasoned and stuffed, it is carved like a boneless roast. If the leg has been butterflied, carve like a beef sirloin roast. If it has been boned and rolled and either oven-roasted or cooked on a spit, carve like any rolled roast.

The *whole loin* is a long piece of meat. It has three sections: the sirloin (nearest the hind), the center and the blade. The center loin, which includes the tenderloin, the 12-inch portion in the middle of the whole cut, is ideal for chops or roasts, plain or stuffed in pockets. The center loin has fewer sinews and interweaving of fibers than the sirloin or blade, and it is tenderer. If the roast is to be served with bones, have the chine bone removed, and crack between the chops before roasting; then carve as you would the same cuts of veal and lamb.

Boning a Loin of Pork

A better presentation can be made with a boned loin, and we will describe this boning process. It can serve as a pattern for boning similar cuts of veal and lamb. Place the meat with the feather bones on the block. Starting from the fatty end, cut straight down against the rib bones, one section at a time, pushing the blade against the bone. The eye of meat lies next to this bone, and you must move the knife blade carefully, to avoid shredding the eye. When you get near the bottom, you will come to a ledge like an S curve lying on its side. Scrape down and over this little ledge, then down again, making an incision close to the bone until you reach the feather bone. Slide the knife under the meat, releasing it from the feather bones.

At this point, you can do several things. You may want to fit the meat and bones together again and use the bones as a rack for roasting. If you do this, season the meat on the side next to the bony rack. You can also stuff the roast between meat and bones, which will retain the meat juices and the flavors of the stuffing. Another possibility is to use the bones as baby spareribs and cook the meat separately. Pork loin is a good cut to roll, by itself or with a stuffing. Tie the rolled roast at intervals of 1½ to 2 inches. Finally, loin of pork is an ideal choice for the spit. Put the spit rod beneath the fatty side, and roll the meat around the rod, without piercing the meat. Roll the meat to a small enough circumference so that the prongs fit on the outside of the roll and will not have to pierce the meat. Be sure to tie the roll firmly around the spit rod. Carving is simple—the same as for any rolled roast.

The *shoulder of fresh pork* has too many sinews for oven-roasting; it is better prepared with moist heat, in stews or braised. Carving the shoulder is easier when it has been cooked with moist heat, but the slices will not be as neat as those from the roasted cut. If you do choose to oven-roast, carve as you would the leg: Cut off the entire top portion above the arm bone, and slice it like London broil. Then cut off the portions on either side of the arm bone, and slice them. Use the meat around the elbow bone just as you would the shank end of the leg.

Cured ham should be carved just like fresh ham. Using a knife with a 12-inch blade, take off the entire piece above the leg bone, and carve it like a London broil, cutting slices at a 45-degree angle toward the shank end of the meat. Treat a half ham—that is, either end of a ham—in the same fashion: Remove the meat above the bone in one piece, and slice it. Remove the leg bone from either whole ham or shank half when it is exposed; carve the meat underneath the bone as you would any boneless roast. To make this easier to do with the shank half, rest the roast on the wider side. The shank half contains only the leg bone, but the butt half has hip and pelvic bones; you will cut around them.

Such other cured meats as corned beef and pastrami should be sliced at an angle, across the grain, like a London broil.

Carving a cured ham on the bone. This is an alternative method. Rest the meat on the widest portion and cut slices from one side of the bone, cutting at an angle.

POULTRY

Birds are so much smaller than meat animals that you cannot avoid dealing with bones. If you understand the anatomy of poultry, you will have an easier time carving. Let's start with the Thanksgiving bird.

Turkey

Place the turkey on a platter or carving board with the legs facing you. With a table napkin in your left hand, grasp the tip of the left leg and push it as far away from the body of the bird as possible. Cut through the skin and flesh between breast and leg in a semicircle until you reach the thigh joint. Bend the leg farther until the joint is loosened, then cut through it, and separate the entire leg and thigh. Transfer the piece to your auxiliary platter. Next, hold the tip of the wing with the napkin, and bend the wing away from the body. Cut through the joint between wing and breast in the same way you tackled the thigh joint.

If your bird is well done, remove the breast on this side in one piece, cutting against the bone. You will be able to carve the breast into even slices like any boneless piece of meat. If the bird is less well done, you will have to slice the breast on the bone. Insert your fork about 3 inches from where you will start to slice. Beginning at the end nearer the wing joint, cut vertical slices; as you continue slicing, you will move closer to the leg joint; move your fork back to get better control. Each slice will start a little higher up, closer to the breast bone.

Now turn to the portions you set aside. If the turkey is small, the drumstick will be one portion. If the turkey is large, you will need to slice the drumstick. Hold the tip in the napkin, resting the joint on the platter. Cut slices on both sides of the bone until you reach the bone. The thigh portion must always be carved. Hold the thigh bone with a fork, and slice up and down on each side, as if carving the breast, until you reach the bone. The thigh of a small turkey will yield 6 to 8 slices, that of a larger bird—22 to 30 pounds—more.

If you have many guests and a large bird, you may want to carve both wing joints, excluding the tip, in the same way.

So far you have carved only one side of the bird. If you expect to serve the whole bird, or most of it, you may prefer to remove both legs and both wings before carving the breast. And you may want to carve both sides of the breast. As you serve individual portions, give each person some of the stuffing if the bird has been stuffed.

If you are new at turkey carving, you may want to place the bird on a carving board with prongs. However, our method of holding the tips of the leg and wing makes it easy to steady the bird on a platter.

Chicken

You may think a chicken should be carved in the same way as a turkey, but the small size of the bird makes this too difficult. It is better to use the poultry shears, with a knife as an aid. Quarter the bird first, then disjoint it.

In Chapter 2, we said you could prepare your own *boneless chicken breasts*, and here is how to do it. A whole chicken breast with its skin has the wings removed. Turn the breast so the bony interior is facing you. With a sharp blow, split the white cartilage, the sternum, at the end of the breastbone. Cut along both sides of the split, making a V on each side. With your thumbs, press down on each side of the bone until the breastbone is partly revealed. With the left thumb, release the meat along the left side; with the right thumb, release it on the right. With a knife, cut along the bone on one side, and split the breast into 2 parts; remove the breastbone completely from the other side. Hold each half in turn, in the left hand, with the thumb on the skin side; with the flat of the knife, remove half of the wishbone. Turn the meat over; toward the narrow end of the piece you will see a small flattened bone end surrounded by white cartilage. Cut under it; with slow strokes, slide the blade flat along the meat, removing the rib cage. When you have loosened about three fourths of it, pick up the bone with your left hand and release it completely. Turn the piece over again, and with your thumb and fingers release the layer of skin, using the knife to help along the edges. There remains a little white cartilage;

Boning a chicken breast. Split the breast, remove the breastbone, cut the wishbone from each side, cut under the cartilage-surrounded bone on the inside and slide the knife blade along the meat, removing the rib cage.

Holding the end of the little tendon between thumb and forefinger slide the knife under the tendon and release it from the meat.

hold it in thumb and forefinger and with the knife peel it out. When you complete both halves, you are ready to cook.

This description will take far longer to read than it would for a professional to do it. And when you have done it a few times you will find it is neither difficult nor time-consuming. However, you can ask your butcher to do this for you. We want to emphasize that the longer boneless white meat of chicken waits before cooking, the drier it will become.

Duck and Goose

Ducks and geese have a different shape from chicken, and the leg joints are hard to sever. The best way to separate them is with poultry shears. If the duck is small, simply serve half as one portion. Or serve just the breast quarters and use the rest for leftovers. A duck is barely adequate for 4 portions, but you can stretch it by cutting it into 8 pieces as for fricassee. The breast portions can be removed either before or after roasting or poaching, to make elegant presentations like chicken *suprêmes*, although the shape is different from the same portion in a chicken.

You will need a long platter to serve a goose. Halve the bird with shears, then cut off the wings. Slice the breast. Also slice the leg meat on the bird, since it is difficult to remove the whole leg from the carcass.

For an unusual presentation with a larger goose, have your butcher bone it completely—do not try this yourself. Stuff with fruit or whatever you like, and bake. Slice like a boneless roast.

Carving is a skill, and like any other it must be learned and practiced. Practice on your family regularly, and you will be successful when you have company.

All these directions are for right-handed carvers. If you are left-handed, reverse everything.

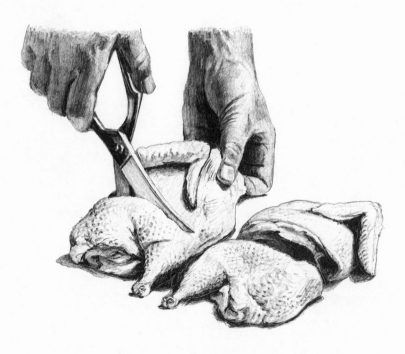

Quartering a duck with poultry shears. Follow the same procedure before or after cooking. For fricassee, cut each quarter again into halves with the shears.

BUFFET

Chapter 21

Aɴʏ ᴍᴇᴀʟ, from breakfast to late-night dinner, can be served as a buffet. The avid reader of British mystery novels will remember descriptions of buffet breakfasts in English country houses, with kidneys and kippers in silver dishes, kept hot over spirit lamps on majestic sideboards. You may want to serve a buffet breakfast, but today this style of service is more often adapted to brunch (see Chapter 7 for a few ideas).

Today, just as in the past, the reason for serving breakfast as a buffet is that members of the same household often eat breakfast at different times, making it impossible to serve the entire meal at once. Buffet service is also ideal when guests are expected at different times, but to make this practical you need devices to keep foods warm or cold, and methods to keep them from drying out. Choose the foods to be served under these conditions carefully.

Another advantage of the buffet meal is that it enables you to serve almost any number of people without help in the dining room and little or none in the kitchen. Because the buffet is such a flexible, informal way to serve, it can be more fun for your guests.

The buffet is said to have originated in France, as a meal set upon boards to feed passengers traveling by coach. It was designed to feed people on the run, and as far as is known they ate standing. This may be encouraging if you have simple facilities; boards will suffice if need be—it is what you serve that counts.

From the meal served on boards, things became more and more elaborate, until Carême was creating architectural masterpieces of spun sugar, and food for important occasions was presented on tiered tables of huge size. No one could reach the top tiers, of course; they were for show only.

Buffets in elegant restaurants were descended from these fantasies, but of course everything was edible. The buffets were designed to give the guests a look at the possibilities offered by the menu, and all the dishes were prepared to have a fine appearance. Many restaurants today continue this tradition. At your buffet meals too everything should look as attractive as possible.

Today the term "buffet" is used for several kinds of meals that are presented quite differently. First, there is the lunch, dinner, supper or outdoor meal with everything except dessert arranged on a serving table, and all the guests arriving at an appointed hour. For such meals, you do not need to worry too much about keeping everything hot or cold.

Another kind of buffet is the reception or "at-home" or evening party at which people come and go over a period of time. It is tricky to have everything just right for such a meal.

Buffets may also differ in the way the food is presented. If you have no help in serving, each dish must be prepared in such a way that guests can serve themselves individual portions with ease. For such meals, serve no large roasts, nothing with bones. If you have many guests and the occasion is important enough to have someone help serve behind the buffet table, you can serve whole roasted turkey, glazed ham or roast beef. As the guests decide what they want, the carver slices individual portions and serves them with appropriate garnishes.

Besides being presented in a variety of ways, buffets may also be eaten in different fashions. Some are eaten standing or sitting very casually, perhaps moving from place to place during the meal. Since the plate must be held in the hand or poised on the knee, you should serve nothing that requires a knife. This buffet must be a one-utensil meal. Even if you have help, do not plan on serving a roast.

If you have enough space, you can set up individual folding tables or card tables. Then you can serve anything, because it will be possible to wield a knife and fork. The guests may settle themselves as they like, or, for a slightly more formal party, you may arrange the seating. At the most formal type of buffet, guests serve themselves from a sideboard, but all come together to dine at a properly set table.

With all buffet meals, dessert is usually served separately, either placed on the sideboard when the main course is removed, or served directly to guests at the table or tables. Coffee and after-dinner drinks may also be arranged in either way.

Help or no help, tables or no tables, summer or winter, the kind of meal, whether your guests will arrive all at once or in stages—you must make these decisions, and what you decide will determine how to set up your buffet meal.

How to serve? There are endless ways. If you have a sideboard or buffet, it will probably be adequate for an average-sized buffet. If not, you can push your dining table to the wall and set everything up on that, or leave it centered so people can move around it. Two card tables fastened together can serve, or even a narrow board securely fastened to wooden horses or other uprights. A desk will do, or even the tops of bookcases. If you will have serving help, the table should be sturdy enough for carving, of a convenient height for the servers, and wide enough to work on; servers should stand in back of the table, and guests will move along the opposite side.

Cocktail parties can be served buffet style too. If you have a huge gathering, it is probably more efficient to have help or friends serve tidbits on trays. For smaller parties, the buffet system can save you a lot of trouble; its chief disadvantage is that everyone tends to congregate around the food. If you have more people than space, those outside the inner circle may feel hungry. For this kind of gathering, during which people eat little bits over a long period of time, it is better to have two or more tabletops, with a selection of everything on each.

Buffet Table

The conventional buffet arrangement consists of a large centerpiece with a serving platter on each side. This may be just what you need, but it would be far more original to arrange everything asymmetrically or according to an imaginative plan of your own. Cover your table, real or makeshift, with something that masks it completely—paper or linen cloths or lengths of any material that suits the theme of your party. If your table is narrow, skip such extraneous decorations as flowers and candlesticks; or use low nosegays arranged in shot glasses, or simply sprays of leaves—beech, lemon, grape—whatever the season offers, instead of anything tall or wide. If the buffet table is round or oval and you expect the guests to move around it, arrange a floral centerpiece or even a construction of fruit and vegetables. But it is nice to be able to see fellow guests across the table, so make the arrangements reasonably low. If the table is against the wall, you can use tall bouquets, candles, or any attractive arrangement to break the line between table and wall; you can even use small pieces of sculpture, piles of Christmas tree balls or Easter eggs, or the dessert, if it is splendid-looking like a *croquembouche*.

If your setup dictates an obvious direction for the movement of guests, use that as a guide. The first thing a guest needs is a plate. If guests are to eat at set places, table napkins and cutlery will be at table. If they are to hold their plates as they eat, utensils and napkins must be arranged on the buffet table. They are usually put near the plates, but it is better to put them at the end, so people will not have to hold them while transferring food to plates. For very informal occasions, wrap the utensils in the table napkins, so that each guest will have only one bundle.

If any dish is served in a sauce with an accompanying starch dish—potato, rice, bulgur—be sure to arrange the starch so it can be served first. When you are planning the menu, consider the mixture of all the dishes on a single plate; will they combine well? Mashed potatoes and gravy do not mix well with salad dressed with vinaigrette. Hot and cold together? Yes, if you plan it carefully, but if the cold preparation is aspic covered or molded, a hot dish will melt it, making a soupy mess of the crystal-clear cold aspic you worked so hard to make. All garnishes must be fresh and crisp; if the buffet must look good for a long time, do not use anything that will collapse easily. Belgian endive will stay crisp much longer than iceberg lettuce, carrot curls longer than parsley sprigs. If it is summer or if you are in the Tropics, you may prefer to use flowers; single hibiscus or geranium blossoms will stay open for a long time even out of water.

Amounts of Food

After planning the menu, make a shopping list. It is harder to gauge servings for a buffet than for a simple sit-down meal. Here are a few guidelines. For a party of 20 or more people, allow 3 to 4 ounces of meat per person. If you have fewer than 20 people, allow a little more than that for display. The platters should never be empty, because you will not want any guest to go away without a serving of any dish he would like. The amount of 3 to 4 ounces is based, of course, on the assumption that you will serve other foods as well as meat. Here is another way to plan: Allow 12 ounces (¾ pound) of *raw* protein for each person; this includes meat, poultry, fish and game.

If you have more than 20 people, consider the general movement of guests. For instance, if you have as many as 50 people—and especially if you have more—plan for two or more tables. Otherwise the line of guests will be terribly long. Your tables should match each other, or, if they are different, it should be an intentional difference.

What should you serve? The most obvious, and the most hackneyed, menu is cold cuts and potato salad. Sometimes, no matter how hackneyed, it may be just right. Serve salami, ham, bologna, liverwurst, sliced turkey and chicken for a good balance. Be sure to remove the casings, and slice everthing quite thin. Arrange overlapping slices, or roll the more flexible meats. Accompany the meats with potato salad and sliced tomatoes, cucumbers, red onion rings or some of each. Pickles, celery ribs, olives and other such picnic fare go well with this menu. Some guests may want to make sandwiches, so split crusty rolls and mustard are good to have. This buffet is appropriate to serve outdoors.

You may prefer to serve several meat dishes and offer a selection of the other dishes as well. Be sure that everything is reasonably harmonious, and consider the problems of coordinating sauced dishes, and combining hot and cold dishes.

Here are some suggestions for dishes that look handsome on the buffet.

GLAZED CORNED BEEF

A well-shaped piece of corned beef can make an attractive presentation. Tell your butcher how you plan to use it, and have him trim it properly, leaving some of the fat on top. Put the meat into boiling water, and simmer for 2½ hours. Let the meat cool in the cooking liquid unless the liquid is very salty. Make a glaze; mix brown sugar, honey, mustard and dry bread crumbs to a rather stiff paste, then add enough fresh orange juice to make it spreadable. Spread over the fatty top of the beef, and stud with whole cloves. Bake in a preheated 250° F. oven for 35 to 45 minutes, until the glaze is shining and well distributed. Let the dish cool, and serve it cold. You can decorate the glaze, if you like, with halves of candied cherries, split almonds, bits of candied citron, or candied lemon, lime or orange rinds. This looks beautiful served whole, but someone must be on hand to slice it. You can slice part of it to start with, leaving the balance whole. Whole cherries, preserved crab apples and green figs are good accompaniments for corned beef.

You can prepare beef brisket or bottom round in the same way. Vary the flavor of the glaze and the garnish if you like.

Veal Round Steak

For another delicious boneless roast, use a 4- to 5-pound round steak of veal. Roast it in a slow oven (325° F.) for 1½ hours. When the veal has cooled, slice it like corned beef, and serve with a velouté sauce made with veal stock, a sour-cream sauce, or a butter and anchovy sauce, either to spoon over the slices or to use as a dip for small slivers of the meat.

Only if you have someone to carve should you serve the larger roasts, those with bones or any cut that presents any difficulty in handling. A roast strip sirloin or shell (both names denote the same cut—see p. 22) is handsome and elegant. Other beef roasts, a whole or half ham, a capon or a turkey can be served cold; the ham and poultry can be carefully garnished. Even a leg of lamb can be roasted, cooled, and served at room temperature if you have someone to carve it, but lamb is not at its best when really cold. Leg of lamb is easiest to carve, of course, if boned and rolled.

These large impressive roasts will look good on your buffet table, but you may want to serve preparations for individual portions.

Chicken Breasts

The easiest and prettiest dishes can be made with boneless chicken breasts or *suprêmes*. If you use *suprêmes*, they will look festive with frills on the trimmed wing bone. Similar dishes can be made with either breasts or *suprêmes*, but it is easier to stuff boneless half breasts. You can stuff them with ham and cheese (like veal *cordon bleu*), sautéed mushrooms or pâté; poach them in chicken stock, then let them cool. If the guests are to assemble all at once, you can serve these plain, even without stuffing, but if your guests will be coming at intervals, or if you expect a delay, aspic is ideal. Brush a thin layer over each chicken piece. When it has jelled, brush on a second layer. You can garnish each piece with a truffle cutout, a simple tarragon leaf or whatever you like; if you do add a garnish, be sure to attach it with aspic. A large silver or china platter filled with these glistening chicken pieces will impress the most fastidious guest.

CHICKEN AVEYRON

We have dubbed another preparation, inspired by chicken Kiev, "Chicken Aveyron." For each serving, prepare a *suprême*, half a chicken breast with the wing bone attached. Remove the other bones, the skin and all sinews. Separate the two lobes, or fillets, but leave them attached at the base, that is, near the shoulder bone. For each chicken piece, cut a slender 1-ounce slice of blue cheese—Roquefort, Gorgonzola, Stilton or Danish Blue. Put the cheese between the two fillets, and press the fillets together around it; there is no need to skewer or sew the pieces closed, because the natural protein juices will hold them together. Arrange in a single layer on a buttered baking sheet, brush with a little melted butter, and cover the sheet with foil. Bake them for 30 to 40 minutes, until they are tender and delicately golden. Do not overcook, because the cheese will leak out and the chicken will become dry. Serve these hot, at once, or at room temperature, or cool them and glaze with aspic. Add a frill to the little wing bone, whether served hot or cold.

Although chicken is not as easy to roll as some other meats, you can try it for another version of this dish. Flatten the chicken, both fillets together, leaving them attached to the wing bone at the shoulder. Make the cheese pieces for this version about 2 inches long and ½ inch wide. Place the cheese at the end farthest from the bone, and roll the chicken with the cheese inside; secure the roll with string or a skewer. Bake or poach the rolls in chicken stock for 20 minutes, until just done, or sauté them (see p. 218).

Of course, you can also stuff chicken *suprêmes* with ham or prosciutto, or with one of these meats and a blander cheese such as Emmental, American Cheddar, or mozzarella. This cannot be called "Aveyron," but invent your own name. Serve hot, cold, or at room temperature, and do not forget to add the little frills.

Whole Small Birds

For another poultry dish, use roasted whole small birds, squab, Rock Cornish game hens or halves of the hens. Their glistening brown exteriors are handsome whether roasted plain or glazed with marmalade, honey or aspic.

Sliced Meats

An even simpler way to present meats or poultry in individual servings is to slice them and arrange the slices on a platter. You can do this with cold beef, veal, turkey, chicken or ham. If the meats are to be kept on the buffet table for a long time, cover them with aspic to keep them from drying. Beef slices can be covered with a little vinaigrette sauce and sprinkled with capers and red onion rings. Slices of ham paired with slices of turkey make a pretty platter and a good taste combination.

With all these meat dishes, whole roasts or individual servings, prepare some sort of grain or starch and one or more vegetable dishes, plain or as salads. Add rolls or good sliced bread, already buttered or plain, or serve garlic butter if it suits the occasion. Salad greens are always acceptable, but be sure to cut or tear them into pieces that can be served without too much trouble. If you know what your guests like, dress the salad; it will save a lot of fussing. If in doubt, arrange a choice of dressings in bowls or cruets.

Mixtures of meats with other ingredients or ground or puréed meats are also good dishes for buffet meals. The possibilities are endless, and we will only suggest a few.

Choucroute

Two famous French classics, *choucroute garnie* and *cassoulet*, make great dishes for hearty buffets. *Choucroute* is sauerkraut, and this dish is basically a casserole of sauerkraut with a selection of pork products cooked with it; there is no set way to assemble this dish and no one combination. Allow about ⅓ pound of sauerkraut and ¼ to ½ pound of meat for each serving. Wash the sauerkraut well. Sauté seasoning vegetables (onion, carrot) and, most important, juniper berries. The berries can be put in a cheesecloth bag or mixed with vegetables. Add the sauerkraut, mix and turn everything into a large casserole. Add white wine, about 1 cup for each pound of sauerkraut; an Alsatian white is preferred, since this dish originated near the border of France and Germany. Some versions call for part stock and part wine, others for Kirsch. A little vodka will accentuate the taste of the juniper berries. Cook on top of the stove or in the oven for about 1 hour or longer if you prefer, but overcooked sauerkraut can be very unappetizing. Cook the pork (tenderloin, thick bacon, various kinds of sausages—whatever you like) separately until almost done; it will probably take longer than the sauerkraut. Then slice the meats, and add them to the sauerkraut. Continue to cook for 30 to 50 minutes, until all the flavors are blended. This is the sort of dish that can continue to cook over low heat if guests are late, and it will remain warm in the casserole for some time. French recipes suggest goose fat or lard for sautéing the flavoring vegetables, but we recommend a small amount of olive oil. If you prepare this for a large group, make it in 2 casseroles. Serve with boiled potatoes sprinkled with chives and caraway seeds.

Cassoulet

Cassoulet is a dish from the French south, Languedoc. It is made with dried beans and meats; white beans are most commonly used, but any kind will do. The meats can be mutton, sausage, pork chops or goose, in any combination. Mutton and goose are not readily available in the United States, but you can make an excellent *cassoulet* with Polish sausage, kielbasy, or with lamb and thick bacon. Cook the meats, cut them into serving pieces, and combine with cooked beans seasoned and flavored to your taste. Bake together until the top is browned and all flavors are blended. This is the kind of hearty dish that requires garlic-buttered French bread, a sturdy salad and red wine.

Pilaf

Pilaf, made with rice and other ingredients, is excellent for the buffet. First, sauté minced onions and other flavoring vegetables with the dry rice in oil. Then add stock that matches the meat you are using and cook the rice until *al dente*. Uncooked meat or poultry can be added at the start; if the meat is cooked, add it toward the end. Serve this in a large casserole, or turn the pilaf into a mold to finish cooking, so it can be turned out to serve; sprinkle the top with parsley, or arrange slivers of avocado around it. Here is our version of a pilaf.

BUFFET CHICKEN AND RICE   6 servings

1 pound boneless cooked chicken	5 tablespoons chopped summer squash,
4 to 6 tablespoons olive oil	green beans or carrots
2 tablespoons chopped onion	1 cup uncooked rice
2 tablespoons chopped green pepper	3 cups chicken stock or water
	1 teaspoon salt

Cut the chicken into bite-sized pieces; there should be about 2 cups, loosely packed. (One 2½-pound chicken will give you about this much, but it will be a mixture of light and dark meat. If you prefer all white meat, buy 2 pounds of chicken breasts, and bone them after cooking. The chicken can be baked or poached, but do not overcook it, because it will be cooked further.) Heat the oil over moderate heat, and sauté the chopped onion and green pepper in it. After 5 minutes, add the other vegetables and the chicken pieces. Sauté, stirring, for 5 minutes longer, then add the rice, and stir until it is coated with oil. Add more oil if you need it to keep the chicken from sticking. Add 2½ cups of the stock or water, and bring to a boil. When the liquid boils, add the salt if using water or unsalted stock, and stir. Reduce to a very low simmer, cover, and cook for 45 minutes. Check once after 30 minutes, and add the rest of the stock if needed. The liquid should all be absorbed and the rice tender. Serve in a large bowl or in a mound on a platter, sprinkled with parsley or mint. You can double or triple this recipe easily, and you can change the vegetables or use another kind of poultry.

Salads

All the salads described in this book can be used for buffets. For gala occasions, you can make them very fancy. Chicken and shrimp salad or chicken and lobster salad are both delicious and unusual. If you plan to have either, be sure to add enough of the chief ingredients. Do not serve a celery salad with only a hint of poultry and seafood.

Molded Dishes

Molded dishes, whether baked and served hot or frozen or chilled and served cold, look fine on a buffet table. Baked mousses, unmolded on a deep plate, can be sauced with a contrasting flavor. Chilled mousses can serve even for winter buffets, and they can be made in advance and kept frozen or chilled until you are ready to unmold them. Chicken, veal and ham make delicious mousses, either cold or hot.

If you want to be very elaborate, poach a large bird like a capon, or several large chickens or ducks. Fill the cooled bird with a mousse—chicken, ham, tomato, mushroom—and spread some over the outside. Finish with a glaze of clear aspic. This is not easy to serve unless you carve the bird first and then reassemble it, attaching the pieces with some of the mousse. If you cook a pair of birds, make a mousse out of one, and use it to fill the other. If you poach in wine-flavored stock and use some of it to make the aspic, the dish will be well flavored.

Daube Glacé

Another delicious molded dish is the New Orleans specialty *daube glacé*, basically braised beef in molded jelly. Although this takes a long time to prepare, it is not difficult. The aspic is made by cooking gelatin-rich bones, and any little bits of meat on the bones are chopped very fine and added to the gelatin. The beef is cooked until tender but still juicy, all the bones and gristle are removed, and beef and aspic are arranged in loaf pans and chilled until firm. Of course, you can use any kind of mold if you are not trying to be authentic.

Slices or small chunks of meat can also be arranged in a mold. For a pretty appearance, arrange a design of vegetables in the mold. This idea can be used for several large molds or lots of small ones. Beef, veal, turkey, chicken and duck can be used.

Parsleyed Ham in Aspic

One of the most beautiful molded dishes is parsleyed ham in aspic, a famous Burgundian dish served at Easter. You can make this in various ways. The ham is fully cooked, then boned. It can be cut into several large pieces or into many smaller portions. The aspic is made with good stock and mixed with a lot of chopped fresh parsley. When the dish is unmolded, the contrast of pink ham and green jelly makes a handsome dish, and of course it tastes delicious. Use a round, oval or ham-shaped mold. For easier serving, you can slice the ham and fit it together with the aspic.

Stuffed Dishes

Many of the stuffed preparations described in Chapter 13 can be adapted to the buffet. If you have a way to keep things hot, serve one of the little meat rolls, which are easily transferred from platter to plate. Stuffed vegetables are also good, and since many of them taste best warm or at room temperature rather than very hot or very cold, they are ideal for the buffet. If you serve such vegetables as eggplant or squash, be sure to select those small enough so that a stuffed half will make one serving.

Stews and Pies

Stews and pies made of small chunks of meat can also serve on the buffet table, if the occasion is not too fancy. A large quantity of stew served in its cooking pot—a sturdy pot of porcelain-coated cast iron or sheet steel—will usually stay hot for a long time. A very large meat pie can look fine, and the filling can be your own specialty. However, you must plan dishes that include pastry carefully, because pastry can become soggy if it sits too long before being eaten, and most pastries used for meat or poultry dishes taste best hot. If you do use pastry, choose the recipe carefully. Beef Wellington and ham *en croûte* are sometimes suggested for buffets, but we think they are better for holidays or special occasions when appearance is important but also when all the guests can be served at once.

Here is an unusual recipe for a stew that is good for a buffet. If your guests will be arriving over a long period of time, prepare several batches, to be ready at intervals. The cooking time can be adjusted by reducing the heat.

CURRIED LAMB AND CHESTNUTS   6 servings

½ cup olive oil
1¼ tablespoons curry powder
20 chestnuts, cooked, peeled, and cut into quarters
3 pounds boneless lamb, cut into 1¼-inch cubes
2 large onions, cut into large pieces

6 carrots, scraped and cut into 1-inch chunks
5 garlic cloves, crushed
1 teaspoon grated fresh gingerroot
½ teaspoon salt
¼ teaspoon ground pepper
½ cup dry white wine
1½ cups shredded red cabbage

Heat the oil in a large skillet, and add ¼ tablespoon of the curry powder. Cook the powder for 1 minute, then add the chestnuts, and brown them quickly. Take them from the skillet, and place them immediately in a Dutch oven. Brown the cubes of lamb in the same oil, and add to the chestnuts. Add onions, carrots, garlic, gingerroot, salt, pepper and the remaining tablespoon of the curry powder to the lamb and chestnuts; mix well. Cook over low heat on top of the stove for 1 hour.

Meantime, discard half of the oil in the skillet, and reheat the remaining oil slowly. Add the wine and red cabbage to the oil, and cook slowly for 10 minutes, mixing occasionally. Lift the lid of the Dutch oven, and stir the contents to mix well. Pour the cabbage mixture, including any remaining oil, on top of lamb. Cover the pot, and cook over low heat for 1½ hours longer. At serving time, mix everything together gently, as if tossing a salad, and transfer to a heated serving platter or bowl. This recipe can be doubled or tripled for more servings, and can be cooked in a 325° F. oven instead of on top of the stove.

Zakuska

We mentioned both *zakuska* and *smörgåsbord* in Chapter 9. An entire buffet meal can be based on either. The Russians are said to have huge appetites, and there are many stories about the innocent outsider eating *zakuski* to a point of satiation only to discover later that it was the prelude to the main meal. For your family, you may serve one *zakuska*, as a first course. However, the large impressive spread, including caviar, herrings, veal or ham salad, some type of salmon, mushrooms, all sorts of vegetable salads, *salade Olivier* (made with chicken) and so on, can make an ample buffet dinner without subsequent courses.

Smörgåsbord

According to some writers, the idea of serving *zakuski* as a prelude to a meal came to Russia from Scandinavia; if so, *zakuska* can be considered a close relative of the *smörgåsbord*. All the Scandinavian countries have a similar presentation in their cookery, but each one is distinctive. *Smörgåsbord* is Swedish, but even in Sweden, a home dinner starts with a simple first course of one or a few selections. The huge service we think of as typically Swedish is actually composed of several courses served at once. First, herrings in various forms; second, cold fish or meat and salad; third, hot dishes; finally, cheese. Mixtures of meat and fish are often used in salads. The hot dishes usually include meatballs; baked chicken wings, lamb and potato hash, liver pâté and game dishes are popular too.

With both *zakuski* and *smörgåsbord*, the idea is to serve several different dishes of each kind; the guests will either choose one or eat small amounts of each. This is quite different from a menu based on a single main dish with its accompaniments. Preparing these huge meals is a lot of work; nevertheless, such a buffet might be just right for a special occasion, and it can be useful for the situation in which guests come and go over a long period of time.

We would like to describe two extremely different buffet meals that we have enjoyed. The first was a luncheon in a country setting. On the sideboard was a beautiful Bayonne ham on a carving rack; a large pâté in a terrine; a platter of cold green and white asparagus; an arrangement of tiny tarts, apple and strawberry, and a large basket of peaches, plums and cherries. Green leaves and flowers were banked around the sides and back of the sideboard. You could copy this kind of meal in any home without turning the kitchen upside down.

The second was a dinner for about 75 people. It included a whole roast turkey, beautifully decorated; orange-glazed roast ducklings; roast guinea hens; roast beef; several kinds of pâté; whole fish in aspic; mounds of shrimps, and varieties of cold vegetables to be served in salads. This buffet required the services of many chefs, not only for cooking, but for making the aspic, the decorations on the meats and fish, and the garnishes. Only professionals can prepare such a meal; and you must have a home with enormous kitchen facilities, especially lots of refrigerator space.

No guest could sample all the different dishes, and even though everything tasted fine, it was the appearance of the meal that was most impressive. For most people, large amounts of a few dishes is an easier arrangement, even for many guests.

Anniversaries, wedding breakfasts, graduation parties and some holidays are often catered, because so few people own enough cups, plates and silver for large gatherings. If you entertain a huge number of guests, you may have no alternative. But it is more fun to have smaller parties, plan your own menus, and invent new recipes that will look and taste delicious and different.

BUFFET LUNCH

Everything in this lunch is served at room temperature. To expand the menu, add a meat dish; a roast veal round served with plain cold mustard sauce will go well.

Melon cubes wrapped with prosciutto
Chicken and shrimp salad
Rice salad in timbales
Green beans vinaigrette in individual bundles
Glazed apple tart with hard sauce

The main course and the vegetable in this lunch must be served hot; be sure to have some device to keep them at serving temperature. To expand this to a larger meal, add baked pâté and baked tomatoes stuffed with crumbs and anchovies.

Chicken Tetrazzini (noodles, mushrooms, cream sauce, Parmesan cheese)
Green peas and mushrooms
Chicory salad
Fresh pineapple

BUFFET DINNER

This is a menu for a warm day, but remember that aspic will melt in extremely hot weather; you could make the aspic stiff enough to avoid melting, but then it would be too rubbery to eat.

Broiled skewered swordfish cubes with lime dressing
Chicken suprêmes stuffed with pâté, garnished and glazed with aspic
Cracked-wheat salad
Eggplant caviar
Endive and watercress
Pistachio ice cream
Brown-edge wafers

This is a menu for fall or winter, and all the items are available in those seasons. You can even use this menu for a party during the weekend after Thanksgiving.

Glazed baked corned beef (see p. 340)
Sliced turkey in Mornay sauce
Individual mounds of duchess potatoes
Steamed cauliflower and broccoli flowerets
Puréed winter squash sprinkled with pecans
Compote of poached dried fruits

This is a menu for an occasion when you have someone to carve; everything is hot except the salad vegetables—provide separate salad plates.

Roast leg of lamb
Red-wine sauce
Molded rice and parsley ring
Celery-knob slivers baked with Parmesan cheese
Vegetable salad (cooked green beans, cooked chick-peas, cooked zucchini rounds, raw cauliflowerets and cherry tomatoes) with anchovy dressing
Individual apricot tarts

NUTRITION
AND
DIET

Chapter 22

Naturally the viewpoint of this book is pro-meat, but we will nevertheless try to be objective when discussing nutrition and diet.

What you believe about early man depends on which anthropologists you trust. Theories about early humans and their diet are based on the study of teeth and jaws, but the samples are very few. Some anthropologists believe that the early primates were vegetarians, others believe they were meat eaters even then. Whatever they began with, today people are dependent on other creatures for their protein, since some essential amino acids are not manufactured by the human system.

The well-balanced diet for human beings living in the Temperate Zone is an ideal that many fail to reach, and many illnesses of civilized man can be attributed directly to nutritional causes. In contrast, the Eskimos, before the radical change in their lives caused by the advance of "civilization," had diets that were almost entirely protein; compared to an ideal diet, it was poorly balanced. At the other extreme are people of various religions who do not eat meat; their practices would seem to contradict what we said earlier about the failure of the human system to produce protein, but even vegetarians drink milk and eat cheese, and many of them do eat eggs; in this way, animal protein is provided.

PROTEIN

The word "protein," from the Greek word *prōteios*, meaning "primary," was coined in 1839 by Gerardus Mulder, a Dutch chemist. Proteins, carbohydrates and fats are the essential elements of the human diet. The role of vitamins and minerals is also essential, but not everything is known about it yet. Protein contains carbon, hydrogen and oxygen, but so do the other essential elements. What distinguishes the large protein molecule from the other essentials is that it contains nitrogen.

Amino Acids

Proteins contain amino acids; eight of these are essential for human growth and maintenance, but they cannot be synthesized by the human body from nonprotein

351

foods. Therefore, human beings must eat foods that contain them. Animal foods supply all the necessary amino acids for human life and health.

So why isn't the human diet composed entirely of animal foods? The Eskimos have survived by eating only meat, and we could mention other cultures that have too, like the African Masai, whose wealth is in their herds and whose diet is derived almost entirely from those herds. Obviously, human beings in most parts of the Temperate Zone lead vastly different lives from those of the Eskimo or the Masai. They occupy heated houses, get much less exercise, and live under different kinds of stresses. But just move someone from one society to another, and the demands of the new life will impose a radical change in diet.

Apparently, food elements are so interrelated that humans need them all to digest each other. For instance, people need adequate protein to absorb enough calcium from other foods, to synthesize enzymes, and to keep metabolism at its proper rate. To utilize all the other food elements properly within the body, vitamins and minerals are needed. Fats are necessary for the storage and use of fat-soluble vitamins. Carbohydrates are needed to help the body use fats.

Animal foods are not the only source of protein. Legumes, including all kinds of dried beans, dried peas and peanuts, contain protein; soybeans and mung beans are particularly good sources. Grains contain some protein, and there are smaller amounts in other vegetables. But none of the vegetable proteins is of top quality; vegetables cannot provide the necessary amounts of all the amino acids that are essential to life. Animal proteins are needed to utilize vegetable proteins, and they must be eaten together to do the job. This explains the importance of bits of salt pork in clam chowder, and crumbled bacon in pancakes.

In addition to amino acids, meat provides large amounts of iron and niacin and substantial amounts of thiamin and riboflavin. The last three are B vitamins. Meat also contains some calcium, but milk is the best source of that mineral. If you make your own stock using bones, especially marrowbones or bones that have been cracked or split, you will gain even more calcium, as well as other minerals, because they will dissolve more easily during cooking.

Some meats provide huge amounts of particular minerals. Liver is the best source of iron, and, Popeye the Sailor notwithstanding, spinach is not in the same league at all! Liver also provides much vitamin A and riboflavin, and most of it is retained in cooking. Some variety meats provide good amounts of phosphorus and other minerals. Pork provides three times as much thiamin as any other food source. As well as being very low in cholesterol, chicken supplies the B vitamins—thiamin, niacin and riboflavin—as well as vitamin A and a lot of calcium.

In recent decades, one of the national health problems in the United States has been overweight. The problem has absorbed the attention and energies of many physicians and nutritionists. Have you read some of the diets proposed by such researchers? They vary enormously. Some direct the dieter to eat no fat. Some direct the dieter to eat no carbohydrates. But almost all of them tell you to eat meat! In fact, meat is one of the few things that makes any reducing diet bearable. Although meat is almost entirely digested by the human body, it takes some time for the process to be completed. Since internal fats in meat slow its movement through the stomach and other digestive passages, meat eaters do not feel hungry for quite a while after eating.

To get the most out of your meat, avoid overcooking it, which may destroy some of the vitamin content. If you prepare meat by a moist-cooking method, be sure to use the resulting liquid to make sauce or gravy, or to enrich soup. If you discard cooking liquid, you will discard water-soluble B vitamins and some minerals along with it.

Let us consider normal human beings at various ages. What does protein do for them, and how should they eat it? Each individual grows and develops from birth to young adulthood. Most of the growth that occurs after that is either replacement or repair.

INFANCY

The greatest amount of growth takes place during the earliest period of life. A child triples in weight during the first year, and protein is crucial for this rapid growth—for muscles, bones, connective tissues, blood and nerves. The soft cartilage of the infant frame must become hard adult bone, and the muscles must grow to keep pace with the bones. Adequate protein is also vital for the proper *rate of growth*, so that the child of two years has the appropriate height and weight for that age.

The temporary teeth that start to push through the gums at about 6 months of age are already in the gums at birth. So are the second, or "permanent," teeth. The advice of the dentist to the patient with poor teeth, that the patient should have picked a different grandfather, is no joke! Can you remember what your baby teeth looked like when they were extracted by the string attached to the door handle? They are usually hollow, because the body reabsorbs the calcium and other elements within the teeth to use again. Good protein is needed to complete dental development, not just from birth, but during pregnancy as well.

Babies start out drinking milk, but at about 6 months they can eat meat. Some pediatricians advise the use of strained meat as early as 6 weeks, and meat-fed babies do not become roly-poly. Steak, lamb chop, liver—almost any meat—can be prepared as baby food. Cut the meat into pieces, and purée it in an electric blender. Leftover cooked meats can be mashed. When a little older, an infant can eat diced, cubed and ground meat. Any of these foods freshly prepared is better than prepackaged infant food, as convenient as that can be. Vegetables are also essential, and they can be prepared separately or with meat or poultry. Later, young children can eat meats and poultry prepared just as adult foods are—by baking, broiling, panfrying, etc. Three well-balanced meals a day composed of good fresh unprocessed food and adequate bulk, for intestinal tone, will support healthy growth.

YOUTH

After the tremendous growth of early childhood, further development toward adulthood is uneven. There are some periods of rapid growth, and these occur at different times in girls and boys. Inadequate protein can cause lassitude and fatigue, then loss of appetite, loss of weight and impaired liver function. Protein is very important in maintaining good resistance to disease and in helping the body develop antibodies.

Protein is stored by the human body only during childhood growth spurts, reproduction and lactation, and recovery from illness. For this reason, everyone must consume some meat, poultry or other protein-rich food every day.

In pregnancy, adequate protein consumption is essential; the unborn child must develop two sets of teeth, among other things. But the health of the mother is also insured by good protein nutrition. Very young mothers, especially those under 20 years, are still growing themselves. And all mothers will produce healthier babies if they were properly fed when they were young.

AGE

As people grow older, they still need protein for repair, good muscle tone, strong bones—many old people have fragile bones—and maintenance of proper metabolic rate.

Well, it is nice to be a "normal human," but suppose you have a health problem that is in some way diet-related. This is not a medical or health book, and we are not qualified to tell you what is wrong with you or what diet to adopt for your condition. We can, however, tell you how to prepare meat and poultry in ways that will be useful for a few common dietary restrictions.

ANEMIA

Anemia is more widespread in the United States than it should be. Amino acids and iron, both contained in animal protein, combine to make hemoglobin, the substance in the red blood cells that carries oxygen from the lungs to other bodily tissues. Anemia is a hemoglobin deficiency. Sometimes it is caused by poor diet, but it appears that it can also be the result of faulty metabolism of protein that is eaten. For simple anemia, which can usually be controlled by diet, it is important to eat rare meats, to prevent mineral loss. Thick steaks broiled rare and rare roast beef are good. Butcher's, or hanging tenderloin, is especially rich in minerals, because it is high in blood content. Liver sliced thick and broiled is the best meat for those with anemia. Beef or steer liver has more blood content and nutritive value than calf's liver.

Butcher's or hanging tenderloin, or hanger, which is near the kidneys, is rich in minerals and high in blood content; a good cut to use for beef tea.

BEEF TEA

For invalids and people who have difficulty chewing, old-fashioned beef tea is ideal. Use butcher's tenderloin or lean neck meat; cut the meat into ½-inch cubes, and put it in the top part of a double boiler over simmering water. Add no liquid to the beef, but a little salt if you like. Cook for 4 to 5 hours, but be sure the water in the lower pot does not cook away; check at least once every hour. A similar nutritious "tea" can be made with the eye of the lamb chop or the round steak portion of leg of lamb. For this, do not use the neck of lamb, because it is too fatty. Serve beef or lamb tea straight, or add barley or rice and serve as soup. You can embellish it with grated carrots and chopped fresh herbs.

OVERWEIGHT

If you are overweight, it is best to get medical advice, because the cause of the problem might dictate a particular diet. If you simply consume too many calories, here are some pointers. Avoid fried foods, no matter how they are prepared. Some internal fats are extracted from broiled or roasted meats during cooking. In frying, the internal fat content of food—except ground meat—is not eliminated at all, and extra calories are added by the coatings and by the amount of fat, however small, that is added for frying. When preparing chicken or turkey in the broiler or barbecue, broil with the skin on, but remove it before serving. In fact, do not eat the skin of poultry prepared in any way. If burgers suit your plans, make chicken or veal-burgers; they are far less fatty than beef. You can make a beefburger with a minimum of fat if you choose the meat cut carefully. Consult Chapter 12 for cuts to use for hamburger; definitely avoid commercially packaged ground beef. Lean lamb and lambburger are both good. Do not eat stews, and eliminate fresh and cured pork altogether. If you choose to panfry or panbroil, cook in a Teflon-coated pan, or use a spray-on nonstick coating. Trim all meats well, of course, and add no extra fat in cooking. When you prepare any dish by moist cooking, let the liquid cool, and lift off surface fat; reheat to serve. With a reducing diet, it is important to make every calorie count; skip all high-calorie snacks and drinks that have little nutritive value; watch your intake of refined sugar; avoid delicious sauces and gravies; but balance the nutritious foods you eat.

UNDERWEIGHT

If you would like to gain weight, eat all the meat and poultry dishes you want: lots of roast beef, pot roast and beef stew. You can have mashed potatoes smothered with gravy, all sorts of buttery sauces, soups garnished with matzo balls and marrow dumplings, steaks and chops, pasta with meat sauces, and stews and casseroles served with buttered rice or barley or kasha.

Some underweight people have reached that state by a vicious circle: Remember, inadequate protein can cause a loss of appetite. For such people, try to present meals carefully; let each meal be as attractive as possible. Do not use flat plates, no matter how contemporary and chic they may be, because they let food cool quickly. A plate with a curved rim helps keep food hot a little longer. Do not overload the plate; a small portion attractively presented may stimulate interest, while mounds of anything may just repulse a flickering appetite. Serve something elegant for the picky eater; save hearty country dishes for those people who enjoy all food.

CHOLESTEROL

In writing a book about meats, we must mention the debate about cholesterol, but we do not intend to get into the ring, since we are laymen as far as medical research is concerned. To a layman, it is puzzling, to say the least, to find statements that are in direct opposition on this subject, both points of view supported by extensive research. Most authorities agree that an increase in serum cholesterol is dangerous and can contribute to arterial heart disease. The fight seems to be over the cause of the increase in serum cholesterol. In one corner is the faction that attributes it to diet, in the other, the faction that minimizes the influence of the diet, blaming instead individual metabolic differences, as well as the life style of the society and the individual. And there is a secondary bout going on, concerning diet; some authorities condemn meats, especially fatty meats, organ meats and meat fats, as well as all other saturated fats, including butter and egg yolks. The opposition says that this relationship is not proved.

Cholesterol is essential for all animal life, including that of humans, and all foods derived from animal sources contain some cholesterol. Cholesterol is a fat-soluble crystalline steroid alcohol, $C_{27}H_{45}OH$; it is synthesized in the human body, apparently in regular amounts. In persons with normal digestion, cholesterol eaten in excess of the necessary amount is discarded by the body with other wastes. What happens with persons with metabolic abnormalities is not really known. Family history, personal life style—inadequate exercise, living only in heated rooms, etc.—and weight problems all contribute to the failure of the human system to utilize food ideally. For such people, dietary changes may provide the answer, and medical advice should be sought on the framing of such a diet.

If you were to omit all foods of animal origin from your diet, you would be left with inadequate protein of low quality. If you were to eliminate all fats, you would not be able to digest the fat-soluble vitamins A and D, and there would be some changes in your nerves and skin. But an individual has idiosyncrasies that may indicate special dietary rules. It is always best to have advice for the individual, rather than following any general rules.

If you are following a low-cholesterol diet, we would like to make a few suggestions. There is only one recipe in this book that you must discard—Filet Mignon on Toast with Butterfly Sauce (p. 285)—everything else can be adapted.

Can people on low-cholesterol diets ever eat fried foods? Yes, occasionally, but certainly not regularly. Use polyunsaturated fats—corn, soybean, safflower, sesame—only; do *not* use animal fats or hydrogenated shortenings. Do not use egg yolks to coat fried foods; instead, use beaten egg white or skim milk. Trim all fats from meat or poultry before dipping it into the liquid, then into flour or crumbs. Often a low-cholesterol diet is combined with a reducing diet. If this is your situation, omit fried foods altogether.

We have recommended olive oil throughout this book, but for low-cholesterol and reducing diets, it is inadvisable. Olive oil is monounsaturated, and therefore less harmful than saturated fats, but it is not as good for these diets as the polyunsaturated oils listed above.

Trim meats well, and when buying, select meats with little internal fat. Do not try to make a hamburger fit the diet by cooking out all the fat or blotting it with kitchen paper; it is much better to choose the right meat cut for your hamburger and grind it yourself without additional fats, but with a small amount of an appropriate oil.

Poultry—except duck and goose—is good for such diets, but be sure to omit the skin. Veal is generally considered a good choice for these diets. Organ meats are not acceptable, nor are fatty meats such as bacon and sausage. And pâté is out!

In recipes prepared with eggs, use one of the egg substitutes; there are several on the market. If you like the Pipérade recipe on page 284, omit all the eggs, use corn oil, and double or triple the peppers; you will have a pepper-and-ham dish instead of an egg dish. If your particular diet forbids all cured meats, then substitute veal strips or partly cooked slivers of chicken for the ham.

Skip all outer-larding with fats or bacon; instead, use cabbage or lettuce leaves for added moisture. Use only small amounts of oil, even the polyunsaturated kind, unless your particular diet requires a specified amount of oil per day, and margarine for cooking. Accept the fact that well-marbled meats are only for special occasions, and plan meals using lean cuts of the permitted meats. Meat salads do not need mayonnaise or oil to taste delicious; try using lemon juice or wine mixed with a little of the meat juice; or stick to polyunsaturated oils, or mayonnaise made with them.

Even such a classic as Beef Wellington (p. 378) can be adapted; instead of pâté in the filling, use minced mushrooms, and make the pastry with oil rather than butter or lard. Use a little skim milk instead of egg wash.

Always use skim milk instead of whole, polyunsaturated margarine instead of butter, and, very important, eat lots of vegetables, fruits and whole-grain cereals.

SALT-FREE DIETS

Throughout the book we have suggested seasoning meat, usually when it is removed from the refrigerator to reach room temperature. If you are living on a low-salt or no-salt diet, you must eliminate salt from the seasoning step. There are several kinds of substitute "salt." If you like any one of them, use it, by all means. However, we feel there is no successful substitute. Every substitute has a taste of its own, unlike salt, which has no distinctive taste but helps develop other flavors and stimulate the flow of saliva. We suggest you try cooking without any substitute; the natural taste of the meat may be adequate, but if you do not think so, try using an herb or an herb salt, one made without sodium. Since meat animals eat salt, the meat will contain some anyway. Of course, for low-salt or salt-free diets, you will have to abstain from salt-cured, brined or pickled meat. And do not do any salt-broiling.

ULCERS

The second most common seasoning, crushed black peppercorns, is on the forbidden list for people with delicate stomachs, especially those with ulcers. Some recent research suggests that spices are not harmful to such stomachs at all, but chunks of pepper can be a mechanical irritant, and any dish that is highly spiced has a certain psychological effect. If someone in your family has an ulcer, omit all spices from the recipes, including mustard. Let other members of your family season their own portions.

Plain broiled or roasted meats and poultry are good for people with stomach problems. Avoid all panfried and deep-fried foods. Sauté only occasionally, and then use a mild oil or a mixture of butter and oil. Poached meats, especially if delicately sauced with cream or milk mixtures, are gentle to the ulcer patient; veal *blanquette* is perfect. Avoid vinegar and acid vegetables in sauces. A ripe fresh tomato, with seeds removed, may be acceptable, but canned tomato products are too acid. Onions are forbidden, but they are so valuable in flavoring that you may find this difficult. One possible solution is to cook an onion in some of the liquid used for the dish; discard the onion—a delicate flavor will remain in the dish. A good trick with all spices and even with herbs is to tie them in a cheesecloth bag that can be discarded after cooking; this will provide ample but not excessive flavor, and the little pieces will not be left to irritate the stomach.

Your own nutritious meat and poultry stocks, cooked with little or no salt and pepper, will be of great value in preparing soups, sauces, and aspics. Use these instead of canned broth or stock, which are usually too salty.

Protein foods help neutralize excess stomach acids, so it is important for ulcer sufferers to eat enough meat.

GOUT

Gout was the disease suffered by Little Lord Fauntleroy's grandfather, who sat with his foot raised on a cushion and let out a shout if anyone touched him. It may seem like a disease of fiction, or at least something gone with the nineteenth century, but it is still with us. This metabolic disease ocurs when too much vitamin A is retained in the system. For this problem, you must eliminate all organ meats and any other meats containing large amounts of purine. You must also consume large amounts of green vegetables and fruits, but not spinach, strawberries or rhubarb. This is one of the few cases in which a low-meat diet is usually specified by a physician. You can still eat chicken and lamb, so there are at least several hundred recipes you can try.

Would you believe that protein foods help you sleep? Tryptophan is one of the essential amino acids that cannot be synthesized by man but must be taken in food. This amino acid is converted into serotonin, which is found in the blood serum, the gastric juices and, in small amounts, in the brain, where it helps put us to sleep. The best sources for tryptophan are meats, poultry, fish, cheeses and legumes.

Meats are vital for rebuilding body tissues after illness or surgery. Proteins help those with diseases of the liver and kidneys, even with diabetes. Even if your diet is not for reducing, the meat or poultry in it, because of its staying power, keeps you from feeling hungry and enables you to avoid the temptation to eat forbidden foods that may be harmful.

The next time you eat that roast beef or broiled chicken, be glad. You are doing what you ought to do.

HOLIDAYS
AND OTHER
GREAT
OCCASIONS

Chapter 23

THE ORIGINAL MEANING OF HOLIDAY was "holy day"—a day of feast and celebration, a day of rest from life's ordinary chores. Most cooks still think holidays call for especially good meals, even if they do not represent a feast after a fast. Traditions influence people strongly in the choice of food for these meals, but when one looks at the menus served in one region or another, it appears that traditions are far from unanimous, except for Thanksgiving, when almost everyone chooses turkey for that most American of all holidays.

THANKSGIVING

If possible, order a fresh bird; if your turkey is frozen, let it defrost in its original wrapping in the refrigerator for 1 to 2 days, according to its size. Then remove to room temperature, still wrapped, and let it stand for 8 to 9 hours. Or follow the method used for frozen chickens (p. 65), which we much prefer. Unwrap the frozen bird, put it in a clean sink, and cover with water. A bird of 12 to 14 pounds gross weight will defrost in about 3 hours. This method prevents loss of juices and protects the meat from airborne organisms while it defrosts.

Any turkey you buy, except a Kosher bird, will be oven-ready, with the neck and giblets packed inside. You will need at least 1 pound per person for the holiday meal, but you will surely want some delicious leftovers for the weekend, so choose the size of the bird with this in mind.

You may follow basic directions for roasting, but we will suggest some other ideas as well. The most familiar Thanksgiving bird is the stuffed whole turkey, still on the bone. The stuffing possibilities are many, ranging from a simple bread stuffing flavored with herbs and onion, to something exotic like wild rice mixed with fresh apricots and almonds. Chestnuts, sausage, oysters, mushrooms—any of your favorite ingredients can be added to a bread or grain stuffing. Allow about 10 cups of stuffing for a 10-pound bird, and for larger birds add another cup for each pound of weight. Remember, however, that some stuffing ingredients will cook down in preparation—bread cubes and vegetables for example. Allow for this when you begin.

Another way to stuff the bird is to follow the description on page 80 for Duck with Peaches; thumb open the skin over the breast, putting about half of the stuffing between skin and breast, and using the rest for the cavity. This keeps the breast from drying and adds flavor, but you will have to make extra stuffing to fill both sections. Dried fruits are good in this kind of stuffing.

Roasting Turkey

All sorts of methods have been suggested for getting a moist juicy turkey. An old-fashioned idea was to enclose the turkey in a brown paper bag; steam could escape through it, so the bird was not steamed but moisture was retained in the meat. We do not recommend this, because today chemicals are used in the manufacture of almost all paper bags, and no food is really enhanced by these chemicals; a bad flavor might be the result. Another idea is to drape the bird with several thicknesses of cheesecloth soaked in oil or butter. This is not a bad notion, but we suggest draping the bird with dry cheesecloth and basting the bird through it as drippings are extracted in baking. Birds baked this way show the pattern of the cheesecloth when done, and this can be quite attractive. The newest idea is aluminum foil draped like a tent over the breast and top of the legs of the bird; leave the foil in place for about half of the roasting time, then remove to let the skin brown.

Self-Basting Birds

Such elaborations are necessary for turkey because the bird is so large that it requires lengthy roasting; in addition, the flesh of turkey, especially a frozen one, can be a little dry. To prevent dryness, the so-called "self-basting" bird has been developed. In these birds, butter alone, or solutions of poultry broth or stock or water and edible fats, including flavor enhancers, are injected into the thick muscles of breast and legs of ready-to-cook birds to provide the basting. These additions may constitute no more than 3% of the weight of the raw poultry and must be included as part of the total weight of the bird when sold. Of course, the labels must state exactly what is included.

You can make your own bird self-basting in several ways. First, you could insert flat slivers of butter between skin and meat, just as you insert a stuffing mixture. Second, and this is the best way, roast the bird breast down for half of the time, then turn it upright to let the top brown.

It is always practical to baste the bird during roasting if you think it is becoming a little dry. Use the pan drippings, or brush with plain or flavored oil, or oil mixed with puréed garlic, or with wine—not too dry because a little sugar in the wine will help in browning. Another trick is to remove part of the pan drippings with a large spoon or a bulb baster and thicken them with flour; use a pastry brush to paint this thickened mixture all over the bird toward the end of roasting for extra browning.

Two other ways to cook the bird are in a plastic bag or in a clay oven. There are oven bags specially made for these large birds. Be sure to follow the directions carefully. If the bird is not browned enough to suit you, slit the top of the bag toward the end and fold it back; brush the bird with drippings or a glaze if you like.

It takes the largest size clay oven to hold a small turkey. Prepare it in the same way as for conventional roasting, but place it on a bed of vegetables—onions, celery, carrots—with apple slices if you like; they will add extra flavor. It will take nearly 4 hours to roast a 10-pound bird in one of these because of starting in a cold oven; 375° F. is the temperature to use.

Boneless Turkey Stuffed with Boneless Capon

For a very elegant Thanksgiving when you have many people, ask your butcher to bone a large turkey completely and stuff it with a boneless capon. This is a job for a professional; do not try to do it yourself. The result will be spectacular, with a lot to eat. A turkey weighing about 12 pounds is split; leaving the skin still in place, all the bones are removed; any pieces of meat separated in the process are set aside, and the liver is also set aside. Next a capon weighing 6 to 7 pounds is cut into quarters, and all the skin and bones are removed. The capon meat and the turkey meat that was set aside are layered inside the turkey, mixing light and dark meat. Butter or chicken fat, lightly seasoned, is added to the layers. When all the meat is used, the turkey is sewn up front and back, keeping the shape of the bird. The leg bones are replaced with a stuffing of the livers of both birds; extra livers are used if necessary. The stuffed bird is tied to help retain the shape, but loosely so that the skin is not marred. Roast at 350° F. for about 3¼ hours, placing the turkey breast down for the first half of the time. When the bird is done, let it rest at room temperature for 30 minutes before starting to carve.

If your family is small, you might prefer to serve a smaller bird. A capon is an excellent choice for Thanksgiving, or even a large beautiful roasting chicken or a pair of roasters.

If your family likes lots of stuffing, it can be prepared separately as well as inside the bird.

Thanksgiving is supposed to have been celebrated for the first time at Plymouth, but Virginians claim it was first at Berkeley Plantation. There is little doubt that in either place it was an outgrowth of the Harvest Festival, still celebrated in early fall in English parish churches with artistic arrangements of the beautiful abundance of the earth. The Harvest Festival probably developed from the rituals of earlier faiths giving thanks for the bounty of the harvest. The Thanksgiving meal should include fall vegetables and fruits—no asparagus or strawberries. Oysters were certainly eaten at the first Thanksgivings; during the seventeenth century, they were plentiful in unpolluted waters along the coasts of the American colonies.

Turkey and other large poultry can be served for any holiday—Christmas, New Year, Easter—or special occasion. At different seasons you will naturally accompany it with other dishes. Roast turkey can be served hot or cold at buffet parties, and smoked turkey is another possibility for any holiday party.

It used to be that Americans ate turkey after Thanksgiving until it was reduced to a carcass, and then it became soup. Today you can buy a bird of a size that suits your needs, and store leftovers in a freezer, to be served at a later date.

CHRISTMAS

Christmas is celebrated so differently in different places that it is hard to think of a meat or poultry that has not served for the great feast. The *pièce de résistance* can be turkey, roast beef, ham or, the delight of Bob Cratchit's dinner, a Christmas goose.

Goose

If your goose is frozen, you may defrost it in two ways. Take it out of the freezer, and leave in the refrigerator overnight; or unwrap it, and defrost it in water—4 to 5 hours should be enough. Take it out of the water, and pat it dry. If the goose is fresh, wash and pat dry. At this point you should be about 24 hours away from serving. Prick the sides of the bird, and drop it into a large container of boiling water; boil for 30 minutes. Drain and pat dry. When the bird is cool enough to handle, season it, and refrigerate it overnight. Choose a fresh fruit; imported apricots are in the market in December and January and they are particularly good. Oranges, grapefruits and pineapples are other possible choices. Use both pulp and juice; blend the fruit in an electric blender. Rub the purée, by itself or mixed with spices, all over the whole goose. Make a stuffing of bread cubes or rice mixed with more of the same fruit cut into slivers or cubes. Roast the goose, turning it to let more fat drain from all sides. You can remove all these drippings with a bulb baster as the roasting proceeds, so they do not burn and spoil your gravy. Chill the drippings so you can remove the fat (for gravy making see p. 314). When you are ready to serve, you can flame the bird at table with a brandy of matching fruit flavor.

Here is another way to prepare a goose, which can be very useful to the cook with small quarters and small pots. Have your butcher machine-cut the goose into small sections. Do not boil the pieces. Make a blended fruit purée, just as for the whole goose, spread it on the pieces and arrange them, bone side down, in a single layer in a baking pan. Cover with foil, and bake until half done, then turn the pieces over with a spatula, cover again, and bake. Toward the end, remove the cover, turn the pieces skin side up again, and let the pieces brown. Pour off the fat, then flame the pieces in the baking pan before transferring them to a serving platter.

Another idea for those with a small kitchen is to cut the goose into quarters and roast them; these smaller portions are a lot easier to handle.

Capon

Capons, which are as flavorful as ordinary chickens but larger, look beautiful on a Christmas table. If you prefer these to turkey or goose, you could prepare two of them for a large gathering. A capon will make 6 to 8 servings. Do not prick the sides of a capon unless it is unusually fatty.

There is a special technique of pricking geese, ducks and other fatty birds. First, do not use a knife, because it would pierce the flesh and release juices as well as fat. For a goose, use a 2-tined fork, and try to pierce through the skin into the layer of fat underneath. For ducks or very fatty capons, use a sewing needle; a fork would make too large a hole. Pricking helps to crisp the skin as it releases fat.

Another traditional Christmas dinner is two large roasting chickens or pheasants.

ROAST ORANGE CAPON

Wash a capon, 6 to 7 pounds, and pat dry. Rub a heavy coating of orange marmalade inside the bird and a light coating over the outside. Use a swivel peeler to take off the rind from 2 oranges. Cut the rind into slivers and blanch them in water for 2 minutes. Drain, then place the slivers in the bottom of your roasting pan. Peel off the white membrane, then with a very sharp knife slice the orange into wafer-thin slices. Arrange some of the slices, as many as will fit, over the breast and legs of the bird; put the rest in the pan with the slivers of rind. Place the capon in the pan and roast in a 325° F. oven for 2½ to 2¾ hours, about 25 minutes per pound, until golden brown and done to taste. Use the juices in the pan to baste the bird as it cooks. Let the capon rest in the oven for 10 minutes, then transfer to a flameproof platter. At serving time heat 2 tablespoons of good-quality orange liqueur, ignite it, and pour it flaming over the bird.

Use this recipe for chicken (pullets) and tender pheasants too. Cook at the same oven temperature, and adjust the timing according to the weight of the bird.

Other good meats for Christmas dinner are roast prime ribs of beef, roast boneless sirloin, roast suckling pig (the present-day version of the medieval boar's head) and crown of lamb, pork or veal.

You might find it easier to serve whole small birds; squabs if you buy them, quails if you have had the good luck to bag them. One squab per serving is ample, but you will need 2 quails to make an adequate serving. Roast simply, brushing with a glaze of some sort to give them a shiny finish. Serve the little birds with wild rice or hominy and garnish with mushrooms or fruits.

NEW YEAR'S DAY

If you have celebrated New Year's Eve with partying, the first day of the year may be best served by ham and eggs. Another practical idea is to have a large piece of meat already cooked that can be served cold or at room temperature, with members of the family serving themselves at their own convenience. Ham is good for this, either on the bone or boneless, and its rosy color is always attractive. Other rolled boneless meats and poultry can also be prepared for such informal service.

If you are at home on New Year's Day and your friends observe the delightful old-fashioned custom of making New Year's calls, you can prepare a proper buffet (see Chapter 21). For an "at home" that extends over many hours, serve a baked Virginia ham with beaten biscuits, a whole smoked turkey with thin slices of whole-wheat bread, bowls of cherry tomatoes and pitted olives, wedges of fresh pineapple, eggnog or punch if your guests like it, or standard drinks, and lots of good coffee. Or assemble other foods that your guests enjoy. Avoid anything that must be kept hot, because it will dry out over a long time. Hot dishes are fine for the reception to which people come all at once; for this you can serve anything, including a large meat pie or a good stew, but keep the party simple and relaxed for this day.

If your family observes the day with a family dinner, serve anything you would for Christmas but not the same menu you did use then. An unusual dish is roast leg of veal, roast outer-larded shoulder of veal, or stuffed veal breast or shoulder. (Do not add any larding to the interior of the shoulder or breast.) Season the veal, then tie on the outer-larding. In place of fat, you could tie on a sheet of aluminum foil or use the "cabbage-larding" idea, only with this, use large lettuce leaves. Just moisten the lettuce to prevent drying of the exterior of the meat. Discard the lettuce before serving. When you are cooking a large piece of veal, just brushing the exterior with oil is not adequate; the oil becomes hot and runs off. Here is one way to prepare a stuffed shoulder.

STUFFED BONELESS SHOULDER OF VEAL   10 servings

1 boneless shoulder of veal, 5 to 7 pounds	grated rind of 1 lemon
2 ounces blue cheese	¼ teaspoon lemon juice
8 ounces mild Cheddar cheese, grated	3 slices of Swiss cheese
2 ounces unseasoned dry bread crumbs	2 hard-cooked eggs, halved lengthwise
2 pinches of salt	1 teaspoon lemon marmalade
½ pound unsalted butter, melted	1 tablespoon liqueur (your choice)
2 teaspoons chopped fresh parsley	1 cup chicken stock
	flour

Have butcher cut the veal open in the center and flatten it well. The meat should measure about 15 by 9 inches and ½ to ¾ inch thick. Mix together blue cheese, Cheddar, bread crumbs, salt, half of the melted butter, the parsley, lemon rind and juice. Arrange the flattened veal on the countertop, and spread the stuffing over the surface. Space the slices of Swiss cheese on top. Start rolling from one of the narrow ends.

Hint: When rolling stuffed meats, always roll with your hands at the ends of the meat and never roll too tightly; remember that the filling will expand in cooking.

When you reach the middle of the meat, place the halved eggs, cut sides down, on the layer of stuffing; finish rolling to the end, then tie the roll with butchers' twine. Tie one string in the center, one on each side of that about 3 inches from the center, and another on each side of those. Add another string the long way around the roll, and then finish with two more strings the short way around, about 2 inches from the others. Tie the strings loosely so the roll does not lose its shape.

Mix remaining melted butter, the marmalade and liqueur, and rub over the outside of the roll. Preheat oven to 350° F. Arrange the veal on a rack in a baking pan, and cover; use foil if your pan has no cover. Bake for 1 hour, then remove cover and turn the veal over. Reduce oven heat to 300° F. and continue baking the veal for 1¼ hours longer. Turn off heat and leave veal in the oven for 15 minutes. Remove from the oven and cut off and discard strings. Transfer veal to a serving platter and keep warm while making pan gravy.

Pour chicken stock into the baking pan and slowly bring to a boil on top of the stove, stirring all the while with a wooden spoon to deglaze the pan. Thicken with flour (see p. 314), and continue to cook until the gravy is thickened. Add more seasoning if needed, and strain the gravy into a sauceboat to serve separately.

Cut the veal into slices ½ to ¾ inch thick.

ST. VALENTINE'S DAY

St. Valentine has been declared mythical, but all around the world people still observe February 14 as a day for sweethearts. There are several delightful dishes that can be made to suggest the traditional symbol of the day. Any good steak trimmed to a heart shape can be used; the trimmed-off portions can be put aside for kebabs or stew. A perfect choice is a butterfly shell steak; broil the steaks— they will keep their heart shape. Chops can be butterflied too, but a butterflied chop has only one good side, whereas the shell butterfly, adequate for 2 servings, will open out flat and look fine on both sides. Boneless chicken breasts and *suprêmes* seem very suitable for Valentine lunches or dinners. The boneless breasts and slices of turkey breast can be trimmed to heart shape. Or you can serve them in their usual shapes and accent the Valentine aspect with the accompaniments—heart-shaped *croûtes* under the chicken, slices of jellied cranberry sauce or anything pink or rosy. Hot or cold jellied meats and poultry or mousses can be prepared in heart-shaped molds.

Butterflied shell steak, two steaks from the short loin, almost split to make a heart-shaped piece of meat perfect for St. Valentine's Day

CHINESE NEW YEAR

For Chinese New Year serve roast squabs with preserved kumquats, or a roast suckling with Sweet and Pungent Sauce (p. 266). Or plan a meal more like a traditional Chinese banquet made of many dishes. Try lion's head (pork balls), chicken with almonds, beef with snow peas, pork with shrimps and mushrooms—there are hundreds of delicious dishes and they are not difficult to cook, although they do take time to prepare. Duck is a great favorite in China; it can be roasted, braised, pot-roasted, poached and even broiled, if you follow the suggestions on page 100. Fruits, gingerroot, choyu (soy) sauce, sherry, other Chinese sauces—these are all used in various duck recipes. The following recipe can be used as a pattern for glazed duck. Alter the seasonings in the first step for a subtle difference in the flavor, and change the glaze if you prefer another fruit.

GLAZED ROAST DUCK   4 servings

2 oranges	1 duck, about 5 pounds
1 bay leaf	½ cup apricot jam
6 tablespoons honey	½ cup apricot brandy
10 whole cloves	

With a swivel peeler, remove the rind from the oranges. Set aside three quarters of the pieces of rind for another use, and drop the remainder into a pot large enough to hold the duck. Cut off the white inner peel of the oranges; cut the fruit into chunks, and add to the pot along with bay leaf and honey. Chop the cloves, or mash them in a mortar, and add them to the pot. Fill the pot with water and boil for 15 minutes. Meanwhile, prick the sides of the duck and tie the legs together. After the 15 minutes, drop the bird into the pot, and continue to boil for 45 minutes. You can set the duck on a rack in the pot if you like; this will make it easier to lift it out. Remove the duck; let it drain and cool.

Preheat oven to 350° F. Heat the jam to very hot, and strain to remove any large pieces of fruit. With a pastry brush, coat the duck on all sides with jam. Place it, breast side down, on a rack in the roasting pan, and roast for 45 minutes. Turn breast up, and roast for 45 minutes longer. Turn off the heat, and let the duck rest in the oven for 10 minutes. Heat the brandy, pour over the bird, and ignite. You can serve it flaming if you like. Prepare more birds for more guests.

ST. PATRICK'S DAY

The New York tradition for St. Patrick's Day calls for corned beef and cabbage. Serve it if you like—there are several good ideas for corned beef in other chapters—but do not think it is typically Irish. Far more likely in Ireland would be a delicious thick steak served with its own juices and a sprinkling of chives and accompanied with some good potatoes. Another meal often served is half of a roast small chicken resting on a large slice of Irish bacon, almost as big as the chicken. You cannot get bacon like that in the United States, but you can substitute a slice of rosy ham. Serve some green vegetables, blanched to set the color, and boiled or mashed potatoes, and garnish everything with shamrocks made of watercress leaves. *Slainte!*

EASTER

Easter is a feast day that carries with it the traditions of spring celebration of many ancient religions as well as the special significance for Christianity. Everything in this holiday suggests spring, rebirth, renewal, and the food of the day should be beautiful to look at as well as good to eat. The traditional meat in the Mediterranean is lamb; in France it is ham; poultry is served often in the United States.

Glazed Ham

When baking a conventional ham, place it on a rack in the roasting pan. Without the rack, the bottom portion of the meat tends to dry, overcook, and become very hard; the rack will give more even heating. Also, all glazes for ham contain sugar in some form; this tends to burn on the bottom of the meat when there is no rack. If your idea is to bake your ham for a long time (over 2 hours), don't put the glaze on until partway through the cooking because it will burn. The average time for baking a precooked ham is 1½ hours in a 350° F. oven, and a half ham needs almost as long. Pour a glass of sweet wine into the bottom of your roasting pan; this helps to keep the drippings from burning, and the wine breaks down the fatty portion of the drippings. When you are making the glaze, make enough for painting on the ham and an additional amount to use as basting during cooking. At the end, remove the drippings, skim off as much fat as possible, and thicken the drippings with flour for an opaque sauce, with cornstarch for a translucent sauce. Serve the sauce over the ham itself—it will cling because it is pasty rather than liquid—or over any accompanying potato or other starch. Ham tastes great with oranges, pineapple, peaches, apples and crab apples, melon balls, sour cherries.

■

If you are serving lamb, a leg is a good choice or, to emphasize the festive character of the day, a stuffed crown of lamb. Basic information about the crowns is in Chapter 13. Try this stuffing:

HERB-FLAVORED LAMB STUFFING FOR CROWN OF LAMB

2 onions, chopped	¼ teaspoon cracked peppercorns
¼ pound butter (1 stick)	1 cup fine dry bread crumbs
¼ cup chopped parsley	1 egg, beaten
¼ teaspoon dried rosemary	1 pound lean lamb, ground
pinch of ground sage	¼ pound chicken breast, chopped
1 teaspoon salt	¼ cup milk

Sauté onions in butter until transparent. Add herbs, salt and pepper, and mix well. Then add crumbs and beaten egg, and mix well. Combine lamb, chicken and milk, and stir well into the rest of the stuffing. Cook over low heat for 15 minutes. Cool. Use to stuff crown of lamb.

Note: The stuffing freezes well alone.

Roast the stuffed crown in a preheated 350° F. oven for 1 hour and 15 minutes. Top the rib bones with frills or pickled crab apples.

Any good poultry dish can serve for an Easter dinner. Serve the first spring peas or, if Easter is early, Brussels sprouts, still at their best in March, with chestnuts or silverskin onions.

Dinner is not the only meal on holidays. Easter has a hunt for what the Easter bunny left, and a good meal is needed either before or after. Here are two ideas that suggest Easter eggs.

Easter Eggs

Scotch eggs: Make a mixture of chopped ham with bread crumbs, milk and eggs, and flavor to taste with dry mustard, salt and white pepper. Hard-cook eggs, shell them, and roll each one in some of the ham mixture. Deep-fry the eggs until crisp and lightly browned. Serve a whole egg, or halve them lengthwise.

Easter croquettes: Make a thick sauce with butter, flour and chicken stock. Stir in a mixture of minced chicken and chopped hard-cooked eggs to make the croquette batter. Season to taste, and chill. Use about 3 tablespoons of the batter for each croquette. Shape into an egg and put a treasure in the center of each—a mushroom, an oyster, a shrimp, 2 or 3 green peas and a pearl onion. Enclose the stuffing completely and deep-fry until golden brown. (See p. 316 for more on croquettes.)

Either of these Easter eggs can serve as a first course at a dinner or luncheon. Another idea is a jellied meat or poultry molded in egg-shaped containers. Round-sectioned ice-cube trays do not make egg shapes, but they are close; you can use these as jelly molds for garnishes too.

Sandwiches for children on all these special days can be cut to special designs: pumpkins, Christmas trees, Easter eggs and so on. But adults too like festive touches, something special for a special day.

MOTHER'S DAY

Roast beef is a good choice for Mother's Day. It is simple to cook, so even inexperienced male cooks can do it and enjoy carving it at the table afterward.

INDEPENDENCE DAY

The great American day July 4 is an occasion for an outdoor barbecue. Cook plain or fancy steaks, chops or hamburgers; or grill poultry or ham steak. Have lots of good salads, bread and watermelon.

SPECIAL OCCASIONS

Holidays are not the only great occasions when you enjoy entertaining. There are also birthdays and other family anniversaries, celebrations of graduations or promotions, engagement parties, wedding receptions, and just parties to spend time with friends. You can adapt any of the holiday suggestions for parties of other kinds, but service of individual portions is also good for dinner parties. Small birds—squabs, quails, Rock Cornish game hens—are always good choices. So are *filets mignons* or *tournedos*, which look extremely elegant and are easy to serve and eat, because they are boneless and tender.

Paillard

A less-common dish is the *paillard*, usually beef, but one can prepare a *paillard* of veal or pork also. For beef, use the first cut of the shell, or Delmonico cut. Have it cut ½ inch thick, with all bone and fat removed. Flatten the steak to ⅛ inch thick. It is flattened so it can be sautéed quickly, in moments. Serve with sauces, or stuff and roll. For veal *paillard*, use the round from the leg; for pork use the center of the rib loin.

Veal scallops can be prepared in countless ways for dinner parties, with many pretty garnishes. *Grenadins* of veal, thicker slices from the same cuts, are usually braised because the added moisture keeps them succulent.

Veal with Bacon

Another good party dish is the stuffed veal shoulder (p. 366). Here is another way to roast veal for a party. Use the shoulder or the sirloin of veal, 4 to 6 pounds, and thick-sliced slab bacon. Season the veal with a mixture of chopped peppercorns, garlic, thyme and salt. Let the meat come to room temperature, then tie bacon around it, covering the outside completely. In a large heavy skillet heat oil until very

371

Paillard of beef, first cut from the shell, with all fat and bone removed

Paillard flattened, to be sautéed briefly for elegant occasions

hot, then brown the roast very well on all sides. Transfer to a rack in a roasting pan and roast in a preheated 325° F. oven for 1¾ to 2 hours, the longer time for the heavier piece.

Filet of Beef

A whole beef filet is another good dish for entertaining. If you know when your guests will arrive so you can plan exactly, preheat the oven to 450° F. and roast the filet for 35 to 40 minutes. If you expect a delay, use a 350° F. oven, and roast the meat for 45 to 50 minutes. In any case, turn off the oven, and let the meat rest in it for 5 minutes. Then transfer to carving board or platter, and slice.

If you cut a Chateaubriand from the center of the filet, broil it, let it rest, then slice at the table.

How would you like to prepare for several dozen people a quail stuffed with an ortolan, the ortolan stuffed with a truffle, the truffle stuffed with a nugget of *pâté de foie gras?* This dish is described in *The Edwardians,* by V. Sackville-West; it was served at Chevron, an English country house modeled on Knole, the house where she grew up. We will not recommend it, because you could not find an ortolan in the United States, and the other ingredients are scarce. Nevertheless, many stuffed dishes are good choices for dinner parties: stuffed pork or veal chops; stuffed beef, pork, veal or poultry scallops; stuffed boned loin of pork.

Fresh Ham

Fresh ham, the leg of fresh pork, is another possibility. Remove the skin and score the fat. Roast at 325° F. for up to 5 hours, half of the time upside down in the pan. If you use a meat thermometer, you can be more confident in cooking this cut; do not overcook it. Toward the end of the cooking, you can glaze the top of the leg. Tart fruits are a good taste contrast with pork; try cranberries or kumquats; melons, if the season is right, are surprisingly good.

The capon recipe on page 365 used for pheasants or pullets is a fine dish for a company dinner. Beef Wellington or other meats baked in pastry cases are natural choices for dinner parties. For less formal occasions, a meat loaf may be appropriate.

Venison

Venison from a tender animal can provide an excellent roast. The round, like the round of veal, is a good choice. The traditional "haunch of venison" is one leg with half of the saddle attached. The saddle is good too. Treat them all like similar cuts of veal, remembering to compensate for the lack of fat. If you are in doubt about the tenderness, marinate first. Or braise the meat instead of roasting. *Noisettes*, little rounds from the eye of the chops or slices from the filet of venison, are as elegant as *tournedos*; cook them like *tournedos*. All venison dishes are good accompanied with chestnuts and a red fruit garnish—lingonberries, red currants, sour cherries, red crab apples. Winter vegetables—turnips, squash, celery knobs, lentils, mashed or puréed—are great with venison dishes.

Carving at the table can be part of the pleasure of a dinner party. Be sure your knives are sharp, and arrange for enough space to work in.

When you are thinking of presents for holidays, don't forget food. A beautiful capon, a box of butterflied shell steaks or a whole beef filet could be the best present you give or receive. Smoked meats are good gifts too, especially ham or turkey.

THANKSGIVING DINNER

Baked oysters casino
Roast turkey
Rice stuffing with dried fruits
Puréed butternut squash
Creamed spinach with pearl onions
Sparkling Burgundy
Mince tarts

CHRISTMAS DINNER

Goose liver pâté on toast
Roast goose
Braised chestnuts with prunes
Steamed Savoy cabbage
Carrots with scallions
Red Bordeaux
Flaming plum pudding

EASTER DINNER

Easter egg croquettes stuffed with mushrooms
Roast glazed ham
Duchess potatoes
Fresh green peas with chives
Rosé
Watercress salad with oranges
Madeira cake

INDEPENDENCE DAY

Cold salmon mayonnaise
Charcoal-grilled steaks
Potatoes wrapped in foil, roasted in coals
Fresh green beans
California red wine
Spinach and mushroom salad
Watermelon

SPRING DINNER PARTY

Broiled shad roe on toast with buttered fiddleheads
Roast Rock Cornish game hens glazed with lime marmalade
Rice
Steamed asparagus
White Burgundy
Meringues glacés

SUMMER DINNER PARTY

Jellied chicken consommé
Veal scallops with white wine
Green noodles
Baked whole tomatoes with herbs
Moselle
Strawberries with ice-cream sauce

FALL DINNER PARTY

Melon with prosciutto
Stuffed Boneless Shoulder of Veal (see p. 366)
Browned potato balls
Steamed diced celery and green peppers
Orvieto
Romaine lettuce with cherry tomatoes
Baked apple dumpling

WINTER DINNER PARTY

Chicken soufflé baked in squash halves
Roast fresh ham
Whole cranberry sauce
Noodles with hazelnuts
Steamed broccoli
White Burgundy
Lemon tarts

PREPARING DINNER PARTIES IN ADVANCE

Chapter 24

When you entertain, there are always many things to do at the last minute. The picture of the cool, calm gracious hostess greeting guests in her party clothes, with everything under control in the kitchen, will probably give many a housewife a great big laugh. Often the true picture shows a hot-faced tired slavey, who may serve a perfect dinner but will probably miss those happy moments when everyone arrives. Even if your house is well staffed, there is a lot to do at the end of the preparation, and if you are doing your own cooking, whether his or hers or theirs, you will be busy.

If your main course is a last-minute only, try to plan for the other dishes to be ready, at least partly, in advance. Some of the most festive meat dishes cannot be prepared ahead. Individual steaks, slices of the filet (*filet mignon, tournedos*), lamb chops, calf's liver, London broil made of flank steak or the first cut of the round, rack of lamb—all these are last-minute dishes only. They must be served as soon as ready or they will bleed and lose taste. Actually, all of these cook in a relatively short time so they are good dishes for any occasion. An 8-chop rack of lamb, for instance, well trimmed, roasted in a preheated 350 to 400° F. oven will be done in 25 minutes. That is a perfect company dish and very easy to carve and serve.

Any meat or poultry that is cooked in liquid, which liquid is often used as a base for sauce or gravy, is a possible choice for a dinner where you want to avoid last-minute efforts. You can time the cooking to fit your schedule, but even if delayed the meat will keep warm in the liquid, with the heat turned off or set at the lowest point on your stove or over an asbestos pad. The liquid keeps it from drying out. You can adjust the cooking time too by reducing the speed of cooking.

BEEF

Beef Brisket

Here is an example. Cook a fresh brisket of beef—braise or pot-roast it—until three-quarters done. Lift out the meat, leaving the cooking liquid in the pot. Cut the meat across the grain into slices ⅛ to ¼ inch thick. The slices won't fall apart because they aren't fully cooked. Return the slices to the liquid. When the dinner hour approaches, continue the cooking until the beef is done.

Many stews can be used for company occasions (see Chapter 21), and these can be prepared ahead, some even a day ahead, to be reheated. They often taste better for the extra time because all the flavors are so well blended.

Beef Wellington

Beef Wellington has been overdone in recent years, and not always well done, but it is still a spectacular-looking dish and can be delicious when everything is just right. The meat used is the filet, either whole or half. It is cooked very quickly to rare, then covered with a mixture of *foie gras* (the genuine article) and truffles, the whole then rolled in pastry (*pâte brisée* with egg) and baked. Recipes for this can be found in many cookbooks, but we are going to tell you how to prepare this in advance.

Trim the meat completely; skin it, and remove all the fat. Many recipes direct the cook to fold the thin ends over; we think it is a better idea to cut off these ends, or just one if you are cooking half of the filet. Use the cut-off pieces for individual steaks or for a very small London broil. Also cut off the side flap of the filet. Remove the meat from the refrigerator early on the day you plan to use it, or up to 2 hours before cooking time. Rub it with oil and season with salt and pepper. While the meat comes to room temperature preheat the oven to 400° F. Roast a 4-pound filet for 15 minutes, to rare. If your filet is heavier, add another 5 minutes. (When the dish is finished, the meat will be medium-rare, since it cooks further while the pastry is baking.) Remove the meat from the oven and let it rest at room temperature until cool. If you have only a few hours to wait, cover loosely with foil and leave in the coolest place in your kitchen, but not in the refrigerator. If you have all day to wait, wrap the cooled meat in foil and refrigerate. Take it out of the refrigerator again 2 hours before you plan to continue.

Meanwhile, make the pastry, roll in plastic wrap, and refrigerate. Make the filling: Skin and bone 1 whole chicken breast (about 1 pound before boning), and grind fine. Add 1 tablespoon oil, and mix well. Sauté in additional oil for 10 to 12 minutes, until the chicken has lost its pink color; pat the chicken dry—it should not be oily. Season the chicken, and mix with an equal amount of *pâté de foie gras*. Refrigerate until 1½ hours before using.

About 50 minutes before serving, spread the filling all over the meat in an even layer. If you have truffles, you can add them, as well as cooked mushrooms. Roll out the chilled pastry into a sheet large enough to cover the meat and wrap it around. Seal the long seam and the ends with egg wash and roll the seam onto the bottom. Preheat the oven to 350° F. Do not start this second cooking in a very hot oven, because it would be too much of a shock to the cool meat; let the meat warm slowly. Brush the roll with more of the egg wash, sprinkle all over with poppy seeds, and put in the heated oven. After 5 minutes raise the heat to 375° F. Bake for a total of 30 to 40 minutes, until the pastry is golden. Let it rest in the oven for 5 minutes before removing to a serving platter.

Beef filet trimmed for a Wellington; the smaller ends have been removed for other uses.

Steak

Steaks to be done over charcoal can stand a small amount of precooking, but it can be done only with thick steaks. Sear them over coals for 3 minutes on each side. Leave the steak at room temperature until you are ready to finish. Complete the cooking over coals for a few minutes on each side.

Blade Roast

Here is another example for the barbecue. Use a blade steak or roast, one of the first three cuts from the blade portion of the chuck; have it cut 3 inches thick. Season and bring to room temperature. Stand up the roast on a rack or on the spine bone and roast in a 300° F. oven, with no cover and no added moisture, for 1 hour. Store at room temperature for up to 4 hours; for longer than that refrigerate. When your guests arrive, finish cooking over the prepared barbecue for 15 minutes on each side, turning the meat every 5 minutes. The same procedure and timing will work with a cut of the shell 3 to 4 inches thick. You can do the same thing with other thick pieces of meat. In fact, it is a good idea even if you are not preparing ahead because the slow oven heat is just enough to keep the barbecued meat from being raw inside.

London Broil

A piece of the shell or top round at least 3 inches thick for a superior London broil can also be precooked for indoor broiling. This does not contradict what we said on page 377, because these pieces are so much thicker. This can be done up to 4 hours before you plan to serve it; refrigerate if the time is longer but be sure to bring to room temperature again before proceeding. Put the beef, uncovered, into a preheated 450° F. oven for 20 minutes. Remove the meat from the oven and let it rest, *not* in the refrigerator, but at room temperature. Cover loosely with foil after the meat is cooled. Just before serving, broil on each side for 10 to 12 minutes.

The meat for beef Stroganoff, ¼-inch-thick slices from the filet or boneless sirloin, cannot be cooked ahead of time, but the sauce can be prepared in advance. At the last minute, sauté the beef in seasoned oil until delicately brown—this takes only minutes—and pour the sauce over it.

Beef fondue and other meats cooked at the table require last-minute processing, but the sauces or condiments used with them can be prepared in advance, and can even be divided among individual sauce bowls; they will keep well if covered tightly with foil or plastic wrap.

Rouladen, made of beef, veal, pork or chicken, can be prepared up to the point where the sauce is puréed. Keep the meat and sauce separate. Just before serving, heat the sauce, with the *Rouladen* in it. Here is an example.

ROULADEN   6 to 8 servings

12 **thin slices of top round steak**	4 **beef bouillon cubes**
12 **paper-thin slices of dill pickle**	1 **bay leaf**
12 **paper-thin slices of onion**	1 **onion, minced**
flour	1 **green pepper, slivered**
15 **slices of bacon**	2 **carrots, scraped and sliced**
1 **cup boiling water**	½ **cup commercial sour cream**

Place the pieces of steak between 2 sheets of wax paper, and flatten to rectangles about 4 by 8 inches and ⅛ inch thick. Divide the slices of pickle and onion among the steak slices. Roll them, and tie with a string at each end. Roll them in flour.

Fry the bacon in a large skillet until crisp. Lift the bacon slices to absorbent kitchen paper, and set aside. Discard all but 4 tablespoons of fat from the skillet. Brown the *Rouladen* on all sides in the skillet, then transfer them to a plate. Wipe the skillet with absorbent paper, then return the *Rouladen* to the pan, and add the boiling water, bouillon cubes, bay leaf, onion, green pepper and carrots. Place the cooked bacon slices over the meat rolls. Cover the skillet, and cook over *very low heat* for 1½ hours. If your burner cannot be adjusted low enough, put the skillet on an asbestos pad. Turn the rolls over twice during cooking. When the *Rouladen* are done, transfer them and the bacon slices to a plate. Discard the bay leaf, and purée everything else from the skillet in either a blender or food mill.

If you are preparing this in advance, cover the plate of meat loosely with foil, and place a sheet of plastic wrap directly on the surface of the puréed sauce. Let both rest in a cool place if you are planning to continue in 2 hours or less. If you must wait longer, refrigerate meat and sauce as soon as they are cool.

About 30 minutes before serving, return the purée to the pan, and add the sour cream. Heat slowly for 5 minutes, stirring to mix in the sour cream. Return the *Rouladen* and bacon to the sauce, and simmer them for 15 minutes. Serve *Rouladen* with the sauce and noodles.

VEAL

Veal presents the same problems for precooking as it does for any other kind of cooking. This very tender, dry meat needs great care to be successful after two cookings. A conventional veal roast made of leg or shoulder is too dry, with too little body liquid, for precooking.

Rack of Veal

On the other hand, a rack of veal can be prepared ahead, and it is an excellent choice for a party. Season the meat very lightly and let it reach room temperature. Roast the rack until three-quarters done (325° F., about 2 hours for a 5-pound rack). Remove the meat from the oven and let it rest at room temperature. When you are ready to continue, add the rest of the seasoning to the meat, then rub it all over with a fruit-flavored brandy and ignite. This flaming refreshes the meat and prevents any stale taste. Return the meat to a preheated 350° F. oven and finish cooking. This works because all those bones keep the meat from drying out.

Veal Scallops

Surprisingly, the thinnest little slivers that you might expect to be only last-minute dishes can be prepared ahead in a few ways. Veal scallops ¼ inch thick or thicker can be breaded and deep-fried until three-quarters done, 5 minutes maximum in fat heated to 375° F. Lift the scallops out of the fat, let them drain, pat gently with absorbent paper towels, and transfer them to a baking sheet. When it is almost time to serve, slide the baking sheet into a preheated oven and bake for 10 minutes.

Another possibility is veal scallops parmigiana. Do the same precooking as for plain breaded scallops. Sprinkle grated Parmesan cheese on top of the cooled scallops just before finishing them. When the cheese is melted, the scallops will be done. Serve them plain or with your own tomato sauce.

Actually, veal scallops cook so quickly that they can be done easily at the last minute, unless you are cooking a great number of them.

LAMB

Shoulder of Lamb

Since lamb is so young and tender, there are very few cuts that can be cooked ahead of time. The chief exception is the shoulder, which has more fatty grain and can stand double cooking without drying out. The shoulder usually weighs 3 to 4 pounds. Bone and stuff it; you can use an herb and bread-crumb mixture, rice with dried fruits or nuts, or whatever you prefer. Roast the meat at 300° F. for 35 to 40 minutes altogether. Let it rest at room temperature, loosely covered with a sheet of foil, for up to 4 hours before serving time. Then finish roasting at 350° F. until done to taste, approximately 1 hour.

Of course, the shoulder can also be braised, and this moist-cooking method eliminates the need for most last-minute preparations.

Another trick with a large partly cooked piece of lamb is to spread it with mint jelly and arrange thin slices of orange with rind removed on top; then finish cooking. You can do this with the shoulder of lamb if the stuffing is harmonious with mint and orange. This dish is both attractive and delicious.

Crown of Lamb

A crown of lamb made from the double rack, spectacular-looking for a special occasion, is nevertheless quick to cook and easy to carve. What needs advance preparation is the stuffing. Cook the stuffing by whatever method serves best— sautéing or baking usually—until three-quarters done. Cook the unstuffed crown in a preheated 500° F. oven for 5 minutes. Keep both stuffing and crown at room temperature. Later on, stuff the crown, season the meat on the outside, and finish cooking in a preheated 400° F. oven for 20 to 25 minutes.

PORK

Pork Roast

A pork roast can be precooked too. Cook it unseasoned, or with only very bland seasoning, but be sure to rub the outside with oil. Roast in a 325° F. oven until three-quarters done. Take it out of the oven immediately, and let it rest at room temperature until you are ready to continue. Season before the second cooking. If the exterior of the meat or the bones are dry, add the seasonings to more olive oil, and rub the mixture over the exterior. Score the fat. Finish roasting at 375° F.

Of course, fresh pork can be glazed like a ham if you prefer. Here is one version of a glaze for fresh pork. Pulverize 10 whole cloves, and mix with 1 to 3 teaspoons dry mustard, according to taste. Add 2 tablespoons orange-juice concentrate and 1 tablespoon honey. Spread over the top of the pork before the last part of the cooking.

Tongue and Ham

Tongue and ham can be fully cooked in advance. Slice them, and, just before serving, reheat them in fruit sauces. Cumberland sauce, made with currant jelly and citrus juices, is delicious with either meat, as are raisin and plum sauce. You can sharpen any of these sauces by adding a little mustard or horseradish or, even better, some minced chutney.

POULTRY

Poultry must be treated specially for precooking. Rub a large roasting chicken, 6 to 7 pounds, inside and out with fruit juice—apricot, orange or pineapple. Roast the bird in the usual way for about 1¼ hours, until about three-quarters done. Remove from the oven immediately, and let it rest uncovered at room temperature until ready to proceed. You may place a sheet of foil loosely over the top, but the bird must not be allowed to steam. When you are ready to continue, rub the bird again, but this time with jam or jelly of the same flavor used at the beginning. Finish roasting the bird, let it rest in the usual way, then pour over it fruit-flavored brandy or other liqueur similar to the fruit you have used. Ignite the brandy, and serve the bird flaming if you like. The flavors of the juice or jam and the liqueur will not be noticeable, but the bird will keep its fresh taste in spite of the double cooking. This method can be used for all kinds of poultry and game birds.

Large birds—capons, turkey, duck, goose—can also be prepared with pieces of fruit. Open the skin over the breast, or have your butcher do it, or loosen the skin with the thumbs, as described on page 79. Cover the breast with very thin slices of fresh apricots or oranges; leave the skin on the apricots, but peel the citrus fruits. The skin of the apricots adds flavor, but the citrus peels may be too acid for some people; there is also considerable variation in the taste of the peel from one piece of citrus fruit to another. If you have opened the skin, fold it back over the fruits, and skewer the edges together. It is more difficult to do this with the legs; use fruit juice or jam on the legs, or on the entire bird, just as described for the smaller birds. Apricots are especially good for turkey; citrus fruits are better for duck and goose, because they help counteract excess fat. Partially roast the bird, then let it rest. For a tangy taste, rub the skin with additional juice or jam before finishing cooking. You can flame these birds with a liqueur too, if you like.

Boneless Breasts

Since the tenderest and most delicate part of the chicken, the boneless breast, takes only a short time to cook, it is usually reserved for last-minute preparation. But even this cut can be prepared in advance. Make a thick orange sauce with butter, orange jelly, sliced oranges with pits and rind removed, and raisins, if you like them. Sauté the chicken breasts in butter over low heat for 3 or 4 minutes on each side, then transfer them to the orange sauce. Leave them in the sauce at room temperature. Just before serving, warm them in the sauce over *very low* heat for a maximum of 25 minutes. If you have less time, increase the heat, but do not let the sauce boil. The chicken will be nearly done after sautéing.

Broiled chicken can also be partially prepared in advance. Place it with the bone side toward the heat source on the broiler, but not too close. Broil for 20 minutes, then remove at once, and let the pieces rest at room temperature. Before serving, broil with the skin side toward the heat until the skin is crisp.

Cold or jellied dishes are good choices when you have limited time immediately before a party. They can be prepared at least a day ahead. Some cold dishes can be frozen many days in advance. Many baked dishes can be fully cooked, to be cooled and frozen. If you have limited space and few dishes, turn the frozen block out of its dish, double-wrap with foil or freezer paper, and store. When you are ready to serve it, unwrap and replace it in the dish you baked it in. Let it defrost and reheat, or follow the directions that apply to your particular recipe. If you have freezer-to-stove casseroles and the recipe makes it practical, you can put the frozen dish directly in the oven.

SOUFFLÉS

Soufflés are elegant-looking preparations for parties. These air-filled masterpieces seem mysterious and difficult to prepare, but any cook can master the simple steps involved. It may sound surprising, but they can be prepared in advance too. An individual soufflé is a good first course for a dinner party, and a large soufflé is a good main dish at a company luncheon. Soufflés can be completely made in advance and can be frozen, or you can complete part of the preparation the day before. The recipe that follows will serve as a pattern. Soufflés can be made with any poultry, ham, cheese with ham, veal and even with other meats, if you use recipes especially adapted for them.

CHICKEN AND MUSHROOM SOUFFLÉ   6 servings

1½ pounds chicken parts	1 tablespoon minced shallots
½ teaspoon salt	4 tablespoons all-purpose flour
1 sprig of rosemary	¼ cup minced fresh parsley
1 cup seasoned strong chicken stock	salt and white pepper
½ to ¾ pound mushrooms	3 egg yolks
3 tablespoons butter	5 egg whites
1 tablespoon olive oil	

Although most recipes for chicken soufflé specify white meat, you can easily use dark meat; for this recipe, about 3 whole legs will do. When the meat is cooked and deboned, you will have about ½ pound of meat if using legs, and ¾ pound if using breasts. Rinse the chicken, cover with cold water and add the salt and rosemary. Bring to a boil, and simmer until the chicken is very tender; let it cool in the liquid. You can use the cooking liquid to add to soup or for cooking vegetables, but do not use it for the stock in this recipe, because the flavor will be too bland. Remove skin, bones, tendons and veins from the chicken, and cut into small pieces. Purée half the chicken, with ⅓ cup chicken stock, at a time, in an electric blender set at BLEND or HIGH; do not try to do it all at once, because it will become too thick within seconds. Turn the mixture into a bowl with a cover, and refrigerate.

Wipe mushrooms with a damp cloth, and peel them. Slice the 6 most perfect mushrooms through stem and cap, making 5 very thin slices from each stem portion. Chop the rest of the mushrooms into pieces the size of dried peas. Melt 1 tablespoon butter, add the oil, and sauté the mushroom slices in it until pale brown; lift them out to a sheet of absorbent paper, then wrap in foil, and refrigerate. Now sauté the shallots (minced onion can be substituted, but the flavor of shallot is more delicate) and the chopped mushrooms together over low heat, stirring occasionally, until the mushrooms are slightly crisp on the edges. Cool, then transfer to a small bowl, and refrigerate. *The steps up to this point can be completed the day before your party.*

To proceed, remove puréed chicken and mushrooms from the refrigerator. Melt the rest of the butter, and stir in the flour over low heat until thoroughly mixed. Add the rest of the stock, and continue to heat and stir until the sauce is very thick. Add the puréed chicken, and stir until well mixed, then stir in the chopped mushrooms and the parsley. Beat the egg yolks lightly, stir in some of the hot chicken mixture to warm the eggs, then mix the yolks into the rest of the chicken. Taste the soufflé; add additional salt if needed and a dash of white pepper. Spoon into a 2-quart bowl. *Up to this point can be completed several hours before your party.* Let the mixture cool, then cover the bowl with foil, and let it rest at room temperature until you are ready to continue. Even if you are planning to finish the soufflé at once, be sure to let it cool before adding egg whites.

About 1 hour before serving, beat the egg whites with a whisk or rotary beater—an electric beater will not be quicker—until stiff. Mix part of the egg whites into the cooled chicken mixture. Then, with a rubber spatula, gently *fold in* the remainder. Spoon the mixture into 6 shirred-egg dishes (each holding 1⅓ cups) or into 6 individual soufflé dishes (each holding 1 cup) or into one 6-cup soufflé dish. Arrange 5 sautéed mushroom slices on top of each individual dish, or all of them on top of the large soufflé. *At this point the soufflés can be frozen; cover tightly, and wrap again after freezing.*

Set a large baking sheet with sides in a preheated 325° F. oven for the small soufflés, or 375° F. for large ones. Pour about ½ inch of hot water into the baking sheet, and set the soufflé dishes in it. Let the little ones bake for about 30 minutes, the large one for 45 minutes. If you are baking frozen soufflés, remove the dishes from the freezer for 1 hour before baking, and double the baking time.

The large soufflé makes 4 ample servings for lunch. If you have some little ones left over, they will flatten out, but they will still taste good. To serve more people, make more soufflés; do not try to make a large one to serve more than 8 people. And do not freeze a soufflé larger than 8 cups, because it will not cook properly in the center.

STUFFED VEGETABLES

If you are preparing stuffed vegetables of any kind, most of the work can be done in advance. Prepare the vegetables to be stuffed, and refrigerate them until ready to proceed; the stuffings can usually be completed in advance. In some cases, you can fill the vegetables, especially if they are not too moist or soft. The hot stuffed mushrooms on page 148 can be completely prepared except for the crumbs and butter on top; at the last minute, you need only enough time to bake them. A reminder: If you bake stuffed vegetables directly from the refrigerator, allow a few extra minutes in the oven. It is better to let them reach room temperature before baking, so you can be sure the center of the stuffing is fully baked.

SALADS

If you are serving meat salads at an informal occasion, you can do everything in advance except combining the ingredients. Lettuces or other greens can be washed, trimmed and cut or torn to the desired size, then rolled in a linen towel or wrapped in absorbent kitchen paper. Refrigerate until ready to serve the completed salad. Other ingredients can be prepared in advance too. The only exception is when you are using avocados or any fruits that turn brown when exposed to air. Leave preparation of such fruits to the last minute. In general, do not season vegetables to be served uncooked, because salt will tend to make them limp. Salad dressings that are stable emulsions, like mayonnaise, can be prepared far in advance. French dressing and its variations taste far better when fresh, especially if the acid ingredient is a fruit juice or wine, which lose flavor rapidly. If possible, combine the ingredients just before you need them.

As you have already read in Chapter 8, vegetables can be blanched in advance, to be reheated at the last minute in butter or by quick steaming. If you are serving many guests, this can save you time; you will discover that there is not room on the stove for all the necessary pots and pans, unless you have done a lot of the time-consuming work beforehand.

Sauces for meats and poultry, or those made with either, can be completely finished except for the addition of that last spoon of butter or marrow for glossiness; that you will add just before serving the sauce. Except for emulsified sauces like hollandaise and mayonnaise, they can all be frozen. If you are making a long-cooking sauce like brown sauce (espagnole) or tomato-meat sauce for pasta, you will spend enough time over it to make it worth your while to prepare a lot. Freeze portions of these sauces; 2-cup containers are the most practical; remember to take them from the freezer in time to defrost.

Homemade bread, pancakes and crêpes can be made in advance and frozen. These are quick to defrost. If you are preparing most of your dinner in the oven, keep in mind that any food baked in the oven needs air space around it; this is especially true of raised breads. Do not try to bake them at the same time as a roast or casserole. Meat and poultry dishes must be surrounded by hot air too.

When preparing for any kind of a party, be sure to clean up as you go along. You need space to maneuver for entertaining.

Even if there is much to do for the occasion, avoid using prepackaged or commercially frozen dishes. They are convenient and time-saving for family meals and emergencies, but a special occasion calls for special effort. Your own recipes, your own taste in seasoning, and your flair for garnishing will make all your parties good times to remember.

MENU
MAKING

Chapter 25

WHEN FRESH ASPARAGUS or corn on the cob are in season, or soft-shelled crabs or shad roe, or strawberries or local melons, one of these treats may be the starting point of a menu, but most meals are planned around the meat or poultry to be served as the main dish. A good main course should include protein—meat, poultry, fish, eggs—and other ingredients to supply necessary nutritional elements—vegetables, fruits, grains. Vegetables and fruits can be served cooked or raw; grains can be served separately or in pasta, bread or other mixtures. The traditional American dinner of meat, potato and a vegetable makes a sound nutritional package. Nevertheless, 365 dinners a year constructed in just that way would be boring. Be adventurous. New foods are new only once, but new combinations can add variety endlessly.

A meal of any kind should have a balance of flavors and textures and should show a balance of colors and shapes as well. Shape and color may seem a far cry from diet and food planning, but these are important in stimulating appetite; the eye as well as the nose helps to make us hungry and gives us pleasure at the table. This does not apply to the main course alone; your whole menu needs to be considered as a unit.

Aside from any special dietary considerations, it is a mistake to plan a meal that is overpowering in any way—too rich, too spicy, too acid, too anything. Do not use the same ingredient in two dishes in the same meal; that does not mean never to use a flavoring ingredient such as parsley, or a basic cooking element such as butter or stock. But never have two dishes made with whipped cream or dressed with whipped cream! Never use nuts or tomatoes or green peppers or cornmeal in two dishes on the same menu. If your main dish is chicken in some form, obviously poultry is out for the first course. If you start with cheese tarts, do not use cheese on anything else. If you start with liver pâté, do not use it to flavor any other dish. Avoid too many eggs; they are used unobtrusively in so many preparations that the cook tends to forget they are there. Skip the custard tart if you have an egg-enriched sauce already planned, and save those stuffed eggs for the picnic menu that does not include any sauces.

Do not flavor everything with the same herbs and spices. If your main course is rich, the accompaniments should be simple, even plain. If your first course is very salty or spicy, the other dishes should be reasonably bland. If you are serving ham or corned beef with a sweet glaze, be sure to strike another note in your dessert.

Texture is very important. If you are using meat in ground form for one course or another, do not use it a second time in the same meal. Do not have several foods that are puréed, and one dish wrapped in pastry is all that any meal can stand. Another thing to avoid—and this may not be so obvious—is the use of several closely related foods; for instance, do not serve melon and cucumber and squash in the same meal, and do not serve more than one variety meat.

A first course implies at least three in the meal, whether lunch or dinner. Plan for that first course to be an enhancing prelude to what follows. You will find many ideas in Chapter 9. With an ample first course like *antipasto*, which usually includes meat, fish and several vegetables, you can forget the meat-potato-vegetable main course and instead serve pasta with sauce. If your main course is based on a dish of delicate taste and appearance—chicken in white-wine sauce, for example—the prelude to it should not be so overwhelmingly spicy or sharp that the palate is ruined at the outset.

Dessert must be considered too. If dessert is a custard-based dish, do not serve *chawanmushi* or quiche to start. If a pie or tart is planned for dessert, skip pastry in any other course.

Let us consider some meat or poultry main dishes and the foods that make good accompaniments for them.

Beef Roasts

Beef roasts seem to call for some kind of potato: baked in the jacket (no foil wrapping for oven baking, please, because foil prevents the escape of steam and the potatoes tend to become soggy; also the skin will not become crisp); mashed or whipped; pan-roasted with the meat itself; cut into rounds, olive shapes or large ovals and sautéed. There's nothing to stop your serving bulgur or rice or pasta if you prefer, but our first choice would be a potato. Do not discard the idea of potatoes because you think they are fattening; eat a medium-sized baked potato without butter or gravy; potatoes are very nutritious.

In season, asparagus is the perfect vegetable; green beans—tiny ones whole, large ones cut or Frenched—make a good choice in any season. A fresh green vegetable is just right with a beef roast.

Since this is a meat you may be carving at table, make your garnishes simple: parsley or watercress bouquets. The slightly peppery taste of watercress is excellent with rich beef. Luxury roasts such as the filet or boneless shell roast are often served with elegant garnishes. You can prepare these if you like, as long as you remember to arrange for removing them to facilitate carving. Whole large mushrooms fluted (carved in patterns), or plain mushrooms upside down and filled with puréed or diced vegetables or truffles; artichoke bottoms filled with sauces or purées; whole small perfect vegetables such as tiny carrots, pearl or silverskin onions, new potatoes, whole green beans, etc., all perfectly cooked—simply blanched, or sautéed, or glazed—and arranged in neat bundles; all these serve as delicious edible garnishes when you are making an effort. You may never think of cooking a salad green, but in France a suitable accompaniment for roast beef is braised lettuce or Belgian en-

Tournedos, slices from the beef filet, cut about 1¼ inches thick, wrapped with beef fat and tied. Broil or sauté these and garnish for a party menu.

dive; use whole heads of small lettuces or halves of endives; the slightly bitter taste is a good foil for beef and neutral-tasting potato.

Steaks

Beef steaks are good with the same foods as beef roasts, but there are other possibilities. Have you tried sweet potatoes with a steak? Do not just save these for Thanksgiving. Bake them in their skins, then peel and mash with butter. Or try buttered noodles topped with crumbs; for a party mix diced mushrooms and slivered blanched almonds into the noodles and add ground almonds to the crumbs for topping. New potatoes, cooked in their jackets and peeled just before serving, are the choice in early summer; roll them in melted butter—only a little is needed if the potatoes are hot—and sprinkle with minced parsley. If you are having butterflied shell steaks for St. Valentine's Day, serve mashed potatoes in a heart-shaped mound, or duchess potatoes.

Any fresh vegetable can be served with a steak; if mushrooms are plentiful sauté them with herbs. Or try this: cut green peppers into shoestrings, sliver mild-flavored onions, and trim whole tiny mushrooms or slice large ones. Sauté peppers in butter, then add onion slivers, then mushrooms; cook until just tender, only a few minutes. Add slivered almonds, and serve the mixture with rice to accompany your steak. Of course, a steak needs no sauce.

Ground Beef

Ground beef served as burgers or patties or in meat loaves tastes good with a leafy green like spinach or broccoli. Spinach mixed with mashed potatoes can be served like a pie.

Pot-Roasted and Braised Meats

Pot-roasted and braised meats are prepared with vegetables, which are cooked until very soft and cannot be served separately. Usually they are puréed with some of the cooking juices and used as a sauce for the meat. If you like just those same flavors, cook some of the same vegetables, whole or in large pieces, separately until just tender. Good choices with pot roasts are braised whole leeks and celery hearts, carrots, white turnips, potatoes.

Veal Roasts

Veal roasts are especially enhanced by carrots, because of the natural sugar in the vegetables. Use small ones whole and cut up larger and older carrots to chunks or slivers of uniform size. Fresh lettuce leaves can be used for color contrast under the carrots, and braised lettuce is good with veal too. Here is another veal and carrot idea: Marinate whole raw carrots—not too large—in a white-wine marinade for 24 hours. Roast the veal, using some of the marinade to add moisture and flavor. Add the drained carrots to the roast about 50 minutes before it is done and let the carrots cook with the meat; turn them to glaze on all sides in the meat juices. At serving time flame veal and carrots with brandy.

Crowns

Veal, lamb and pork crowns will require lots of parsley; the whole crown may be served on a base of leaves—lettuce, cabbage, grape, lemon. Cabbage leaves are most easily available and less perishable than lettuce. Additional garnishes of fresh onion slices, halved or quartered fresh tomatoes, whole crab apples or small lady apples, slices of large candied apples or cranberries are appropriate.

Stuffings for crowns usually include meat, but grains or vegetables can be used; and for pork crowns, fruits are especially good. Consider the stuffing and the garnish when choosing a vegetable. If you are not using a grain in the stuffing, then browned potato balls or steamed new potatoes are good. If the crown is garnished with greens, use an orange or red vegetable. With rosy crab apples as a garnish, fresh green peas, cauliflowerets or green beans are preferable.

Veal Scallops

Delicate veal scallops can be garnished with a great variety of accompaniments, which can serve also as the main vegetable if plentiful enough. Mushrooms, cauliflowerets, green peas with pearl onions, vegetable purées—carrot, green pea, spinach—are all good. Thin noodles, *linguine*, are excellent with all veal dishes, and so is rice.

Chops

Chops, which become routine when accompanied with the same old things, can be served in so many ways that we could write a chapter of chop menus. Potatoes might be your first choice, but how about curried rice? It is great with all kinds of chops. Good vegetables are pearl or silverskin onions, buttered artichoke hearts, asparagus in season. Spinach baked in filo pastry in the Greek fashion is a delicious and different accompaniment. As a garnish, use whole cranberries or applesauce flavored with brandy or mint.

Roast Lamb

Roast lamb, baked potatoes, green peas, mint sauce—a familiar tradition and still good. Other vegetables that complement lamb are buttered carrots and red or white cabbage, slivered and sautéed with caraway seeds. Vegetable tarts with or without custard—without if you have custard or eggs elsewhere in the meal—can serve as both starch and vegetable. Good choices for starch are puréed mixed turnips and carrots or sweet potatoes and carrots. If you prefer plain potatoes, they are good pan-roasted; cook them in the roasting pan as the lamb is finishing. With tender spring lamb, asparagus is right in season; for a fine taste fillip, arrange the finished lamb and asparagus on a heatproof platter and flame them with Cognac just before serving. Mint sprigs can be arranged on top of a lamb roast or under it before flaming to add a fine bouquet. Mint is a good garnish, or mint and parsley together.

If you want a cold accompaniment with a lamb dish, gently mix slivered raw cabbage, carrot and cauliflower and dress with just a little oil and wine vinegar to make a delicate vegetables vinaigrette. Pickled beet salad is good with lamb and with pork too; in fact, it is an excellent choice with all cured and fatty meats.

Saddle of Lamb

A saddle of lamb can be served on a bed of shredded lettuce or parsley; these garnishes will not interfere with carving, since the bony framework of the saddle will serve as a carving rack. For a beautiful way to present a saddle, gently separate the uncooked meat from the bony framework along the spine bones and for the same distance along the rib bones, making an L-shaped opening on each side of the spine. Fill this with a flavorful stuffing, packing in just enough to make an even layer about ½ inch thick. When the saddle is roasted it will be beautifully flavored and none of the seasoning will be lost in the pan. Each slice should have a narrow edge of the stuffing served with it.

To garnish the saddle, serve whole tomatoes with a thin slice cut from the top; sprinkle with butter, crumbs and seasoning, and broil; for another version top with a mushroom and broil tomatoes and mushrooms together. Another good garnish is orange and mint together; slice oranges ⅛ inch thick and remove the peel (if you find it easier to peel first and then slice, do it that way); macerate the slices in orange-flavored brandy, with a few mint leaves mixed in, for several hours or over-night. Arrange the orange slices and more mint leaves on the top of the roast; use the remaining brandy to flame the roast at the end. This is good for other roasts be-sides saddles, and can even be used for meats other than lamb.

Fresh Pork

We have already mentioned pork crowns and chops, but other meals based on fresh pork can be beautifully complemented with the right choice of foods. Rice or wide noodles are especially good with pork. Sautéed or steamed new potatoes go well with roasts, broiled or barbecued cuts like spareribs, and pork stews. An ex-cellent garnish for pork is some kind of fruit—poached apple or pear slices or quarters flavored with cinnamon, made rosy with cranberry juice, if you like. Poached dried fruits can be rolled in butter flavored with cinnamon or curry.

Two harmonious vegetable accompaniments for pork are cauliflower and egg-plant. Cut raw cauliflower into thin slices, and sauté quickly in butter; do not over-cook the cauliflower—it is best when still slightly crunchy. Eggplant absorbs a lot of butter or oil when sautéed. If this presents a dietary problem for you, try cutting the eggplant into chunks and steaming it. It will be fully cooked in less than 8 min-utes. Steamed eggplant can be prepared in advance. Just before you need it, toss it into a small amount of butter to reheat; minced onion and fresh tomato, or minced green pepper or pimiento can be added. For a different taste that goes well with lamb or pork, season the eggplant with curry powder or ground cuminseed just before reheating it in the butter. Cauliflower and eggplant can be combined for an interesting dish; the crunchy and smooth textures make a good contrast.

Cured Meats

Cured meats are usually enhanced by sweetness in the accompanying dishes. Ham is good with baked or mashed sweet potatoes. Spoon the mashed cooked sweets while still hot into a shallow casserole; mix in some honey, and brown the top of the potatoes in the oven or under the broiler. Mashed cooked butternut squash is good buttered and sprinkled with cinnamon; or serve gently sautéed or steamed crosswise slices with a sprinkle of cinnamon. Brussels sprouts and silverskin onions together are a good dish with ham; the sweetness in the onions adds just the right note of flavor. Glazed vegetables are fine with ham; cook carrots, whole small onions and small white turnips until just done but not mushy; drain them, then roll in butter in a heavy skillet; sprinkle with brown sugar or honey, and turn them over and over on low heat until they are shiny and glazed on all sides. These are good with beef pot roast too.

A different sort of menu based on ham substitutes salad for the conventional vegetables. Fruits or vegetables or mixtures of both can be excellent, and practical if you have a tiny kitchen or limited serving space. If planning a fruit salad, do not forget some unusual fruits like figs, pomegranates and persimmons. If you prepare this in advance, be sure to brush cut fruits with lemon juice to prevent browning. For an attractive presentation, surround the ham with individual bowls or plates of the salad.

The traditional accompaniments for corned beef are boiled potatoes and cabbage. Fine if you are a traditionalist. But how about cauliflower with butter and nutmeg (good with ham too), or a salad of uncooked fresh peas with cherry tomatoes, or corned beef with two salads—cucumber and potato?

Green vegetables provide good color contrast to cured meats, but this is one place where you can use pale vegetables like cauliflower, onions and parsnips. Canadian bacon roast, another rosy meat, is delicious with creamed onions or cauliflower polonaise.

Variety Meats

Such delicate-tasting variety meats as brains and sweetbreads require careful menu planning. Their texture is so soft that at least one dish should be crunchy or firm. And they are so pale that color contrast is needed. Mushrooms are particularly good with sweetbreads, but be sure to add a green vegetable as well. Brains need something acid for contrast, especially if you do not use lemon juice or vinegar in the preparation. Baked tomatoes are a good choice, for their acidity and color as well. A green vegetable with lemon butter and a cold vegetable vinaigrette are other good choices. Chopped nuts could be combined with something in such a meal; and there are many others besides the overused almonds. Try hazelnuts, pecans, walnuts, pistachios, even the humble goober. Creamed onions with peanuts is a famous Virginia dish and very good served with variety meats.

Slightly bitter-tasting or acid vegetables are also good with liver and kidneys: raw or cooked endives, tomatoes, asparagus. For a plain meal at home, home-fried potatoes are suitable accompaniments, but rice and noodles are also good with these organ meats. If you use a wine in the preparation of kidneys—or any variety meat, for that matter—try to match it to your table wine; although this is a good general rule when cooking with and serving wine, it might not seem so obvious with meats, like kidneys, that taste strong enough to mask the distinctive flavor of any wine. However, the flavor of the completed dish with its sauce will be subtly enhanced by using the same kind of wine at table.

Stews

Meats that are cooked for a long time to release the collagen in the joints and the nutrients in the bones, such as those usually used for stews and some casseroles, can be accompanied by vegetables that also require long cooking. Dried beans, lentils, chick-peas and dried yellow or green peas are obvious examples; they add extra protein, and their flavors will be greatly improved as a result of being cooked with the meat. Root vegetables need somewhat longer cooking than leafy greens, but even potatoes and parsnips will become mushy if cooked for hours. If you must cook root vegetables for a long time and if you intend to serve them as vegetables rather than as part of a sauce, cut them into large pieces, or leave them whole if they will fit in the pot. To keep vegetables firm, make sure that you never let a stew or casserole boil. Since most long-cooking meats become more tender with prolonged gentle heat, this is best for all the ingredients in the recipe.

Poultry

All poultry is good accompanied by rice as the starch. Serve noodles with delicious Middle European dishes like paprika chicken. Either noodles or rice can be used in a poultry stuffing. Bread is more common, but it is by no means the only possibility; Pennsylvania Dutch cooks use mashed potatoes for stuffing. Sweet potatoes are good to accompany chicken and turkey. If you are not using sweets, another good choice is a yellow squash—butternut, Hubbard, acorn—or yellow turnip (rutabaga).

All green vegetables are good with poultry: green peas, asparagus, green beans and Italian beans, broccoli, spinach, fresh lima beans, braised endive, Brussels sprouts with chestnuts, fiddleheads in the early spring, leeks cooked in wine. There is scarcely a vegetable that cannot be served to good advantage with poultry. Tangy vegetables are good with the fattier birds—duck and goose—but duck is also beautifully accompanied by green peas, because the starch in the peas helps absorb the fat of the bird.

Starches

When planning a menu, do not fall into the trap of thinking of potatoes as a necessary part of every meal. We are not trying to diminish the nutritious, delicious potato, but it is superfluous if your menu includes a starchy stuffing, a stew served with dumplings, or spoon bread or corn muffins. Other good starches besides rice and noodles are bulgur (cracked wheat), barley, kasha (buckwheat groats), hominy and grits and cornmeal, and little pasta like *spaetzle* or *tarhonya* (egg barley). The grains add enough starch and lots of nutrition (vitamin B), and they are especially good if your main dish is a stew or cooked in a sauce. Rice can be flavored in countless ways, and there are many kinds of rice: white, brown, long-grain, round-grain. Rice from Italy (Piedmont) or India (Patna) tastes quite different from ours. All these grains can be simply boiled or baked, or they can be made into pilafs or casseroles with additional ingredients. Rice, barley and noodles can be baked in large or individual molds, or in ring molds to serve as containers for the meat or vegetable. Cooked cornmeal or hominy grits can be cut into little rounds or other shapes, to be used as bases for unmolded timbales or small servings of variety meats or game; the little bases will taste better and look prettier if sautéed—as if making fried mush—plain or first dipped into egg and crumbs.

Garnishes

Aside from the vegetable you plan to serve as a substantial part of the meal, you can use others as edible decorations: a few asparagus tips; frilled cucumber slices or sections of cucumber filled with a tiny salad and dressing; marinated vegetables; small perfect vegetables, perfectly cooked and arranged in a decorative fashion; stuffed mushroom caps or artichoke bottoms. The glossy green leaves of uncooked fresh spinach make a striking contrast to any meat; endive leaves and Bibb lettuce add a paler green. Be sure to wash spinach and Bibb lettuce with great care, because the little folds can contain sand grains.

Fruits

Do not forget fruits. Everyone is used to oranges with duck and cranberries with turkey, but there are so many other combinations. If figs and melons are good with prosciutto, they are bound to be delicious with other cured meats. Cold or poached or broiled peach and apricot halves are fine with cured meats and others as well, especially poultry. Both green and black olives can be sliced, chopped or used whole in recipes or as separate garnishes. For color, try combining applesauce and cranberry sauce—good with poultry and pork. For meats that need a touch of acid, use citrus fruits, sculptured halves or sections of lemons or oranges; if you have time for more fussing, make lemon or orange baskets, and fill them with a mixture of fruits, a preserve, or a citrus-flavored sauce. Limes and kumquats, used less often, can make beautiful little garnishes; poach the kumquats to make them tender if you plan to eat them, or cook them in sugar syrup, as if making a preserve. Twist lemon and lime slices together. Use a melon-ball cutter to prepare a mound of melons, pears, apples or avocados; just be sure to sprinkle them with lemon juice to prevent browning. Plain or frosted grapes can make beautiful decorations, and the juice of fresh grapes (verjuice) is an exotic addition to sauces, and can be used in cooking meats and poultry for the tenderizing effect of the acid. A great classic sauce for fish, especially mackerel, is made with gooseberries; these interesting berries can sauce meat and poultry as well. Try them with cured or fatty meats; the acid of the berries gives good taste contrast.

Special menu problems require special solutions. To plan menus around dietary restrictions, see Chapter 22. Ideas for breakfast, luncheon, buffet and holiday menus are in separate chapters, and you will find other menus throughout the book.

The aims of all menu planning are twofold: good nutrition in the food itself and a presentation that stimulates the appetite. For the second, consider color, shape, texture, taste and smell. Be creative. Use imagination. Despite centuries of complicated menu making, you can still devise new combinations to make delicious and good-looking meals that suit the simpler style of today.

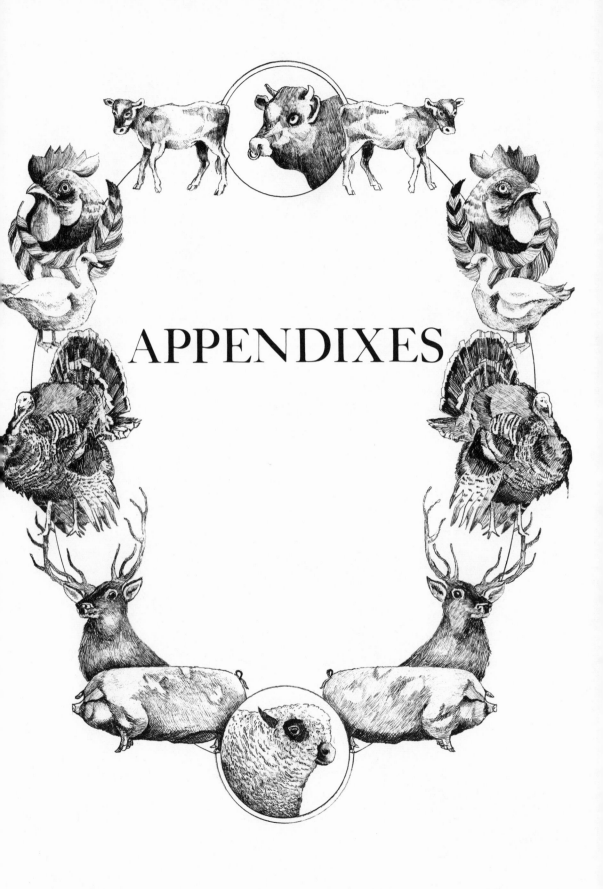

APPENDIXES

Appendix I

CALORIES, PROTEIN AND FAT

T HE TABLES THAT FOLLOW are based on information published by the United States Department of Agriculture. If you want more details on food nutrients, there are many USDA publications that give mineral and vitamin content, as well as information on foods other than meat and poultry.

The statistics in these tables are based on 100 grams, or about 3½ ounces, of the edible portions of each meat item, including both fat and lean, either cooked according to the method listed or raw. We have chosen to list the statistics for only medium-fat cuts of Choice grade, but USDA publications list statistics for all grades and percentages of fat. Because Prime beef is heavily marbled, which accounts for the tenderness of the grade, it is higher in fat content than Choice beef. As a result, Prime beef has more calories per unit of weight. On the other hand, Prime lamb is somewhat leaner than Choice. Meats with large amounts of external fat will always contain more calories unless well trimmed. Meats with large amounts of internal fat will also be high in calories, but the fat content can be somewhat reduced by certain cooking methods (see Chapter 6). Even fatty poultry is reasonably low in calories and fat when the skin has been removed.

The cooking methods listed do not represent our recommendations of ideal methods for the cuts listed; they are simply the methods used in computing the calories and nutrients in the tables. You will notice in a few places the use of the word "uncooked," rather than "raw," to describe the state of a particular item; this applies to items that have been processed in some way before they are sold.

We have not listed carbohydrate content in these charts, because it is negligible in meats. There are small amounts in hearts, livers and tongues, in chicken, and in cured ham as a result of the ingredients used in curing.

Not every conceivable cut is listed, but we think enough typical cuts are in-

401

cluded so that you can use the tables to compute approximate statistics for most of the meat and poultry you buy.

A calorie is a unit of measure to designate the amount of heat required at a pressure of 1 atmosphere to raise 1 gram of water 1 degree Celsius. Tests to determine caloric content are carried out under laboratory conditions, not *in vivo*, so the figures listed in the tables are only indications of energy potential, and each piece of meat will vary somewhat from the specific example tested. A gram of fat provides almost twice as many calories as a gram of protein. If the food you eat provides more calories than you burn, the unused calories are stored in the body as fat.

	Cut	Cooking Method	Lean %	Fat %	Calories	Protein Grams	Fat Grams
BEEF	chuck rib	braised	69	31	427	22.4	36.7
	chuck arm	braised or pot-roasted	85	15	289	27.1	19.2
	flank steak	braised	100		196	30.5	7.3
	hindshank	simmered	66	34	361	25.1	28.1
	porterhouse steak	broiled	57	43	465	19.7	42.0
	T-bone steak	broiled	56	44	473	19.5	43.2
	club steak	broiled	58	42	454	20.6	40.6
	sirloin steak						
	wedge, or round, bone	broiled	66	34	387	23.0	32.0
	double, or flat, bone	broiled	66	34	408	22.2	34.7
	hip, or pin, bone	broiled	55	45	487	19.1	44.9
	short plate	simmered	58	42	474	20.6	42.8
	rib	roasted	64	36	440	19.9	39.4
	rib, sixth, or blade	braised	70	30	437	22.1	38.0
	round	broiled	81	19	261	28.6	15.4
	rump	roasted	75	25	347	23.6	27.3
	ground beef	panfried	lean		219	27.4	11.3
			regular		286	24.2	20.3
	corned beef	simmered	medium fat		372	22.9	30.4
	chipped beef	uncooked			203	34.3	6.3
	brains, all kinds	raw			125	10.4	8.6
	heart	braised			188	31.3	5.7
	kidney	braised			252	33.0	12.0
	liver	panfried			229	26.4	10.6
	sweetbreads	braised			320	25.9	23.2
	tongue						
	fresh	braised	medium fat		244	21.5	16.7
	smoked	simmered			267	19.3	20.3
	tripe	uncooked			100	19.1	2.0
	suet	raw			854	1.5	94.0
VEAL	shoulder	braised	85	15	235	27.9	12.8
	flank	stewed	60	40	390	23.2	32.3
	foreshank	stewed	86	14	216	28.7	10.4
	loin	broiled	77	23	234	26.4	13.4
	breast	stewed	73	27	303	26.1	21.2

	Cut	Cooking Method	Lean %	Fat %	Calories	Protein Grams	Fat Grams
	rib	roasted	82	18	269	27.2	16.9
	round with						
	rump	broiled	79	21	216	27.1	11.1
	brains (see under Beef)						
	heart	braised			208	27.8	9.1
	kidney	raw			113	16.6	4.6
	liver	panfried			261	29.5	13.2
	sweetbreads	braised			168	32.6	3.2
	tongue, fresh	braised			160	23.9	6.0
LAMB	leg	roasted	83	17	279	25.3	18.9
	loin, chops	broiled	66	34	359	22.0	29.4
	rib, chops	broiled	62	38	407	20.1	35.6
	shoulder	roasted	74	26	338	21.7	27.2
	brains (see under Beef)						
	heart	braised			260	29.5	14.4
	kidney	raw			105	16.8	3.3
	liver	broiled			261	32.3	12.4
	sweetbreads	braised			175	28.1	6.1
	tongue						
	fresh	braised			254	20.5	18.2
	smoked (see under Beef)						
PORK, FRESH	leg	roasted	74	26	374	23.0	30.6
	loin	roasted	80	20	362	24.5	28.5
	loin chops	broiled	72	28	391	24.7	31.7
	Boston butt	roasted	79	21	353	22.5	28.5
	picnic	simmered	74	26	374	23.2	30.5
	spareribs	braised			440	20.8	38.9
	heart	braised			195	30.8	6.9
	kidney	raw			106	16.3	3.6
	liver	panfried			241	29.9	11.5
	tongue	braised			253	22.0	17.4
	lard				902		100
PORK, CURED	ham						
	country-cured, dry	simmered			389	16.9	35.0
	moist-cured	roast	84	16	289	20.9	22.1
	Boston butt	roast	83	17	330	22.9	25.7
	picnic	roast	82	18	323	22.4	25.2
	canned, with juices				193	18.3	12.3
	bacon	broiled or			611	30.4	52.0
	regular	panfried, drained					
	Canadian	broiled or panfried, drained			277	27.6	17.5
	salt pork	uncooked			783	3.9	85.0
	pig's feet	pickled			199	16.7	14.8
GAME	rabbit						
	domestic	stewed			216	29.3	10.1
	wild	raw			135	21.0	5.0
	reindeer	raw	84	16	217	20.5	14.4
	venison	raw	lean		126	21.0	4.0

	Cut	Cooking Method	Lean %	Fat %	Calories	Protein Grams	Fat Grams
SAUSAGES	blutwurst				394	14.1	36.9
	bockwurst				264	11.3	23.9
	bologna, all						
	meat				277	13.3	22.8
	braunschweiger				319	14.8	27.4
	brown-and-serve	browned			422	16.5	37.8
	capocollo				499	20.2	45.8
	cervelat, dry				451	24.6	37.6
	country-style,						
	smoked				345	15.1	31.1
	deviled ham				351	13.9	32.3
	frankfurter	simmered			304	12.4	27.2
	headcheese				268	15.5	22.0
	knackwurst				278	14.1	23.2
	liverwurst				307	16.2	25.6
	luncheon meat,						
	pork				294	15.0	24.9
	mortadella				315	20.4	25.0
	kielbasy				304	15.7	25.8
	pork sausage,						
	links or						
	bulk	panfried			476	18.1	44.2
	salami, dry				450	23.8	38.1
	scrapple				215	8.8	13.6
	souse				181	13.0	13.4
	thuringer				307	18.6	24.5
	vienna,						
	canned				240	14.0	19.8
POULTRY	chicken						
	broilers	broiled	no skin		136	23.8	3.8
	fryers	fried	no skin		209	31.2	7.8
	light meat only				197	32.1	6.1
	dark meat only				220	30.4	9.3
	breast only				203	32.5	6.4
	legs and thighs				236	30.9	10.8
	roasters	roasted	with skin		248	27.1	14.7
	light meat only		no skin		182	32.3	4.9
	dark meat only		no skin		184	29.3	6.5
	hens	stewed	no skin		208	30.0	8.9
	capons	raw			283	21.4	21.2
	canned chicken				198	21.7	11.7
	gizzards	simmered			148	27.0	3.3
	hearts	simmered			173	25.3	7.2
	livers	simmered			165	26.5	4.4
	duck						
	domestic	raw	no skin		165	21.4	8.2
	wild	raw	no skin		138	21.3	5.2
	goose,						
	domestic	roasted	no skin		233	33.9	9.8
	liver	raw			182	16.5	10.0
	pâté de foie gras,						
	canned				462	11.4	43.8
	guinea hen	raw	with skin		158	23.4	6.4
	pheasant .	raw	no skin		162	23.6	6.8
	quail	raw	with skin		172	25.4	7.0
	squab	raw	no skin		142	17.5	7.5
	light meat only				125	20.4	4.2
	turkey						
	young birds	raw	with skin		151	19.8	7.4
	(24 weeks or						
	less)						

Cut	Cooking Method	Lean %	Fat %	Calories	Protein Grams	Fat Grams
medium-fat (26 to 32 weeks)	raw		with skin	197	21.6	11.6
fat (over 32 weeks)	raw		with skin	343	18.4	29.3
canned				202	20.9	12.5
gizzards	simmered			196	26.8	8.6
hearts	simmered			216	22.6	13.2
livers	simmered			174	27.9	4.8

The foods with the largest amounts of saturated fatty acids are bacon, beef fat, butter, coconut meat in any form, cooking fats, lard, and margarines made of any liquid oils or hydrogenated fats that are high in saturated fatty acids. The foods with the greatest amount of cholesterol are brains, butter, caviar or other roes, crab, egg yolk and whole egg, kidney, liver, oysters and shrimps.

Appendix 2

STORING
MEATS AND POULTRY

INFORMATION ON STORAGE OF FRESH MEATS can be found in Chapter 5, on frozen meats in Chapter 4, on cured meats in Chapter 3 and on cooked meats and poultry in Chapter 19. In the tables that follow we have assembled information on meats and poultry in all these states.

Meats and poultry in completely sealed cans or jars with no dents or bulges can be stored for 9 months without loss of flavor or nutritive value. They should be kept in a cool dry place. Food in jars should not be exposed to light. Do not let canned goods freeze and thaw; one freezing and thawing will not cause spoilage if the can has not been damaged, but it will affect the flavor adversely. If canned goods are frozen more than once, it is best to discard them. Although some sources say that canned products can be stored indefinitely, we advise against it. Even under good storage conditions, there will be loss of flavor over a long period of time, and meat will tend to become mushy because of the preservatives used. Rotate your canned goods, using first those you purchased first. At present, many large chain stores have freshness codes, giving date of packaging or last permitted date of sale. It will be to your advantage to know the code if you regularly use canned meats and poultry.

Some kinds of canned meat must be refrigerated; the chief example is ham. If these are kept at a steady temperature that does not rise above 40° F. (4.4° C.), they can be kept for 2 years.

Fresh meats and poultry require scrupulous care. Mild to severe food poisoning caused by various organisms of the genus Salmonella is one of the chief food-connected illnesses in man, and 70% of the cases of salmonellosis in the United States from 1961 to 1971 were caused by red meats and poultry. There are over 1300 types of these pathogens, and they enter meats partly through the feed of the live animals and partly because of poor sanitation in the handling of the meats. Neither freezing nor drying destroys these organisms, but they cannot grow in meat refrigerated below 45° F. (7.2° C.). Keep your refrigerator between 34 and 38° F. (1 and 3.3° C.). There are meat keepers that maintain 29° F.; this is not cold enough to freeze meat, but it will give meat a hard chill, enabling you to keep it for 2 days longer than under normal refrigeration. However, meat does have a tendency to dry out when stored at such a low temperature. One special point: The prohibition against stuffing poultry in advance of roasting is important because of salmonella; even if the stuffed bird is refrigerated, it takes too long for the stuffed interior to reach a safe low temperature.

Freezer storage at − 10° F. (− 23.3° C.) will not diminish the flavor or nutritional value of meat. If your machinery fails, it is safe to refreeze meats and poultry if the pieces still have ice crystals in them and if the temperature has not risen above 40° F. (4.4° C.). However, the safe storage time will be halved after thawing and refreezing. If meat has been at 40° F. for 2 days or longer, do not attempt to refreeze it; there will be loss of quality, flavor, nutritive value, and considerable loss of juice; if possible, cook these meats without delay. Thawing meat (described on p. 62) can be done at room temperature, but it is better to thaw in the refrigerator to prevent the growth of salmonella, which flourishes between 60 and 115° F. Even when thawing under water (described on p. 65), the water should be cool—below 60° F. (15.5° C.).

Notes on the tables: The times given are for optimum storage, with no loss of flavor or nutritional value. You can keep meats longer without spoilage, but they will not taste their best, and they will not be as good for you.

FRESH, UNCOOKED, REFRIGERATED: This means meat or poultry as you buy it, stored before cooking at ideal temperatures of 34 to 38° F. In general, a rise of 5° in temperature will halve the storage life of foods. Also, we are talking about food that is truly fresh when you buy it; if fresh sausage links, for example, have been in the butcher's case for 3 days, your home storage time should be reduced to 4 days rather than 7. Sausages or other meats in casings that are sealed in plastic can be kept for an additional 1 to 2 weeks without harmful effects. If they are opened and sliced, you must cut in half the storage time listed in the table. Cured meats and sausages represent these products as you buy them, before any baking or heating done in the home.

MARINATED OR PICKLED, REFRIGERATED: This refers to larger pieces of beef, lamb or venison that have been marinated; the actual time of marination may not be longer than 2 days (for sauerbraten or venison, see p. 133), but the acid in the marinade has a preservative effect that makes it possible to store meats for some days longer after marinating. Such pickled foods as corned beef, pickled pig's feet and pickled tongue can be stored, still in the pickling liquid, under refrigeration for longer than similar cuts of fresh meat.

COOKED, REFRIGERATED: We assume cooked meat or poultry has been cooled as quickly as possible, has then been properly wrapped, and is stored at 34 to 38° F. Meats and poultry that have been partially cooked count as cooked for storage purposes.

FROZEN UNCOOKED: Freezer temperature is − 10° F. (−23.3° C.); food must be properly wrapped (see p. 60), and we are assuming it is stored in a separate, self-contained freezer. Reduce the time by one third for a side-by-side refrigerator-freezer, and halve it if you have only a freezer compartment in a refrigerator.

DEFROSTED, REFRIGERATED: After defrosting, frozen meats are more perishable than fresh meats. Plan to cook them as soon as possible.

FROZEN COOKED: It is not safe to freeze everything after cooking. Ground meat and delicate organ meats, for instance, should not be frozen after cooking; the meat is too dry, the texture will be spoiled and most of the flavor lost. Most cured meats should not be frozen after cooking, because freezing forces the salt to the surface, making the exterior too salty.

DEFROSTED, REFRIGERATED: Meats and poultry frozen after cooking should be used within 2 days or less; the only exception is a meat stored in pickle, like corned beef. The more delicate the item, the shorter the storage time, because such meats dry out rapidly and can spoil.

	Meat	Fresh uncooked refrigerated	Marinated or pickled refrigerated	Cooked refrigerated	Frozen uncooked	Defrosted refrigerated	Frozen cooked	Defrosted refrigerated
BEEF	large cuts	4 days	7 days	3 days	6 mos.	2 days	3 mos.	2 days
	steaks	3 days	——	2 days	6 mos.	2 days	2 mos.	2 days
	pieces in gravy (stews, etc.)	——	——	3 days	——	——	2 mos.	2 days
	small pieces	2 days	——	2 days	4 mos.	2 days	1 mo.	1 day
	ground	1 day	——	1 day	4 mos.	1 day	——	——
	marrowbones	4 days			6 mos.	1 day		
	marrow	2 days	——	6 days	2 mos.	1 day		
	other bones	2 days	——		6 mos.	1 day		
	corned beef	——	7 days	5 days	1 mo.	5 days	2 mos.	5 days
	chipped beef	2 weeks	——	2 days	——	——	——	——
	fat	7 days	——		6 mos.	2 days	——	——
VEAL	large cuts	3 days	——	3 days	3 mos.	1 day	3 mos.	2 days
	pieces in gravy	——	——	3 days	——	——	2 mos.	2 days
	slices, chops	2 days	——	2 days	1 mo.	1 day	1 mo.	1 day
	ground	1 day	——	1 day	1 mo.	1 day	——	——
	bones	2 days	——		6 mos.	1 day	——	
LAMB	large cuts	3 days	5 days	3 days	6 mos.	2 days	3 mos.	2 days
	shanks	2 days	——	3 days	4 mos.	2 days	3 mos.	2 days
	chops	2 days	——	2 days	4 mos.	1 day	1 mo.	1 day
	pieces in gravy	——	——	3 days	——	——	4 mos.	2 days
	ground	1 day	——	1 day	3 mos.	1 day	——	
PORK, FRESH	large cuts	3 days	——	3 days	4 mos.	2 days	3 mos.	2 days
	chops	3 days	——	2 days	3 mos.	2 days	1 mo.	1 day
	spareribs	3 days	3 weeks	2 days	4 mos.	2 days	——	——
	ground	1 day	——	1 day	3 mos.	1 day	1 mo.	1 day
	fresh fatback	6 days	——		12 mos.	6 days	——	——
	lard	2 mos.	——		12 mos.	1 mo.	——	
PORK, CURED	ham (whole or half)	7 days	——	7 days	3 mos.	6 days	——	——
	ham steaks	4 days	——	3 days	1 mo.	4 days	——	——
	spareribs	5 days	——	4 days	3 mos.	4 days	——	——
	bacon, sliced, in sealed wrap	7 days	——	2 days	1 mo.	1 day	6 weeks	1 day

STORING MEATS AND POULTRY

	Meat	Fresh uncooked refrigerated	Marinated or pickled refrigerated	Cooked refrigerated	Frozen uncooked	Defrosted refrigerated	Frozen cooked	Defrosted refrigerated
	bacon, slab	2 weeks	———	2 days	3 mos.	3 days	6 weeks	1 day
	bacon Canadian slices	3 days	———	1 day	3 weeks	1 day	———	———
	Canadian whole	7 days	———	5 days	6 weeks	2 days	———	———
	salt pork	1 mo.	———	———	1 year	3 weeks	3 mos.	2 days
	salted fatback	1 mo.	———	———	1 year	2 weeks	3 mos.	2 days
GAME	rabbit	2 days	2 days	2 days	3 mos.	2 days	2 mos.	2 days
	venison after hanging	4 days	7 days	4 days	3 mos.	2 days	3 mos.	2 days
VARIETY MEATS	brains	2 days	———	2 days	3 mos.	1 day	———	———
	heart	3 days	5 days	6 days	6 mos.	1 day	4 mos.	1 day
	kidneys	2 days	———	4 days	6 mos.	1 day	1 mo.	1 day
	liver	2 days	———	1 day	4 mos.	1 day	———	———
	sweetbreads	2 days	———	1 day	4 mos.	1 day	———	———
	tongue fresh	3 days	7 days	3 days	6 mos.	3 days	4 mos.	1 day
	smoked	8 days	———	4 days	6 mos.	5 days	4 mos.	2 days
	tripe	2 days	———	2 days	4 mos.	1 day	1 mo.	1 day
	oxtails	3 days	———	4 days	2 mos.	2 days	3 mos.	1 day
	calf's feet	2 days	———	4 days	4 mos.	2 days	2 mos.	2 days
	pig's feet	2 days	10 days	4 days	4 mos.	2 days	2 mos.	2 days
SAUSAGES	fresh links or meat	7 days	———	———	6 mos.	2 days	———	———
	fresh smoked	7 days	———	———	6 mos.	2 days	———	———
	cooked	2 weeks	———	———	6 mos.	2 days	———	———
	cooked smoked	2 weeks	———	———	6 mos.	2 days	———	———
	semidry	3 weeks	———	———	6 mos.	2 days	———	———
	dry	3 weeks	———	———	6 mos.	2 days	———	———
	bologna, chunk, not sliced	5 days	———	———	3 mos.	2 days	———	———
	frankfurters, loose, unwrapped	1 day	———	———	3 mos.	2 days	———	———
	liverwurst, chunk, not sliced	7 days	———	———	———	———	———	———
	cold cuts, sliced	3 days	———	———	1 mo.	1 day	———	———
POULTRY	chicken	2 days	———	2 days	6 mos.	2 days	1 mo.	2 days
	chicken, cut up	2 days	———	2 days	3 mos.	2 days	1 mo.	2 days
	chicken pieces in gravy	———	———	3 days	———	———	3 mos.	2 days
	duck	3 days	———	2 days	6 mos.	2 days	1 mo.	2 days
	goose	3 days	———	3 days	6 mos.	3 days	3 mos.	2 days
	turkey whole	3 days	———	3 days	6 mos.	3 days	3 mos.	2 days
	cut up	3 days	———	3 days	3 mos.	2 days	1 mo.	1 day
	guinea hen	2 days	———	1 day	2 mos.	1 day	1 mo.	1 day
	quail	2 days	———	1 day	2 mos.	1 day	1 mo.	1 day
	Rock Cornish game hen	2 days	———	1 day	2 mos.	1 day	1 mo.	1 day
	squab	2 days	———	1 day	2 mos.	1 day	1 mo.	1 day
	poultry livers whole	2 days	———	1 day	2 mos.	1 day	———	———
	ground	1 day	———	———	———	———	———	———
	gizzards	3 days	———	2 days	3 mos.	2 days	2 mos.	1 day

Meat	Fresh uncooked refrigerated	Marinated or pickled refrigerated	Cooked refrigerated	Frozen uncooked	Defrosted refrigerated	Frozen cooked	Defrosted refrigerated
hearts	3 days	———	2 days	3 mos.	2 days	2 mos.	1 day
bones	2 days	———	———	1 mo.	1 day	———	———
turkey, smoked	7 days	———	———	6 mos.	2 days	———	———
capon, smoked	4 days	———	———	6 mos.	2 days	———	———
chicken, smoked	3 days	———	———	6 mos.	2 days	———	———

MISCEL-LANEOUS

Meat	Fresh uncooked refrigerated	Marinated or pickled refrigerated	Cooked refrigerated	Frozen uncooked	Defrosted refrigerated	Frozen cooked	Defrosted refrigerated
stocks, meat and poultry, plain or jellied	———	———	6 days	———	———	4 mos.	2 days
meat or poultry pies, with pastry	———	———	2 days	3 mos.	1 day	2 mos.	1 day
casseroles of meat or poultry	———	———	3 days	3 mos.	1 day	3 mos.	1 day

CONVERTING TO
THE METRIC SYSTEM

W<small>HEN WE BEGAN TO WORK ON THIS BOOK</small>, we expected the metric system to become standard in the United States within a decade. Now, several years later, we think it may be longer. Many professional engineers and some large corporations have resisted the change because of the tremendous job of retooling. However, the trend has begun, and the change is inevitable. Our current system, the U.S. Customary System, is based on the British Imperial System. Even though it uses the British system of weights and measures, the United States already uses a monetary system based on 10, and the metric system has been legal in this country for over 100 years. The International Metric System is now used by 90% of the world's population, and the United States is part of a shrinking minority. The units of measure currently used for volume, weight, distance and temperature are not coordinated, whereas everything in the metric system is. The old saw "a pint's a pound except lead and feathers" was never strictly true, but probably no one noticed the discrepancy in a country like England, where there were three kinds of gallons and at least two kinds of pounds. Cooks are still hampered by the gallon problem when reading British and Canadian recipes. The Imperial gallon has $1^1/_5$ times the volume of the U.S. gallon, the Imperial quart contains 5 cups or 40 ounces, and the Imperial pint contains 2½ cups or 20 ounces.

The tables that follow should help you adjust from one system to the other in using cookbooks based on the metric system and in shopping by gram and kilo in the near future.

CONVERTING TO THE METRIC SYSTEM

VOLUME MEASURES IN THE U.S. CUSTOMARY SYSTEM
COMPARED WITH OTHER VOLUME MEASURES,
WEIGHTS GIVEN IN OUNCES AND GRAMS

			1 teaspoon	4.7 grams	
		3 teaspoons	1 tablespoon	14.3 grams	
	1 ounce	6 teaspoons	2 tablespoons	28.35 grams	
	2 ounces	¼ cup	4 tablespoons	56.7 grams	
		⅓ cup	5+ tablespoons	72.0 grams	
	4 ounces	½ cup	8 tablespoons	113.4 grams	
	6 ounces	¾ cup	12 tablespoons	170.1 grams	
	8 ounces	1 cup	16 tablespoons	226.8 grams	
1 pound	16 ounces	2 cups	32 tablespoons	453.6 grams	0.4536 kilogram

All the weights given here are for liquids measured in containers of the listed sizes. Liquids include such items as water, milk, butter and sugar, all of which count as liquids in cooking and weigh approximately the same. Dry ingredients weigh less. Although these items do not weigh the same, the weight of conventional all-purpose flour can be used as a standard. This will make conversion to the metric system possible and simple in the kitchen, but it is only approximate and will not serve for any scientific purpose.

1 teaspoon	3 grams
1 tablespoon	9 grams
¼ cup	36 grams
⅓ cup	46 grams
½ cup	72 grams
¾ cup	108 grams
1 cup	144 grams

There will be times when you may need to convert your measures in the other direction. For a rough approximation, divide the number of grams by 31 to get the number of ounces.

$$1 \text{ gram} \times 1000 = 1 \text{ kilogram}$$

1 gram		.0353 ounce	1/28 ounce AVDP
4.7 grams	1 teaspoon		
10 grams		.353 ounce	
14.3 grams	1 tablespoon	½ ounce	
28 grams	2 tablespoons	1 ounce	
100 grams	7 tablespoons	3½ ounces	
200 grams	14 tablespoons	7 ounces	⅞ cup
226.8 grams	1 cup	½ pound	
453.6 grams	2 cups	1 pound	7/16 kilogram
500 grams		1⅑ pounds	
1000 grams		2.205 pounds	1 kilogram

When comparing liquids by volume only, use the liter and milliliter. Since all the units in the metric system are interrelated, a liter is equal to 1 kilogram or 1000

414

cubic centimeters. A liter is only slightly larger than a quart, so in most recipes it is possible to substitute one for the other.

$$1 \text{ milliliter} \times 1000 = 1 \text{ liter}$$

1 ounce	2 tablespoons	29.573 milliliters	
8 ounces	1 cup	236.588 milliliters	.2365 liter
16 ounces	1 pint	473.176 milliliters	.473 liter
2 pounds	1 quart	946.35 milliliters	.946 liter
	1 gallon		3.79 liters
	(4 quarts)		

1 milliliter = 0.033 ounce
1 liter   = 2.113 pints or 1.057 quarts or .264 gallon

In case you find measurements given in centimeters and meters, here are the basic equations.

$$1 \text{ centimeter} \times 100 = 1 \text{ meter}$$

1 cubic inch   = 16.39 cubic centimeters
1 cubic centimeter =   .061 cubic inch
1 cubic foot   =   .0283 cubic meter
1 cubic meter   = 35.3 cubic feet

Another problem concerns temperature readings. There are three systems: Kelvin (K), in which 0° is absolute zero ($-459.67°$ on Fahrenheit scales), which is chiefly used for scientific work; centigrade (C), or Celsius (the name of its inventor), in which 0° is the temperature at which water freezes; and Fahrenheit (F), in which 0° is 32 points below freezing. Most American food books, including this one, use Fahrenheit to indicate temperatures for cooking and freezing. However, books published where the metric system is used will use Celsius. To convert from Fahrenheit to Celsius, subtract 32 from the Fahrenheit figure, multiply by 5, and divide by 9. To convert from Celsius to Fahrenheit, multiply the Celsius figure by 9, divide by 5 and add 32.

	° *Celsius* (C)	° *Fahrenheit* (F)
	−50	−58
	−40	−40
	−30	−22
freezer	−23.3	−10
	−20	−4
	−10	14
water freezes	0	32
	10	50
	20	68
	30	86
	40	104
	50	122
	60	140

(table continued on pg. 416)

	° Celsius (C)	° Fahrenheit (F)
water freezes	70	158
	80	176
	90	194
simmering	95	203
boiling	100	212
	110	230
	120	248
	130	266
	140	284
	150	302
roasting (mod)	177	350
	200	392
	250	482
broiling (high)	260	500
	300	572

The temperatures given for boiling apply only at sea level. For each 550 feet above sea level, liquid will boil at 1° F. lower.

Ovens are marked differently also in countries using the metric system, and some are still marked with words instead of figures. This may help you adjust:

	° Celsius (C)	° Fahrenheit (F)
warming	95 to 120	200 to 250
very slow	120 to 135	250 to 275
slow	150 to 165	300 to 325
moderate	175 to 190	350 to 375
hot	205 to 220	400 to 425
very hot	230 to 245	450 to 475

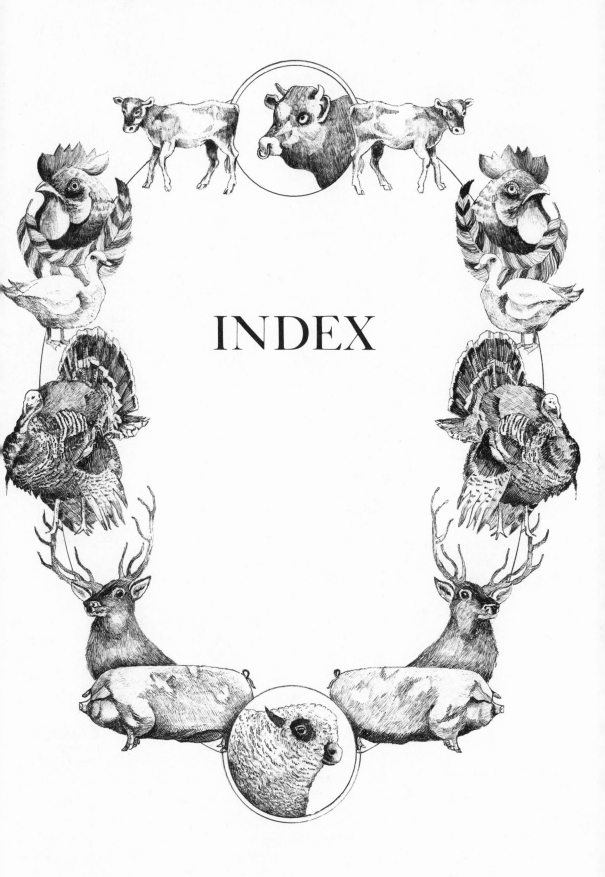

INDEX

INDEX

Although this book contains many suggestions or descriptions of recipes, it presents relatively few that are completely spelled out, with ingredient lists or measured proportions. To help you locate these complete recipes, we have indicated them with the letter (R) just before the page number.